The Doppelgänger

The Doppelgänger
LITERATURE'S PHILOSOPHY

Dimitris Vardoulakis

FORDHAM UNIVERSITY PRESS   *New York* 2010

the modern language initiative

THIS BOOK IS MADE POSSIBLE BY A COLLABORATIVE GRANT FROM THE ANDREW W. MELLON FOUNDATION.

© 2010 by Fordham University Press

All rights reserved. No part of this publication may be reproduced, stored in a retrieval system, or transmitted in any form or by any means—electronic, mechanical, photocopy, recording, or any other—except for brief quotations in printed reviews, without the prior permission of the publisher.

Fordham University Press has no responsibility for the persistence or accuracy of URLs for external or third-party Internet websites referred to in this publication and does not guarantee that any content on such websites is, or will remain, accurate or appropriate.

Library of Congress Cataloging-in-Publication Data

Vardoulakis, Dimitris.
  The Doppelgänger : literature's philosophy / Dimitris Vardoulakis.
     p. cm.
  Includes bibliographical references and index.
  ISBN 978-0-8232-3298-7 (cloth : alk. paper)
  ISBN 978-0-8232-3299-4 (pbk. : alk. paper)
  ISBN 978-0-8232-3300-7 (ebook : alk. paper)
  1. Philosophy. 2. Literature—Philosophy.
3. Subject (Philosophy)   I. Title.
B66.V36 2010
190—dc22
                              2010012138

12 11 10   5 4 3 2 1

First edition

For Andrew Benjamin

CONTENTS

Preface	ix
Preamble, or An Other Opening	xi
Introduction, or The Reflections of the Doppelgänger	1
1. The Critique of Loneliness: The Genesis of the Doppelgänger	11
Isolation: Toward a Political Placement of the Doppelgänger	11
Harrington's "Flies": Kant's Madness	16
The Black Nothing and the White Nothing: Jean Paul's *Clavis Fichtiana*	23
The Return of Negation: Freud's "The 'Uncanny'"	37
"Double Acts" and Transformation	53
2. The Subject of Modernity: Law and Temporality in Alexandros Papadiamantes	66
...and...: The Doppelgänger as the Subject of Modernity	66
Community with the Dead: Self-Confession in *The Murderess*	75
The Penumbra: Obligations	90
3. The Task of the Doppelgänger: Jean Paul as Collocutor of Maurice Blanchot	106
4. The Politics of the Doppelgänger: Universal History and Cosmopolitanism	135
Automatism, Autonomy	135
The Subject of History in Walter Benjamin	144
Displacement: Figuring the Cosmopolitan in Alasdair Gray's *Poor Things*	165

5. Self-Inscriptions: Failing Kafka and Benjamin 192
   The Pure Machine's Gambit: Benjamin's "Thesis I" 192
   World Theater and Nature Theater 202
   Kafka's "Lost Gesture" 218
   Lying with Benjamin 232

Notes 249
Bibliography 307
Index 325

PREFACE

A project that has been carried out, in various stages and in different places, for almost a decade will inevitably be indebted to a large number of friends. At the same time, this makes it difficult to acknowledge everyone. Thus, only those with the most immediate impact on the book can be mentioned here. Tina Weller's help has been invaluable. Walter Veit has offered wise counsel and support. Thanks to Gail Ward, Carlo Salzani, and Sabina Sestigiani for their friendship. Leslie Hill has been instrumental in forging the presence of Blanchot in these pages. Chris Danta's intellectual insights have always been highly valued. The input by Stathis Gourgouris, David Ferris, and Ewa Ziarek has been crucial in bringing this project to completion. An Alexander von Humboldt Fellowship, undertaken at the Peter Szondi-Institut für Allgemeine und Vergleichende Literaturwissenschaft, at the invitation of Winfried Menninghaus, made it possible to complete a full draft of the manuscript. The final draft was completed during a sabbatical that was organized by Peter Murphy and the School of English, Communication and Performance Studies at Monash University. Sarah Anderson was a supportive companion during the writing of this book.

Finally, this book was supported by the College of the Arts, University of Western Sydney.

The spelling of the German word "der Doppelgänger" has been normalized to the English spelling "doppelgänger," except when German texts are cited.

In the absence of a reference to a published translation, translations are mine. On occasion, cited translations have been altered in order to amend mistakes or to retain terminological continuity or the stylistic tenor.

All references to Jean Paul's works are to the Norbert Miller edition, unless otherwise stated: Jean Paul, *Sämtliche Werke*, edited by Norbert Miller (Darmstadt: Wissenschaftliche Buchgesellschaft, 2000).

All references to the works of Alexandros Papadiamantes are to the Triantafyllopoulos edition of the *Complete Works* (*Hapanta*), 2d ed. (Athens: Domos, 1997), volume number followed by page number.

All references to the German edition of Walter Benjamin's work are to *Gesammelte Schriften*, edited by Rolf Tiedemann and Hermann Schweppenhäuser (Frankfurt am Main: Suhrkamp, 1991), abbreviated *GS*. All references to the English translations of Benjamin's work are to the *Selected Writings*, 4 vols., edited by Michael W. Jennings et al. (Cambridge, Mass.: Harvard University Press, 1997–2003), abbreviated *SW*. All references to *The Arcades Project*, translated by Howard Eiland and Kevin McLaughlin (Cambridge, Mass.: Belknap, 1999), are given by the number of the Convolute entry, which is identical in the English and the German editions.

PREAMBLE, OR AN OTHER OPENING

What is proper to a culture is not to be identical to itself. *Not to not have an identity, but not to be able to identify itself, to be able to say "me" or "we"; to be able to take the form of a subject only in the nonidentity to itself or, if you prefer, only in the difference* with itself. *There is no culture or cultural identity without this difference* with itself.

JACQUES DERRIDA, *The Other Heading*

According to Jean-Joseph Goux, the figure of Oedipus represents the first philosopher. Oedipus can claim to launch the entire philosophical tradition of the West because he presents a subversion of the traditional mythic pattern of a hero's trial in order to become king. Instead of the hero's using physical force to overcome the monstrous, Oedipus uses only his mind against the Sphinx. As a consequence of Oedipus' self-reflective act, the subject can aspire to self-identity. This represents the humanist insistence on self-knowledge.[1] There are two dangers inscribed in this act that have accompanied philosophy ever since. First, Oedipus' use of ratiocination can set him apart from all other humans. He can be called a *last man* in the sense that his reason creates a space separate from his fellow humans, a space where he remains forever trapped.[2] His bypassing of bodily combat with the Sphinx condemns Oedipus to a desolate space of reason from which there is no escape. Second, Oedipus' revolutionary act of overcoming the Sphinx is not directed merely against myth but also has profound repercussions for the sovereign power that it bestows on him. That power is also supported by the spilling of blood, initially the blood of his own father, and subsequently that of his mother, who was driven to suicide. Oedipus as a *first man* cannot disengage himself from a founding act of violence. Separation and its accompanying violence challenge the humanist assumption of a self-consistent subjective identity—and this is a challenge to the first philosopher no less than to the foundations of the philosophical tradition he inaugurates.

What would it be like to think of another opening to the philosophical tradition? How is it possible to think of the philosophical without being seduced by the desire for self-identity? Henri Lefebvre suggests in the second lecture of his *Introduction to Modernity* that such an opening consists in recognizing the inherently political dimension of Oedipus' answer to the riddle. Lefebvre presents the blind Oedipus groping his way toward Colonus and wondering what he did wrong. Being fully aware of his importance as a first philosopher, Oedipus is unable to see his error. At this point the "voice of the Unseeable" intervenes to remind Oedipus of his crime, the blood that he has spilled. It is because of this crime, says the voice, that Oedipus is guilty. Lefebvre abruptly concludes with the following statement: "The voice is lost in the tumult. A cloud of dust rises from beneath the feet of soldiers marching by. They laugh at the blind old man. They come from the little town towards which Oedipus is groping his stumbling way: Athens."[3] What the marching soldiers of Athens—the first colonial power in the country that gave birth to the first philosopher—remind Oedipus, along with the "voice of the Unseeable," is that Oedipus' crime was neither a mistake in the way he rationalized his circumstance nor the spilling of the blood his action precipitated. Rather, his crime was that both his ratiocinations and his actions ignored the structures of power. Oedipus failed to take responsibility for the political, even though—or, perhaps, because—he assumed sovereignty. Man's self-knowledge cannot justify or legitimate the use of this knowledge in perpetrating acts of political violence.

Recognizing the emergence of the political in the discrepancy that persists between any configuration of knowledge and power characterizes, according to Lefebvre, modernity. The other opening to the philosophical is made possible in modernity. What is, however, the nature of this other opening? How is its political agenda to be understood? Discussing *Oedipus at Colonus* in his lectures on hospitality, Jacques Derrida suggests that this other opening requires an unconditional acceptance of the other. The stranger must be welcomed as the most intimate friend, as the one whose unconditional acceptance is determinative of the host's identity.[4] This is both an ethical and a political responsibility. Through this responsibility, the individual can attain singularity, which is to say, that it renounces self-knowledge; it is no longer "able to say 'me' or 'we,'" as Derrida puts it in the epigraph above. As Derrida further explains, such a subject does not renounce identity altogether but can locate identity "only in the non-identity to itself or . . . only in the difference *with itself*."

At the same time, it is a responsibility that challenges the autonomy of philosophy in modernity. If philosophy is to account for the other, if it is to find another opening, then philosophy has to welcome its own other, namely literature. Even more emphatically, the welcoming of philosophy's other is not a matter of choice for modernity but the chance for philosophy to rise to its own potential. That potential can be called "literature's philosophy." But it should never be forgotten that "literature's philosophy" would have been unthinkable in modernity without Oedipus. The first philosopher—and this means, most emphatically, the first subject also—cannot be summarily rejected, thrown in the dustbin of the history of ideas. Modernity is called to respond to the construction of self-identity. This response will be traced in the following pages through the figure of the doppelgänger. The doppelgänger overcomes the sovereign, self-identical subject by disrupting the nexus of knowledge and power. As such, the doppelgänger emerges as the other that literature has to grapple with in order to give philosophy a chance.

Introduction, or The Reflections of the Doppelgänger

Mirroring is the primary phenomenon of ideology.

THEODOR W. ADORNO, *Metaphysics*

The doppelgänger makes possible an ontology of the subject. This does not entail a lapse into metaphysics. The doppelgänger, rather, eschews attempts to reduce the subject to mere presence. A first thesis of this book is that *the resistance to presence indicates the doppelgänger's ontology, bringing literature and philosophy into productive and mutually illuminating contact.* The thesis about the doppelgänger's resistance to presence does not entail a simple opposition to, or negation of, presence. Such a move would have resulted in an essentialization of absence as constitutive of subjectivity. Instead, it will be shown that the subject persists through its resistance to both presence and absence, and, therefore, what matters is the manner in which it persists. The subject's persistence is evidenced not only by the continuing use of the concept in philosophy but also by the necessity of having characters in stories and novels as well as by the necessity that criticism address those characters. The poststructuralist insistence on the death of the subject, the author, and so on does not entail equating death with complete absence.[1]

The doppelgänger, it will be argued, is an *operative* or *effective presence* to the extent that it effects the undoing of the framing of the subject by the opposition between mere presence and absence. Such an operation indicates a function of relationality—the various relations that structure the subject's ontology. This relationality is what is called here the doppelgänger. The relationality is formal, and for this reason the doppelgänger will be referred to by the neuter pronoun, the "it," despite the fact that "der Doppelgänger" is a masculine noun in German. This is not to deny that the relations established in the subject are gendered.

1

On the contrary, it follows from the acknowledgment that the relations are always gendered because they are always particular. Hence, the neuter is preferable so that neither the masculine nor the feminine appear privileged.

What are the doppelgänger's relations of? What is being related? The problem of approaching the relationality proper to the doppelgänger by an inquiry into its "what" will always encounter the problem of essentializing relationality itself. In other words, by starting with "what," relationality is already presupposed. The doppelgänger is neither solely a product of relations nor simply produces them, so that it unfolds outside the bounds of this neither/nor. The question is about the manner in which the unfolding occurs. *How* is the doppelgänger operative? Or, *how* does the subject figure as the doppelgänger? The relations proper to the subject should neither be equated with the aggregate of empirical attributes of a specific subject nor lead to an abstraction of a subjectivity as such. Rather, the relations will unfold in particular sites, which will always be historically determined. Such determinations will be provided in this book by literary texts. This is not an arbitrary choice, given that the doppelgänger has been prevalent in literature. The focus on specific literary texts means that the particular endures. There is always a historical context. At the same time, the context is not occluded: the literary contains immanently in itself possibilities for its criticism, and both the literary and the critical are also organized by various protocols that entail a propriety leading to the ontological and the philosophical.[2] So long as relationality is an operative presence, it enables the staging of different discursive fields (here, the literary, the critical, and the philosophical) as well as that which is being staged by those fields. The doppelgänger is this double staging—or chiasmus—of relationality.

Tackling the doppelgänger through literature is due to its historical development, but still this approach should not be taken as exemplary. A number of alternative approaches can be envisioned. For instance, Debra Walker King summarizes the doppelgänger as "the collision between real bodies and an unfriendly informant: a fictional double whose aim is to mask individuality and mute the voice of personal agency. Although this double is created and maintained most often by forces beyond ourselves (television, magazines, cultural mandates and myths), we bear its markers on our bodies, particularly those of age, race and gender. In this way, the fictional double is always with us.... Unfortunately the informant they see, and to whom they are willing to listen, lies. Instead of telling a story of individuals living in social reality, this cultural construction of racialized, gendered, or sexual body fictions disfigures or conceals women beneath a veil of invisibility, threatening economic, political, emotional, and spiritual suffocation."[3] The first thesis, stated above, about the doppelgänger's resistance to presence is in accord with King's assertion that the "double is always with us." The doppelgänger's effective presence could be pursued from the point of view of technology, the media, or feminism, as is suggested by King. But this intimates a second thesis of the book, namely that *the doppelgänger is in a process of construction—its effective presence is transformative.* Consequently, it is possible to thematize the doppelgänger in different ways. There is no ipso facto privileged mode of access to the doppelgänger. However, this book diverges from King's proposal in one significant respect. It does not read the doppelgänger as a symptom of impotence or as an evil presence. Moreover, as it will be argued throughout, a nostalgic restitution of the individual is not amenable to the doppelgänger, whose operative presence undoes individuality. The doppelgänger is neither good nor bad, but rather it is the element of formal relationality that structures the subject's ontology.

| | |

The distinction highlighted above between the "what" and the "how" of the doppelgänger can also be the starting point for distinguishing two kinds of reflection vis-à-vis the subject, which bring to the fore literature's import for philosophy. The first kind of reflection, which pertains to the "what," is instrumental for an understanding of the doppelgänger insofar as it designates the relation that is reconfigured by it. (Crucially, the movement from the "what" to the "how" is a reconfiguration, not a rejection or an overcoming. As it will be argued later, there is no sublation or synthesis to guarantee the reflection proper to the doppelgänger.) This first reflection can be called metaphysical and is linked to the genesis of the word "Doppelgänger." It is the reflection between a subject and the subjectivity underlying it. The subject is the phenomenal self, every single one of "us." The subjectivity is that "us" itself, a generalized notion of the subject—not a single man but humanity, not an individual but the individuality of the people(s), not a human but man in the image of God. The relation between the subject and subjectivity is a self-reflection. As it will be shown, self-reflection always requires a clear distinction between the two structural terms—the subject in its particularity and in its universality—but the doppelgänger always intervenes and destabilizes the distinction.

The metaphysical self-reflection does not merely indicate that subject and subjectivity mirror each other. What is also necessarily involved is a reference to the "world." Specifically, if this image is not to be simply tautological, it requires the mediation of a third term. But to the extent that what is enacted between the particularity of the individual and the universality of subjectivity is a relation between the finite and the infinite, then the third term would also be constructed by that relation. For this reason, the third term is the setting of self-reflection, the "world" or "reality" of the subject. If the reflections between a self and selfhood construct reality, then what tends to be forgotten is the ineliminable web of interests on the part of the subject, which are refracted through the reflection. No matter how many precepts are prescribed to regulate action, self-reflection will always be aligned with self-interest. To repeat Adorno's assertion from the epigraph, "mirroring is the primary phenomenon of ideology." Reflection's import is that there is always a politics of the subject.

Self-reflection, as a unilinear relation between the infinite and the finite, can take two forms, depending on which term is given primacy. First, the move from the infinity of reason to the particularity of action characterizes the philosophy of Johann Gottlieb Fichte. Following in the footsteps of Kant, Fichte developed a philosophy by positing apperception or a transcendental subject as a first principle from which all the laws about the subject will be derived. As will be shown in Chapter 1, the German author Jean Paul coined the word "Doppelgänger" to criticize Fichte's "I-philosophy."[4] Jean Paul's Doppelgänger illustrates that the move from the infinite to an actual place or setting is always curtailed, with the result that the subject is lost in the infinity of reason—in an absolute loneliness. This is what Nietzsche calls "the last man," a placeless subject. Second, the opposite move can be adopted, namely from the particular to the infinite. As it will be shown in Chapter 2 through a reading of Alexandros Papadiamantes' novella *The Murderess*, this requires a continual negation of the particular in order to attain to a complete self-reflection. Negating reality is, according to Hegel, the solving of the riddle about the human by a "first man," who institutes the laws of subjectivity. Because the negations are endless, this self-institution is timeless. The legal framework of subjectivity will accord with the infinite. However, what dies in the progression toward subjectivity is the particular subject—there is a murder of the subject in that its future is foreclosed. This explains the often murderous intention of doppelgänger characters and also shows another loneliness operating here. It is the loneliness of the subject struggling for the atemporal, which takes the guise of an accessible future. This struggle is curtailed; the future cannot present a complete self-reflection; and hence, just like the last man, the first man also fails.

This dual failure of self-reflection—the failure of the institution of the subject through subjectivity and the failure of the subject to institute subjectivity—will make it possible to stage a different relation of the subject to the law. It will be a relation arising out of a small remainder in the law, a penumbra, which always destabilizes the law and which cannot be identified with it. This taint in the mirroring of self-reflection leads to a notion of justice—to the tain of the mirror, as Rodolphe Gasché puts it.[5] A justice which is premised, on the one hand, on the dismantling of individuality and subjectivity and, on the other, on the blurring of the outlines of the autonomous and independent subject. In other words, justice cannot accommodate the distinct terms—the empirical and the transcendental subject—that structure the metaphysical self-reflection. The second notion of reflection will arise from the failures of metaphysical self-reflection.

This second reflection, the doppelgänger, will be a critique of infinite subjectivity no less than a critique of the law. In the doppelgänger's reflection, both the subject and the law can only be present as absent—that is, not framed by the opposition between presence and absence. As it will be shown in Chapter 3, Jean Paul as this absent presence is a collocutor of Maurice Blanchot. This allows for the operative presence of the doppelgänger, which unfolds on the fault lines of literature, criticism, and philosophy. The doppelgänger arises at the points where each inquiry reaches a limit, transforming itself into something else. The collocution of Jean Paul and Blanchot entails that the canon is not merely a list of authors compiled by the critic but arises out of the absent presence of the doppelgänger. Thus, the doppelgänger becomes a medium of reading the work, and hence constitutive of writing. This process of the mutual limiting and interacting between—the imbrication of—literature, criticism, and philosophy is, then, an initial feature of the reflection proper to the doppelgänger.

To allow for the doppelgänger's reflection to exceed the laws of subjectivity—the self-reflection of a particular and a transcendental subject—is a political project. However, the political should not be assumed to be given within the empirical. The finite and particular human activities that comprise the sphere of politics should not be confused with the political that enacts the excess proper to the doppelgänger, and hence escapes the merely present. Nor should the political be equated with an ideal. As already intimated, the doppelgänger counteracts the attempt to base the subject on a principle of infinity. The political comes to the fore precisely as the mutual delimitation enacted between the finite and the infinite. Or, to put it in another way, the political is the *interruption* of the relation between the infinite and the finite.[6] In Chapter 4, such an interruption will be shown to be associated, first, with the enactment of judgment, as understood by Walter Benjamin's materialist historiography, and, second, with a notion of the cosmopolitical, independent of the humanist ideal of an autonomous individual but rather, as is argued with recourse to Alasdair Gray's *Poor Things*, with intermingled autonomy and automaticity. The political is an interruption of metaphysical self-reflection and hence a rupture of the politics of self-interest.

The doppelgänger is political in the sense that it allows for an extrapolation of the conditions of the possibility of action. The doppelgänger allows for a staging of the fissure between the two totalities of the phenomenal and the universal—a staging that reflects the political in the sense of not allowing the infinite and the finite to reconcile. What matters is the staging of this fissure, not its bridging. Consequently, as it will be argued in Chapter 5, theatricality—as that staging—is crucial for an understanding of the doppelgänger. Walter Benjamin's work on Franz Kafka is structured by the opposition between life and work. However, this opposition offers three different stagings, or three kinds of theater. Privileging the author's work turns the subject into an actor on a cosmic stage where conciliation has been achieved. Opposed to that is the privileging of life, which turns the subject into an actor mired in the ambiguities of mythic contingency. The third staging is an oscillation between the previous two, in which the subject is never allowed to find a resting place. Oscillation is important because, no matter how seemingly opposed life and work are in the first two extrapolations, they are ultimately allied. Their alliance is premised on an insistence on sameness, the retention of an essential quality as that which defines the subject's self-identity. This shows that, at the end, the self-reflections of the first and the last man have a common metaphysical foundation—the assumption that an equation between the empirical and the transcendental selves is possible.[7] Conversely, an interruption of the relation between life and work in the manner of a mutual transformability or oscillation between them is an insistence on difference. This difference is due to the operative presence of the doppelgänger. The doppelgänger figures the political in the sense that it enacts a configuration and disfiguration of that which seeks to deny difference. The political figures as, or is reflected by, the doppelgänger.

For such a figuration to take place, reflection cannot be expunged.[8] A total rejection of metaphysical self-reflection will only result in the sublation of the concept of subjectivity into something even more totalizing and into a sublimation of the subject into a higher entity. Rather, owing to the interruption, reflection is to be retained. Interruption resists the final synthesis of a sublation or a sublimation. The subject persists in the figure of the doppelgänger. But it is a persistence in a process of formation, and hence a being as transformation. There is no *forma finalis*; rather, form is constantly deformed and reformed. The doppelgänger is always in a process of construction, very much as the discourses it reflects—literature and philosophy.

This endless transformation entails that the doppelgänger is never always already political. Rather, the doppelgänger is the interruption of the "always already" in its relation to the political. In other words, interruption has to be achieved; it does not simply exist—interruption is a praxis. Thus, the doppelgänger retains reflection but is not itself simply a reflection: the interruption is not only creative but also created. The doppelgänger is the medium of reflection, that is, that which allows for the interruption to take place. The doppelgänger is this staging in the interstices of the literary, the critical, and the philosophical. By being the condition of the possibility of this staging, the doppelgänger follows the political like a shadow but without ever being allowed to fully coincide with it. Thus, as is argued throughout this book, the doppelgänger is always in a process of formation and hence transformation; it remains to be elaborated; it *is*, but its being, its ontology, its presence, is not only linked to a past but also laden with a future.

| | |

Some of the most important works directly dealing with the doppelgänger, such as Freud's "The 'Uncanny'" and Andrew J. Webber's *The Doppelgänger*, will be discussed in their appropriate context later in the book. It should be noted here, however, that these important works are the exceptions to the two main approaches to the doppelgänger. The main approaches represent the two common and easy ways to miss the significance of the figure of the doppelgänger to present literature's philosophy.[9] The first approach bypasses the doppelgänger's transformability altogether, whereas the second obviates the effort required by the enactment of the interruption and transformation. In other words, these two approaches directly contradict the two theses about the doppelgänger indicated earlier—namely, that the doppelgänger persists in a process of construction and that its presence is effective. The result is that both these approaches lead to thoroughly unbalanced relations between literature and philosophy.

The first approach posits the doppelgänger as an immanently psychological category by insisting on a syncretism between author and character as well as between critic and analyst.[10] What is lost in the gap between the two syncretisms is literature itself—or, rather, literature is discussed only in terms of self-reflections. Ralph Tymms, who wrote one of the first and most influential studies of the doppelgänger in English, offers a succinct and instructive example of this psychological approach. The first sentence of Tymms's book asserts that "superficially, doubles are among the most facile, and less reputable devices of fiction."[11] This superficiality is dispelled, Tymms argues, so long as the doppelgänger is seen as a representation of the author's psychic process.[12] Thus, Tymms concludes, dark fantasies about subjective doublings should "be treated with the objectivity of a psychiater's casebook."[13] If that were so, then the literature of the doppelgänger would be merely a manifestation of the author's symptoms, and Tzvetan Todorov would have been correct to say that, as a category of psychoanalysis, the doppelgänger has lost its import for literature.[14] This approach posits the doppelgänger as exhausted, as having reached its end for literature. The syncretism of this approach is premised on a notion of something secret in the psyche of the human, which can be either fully confessed or never revealed. Conversely, as it will be argued in various points in this book, the doppelgänger resists an equation of subjective identity with either something entirely hidden or with that which is to be disclosed. Thus, the psychology allowed by the doppelgänger focuses on the staging of such resistances, no less that it is being staged by them.

Whereas the first way to miss the doppelgänger's significance for the relation between literature and philosophy consists in a contraction of the literary, the second way argues for its enormous expansion. Such an expansion has two variations: The first renders the doppelgänger either meaningless or theological. For instance, Hillel Schwartz defines the doppelgänger as that which exhibits a duplicity. This allows Schwartz to amass examples, having ignored all the while to specify what is meant by "duplicity." Everyone becomes a double of everyone else; everything is a copy of something. There is *no end* to doubling and copying.[15] On the contrary, taking the issue of the end seriously entails inquiring into what is meant by "everything." The "everything" opens up a realm of pure differentiation, a totality which seeks to deny that there is anything outside, and hence it is a theological impulse. As it will be shown, such a totality seeks to deny difference, but the operative presence of the doppelgänger always reinscribes difference as it counteracts the mystique of reconciliation. The second way of broadening the scope of the doppelgänger tends to overlook the resistances offered by the figure of the doppelgänger as well as the effort required for interruption and the political to occur. What characterizes this approach is that there is *no beginning* to the doppelgänger. Typically, the canon of the doppelgänger is pushed back to antiquity, evoking a series of more or less standard examples, such as the discussion of the "other half" by Aristophanes in Plato's *Symposium*, or the motif of *Amphitryon*, the myth of Narcissus, comedies of anagnorisis, not to mention all the examples of doubling and the shadow that anthropology has highlighted.[16] This results in studies of the doppelgänger which are usually learned and often contain astute readings of literary texts, but which completely miss the doppelgänger's philosophical significance.[17]

Once the doppelgänger is effortlessly pinpointed in any canonical text of its genre, then there is no scope for thinking about the resistances that characterize the subject and which necessitate the interruptions of the political. The present study avoids both a contraction and an expansion of the doppelgänger. The beginning of the doppelgänger is pragmatically determined by Jean Paul's coinage of the word "Doppelgänger" in 1796. Yet given the ontological structure of the doppelgänger, its effective presence is not reducible to any pragmatic context nor to any single historical narrative. Therefore, so long as the doppelgänger's relationality—its being creative *and* created—is shown to be operative in a text or discourse, the date 1796, is of secondary importance. This allows for the doppelgänger to be discovered—that is, actively sought—in any text where the interruption of self-reflection can be discerned. In other words, the doppelgänger appears the moment a text is shown to be political.

The doppelgänger is not framed by an absolute beginning or an absolute end. The approaches that miss the doppelgänger—either by contracting or by expanding it—have all in common an essentializing of the limit. Conversely, the doppelgänger does not end with psychoanalysis; nor is it endless simply because there is an indefinite number of examples of it. Furthermore, because it eschews a metaphysics of origin, the doppelgänger does not have *a* beginning or *many* beginnings. Far from essentializing the limit, the doppelgänger is an interrogation of the limit and on the limit—its interruptive power consists in the necessity of the limit as well as its equally necessary delimitation or transgression. Therefore, unlike the approaches that essentialize the limit, the doppelgänger puts the notions of beginning and end into question. If there is an endlessness proper to the doppelgänger, it is the infinite possibility of interruption between an absolute beginning and an absolute end. The doppelgänger enacts the interruption between a first and a last man, no less than the relation between the emergence and the exhaustion of novelty. But this is enacted on sites historically determined—the work of particular writers soliciting a response. Thus, this book does not pretend to have identified exemplary instances of the doppelgänger because there are no texts that are canonical doppelgänger examples. The corpus of the doppelgänger is growing and diminishing depending on the responses offered to particular texts. The canon of the doppelgänger does not have an end or a beginning because the doppelgänger does not have a measure—in the sense that the doppelgänger is that which interrupts the opposition between the measurable and the immeasurable. The operation of the subject can no longer be equated either with individual perceptions or with a generalized subjectivity. Rather, as both delimit themselves, they set in motion a chiastic relationality between being creative and been created, that is, the ontology of the doppelgänger, the liminal subject.

CHAPTER ONE

The Critique of Loneliness

The Genesis of the Doppelgänger

> I call myself the last philosopher, because I am the last man. No one speaks with me but myself, and my voice comes to me like the voice of a dying man! Let me associate for but one hour more with you, dear voice, with you, the last trace of the memory of all human happiness. With you I escape loneliness through self-delusion and lie myself into multiplicity and love. For my heart resists the belief that love is dead. It cannot bear the shudder of the loneliest loneliness, and so it forces me to speak as if I were two.
>
> FRIEDRICH NIETZSCHE, "Oedipus:
Soliloquy of the Last Philosopher"

ISOLATION: TOWARD A POLITICAL PLACEMENT OF THE DOPPELGÄNGER

A consideration of the political has to start with a distinction between politics and the political. This distinction, here, is drawn in relation to the place of the subject. Both politics and the political require a locus in which interaction between human beings occurs. Both terms require that the subject is not isolated but that it is placed in an area where there is contact with other subjects. The subject's isolation, as the locus that resists or counters sociality, is central in identifying the subject of both the political and of politics. Isolation puts the subject in a place devoid of other subjects. However, when subjectivity emerges as a crucial element of human interchange, then subjective identity also leads to a differentiation between the realms of politics and the political. The two questions—who is the political subject? and who is the subject of politics?—receive, then, divergent answers. For the subject of politics, the locus of human interchange is the sovereign state within which the subject exists as citizen. As such, the laws of the state define the subject of politics. Isolation occurs when the subject is firmly outside the law—the law in the narrow sense, the law as statute. In contrast, since the political subject is not confined to this or that sovereign state, its locus does not exist narrowly on a phenomenal plane. Thus, for the political, isolation is not conceivable as simple physical exclusion. Sociality is a regulative principle of the political only if it is not reduced to content. Nor can isolation, as the opposite of sociality, be equated with physical space. In relation to the political, it is better to view isolation as a topos. A topos is not merely in the service of oration (this would constrain it to politics). What is more, since Aristotle in the *Topics* links it to the general opinions of humans, topos brings along at least two interrelated aspects: a concern with argumentative strategy and the insistence of topicality. The former aspect is inseparable from language, whereas the latter is tied to historical actuality. The two aspects are interrelated since they presuppose an effective community. In this sense, the topos has a genuine significance for the political.[1]

Isolation will be crucial in identifying the place of the political subject inasmuch as isolation—as a topos—affirms sociality even though it seeks to disavow it. (Perhaps it is more accurate to say that isolation affirms sociality *by* seeking to disavow it. Thus it is made clear that what isolation introduces is a distancing from an identitary logic and a move toward a differential logic.) The significance of isolation for the political is that since the place of the political cannot be defined as this or that place, it brings along with it a problem, namely the danger of its complete identification with the ideal. The spaces of politics and the political would thus be completely segregated. The contention here is that isolation, as the negativity of an ideal space, counteracts a metaphysical conception of the place of the political. Or, to put it from the perspective of the political subject: with isolation arises the question of whether the subject is completely severed from particularity. It will be argued that this threat of severance—a threat also to the very possibility of judgment and thus to the political as a site of conflict or debate—is constitutive of the political subject.

The severance from particularity along with its implications is pertinent in order to broach the doppelgänger. Not only is the doppelgänger as a conception of subjectivity in jeopardy, but the threat of isolation is also as instrumental to the doppelgänger as it is to the political subject. Paul Coates has noted that the political, place, and subjectivity interact and intersect in the doppelgänger. Further, Coates identifies the severance from particularity as ideology, which "brings forth the Double."[2] With ideology, at least two important elements are introduced: a sense of community and a set of ideas held by that community. What governs both elements, for Coates, is an internalizing movement.

> [T]he essence of ideology lies in the institutionalised bipartisanship of the imperative to "see the other side of the question," which transforms the potential for change inherent in contradiction into a steady state of balance. Ideology socialises the individual by bringing him or her to *internalise* the dividedness of a class society in the form of the structure of "objective, value-free judgement"—thereby enabling the system to rule the subject, by dividing it. The antithesis between the "here" of the individual and the "there" of others is translated into *internal space*. Perhaps its main agents are the media, which create a society that is mediation and phantasmagoria, never encountered directly.[3]

What the doppelgänger presents, according to Coates, is a subject that is permitted to make distinctions only internally. This inward direction of thought is underpinned by a self-identical subject. One who says "I am I," thereby believing to be stating an objective judgment dictated by the commands of reason, is also logically impelled to grant others the same capacity. However, with regard to political praxis, such a logic of the same further impels one to grant the other "the right to be right." This is not a premise of the political organization of a society, of a polis—it has nothing to do with the articulation of the democratic nature of the state. "The right to be right" remains internalized, granted on the conceptual realm, where reality is still not an issue. The invidiousness of such a phantasmagoria is obvious in its institutionalization, that is, when the concept becomes an imperative regardless of the specific situation. The subject is under the sway of "the system." The most significant upshot of such a state of affairs is the disavowal of contestation. The conditions of the possibility of conflict are replaced by "a steady state of balance" as the condition of the possibility of self-identity and ideology.[4]

The origins of the doppelgänger testify to a similar concern with the internalizing performed by the subject. The word "Doppelgänger" was coined by the German Romantic author Jean Paul.[5] In the doppelgänger's own words, the threat of the severance from particularity is identified as loneliness.

> Around me an expanse of petrified humans. In the dark, uninhabited silence glows no love, no admiration, no prayer, no hope, no aim. I, totally alone, nowhere a pulse-beat, no life; nothing around me and without me nothing other than nothing. There is consciousness in me only of my highest Not-Con-sciousness. Inside me the mute, blind, concealed and labouring demogorgon, and I am he himself. I came, then, from eternity, and head into eternity——[6]

The lonely subject is, in Nietzsche's formulation from the epigraph, the last man, a subject trapped in the kingdom of reason and unable to reach the particular. Here, loneliness functions as the register of the complex that isolation presents as a challenge to sociality. An explication of this citation, to be carried out in this chapter, will unfold this complex under the rubric of the doppelgänger's loneliness. After showing the way that madness figures in the matrix of loneliness, the discussion will focus on the way that the "nothing" is understood in this citation. This will disclose some of the issues that are pertinent to the political constitution of the doppelgänger. An examination of Freud's paper on the uncanny will not only give a historical perspective of the doppelgänger as understood by psychoanalysis, but it will also capture the ontology of the subject it introduces. The final section of this chapter shows the importance of technique in relation to the subject's ontology with reference to the "mute, blind, concealed, and labouring demogorgon" that is identified with the subject. This has implications for the reciprocal relation between philosophy and literature staged by the doppelgänger.

The passage quoted above occurs almost at the end of a letter that the doppelgänger writes. The title of the piece in which this letter appears announces an initial differentiation from Coates's conception of the Double: the title is *Clavis Fichtiana seu Leibgeberiana*. The key or cipher (*clavis*) to the thought of Fichte or Leibgeber. Leibgeber is one of the names that the doppelgänger dons as it transverses a number of Jean Paul's works, while Johann Gottlieb Fichte is the self-avowedly Kantian philosopher who exercised an enormous influence on the formation of the Romantic movement in Germany at the turn of the nineteenth century. Therefore, Jean Paul does not orient his doppelgänger toward a "critique of ideology" in general; rather, Jean Paul's doppelgänger is specifically related to subjectivity as it was conceived by Kant and by Fichte.[7] The subject's internalizing movement, the "I came, then, from eternity, and head into eternity," is Jean Paul's way of questioning the relation of reason and understanding as it is explicated by the two transcendental or "critical" philosophers. In other words, Jean Paul is arguing here against subjective autonomy (*Selbstständigkeit*), a defining characteristic of the Enlightenment subject.

Besides the different context, there is another difference between Jean Paul and Coates that is more pivotal in an understanding of the place of the political that the doppelgänger introduces. For Coates, the double presents a concept of experience that is regulated by a constitutive loss or deficiency. The divided self's experiences are always lacking, since reality is "never encountered directly." The subject is at an impasse. For Jean Paul, the doppelgänger still retains the potential for a release from this state of affairs. Jean Paul argues for a residual transcendence inherent in the autonomous self. By conducting a *critique of loneliness* Jean Paul shows that the space of loneliness, despite being the other of the space of communicability, is nevertheless still related to a place of sociality. The loneliness of the doppelgänger exposes a lack in the autonomous subject, but this does not mean that the subject as such is rejected. To the contrary, the lonely subject, the last man, inscribes the potential of its overcoming—the overcoming of lack and the overcoming of autonomy. Thus, the doppelgänger can be seen as an overcoming of the idealist, autonomous subject, a subject that is premised on the ability to have an immediate access to its internal functions.

Jean Paul's critique of loneliness will be conducted, first, as a critique of the function of place in Kant and in Fichte. Kantian epistemology approaches experience and ethics by the division between the faculties of cognition and reason. The subject that cognizes does not find itself in a particular space, but rather in a space coordinated by the separation of reason and understanding—what will be called a *limit spacing*. Fichte intensifies Kant's lesson, arguing for the autonomy of reason that in turn underwrites the autonomy of the subject. Thus, the absolute I is placed firmly within reason—in what will be called the *unlimited limit spacing*. Friedrich Jacobi, a close friend of Jean Paul's, attacked transcendental epistemology in his open letter to Fichte, which, as it will be shown, exercised a decisive influence on the composition of Jean Paul's *Clavis* and thus the conception of the doppelgänger. Departing from a similar rejection of epistemology, it will be demonstrated that Jean Paul's second aspect of his critique of loneliness shows that loneliness can be become the basis of critique, that is, loneliness opens up the possibility of the subject to make decisions and thus to become part of the polis. The critique of loneliness is now the critique as the possibility of meaning and judgment that loneliness enacts. The transfiguration of loneliness from what leads to isolation to that which makes it possible for the subject to return from isolation is essentially an attempt to give a place back to the subject. This is a place that is no longer severed from particularity, no longer the eternity of reason—rather, what will be called a *limiting space*.[8] Jean Paul arrives at this alternative conception of place by emphasizing the priority of art over epistemology. Artistic expression is always related to specific linguistic use, and as such specificity is ineliminable in it. The political significance of place is, then, linked to the political significance of art to the extent that the critique of loneliness as it is carried out by the doppelgänger returns to the subject not only its argumentative power but also its positioning in historical particularity.

However, as the discussion of the ontology introduced by Freud's uncanny will show, the placement of the subject is liminal. Neither the finite nor the infinite is privileged, and neither the particular nor the universal. Rather, what matters is the type of relation established between them. A relation that is not amenable to absolutism but ceaselessly endeavors to retain openness. Further, as it will be argued in the final section of this chapter, this relation has a transformative effect. Thus, the critique of loneliness does not seek an overcoming as dialectical negation or sublation. Rather, what is introduced is a kind of denial that is also an affirmation. This is crucial to the definition of the doppelgänger.

HARRINGTON'S "FLIES": KANT'S MADNESS

A presentation of Jean Paul's critique of the space that loneliness opens up in Kantian philosophy will be an explication of the doppelgänger's expression of its own loneliness: "I, totally alone, not even a pulse-beat, no life; nothing around me and without me nothing other than nothing.... I came, then, from eternity, and head into eternity." What this passage initially introduces is the problematic relation between reason and madness. The confinement of the subject in a desolate place was a standard metaphor for the state of the madman. As Foucault has argued, the connection between the place of exclusion of madness and the eternal but empty space of reason had been established at least since the Renaissance: "The ultimate language of madness is that of reason."[9] A well-known example from the time of the genesis of the doppelgänger in Germany attests to the use of loneliness as a metaphor for madness.[10] It comes from book 7, chapter 4 of Goethe's *Wilhelm Meister*. The doctor reports the Harper's own description of his mental ailment: "'I see nothing before me, and nothing behind me,' he [the Harper] would say, 'nothing but the endless night of loneliness in which I find myself. I have no feeling left.... There is no height or depth, no forwards or backwards, nothing to describe this continual sameness.'"[11] Loneliness is the main characteristic that the madman uses to describe his condition. Although madness runs implicitly through the whole of the *Lehrjahre*, its most explicit articulation is in relation to the figure of the

Harper. Similarly, the doppelgänger's behavior in *Siebenkäs* is always regarded as transgressing beyond the standards of "normal" behavior, and, indeed, in *Titan* it ends up confined in a lunatic asylum.[12]

The evocation of loneliness is not made in the name of a phenomenal description of human nature; nor is loneliness construed by either Goethe or Jean Paul as an existential condition. In addition, it should not be forgotten that, as literary texts, they are not concerned with a symptomatology or aetiology of madness. Rather, extreme loneliness is a tropological description of the madman, *in the first person*, of his own self-consciousness. Man soliloquizes, just like Oedipus the last man. As such, what emerges as an issue is narration itself. Now, the nexus of confinement, internalization, and expression should not be seen to subsist as a mere trope. The loneliness that madness demands is not just a turn of phrase, but rather, it has a dual significance. First, internalization is forced on the subject by contingency itself, or as Blanchot puts it in his review of Foucault's book: "The demand to shut up the outside, that is, to constitute it as an *interiority* of anticipation or exception, is the exigency that leads society—or momentary reason—to make madness exist, that is, to make it *possible*." Second, the linguistic manifestations of this "exigency" do not allow themselves to be neatly distinguished from works of art. Thus the work of art, instead of a demarcation, rather "designates the point where there would be an exchange between aberration and creation, where ... all language would still hesitate."[13] Not only is, then, this internalization linked to the cognitive urgency. In addition, the wavering between "aberration and creation" installs art at the fault line between madness and cognition. This fault line will be crucial for an understanding of the space of madness in Kant.

Apropos of the subject's loneliness, Kant's own definition of madness in the *Anthropology* is crucial. This definition leads to an interpretation of the space of the autonomous subject, and thus to an interpretation of the loneliness of the doppelgänger as it is articulated in Jean Paul:

> The only general characteristic of insanity is the loss of a sense for ideas that are common to all (*sensus communis*), and its replacement with a sense for ideas peculiar to ourselves (*sensus privatus*) [*Das einzige allgemeine Merkmal der Verrücktheit ist der Verlust des Gemeinsinnes* (sensus communis) *und der dagegen eintretende logische Eigensinn* (sensus privatus)].... It is in just this that illusion consists, something which is said to be deceptive, or rather something whereby one is misled into self-deception in the application of a rule. He who does not bother

about this touchstone, but gets it into his head to acknowledge his own private opinion as already valid without regard for, or even against, common opinion, has submitted to a play of thoughts in which he proceeds and judges in a world not shared with other people, but rather (as in a dream) he sees himself in his own little world.[14]

Despite the lack of dramatic intensity, there is still here a clear statement of the loneliness of the madman. The madman is enclosed in a private world that resembles a dream. It is important not to confuse the *sensus communis* here with the common sense (*Gemeinsinn*) of the *Critique of Judgement*. Kant himself indicates the difference in section 20 of the *Critique*: while *Gemeinsinn* starts with a feeling, that is, with a particular, the *sensus communis* is linked to the faculty of understanding and thus to the cognition of objects. "The judgement of [the *sensus communis*] is not one by feeling, but always one by concepts, though usually only in the shape of obscurely represented principles."[15] Clearly, the judgment of the *sensus communis* is an objective judgment, a judgment about the cognition of objects. It is not a reflective judgment. With regard to the subject, it would have been tautological to attribute the loneliness to the lack of *sensus communis* if the latter indicated merely the physical presence of others—in other words, it would have been conflating politics with the political. Thus, contrary to Blanchot, Kant holds to a very sharp demarcation between madness and art, which for him follows from the cognitive faculty as it is related to sociality.[16]

According to the *Anthropology*, madness misapplies the laws of understanding, while the *Critique of Judgement* makes the additional point that the *sensus communis* is needed when the understanding applies obscure rules. Nevertheless, a parallel reading of Kant's quick extrapolation of *sensus communis* in the two books only generates ambiguities. For, despite the caveat of the *Critique*, the first example offered by the *Anthropology*—the case of whether there is really a lamp on the table or whether the lamp is an illusion—does not seem to warrant any peculiar application of the categories. And a second example, provided immediately after the passage cited above, not only tends to implicitly remove any functional sense of community from the *sensus communis*, but it also, if it is related back to the *Critique of Pure Reason*, creates a significant strain within Kantian epistemology. Kant refers to the case of James Harrington, who claimed that he was seeing "flies." However, Kant argues, the "flies" were not inexplicable hallucinations but rather Harrington's idiosyncratic way of referring to his beads of perspiration.

The argument is that "terminology" that describes real perceptions can be made to accord with the *sensus communis* of the understanding, as long as it is realized that idiosyncratic expressions "point out only the similarity" between the term used and the actual concept.[17] Thus Harrington's expression "flies" is merely a peculiar way of describing the perspiration jumping off the skin. The crucial terms here are "terminology" and "similarity." They stand, so to speak, a step lower than cognition and representation, but, Kant contends, this lower standing can be amended by the cool-headed, terminology-neutral critical philosopher. The problem is that, beyond mere conjecture, it remains impossible to decide whether an individual's terminology is just a case of private perception, of *sensus privatus*. Further, undecidability also pertains to similarity, since only a few pages earlier Kant had defined *Wahnwitz* or *insania* as a state "in which the mind is deceived by analogies, which are being confused with concepts of similar things."[18] These are not merely pedantic observations about loosely used examples in the *Anthropology*. Rather, Kant's inability to find a proper example for the madman's use of the understanding discloses an imbroglio in the demarcation between understanding and reason that is central to Jean Paul's critique.

To clarify this, what is required is a consideration of subjectivity as it is conjoint with an implicit notion of place in the first *Critique*—a book, incidentally, in which the deliberate abjuration of examples is striking. From the opening of the *Critique of Pure Reason*, the Transcendental Aesthetic, space is explicitly internalized: "Space is essentially one; the manifold in it, and hence also the universal concept of spaces as such, rests solely on [our bringing in] limitations."[19] The space of the Aesthetic is given by the delimitations of the cognitive subject. However, the function that this internalized space performs is gleaned by starting from the subject itself. The Kantian subject is often described as "empty." This intends to indicate that the subject is stripped of all content, that it is pure form. This move is made in order that the subject be capable of cognizing objects through the use of the categories. Cognition happens through the faculty of understanding that finds a concept for the object. As for reason and metaphysics, Kant's well-known comment in the introduction contends that their fate is to easily go into a flight in the air, irrespective of a secure foundation. This is nowhere more obvious than in the examination of the antinomies in the Transcendental Dialectic. The descent from the universal to the particular is impossible if thought is dealing with a transcendental idea. Such an idea is totally unconditionable, impossible to be determined by the subject, and thus it can never become constitutive. The grounded cognition through concepts and the flight of metaphysical ideas seem to make a distinct cut between the two faculties, understanding and reason. What guarantees such a neat division is a notion of subjectivity that is defined by the use of rules. Not only is the subject "empty"; its defining function, its potential to employ the categories, does not occur in a place that has geographical coordinates. The rules that regulate the subject's functions create instead a spacing. The purpose of this spacing is to facilitate the subject's application of the rules. More precisely, it is the rules themselves, as a defining feature of subjectivity, that create a spacing between subject and object. The epistemology of the *Critique of Pure Reason* installs the subject in a place that is delimited by the rules of understanding—a place that can be called *limit spacing*. In the case of reason, this limit spacing leads to the conclusion that the rules are inapplicable, or that metaphysical ideas are distinct from the concepts of understanding. What is emphatically not permitted within this limit spacing is specificity: the object is either placed at one remove, as a representation that corresponds but is not qualitatively identical to it, or the object is something ethereal, a noumenon, whose function is strictly regulative.

Such a seemingly neat division between understanding and reason remains, nonetheless, precarious. Examples such as Harrington's "flies" expose a fateful weakness to the whole edifice. Any word that does not immediately, automatically conform to a concept—and, how often does this happen? what is the nature of such a word?—any word that is meant to be dealt with by the understanding but resists relinquishing its particular subjective reference, creates a disturbance in the tranquil compartmentalization. The crucial terms, as already intimated, are "terminology" and "analogy." It is a characteristic of idiosyncratic expression that it resists divorce from the particularity of its enunciation. Now, this would not be a problem, if its similarity to a concept could be decided conclusively. If the word "flies," as a metonymy, is a substitute for "beads of perspiration," then the understanding has indeed claimed its province and has the power to say whether the experience is true or an illusion. However, words are not always so pliant; words often offer great resistance. What if the word "flies" is a metaphor? What if, instead of a one-to-one substitution, a whole series of variant words is referred to here? The word now, through its tropological function, has suddenly acquired a peculiar characteristic: it becomes unconditionable; what falls under it can be potentially expanded or contracted infinitely as much as one pleases.[20] This quality of resistance can, almost surreptitiously, usurp for certain words the properties of universals, but without thereby obliterating the word's particularity. Precisely at this point the metaphorical description of madness as loneliness is used by Jean Paul as an argument against Kantian subjectivity and epistemology.

The word as image that has taken up the properties of the universal without thereby losing its particularity, its reference to the thing, is Jean Paul's weapon against Kant. The doppelgänger, in what *may* be insane ravings induced by its submersion in critical philosophy, offers a "proof" about the systematic coherence of its philosophy: "whatever the human understanding cannot explain as mad is not pure philosophy for us."[21] Transcendental philosophy *requires* the indecision before the object. At this moment the editor, that is, Jean Paul himself as one of the *dramatis personae*, intervenes to offer "a few general philosophical exercises [*Exercitationes*]" for the purpose of clarifying metaphysical mistakes.[22] The announcement, "Therefore I am of the opinion," indicates that the *Exercitationes* present a clear, direct, and damaging critique of such illusions.[23] This task is pursued with a discussion of "language" (*Sprache*). The crucial sentence states:

> [E]ach image and each signification must be also something in addition, namely also itself a primordial image and a thing, which one can repeatedly depict and signify and so forth.[24]

The force of the adverb "repeatedly" (*wieder*) is to indicate that particularity cannot be eliminated, even in the infinity of the universal. What is precluded here is a state in which the image and the sign will exist in identity. The relation is not foreclosed; rather, the relation is repeatable. The power of the image, the metaphoric element of the word, consists in an open relation that persists between the reality and the ideality of the referent. The metaphor as image *and* signification contravenes an epistemology that bifurcates subject and object. Such an epistemology, which has to account for the separation between understanding and reason in order to account for the validation of the object and the freedom of thought, is unable to decide between the imagistic and the significatory function of the word as universal. Kant's wavering before Harrington's "flies" in the *Anthropology* shows that Kant's own terms, "terminology" and "analogy," cannot be fitted to the subject or the object respectively. It is only conjecture that will either assign the thing that such a word signifies through the peculiar application of the categories as it is guaranteed by the *sensus communis*, or assign madness to the subject whose terminology is incommunicable because, since it lacks a community, it is demoted to a *sensus privatus*. This wavering, due to the absence of a criterion to distinguish between error and madness, puts the subject of limit spacing in extreme uncertainty. For every time that the subject makes a reference, every time that a word is uttered, there is the danger that the thing signified is a spectral metaphysical idea. The subject may not be physically alone, but loneliness still features as that which removes communication—and thus sociality—as a possibility. There is no longer anything to return the subject to the polis. Any possibility of action is premised on the subject taking its own actions as exemplary—regardless of others.

Limit spacing places the subject in a region where its own autonomy or "self-standing" (*Selbstständigkeit*) has become detrimental. Jean Paul describes the conception of such a subject as an expanding membrane that seeks to encompass reality, but language always indicates the mistake of such a procedure:

> Now, if a philosopher wants to spread out his epidermic calculus and to arrive thereby at a transcendent chain of calculation, then the language alone shows him three certain ways to miscalculate.[25]

So long as particularity does not feature in the distinction between understanding and reason, there is always the possibility that the utterances of the subject will never be guaranteed by an object and their flight will not find a secure ground. And, so long as this guarantee is wanting, the subject's words remain hollow. From the three above-mentioned ways of language's miscalculations, the third, "the best piece of art," is to pose an "identity in language between the sign and the object."[26] In other words, the philosophy for which everything is "cut to size out of the I's skin" is premised on the impossibility of a word as universal, of a word where sign and object are never allowed to coincide.[27] However, it is precisely the unconditionality of the word—the *incoincidence* of word and sign—that is allowed by the repeatability of the word, which in turn allows for the possibility of meaning, judgment, and communication.

From here, it is easy to make sense of Jean Paul's rejection of the subjectivity and epistemology of transcendental philosophy due to that philosophy's inability to sustain the distinction between understanding and reason. The doppelgänger's "proof" that "whatever the human understanding cannot explain as mad is not pure philosophy for us" is, then, not at all a deranged raving, but the most accurate description of limit spacing. The whole critical project was undertaken in the name of the cognitive emancipation of the transcendental subject. However, such a subject is only ever allowed at the limit spacing, where the rules of understanding can only make tentative conjectures about the relation of "terminology" and "analogy." If critical philosophy is to persist on the identity of sign and object, this identity cannot be found in the conjectures of the understanding. The identity ultimately rests on reason alone, in whose eternal space the particular is absent and the different can become the same. The limit spacing of understanding collapses into the eternal monotony of reason. Or, to unravel Jean Paul's own imagery, the subject spreads its skin from within eternity, but the price it has to pay is that "words do not even outline a silhouette"; reality is not even a representation of a representation.[28] The subject can no longer dispute about anything, it can no longer encounter any resistance, not even from words.

If a characteristic of madness is arbitrary analogy, then the transcendental subject is mad, since all its analogies are arbitrated by conjectures. What the closing of the doppelgänger's letter put at stake was the relation between particular and universal. The faculty of reason in the Kantian scheme is the movement toward particularity through the universal. The articulation of the doppelgänger's loneliness as a sojourn firmly *within* eternity, its entrapment in eternity ("I came from eternity and head into eternity"), amounts to an admission that the universal has failed to attain particularity. So long as the protoplast doppelgänger's first step was taken inside the kingdom of eternity, there is no way of stepping out of this region. The subject may be told by its categories that it occupies a world of objects, but the subject (a last man, alone in eternity) is still unfit *to name* any objects.

THE BLACK NOTHING AND THE WHITE NOTHING: JEAN PAUL'S *CLAVIS FICHTIANA*

Yet, the last contention is not strictly true. As the doppelgänger itself puts it: "Around me nothing, and without me nothing other than nothing." The subject is unable to name any objects, except for one, the *Nothing*. Nothingness may appear as a synonym of the space of loneliness, and as such to reinscribe the madness of the autonomous subject. This could be supported by the conclusion of the most influential writing on madness of the first decade of the nineteenth century, *Die Nachtwachen des Bonaventura*. After describing a number of scenes where madness unfolds, the book ends with the following evocation: "On the grave beyond, the visionary [*Geisterseher*] is still standing and embracing Nothing! And the echo in the charnel-house cries for the last time—*Nothing!*—"[29] Upon reading the *Nachtwachen*, Jean Paul believed that Schelling (whom he assumed to be the anonymous author) had imitated his character Giannozzo, which is the name of the doppelgänger in the first appendix to *Titan*—one of the many names that doppelgänger assumes in Jean Paul's works.[30] However, the ability to name "nothing" is not restricted to the madness that the autonomous subject is unable to dispel. In addition, it is this naming itself—the naming of "nothing"—that announces the possibility of finding a different place for the subject, a place that attains particularity.

The relation of the "nothing" to Jean Paul's doppelgänger is multivalent, and some of its repercussions will be demonstrated soon. Meanwhile, it should not be overlooked that what the "nothing" brings to the fore is what has been indicated as the *incoincidence* of word and sign, that is, the word as universal. Max Kommerell understands the importance of this point perfectly well and expresses it succinctly in his discussion of the *Clavis* by saying that Jean Paul is "based on an empty magic-word [*auf einem leeren Wortzauber beruhe*]."[31] The word is *empty* so long as it is uttered by a subject in the limit spacing of transcendental philosophy, where it cannot help but be threatened by its enclosure in reason. However, the *magic* of the word consists in the recognition that despite its emptiness, the word has nevertheless defined a particular place. What is needed to accommodate this is a contrary movement, a *reversal* whereby the emptiness of the word forces a delimitation of the space from which the subject speaks. It is a different metaphysics of place, one that reduces space by moving out of pure infinity and into particularity, one that can be described as *limiting space*. Rules no longer circumscribe the epistemological power of the subject. Rather, the subject's utterances resist a severance from particularity that limits the subject to a space that could no more be the eternity of reason.

The result of this maneuver, whose execution still has to be demonstrated, is that the subject is liberated from the hold of identitary logic. In the eternity of reason a position and its antithesis are still mutually inclusive precluding disagreement on specific situations. The limiting of space, on the contrary, installs the subject in a specific place that is agonistic. It is a place where decisions on language are offered as possibilities and where judgment, although still regulated by laws, is nonetheless coextensive with those laws and not limited by them. The primacy of the cognizing subject has given its place to the disputing, the political subject. It is crucial that the transfer to a different place—a differentiating place, the limiting space of the political—is achieved with the *Wortzauber*. The doppelgänger, then, undoes the autonomy of the subject of epistemology with recourse to literature. Art becomes a privileged site for the enactment of the political. The move from literature to art is solicited by the aporia indicated, in Blanchot's way of putting it, as the madness of the work: the indecision "between aberration and creation" that creates a space where "all language would still hesitate." The point is that the hesitation does not have to be dispelled by drawing generic differentiations, that is, by the imposition of a rule. Genres can never be absolutely or definitively delimited—a point that will be taken up in detail and in relation to the doppelgänger in Chapter 3.[32] Rather, it is in this site opened up by hesitation, the site of art as such, that the subject can find a place where decisions, meaning, and judgment are germane. (Hesitation will be linked in Chapter 2 to justice.) The word-magic is a political act to the extent that it allows for criticism. Word-magic claims a place for the subject by making art possible. And art creates a space that is not only linked to particularity but is also not foreclosed. The political subject is thus given the conditions of the possibility for dispute by overcoming the conditions of the possibility of removing dispute as such.

The rejection of the static confrontation between subject and object in favor of a dynamic coarticulation of subject and place is an effect of the presentation of the *leere Wortzauber* and the presence of art. Art effectuates the limiting space that transfigures the presentation of the emptiness of limit spacing. A return has to be made to Jean Paul's interconnection of presentation and presence in the citation from the doppelgänger's letter. This return is necessitated by Jean Paul's own insistence on the return or repetition of the relation between sign and image, on the *wieder* that governs their relation. But this return has to carry out a focusing on particularity, in this case, a focusing on the way that loneliness in the *Clavis* effectuates the passage from an autonomous subject to the political subject. "I, totally alone, not even a pulse-beat, no life; nothing around me and without me nothing other than nothing." The magic in this instance is performed by the word "nothing." The resistance that this word offers, and which forces a return to it, is linked to the doppelgänger. To explicate this subject is not a straightforward task, since the torsions around the word "doppelgänger" relate, on the one hand, to the composition of three works by Jean Paul, *Siebenkäs*, *Titan*, and the *Clavis*, and, on the other, to the history of Jean Paul's contact with the philosophy of Fichte.

The statement of paramount loneliness in the *Clavis* is the doppelgänger's last word within Jean Paul's chronology of publications. Prior to the *Clavis*, the doppelgänger expired in *Titan* just after uttering "Ich auch, Ich gleich Ich."[33] This statement can be translated either as "Me too, I resemble myself," or "Me too, I equals I"—and, as it will be demonstrated, a lot hangs on the relation of the two possible translations. The *Clavis* is an appendix to the first appendix of *Titan*. It consists of a letter that the doppelgänger sent to Jean Paul, in which it discusses the implications of its conversion to the philosophy of Fichte. This conversion was already announced in *Titan*, but it appeared in a somewhat abrupt, almost ad hoc manner. *Titan* is the story of young Albano and his search for his real parentage. Schoppe, one of Albano's companions, embarks on a trip to Spain in order to assist his master in his pursuit. However, his route must have gone through Jena, since upon his return Schoppe suddenly declares that "*der Ich könnte kommen*" (the I could come).[34] Albano is puzzled about who this I, *der Ich*, might be—not *das Ich*, not the personal pronoun in the neuter indicating a self, but the personal pronoun in the masculine, as if the pronoun is flesh-and-blood, one particular self. In response to Albano's puzzlement at such a strange terminology, Schoppe contends that he is not mad and that it all makes perfect sense for someone like him, who is immersed in the philosophy of Fichte. A student of Fichte's, Schoppe contends, can contemplate the possibility of *der Ich* appearing in all seriousness. It is an expectation premised on the fact that "das Ich setzt Sich und den Ich samt jenem Rest, den mehrere die Welt nennen."[35] It is better to paraphrase this passage, since a literal translation is bound to be misleading: The I, the neuter, impersonal I posits Itself, as a real entity, and then posits also the I, the masculine flesh-and-blood I, and along with it everything else that is commonly called the world. With the notion of "positing," the philosophy of Fichte is evoked. Suffice it to say here that, for the doppelgänger, the positing of the I does not merely introduce a self that is separated from "the rest," that is, everything but the I itself, a space where the doppelgänger stands alone. Further, the play between the neuter and the masculine personal pronoun indicates that what performs this topographic separation is a linguistic act.

All this, of course, is far from clear to Albano. Despite his perplexity, Albano remains receptive to his friend's idiosyncratic statements, but the rest of the world is not so kind. Schoppe is locked up in a lunatic asylum, where in isolation the fear of the impending arrival of *der Ich* is further accentuated. His escape from the asylum turns tragic when Schoppe suddenly encounters Siebenkäs, the character of Jean Paul's previous novel to whom Schoppe looks identical. *Der Ich* has appeared before him and Schoppe dies of shock, with the words "Ich auch, Ich gleich Ich" escaping his mouth. The fateful meeting with Siebenkäs reintroduces the doppelgänger. Siebenkäs recognizes in Schoppe his long lost friend Leibgeber, with whom he had previously exchanged names. In the novel *Siebenkäs*, the extraordinary similarity in appearance between Siebenkäs and Leibgeber means that an onlooker would mistake one for the other. Indeed, they are so similar, that they are "Doppeltgänger." They constantly feel each other's presence; they are constantly together, even though they might be apart. Indeed, the word "Doppeltgänger" is introduced when Leibgeber is going away, separating from his look-alike, his *sosie*.[36] Even though they are going their separate ways, Siebenkäs and Leibgeber are still united, like a wanderer and his shadow or like a "double-walker."

Fichte is not merely a name that is introduced as an aside to the relation between Siebenkäs and Leibgeber at the end of *Titan* and its second appendix. Fichte's philosophy is inextricably linked to the conjunction—so crucial for *nothing* and subjectivity—between *das Ich* and *der Ich* posed by the Doppelgänger, despite the fact that Jean Paul was not versed in Fichte when he wrote the word "Doppeltgänger" for the first time in *Siebenkäs*. In a letter to Jacobi dated 4 June 1799, Jean Paul wrote that he had only read the "Outline of the Distinctive Character of the *Wissenschaftslehre*," a few bits of Fichte's moral philosophy, and the criticism of others.[37] Jean Paul felt the need to inform Jacobi that he had not read Fichte's *Wissenschaftslehre*, since Jacobi had sent him his letter to Fichte before making it public. Jean Paul agreed with Jacobi, but he could not comment in detail. By the beginning of October, Jean Paul had started going over Fichte's writings, and a month later he admitted to Jacobi that he studied Fichte long and hard, but "in disbelief."[38] On 10 November Jean Paul wrote Jacobi his criticism of Fichte's philosophy, which contained in a nutshell all the points that were to be employed against Fichte in the *Clavis*. Indeed, this second November letter was followed on 22 December by Jean Paul's sending Jacobi the first complete draft of the *Clavis*. What this correspondence shows is the influence that Jacobi's letter to Fichte had on Jean Paul, who thus turned to the philosophy of Fichte, and, within a very short time—indicative of the intensity of Jean Paul's immersion in Fichte's philosophy—*Clavis* was produced. At that time, *Titan* was in preparation, but its composition did not start in earnest until shortly after and was only fully published a whole four years later. Meanwhile, Jean Paul initially published the *Clavis* as a separate pamphlet in March 1800, that is, only months after he started reading Fichte. Its connection to the doppelgänger is clear in relation to *Titan*, to which the *Clavis* was added as an appendix to the appendix. In *Titan* Schoppe's real identity is revealed—the student of the "I-philosophy" was Leibgeber, that is, the doppelgänger from *Siebenkäs*.

Since the *Clavis* is dedicated to Jacobi, and since Jacobi's letter incited Jean Paul's turn to Fichte, an examination of this open letter is indispensable in understanding the nature of the doppelgänger's subjective ontology.[39] It is precisely in this letter that Jacobi introduces nihilism as an epistemological concern and thus the polemic with Fichte is linked to the notion of the "nothing." It may appear that polemic is not the right word, since Jacobi seems to be laudatory of Fichte at the start: "I consider you the true Messiah of speculative reason, the genuine son of the promise of a philosophy pure *through and through*, existing *in* and *through* itself."[40] However, the intention is certainly polemical, and the word "Messiah" in this context is anything but unqualified endorsement. For Jacobi, a clear either/or decision is unavoidable: either "God is, and is *outside me, a living self-subsisting being*; or I am God. There is no third."[41] Clearly, Fichte has opted for the latter alternative, he has posited himself as Messiah, while Jacobi stands for the former, a staunch defender of Christianity. In other words, according to Jacobi a choice has to be made between "either a rational skepticism or an irrational faith."[42] This is Jacobi's unavoidable epistemological dilemma. Fichte is a rationalist insofar as he trusts in reason and uses reason as the primary instrument of his system. Jacobi is an irrationalist insofar as he denies the primacy of reason. For Jacobi, a rationalist is forced to a skeptical position since it is impossible for reason to underpin reality as something other than itself—in other words, there is nothing but reason. To avoid nothingness, one has to turn to faith, a belief in God that is not premised merely on an internal law but also on an ontological *salto mortale*.[43] The choice then is between "chimerism," mysticism, pietism on the one hand, and nihilism, atheism, egoism, on the other; one is either an "*Unphilosoph*" or a solipsist.[44] For Jacobi, there is no third option that can be discovered within philosophy itself.

Denying that a third alternative is possible strikes at the very heart of Fichte's philosophy: it strikes at Fichte's conception of the self, of the *Ich*. Before sketching Fichte's absolute I, it has to be recalled that Fichte is a transcendental philosopher. He regards himself as a follower of Kant; he even implies that he has understood Kant better than Kant understood his own philosophy.[45] Fichte's aim is to unify the three Kantian faculties. To do so, he reworks the conditions of the possibility of experience based on the conception of subjectivity. Thus, the absolute I is born. In other words, Fichte, on the one hand, regards the distinction between cognizable object and noumenon as redundant; although this point is not addressed in these terms, it is nevertheless made clear, for instance, when he describes the activity of the absolute I as the original or intellectual intuition of the I.[46] On the other hand, Fichte attempts to derive the rules of understanding, the power of judgment, and reason from a single source, the absolute I. Thus, Fichte's *Ich* has a transcendental function; as such, it is not experiential (it cannot be encountered in the world); it is simply something that is necessary for experience.

This transcendental function of the I is explicated in the *Wissenschaftslehre* in three principles or *Grundsätze*. These principles are laid out in the first three sections of the *Wissenschaftslehre* (§§1–3). The first is the principle that the I posits itself absolutely. Fichte explicitly states that this is a proposition which cannot be proved. Fichte also expresses this principle by saying that the I is self-identical, or "Ich gleich Ich" (I equals I), and even writes it as "I = I." (The "Ich gleich Ich" are, of course, the very same words that the doppelgänger utters before its death.) The I's self-reflection is the axiom of the existence of subjectivity. This positing also logically implies its negation, or *Vernichtung* in Fichte's terminology. The I counterposits the not-I. In other words, at the moment that the I is posited as a logical necessity, it is logically necessary to also posit its opposite. The not-I is, then, what is not the I, the rest of the world as a logical necessity. Thus, the principle of negation presents the "nothing" as that which is solely defined by the subject's rational function and yet in contradistinction to the subject itself. Obviously, Fichte's absolute I and not-I need to escape from these purely formal relations and find a way of having a real experience. To explain how this happens, Fichte has recourse to a third principle that is logically implied by the previous two principles. He argues that the absolute I and the not-I interact with each other, or limit each other. Out of this self-limiting activity, or the self-reflection proper to subjectivity, the empirical self is formed.

Three observations are needed here: the first about what is a foundational claim in the *Wissenschaftslehre*; the second about the space that the absolute subject occupies; and the third about an initial dissonance between Fichte's space and the space as it was explicated by his "student" Schoppe, or the doppelgänger, in *Titan*. All three elements will be crucial for Jacobi's rebuke of Fichte, as well as for Jean Paul's reworking of the concept of the "nothing." First, then, Fichte's three principles are necessary but not experiential for a number of very good reasons, one of which is that Fichte *has to* deny that the self is a substance, in the sense that the self is neither an object nor a soul.[47] To avoid this consequence, Fichte insists on the independence of reason. The three principles are firmly within reason, a fact that accounts for the autonomy of the self. The nonsubstantiality of the self, self-autonomy, and the autonomy of reason are all indispensable for Fichte's system to work. Second, the limiting introduced with the third principle is the product of negation, in the sense that the third principle is implied in the previous principle. However, it will be deceptive to understand the terms negation and limitation as stages of a dialectic—or, at least, a dialectic in the Hegelian sense. The autonomy of reason, within which the limitations of the empirical self occur, does not introduce a movement between subject and object. At this stage, cognition is still not an issue. Moreover, the absence of an object also distinguishes Fichte's conception of limit from Kant's own limit spacing. Fichte does not merely internalize space, as Kant does in the Transcendental Aesthetic. Fichte's spacing is also precognitive, that is, it has no relation to an object and is firmly within reason itself. The internalizing of space means that for Fichte there is a kind of limit spacing. But the inclusion of the limitations of the empirical self—or, rather, subjectivity—firmly within reason makes this spacing eternal: it is an *unlimited limit spacing*. This is the place of the Fichtean subject—and it is not a coincidence that both the subject and reason share for Fichte a common epithet: autonomous.[48] Third, if the empirical self of Fichte's third principle is compared with *der Ich* whom Schoppe dreads in *Titan*, it will be noted that the two are not the same. While Schoppe entertains the possibility of encountering *der Ich*, and indeed he does so with fatal consequences when he meets his *sosie*, it is still strictly impossible to come across the empirical self of the third principle. The empirical self remains within reason, and differs from the absolute I only in that it is derivable from the previous two principles. *Der Ich* is differentiated from the empirical self, because *der Ich* is dependent on language. While Jean Paul, as already intimated, creates a linguistic space with the interplay of *das Ich* and *der Ich*, Fichte's strategy is to denounce any linguistic influence in pure philosophy.[49]

The first two aspects are directly addressed in Jacobi's letter to Fichte. The dilemma between rationalism and skepticism is essentially dealing with the way space is conceived by the subject. Either God is admitted as separated from the human being, or the subject internalizes God. The epistemological nihilism that this dilemma introduces undercuts the spacing that the nonsubstantiality and autonomy of the self and the independence of reason have assumed as a foundation to the Fichtean System. Jacobi's indictment is essentially that the Fichtean self is a substance, and this strikes at the heart of Fichte's philosophy. What propels Jacobi's criticism is the placement of the absolute I in predialectical negation, that is, the way space is conceived when the second and third principles of the *Wissenschaftslehre* are deduced from the first axiomatic principle of self-identity. This is made clear when the relation between nothing and substance is examined. Although this relation in 1799 would have been viewed within the context of contemporary public debates,[50] it is nevertheless more fruitful to examine Jacobi's objection with recourse to the Aristotelian definition of substance. This is not an arbitrary choice: Aristotle's definition of substance had been accepted by the philosophical tradition and is still operative in both Jacobi and Fichte.[51] A substance, says Aristotle, "is that which is neither said of a subject nor in a subject."[52] What exists as a substance needs *nothing else in order to exist*. Now, Aristotle did not formulate the problem of substantiality in terms of the subject-object relation, and nor did Greek philosophy. Yet, given the terms of Jacobi's letter to Fichte, it is precisely the subject-object relation that is involved in substantiality. In other words, what is pursued by Jacobi is an examination of idealist epistemology in terms of substantiality. Jacobi's term "nihilism" makes sense as the topography that substance demands: *nothing* is excluded from substance. Clearly, the word "nothing" here has a double significance. It is a logical operator, an ancillary word that performs a function within reason, that is, it shows what reason itself excludes with recourse solely to its own rules. This is the meaning of "nothing" in Fichtean negation, where it performs the transition from the first to the third principle. Besides the *logical nothing*, there is also the *ontological nothing*. Nothing is that which is left out of the substance, that is, substance is treated as a space whose existence is defined by what is excluded from it. The theological implications of the ontological nothing are portrayed in Jacobi's appropriation of the label "nihilism" to designate his epistemological theism. According to Jacobi, for the egoist the "nothing" is nothing, while for the faithful the "nothing" is everything. From this point of view, Fichte's absolute I is substantial "in the concept of a pure absolute exodus and return (*from* nothing, *to* nothing, *for* nothing, *into* nothing)."[53] If the I's self-reflections are substantial, then the Fichtean subjectivity needs an ontological negation, or, in other words, it is ontologically the same as God.[54] Thus, self-reflection cannot be ontological. Jacobi grants logical consistency and logical truth to the peregrinations of the Fichtean I; but these peregrinations are forever banned from solid ground, from the surface of the earth. To repeat the same point in the terminology employed by the doppelgänger, *das Ich* is forever a logical function so that it is never possible to encounter *der Ich*.

The echo of Jacobi's critique is audible in Jean Paul's *Clavis*. "Nothing around me and without me nothing other than nothing." The loneliness of the doppelgänger is the loneliness of the absolute I that is enclosed within the borders of the totally independent reason, that is, in the unlimited limit spacing. The absolute I pretends to be a mere logical necessity that posits the rest of the world. However, logic cannot eschew the ontological implication that such an I, enclosed as it is within the independent kingdom of reason, at bottom claims a similarity to God. Yet being a reflection of God also means that absolute subjectivity can never be particularized—it is a last man. Jean Paul explicitly appropriates the distinction between the two "nothings" in the *Clavis*:

> Reason as such cannot escape from itself. . . . After the *crushing* Kant, who still left behind huge chunks, like the things-in-themselves, had to rise up the *annihilating* [or, negating, *vernichtende*, the one who performs the negation, or *Vernichtung*, of Fichte's second principle] Leibgeber . . . who also calcified them and left nothing standing except the white Nothing [*weiße Nichts*] . . . namely the ideal *finitude* of the infinitude. If that was also to be done away with (and Fichte gave certain indications to that effect), then only the *black Nothing* [*schwarze Nichts*] would still remain, the infinitude, and reason would need to explain nothing else since reason would no longer be in existence.[55]

There is here an either/or operating. Nothing is either "white," that is, the ontological nothing that corresponds to the ideal finitude, the everything that is left out of the substance God. Or, nothing is "black," the logical nothing that resides in a metaphysical region, nowhere to be found except in the nonexperiential infinitude of reason, "since neither concepts nor intuitions belong or persist in this ether."[56] Fichte has indeed avoided the Kantian undecidability between reason and understanding. However, Fichte has done so by further radicalizing the internalization of space. Jacobi's dilemma catches the *Wissenschaftslehre* between either theology or solipsism. Both make a mockery of the absolute I, the former by implying that it is no longer part of philosophy as such, while the latter locates it in a region completely severed from reality. These are the only placings admitted from Jacobi's epistemological-philosophical perspective.

The distinction between the "white" and the "black" nothing, a distinction that the doppelgänger itself draws, reenacts Jacobi's dilemma, but not exactly.[57] A difference emerges in the final sentence of the citation: with the "*black Nothing* . . . reason would need to explain nothing else since reason would no longer be in existence." The terms of reference are adjusted from the moment that explanation and existence become correlated issues. What is propounded here is that meaning is related to an existing place, a space of particularity. This adjustment is gleaned by the curious positioning of the doppelgänger, who does not fully identify itself with either Kant or Fichte. Thus, the loneliness at the end of the *Clavis* is not, strictly speaking, the loneliness that the Kantian undecidability enforced as madness. Nor is it an unadulterated affirmation of the independence of reason, a purely solipsistic position. The difference with Fichte is also implied in the encounter with *der Ich* at the instant of the doppelgänger's death. Such an encounter is, as already intimated, impossible within the purview of the *Wissenschaftslehre*. The "white nothing," then, does retain the possibility that a third alternative, *pace* Jacobi, might be achievable, an alternative that is given by language.[58] Jean Paul is not satisfied with Jacobi's separation of two realms, the logical one regulated by reason and the ontological one where substances as well as substance as such—God—persist. Rather, the "white nothing" undoes this opposition—and it is for this reason that a nonessentialist ontology of the doppelgänger is possible, as it will be shown in the following section.

The new positioning of the doppelgänger as the subject that takes seriously the "white nothing" can be approached with reference to Schoppe's exclamation at the moment he sees Siebenkäs, the instant before he dies. At that moment the doppelgänger says: "Ich auch, Ich gleich Ich." The difficulty with a translation of this phrase has already been noted. This is because the "Ich gleich Ich" implies *both* a purely logical relation of subjective self-identity *and* a pure ontology inscribed in the self-reflexivity. Jean Paul's expression frames both of these antithetical possibilities, thereby making them impossible. It is, nevertheless, an impossibility which will yield a third possibility. The first alternative is to translate the expression "Ich gleich Ich" as "Me too, I equals I." Thus, the doppelgänger is seen to repeat Fichte's first principle: There is an axiomatic self-identity, which implies that there is something that negates subjectivity but that is also definable from within that subjectivity itself. The I is both an I and a not-I even though that negation is still a repetition of the I. However, the "gleich" that the doppelgänger articulates in *Titan* cannot be the same as the sign of identity. It cannot be a translation of the "=." The translation cannot be "I equals I." The scene of this utterance is very clear: The other I is present, it is standing in front of Schoppe/Leibgeber in the shape of his lost friend and *sosie* Siebenkäs. Nevertheless, the alternative translation is equally unsatisfactory. The phrase could also be translated as "Me too, I resemble me." The problem here is that the "gleich" stands for a cognitive function. The meaning of the phrase is sustained only so long as the perception of the "me" can be validated. But with the translation "I resemble me" the issue of linguistic usage reemerges and with it the specter of the Kantian undecidability. For who is, in this instance, *das Ich* and who *der Ich*? Schoppe/Leibgeber or Siebenkäs? Only conjecture could designate who is the subject and who the predicate. The similarity between the two, their identical appearance, makes the decision on terminology and analogy impossible. Both translations fail. The two possibilities are both impossible. Yet, not all is lost. The third way of the doppelgänger should be sought at the possibility that is announced by the two impossibilities.

This new possibility, the possibility inherent in the *white Nothing*, is not to be found within Jacobi's dilemma, that is, it is neither within philosophy nor in the subject-object epistemology. It is to be found instead within the site of art. A site, a place, that is articulated by the interplay of presentation and presence. This is an interplay in which the two impossibilities are intertwined. On the one hand, the utterance "Ich auch, Ich gleich Ich" presents the Fichtean impossibility of immediate self-identity. On the other hand, the undecidability between object and noumenon is written down in the doppelgänger's enigmatic phrase in *Titan*. However, the writing down, in a work of literature, is no longer *within* philosophy—or, more accurately, within a philosophy under the sway of representation (*Vorstellung*). What art makes present is an undecidability that is removed from the epistemological concerns of Kantianism. This removal is made possible with the subject's passage through the presentation of its formally functional self-identity. What is conducted here is a maneuver with the help of language. This maneuver is premised on Jean Paul's insistence that the relation between image and sign is infinite. Infinity is retained as the presence of the undecidability in the relation between image and sign. At the same time, nevertheless, this infinity has to go through finitude, through the thing (*Ding*) that sustains the relation—in this instance, the specific philosophy that Fichte developed. That relation is the ineliminable presentation of particularity. This is achieved within language, the artistic language that is based on a word-magic. Jean Paul is very clear on this point: the *white Nothing* is "the ideal *finitude* of the infinite." Particularity is not simply part of infinitude, but is also implicated in it.

The interplay of presence and presentation enacted by the "white nothing" can also be explicated from the point of view of the subject. This is no longer the autonomous subject of transcendentalism. Rather, it is the subject that the critique of loneliness augurs—it is the doppelgänger. The important point is that the subject retains its particularity without relinquishing reason. Thus loneliness, as a topos, has the capacity to present a historically conditioned position—in this instance, the critique of loneliness presents the Kantian and the Fichtean subjects. This, despite the fact that these subjects lose their foothold on reality and are trapped within the infinity of reason. Loneliness simultaneously raises the issue of the site in which this presentation takes place, that is, the site of art. Since the presentation has actually taken place in art, and in ways that affirm this very presentation, the subject has thereby acquired a place. What happens is that the relations of the subject qua subjectivity are radically altered, but only by the use of what is already there. The loneliness of the transcendental subject was its enclosure in a nonplace where it was merely placed in a spacing delimited by reason. Loneliness had thus become absolutized, an absolute feeling. However, it has had the potential to be related back to existence by focusing on its linguistic expression. From within the spacing where the subject is lost, this expression takes the guise of a critique of its own subjectivity. The expression of loneliness with which the *Clavis* concludes is thus a lamentation only to the extent that it is an indictment of the type of relationality that put the subject in the position of the last man. However, the expression of this critique from within loneliness itself enacts the reversal of this relationality, because expression becomes co-implicated in the relations that are thus established. What is denied is that there are any laws independent of the relations between universality and particularity, so that it becomes illegitimate to assert that the movement from the former to the latter is either attainable or unattainable. Consequently, the expression and its meaning are consuponible with the laws that give meaning. In other words, expression depends on the subject's finitude. The feeling—loneliness—is not absolute any more.

From this perspective, the doppelgänger's expression of loneliness can no longer be taken at face value as a lamentation. The power of the reversal—the power of particularity—is to introduce a logic that, by calling attention to its own enunciation, raises contradiction as its governing principle. Thus, this final utterance of loneliness is transfigured into an expression of mirth.[59] Here is the doppelgänger's laughter at the logic of identity that had sought to pin it down. It is a laughter in the face of the forces that sought to remove its ability to communicate *as well as* its joy in communicating by appropriating these very forces. The detrimental has turned into something useful. Jean Paul indicates this reversal in a comment that introduces the passage in which the doppelgänger makes the distinction between the "white" and the "black" nothing: "The overall *Clavis* shines through with his [Leibgeber/ Schoppe's, the doppelgänger's] original intention to make fun of [Fichte's] *Science of Knowledge*; whenever he tries to expand and to present something stylistically difficult, serious or sober, he soon reverses [*wiederstellen*] (due to his amusingly grotesque nature) everything to such comedy, that he downright stultifies simple readers."[60] What is essential to the subjectivity of the doppelgänger is this repositioning, the return of a certain positioning that is simultaneously a resistance to give in to the original positioning. This wieder-*stellen* of the doppelgänger recalls the *wieder* in the relation of image and signification that, according to Jean Paul, gives meaning. Here Jean Paul indicates this return or repetition in terms of the situatedness of the subject. The doppelgänger is situated there where it can criticize what is already in place. In addition, the doppelgänger is situated so that it can express a meaning. These two aspects, both already at work within *Stellung* (in *wieder*-stellen), which implies placement as well as opinion, are united in the laughter of the doppelgänger. Criticizing by poking fun is in the nature of Leibgeber. Although it may appear that he meanly ridicules "simple readers," as a matter of fact his disposition thrusts interpretation to the fore and raises communication as an issue. Through this posturing, explanation becomes possible.[61] Additional implications of the doppelgänger's ironic disposition will be adumbrated in terms of technique in the final section of this chapter. Suffice it here to say that the subject has gained the capacity to express itself, to say something meaningful. Leibgeber (a name which literally means the "giver of the body," that is, the one who gives the gift of corporeality) has given particularity to the subject. The subject of the critique of loneliness is criticizing and judging because loneliness has given it the topos to acquire meaningfulness.

The doppelgänger is the divided subject. So far the subject has been divided in three distinct ways. All these divisions contest the notion of place. In Fichte's unlimited limit spacing, the subject is divided within itself, but it is also denied an exit, a foothold in reality. In the Kantian limit spacing, the cognizing subject's object is divided such that a decision cannot be made about it. Although these divisions are part of the doppelgänger, the decisive division of Jean Paul's original doppelgänger is that enacted by the maneuver. This latter division is the twofold aspect of the critique of loneliness, that is, loneliness as the critique of the Fichtean and the Kantian spacings as well as the appropriation of loneliness in order to engender critique. The loneliness of the doppelgänger gives a meaning to the words of the subject by emphasizing that judgment and decision are intertwined with existence. As the "white nothing" attests, reason can explain only if it is implicated with finitude. Limiting the space of the subject gives the subject its particularity. The subject has to pay with its autonomy. However, autonomy has proved an illusion and a detriment. Moreover, the subject now is placed in a position to make judgments: it is placed within a polis.

The disjunctive relation between the black and the white nothing is then governed by the reversal. With the reversal the doppelgänger has become a political subject. But more is at stake here: for, as it will be shown with recourse to Freud's understanding of the doppelgänger, the differential identity of the doppelgänger is crucial for its ontological constitution. This differential identity has already been introduced as the overcoming of the absolutism of pure loneliness. Thus, what is opened up is the possibility of an ontology beyond the hold of identitary logic, the logic of the same. This is an ontology that embraces contradiction and the logic of the chiasmus.

THE RETURN OF NEGATION: FREUD'S "THE 'UNCANNY'"

In Jean Paul's adumbration, the doppelgänger is the *relationality* that establishes the subject's identity and difference. Two points arise here: First, regarding its *definition*, what the doppelgänger is, is given through and regulated by this relation. The critique of loneliness, as shown, rests on relationality. It follows that the number of individuals or persons or characters related is at best a secondary concern: the doppelgänger subsists in a relation, regardless of whether this relation is enacted within one, or between two, three, or a million persons. Thus, for instance, novels that deal with the so-called multiple personality disorder do not ipso facto form a subgenre of a doppelgänger theme, and they might even not be commensurate with the doppelgänger insofar as the reversal is entailed therein.[62] The second point comes at the heels of the first one: the gift and organization of this relationality poses an *ontological* problem. It concerns the nature of subjective experience that is given by nothing, which, however, can never be an absolute nothing or a pure loneliness. The doppelgänger's espousing of the "white nothing" has this unavoidable implication: the subject is no longer determined in terms of content, regardless of whether that content consists of the representations that the subject organizes, or any affects or empirical feelings. Instead, the ontological constitution of the subjectivity of the doppelgänger is formal. It is the openness that precedes the empirical and makes the empirical possible.

It is crucial to hold these two points together. Without the caveat introduced by the ontology of the doppelgänger, the type of relation taken to be the defining feature of the doppelgänger can slide from content to content, and its definition would then be not only capricious but also, more importantly, occluded. This occlusion is precisely what has to be avoided. For instance, if the definitive feature of the doppelgänger is taken to be autoscopy, following to the letter Jean Paul's own explanation of the term when he coins the word "Doppelgänger,"[63] then the doppelgänger would be both too broad a concept and at the same time too narrow. It would be too broad because it would be applicable to many different contexts, texts, or experiences; but it would also be too narrow since its dependence on these specific contexts, texts, or experiences would confine it to specific examples. Thus, anthropological studies have shown that the notion of the double is deeply imbedded in almost every "primitive" or "civilized" culture—e.g., James G. Frazer's *Golden Bough* (in particular the chapter titled "The Soul as a Shadow and a Reflection") did much to promote this awareness, and it was taken up in *The Double*, by Otto Rank, who explained it in terms of narcissism.[64] Ancient civilizations incorporated the double in their religious beliefs. Thus, the "Egyptians believed that not just humans but all things—trees, boats, stones, and knives—had their precise duplicate, the *ka*."⁶⁵ The myth of Narcissus from Ovid is a Greco-Roman mythical double. The youth's face reflection in the water may be regarded as self-seeing. But it should not be forgotten that doubles appear in Greek literature much earlier. In his famous speech in the *Symposium*, Aristophanes claims that everybody is a half and man's destiny is to find his other half.⁶⁶ Todorov has argued that the doppelgänger's appropriation by psychoanalysis and specifically Otto Rank has signaled its death for literature.⁶⁷ Todorov is perfectly correct insofar as the doppelgänger is taken to be conclusively defined and usurped by a certain discourse. However, since the very ontology of the doppelgänger precludes its narrow collapse into specific content, such an obituary is premature—or even an obituary about the wrong doppelgänger.⁶⁸ The doppelgänger addressed here could only be "definitively defined" as lacking any proper definition, as resisting definitive definition, not merely in the sense that it negates or transgresses attempts to define it, but rather, as the type of subjectivity that persists on the limits of definition, a liminal subject whose formal frontiers are open.⁶⁹

If the doppelgänger can escape occlusion by specific contexts or discourses, it should also be able to avoid occlusion by specific persons. Jean Paul holds a singular importance for the doppelgänger because he coined the name; however, this does not mean that his conception was unique, unrepeated, and unrepeatable. If a turn to Freud's paper on "The 'Uncanny'" is called for here, this is to show, primarily, an instance of a similar conception of relationality vis-à-vis the doppelgänger. However, a secondary or implicit concern is to indicate that, despite Rank's appropriation, psychoanalysis still has the potential to address the doppelgänger without thereby foreclosing it. The analysis of Freud's article does not aim at a detailed exegesis. The aim, instead, is to glimpse precisely the ontological relationality of the doppelgänger as it is developed by Freud, and thus any divergences that would lead to either a close look at the paper as a whole or to its tributaries in Freud's system will be avoided as much as possible.

Prior to augmenting with Freud, it is useful to draw a brief outline of the critique of loneliness. What Jean Paul's doppelgänger seeks to efface is a conception of the subject that lends itself to absolutism. Apperception and the absolute ego are rejected as mere abstractions that ineluctably lead to a feeling of complete severance from the world: an absolute loneliness. "Nothing" and "negation" have been the crucial coordinates in the attempt to navigate through the polemic between Kant and Fichte, on the one side, and Jacobi and Jean Paul, on the other.

If transcendental philosophy sought to clearly distinguish the logical nothing from the ontological nothing and its negating function, Jacobi argued that the two are in fact completely severed, not just conceptually distinct. However, Jean Paul went a step further. The *Clavis* also offers a positive articulation of the absolute ego, or rather a rearticulation that augments with the "ideal finitude of the infinitude" of the "white nothing." The infinitude of reason is retained as the inherent undecidability of language. This infinity is premised on finitude, on particularity. It is the doppelgänger itself that supposedly composes the *Clavis*, and with the act of writing the doppelgänger has managed to place itself; it emphasizes its very corporeality. This is the meaning of the reversal that is at the core of the subjectivity of the doppelgänger: the presentation of the infinite through the finite. In other words, Jean Paul does not throw out— expunge—the nothing from subjectivity; rather, he develops a notion of the subject that has to go through the transcendental idealist conception of the absolute I; but this very passage and the resistances that are encountered therein are experienced as particular and individuating feelings—thereby overcoming abstraction, reversing the relational priority between infinite and finite. The nothing, as a site of resistance, is repeated, but not as a purely logical or ontological quality—rather, as that which makes interpretation possible through the excess, and simultaneous deficiency, of meaning.

Therefore, what the doppelgänger's critique of loneliness rejects is a conception of the absolute ego as a self that is, first, immediately self-conscious since it has unmediated access to its own self-positing; second, cannot negate its own content, given that Jacobi has shown that the ontological nothing deifies the ego; and, third, admits of absolute feelings. Conversely, what the critique of loneliness makes possible is a notion of subjective difference that is not underpinned by subjective identity—it makes possible a subject that is individuated but not purely particular. Or, to put the same point in a formulation whose significance will become apparent soon: the reversal that is enacted by the doppelgänger is all about a type of subjective relationality—not about what the subject is related to. It is about the *how*, not about the *what*.

Negation offers a way of approaching Freud's paper on the uncanny.[70] This is obvious from the word *das Unheimliche* itself, since "the prefix 'un-' is the token of repression," as Freud puts it.[71] The nothing that persists in the ego as repression is indicated by Freud in one of the case studies. When Freud confronts Dora with the supposition that she had been in love with her father from an early age, she replies that she has no such recollection. And she immediately embarks on the anecdote of a young cousin of hers whom Dora visited shortly after the cousin's parents had had a quarrel. The cousin whispered to Dora that she hated her mother and that when her mother died she would marry her father. Such an association, as Freud comments on the story, has no other function than to affirm his original supposition. "There is no such thing at all as an unconscious 'No'," contends Freud. And he elaborates a page later: "The 'No' uttered by a patient after a repressed thought has been presented to his conscious perception for the first time does no more than register the existence of a repression."[72] In sum, repression knows of no negation. The unconscious does not have "No" in its vocabulary. Further, in a short paper that Freud wrote in the mid-1920s, negation is a hallmark of *thanatos*,[73] and this directly links negation to the "return of the repressed." The "return of the repressed" which, according to Freud, is one of the characteristics of the doppelgänger, may, then, be paraphrased as the "return of negation." The confrontations, in consciousness, of what the unconscious cannot deny. Negation does not merely signify an area of resistance where the conscious self is unable to exercise judgment, and it does not merely construct an excluded zone in the topography of the ego. Rather, through ambiguous expression, negation facilitates relations between the different regions of the ego's topography. The exercise of consciousness, then, is a function of excess—consciousness is a response to the challenge offered by the ego's limits, the fluidity that partakes of the components of the ego, through the use of language.

The contention here will be that there is an affinity between the Freudian uncanny and the doppelgänger's formal relationality as it unfolds in the reversal described in the *Clavis*. This affinity will be recognized once the same structure of relationality is seen to operate in the uncanny. The mediating term for the comparison is the nothing. The possibility of negation is linked to the possibility of meaning. Negation makes interpretation possible. And this possibility is dependent on the limits that negation draws. Just as the topography of Fichte's absolute self is inaugurated with the not-I, in the same manner negation draws the line between conscious and unconscious in Freud. Meaning becomes a function of the negotiation between those regions. The reversal performed by the doppelgänger counteracts absolutism by making excessive what seeks to become absolute. Excess undoes occlusion. The limits of the conceptual immediacy that gives the absolute I is exceeded through meaning's dependence on particularity. And the absolutism of feelings is exceeded by the formalism of relationality that is not depended on the bifurcation between interiority and exteriority. By enacting the reversal, the doppelgänger is in excess of both aspects of absolutism. The upshot is that the nothing has been transformed. The nothing no longer draws sharp limits. Instead, the excessive nothing of the doppelgänger is constantly transgressive of the limits. (*Its compulsion is its insistence on transgression.*) Freud will be shown to present the formal relationality of the reversal in the form of a chiasmus, which is to be found in a long footnote in the article "The 'Uncanny'." The great value of this chiasmus would be that a positive articulation of subjectivity will thereby be made possible. There will be an ontology of the subject. The doppelgänger will no longer be the harbinger of abject loss and failure.

Before turning to Freud, a digression is called for. It is necessitated by Andrew J. Webber's *The Doppelgänger: Double Visions in German Literature*. On the one hand, Webber's book stands out as the most cogent investigation of the doppelgänger in German literature. Webber provides incisive analyses of the texts he is dealing with, usually with the use of psychoanalytic theory, occasionally with recourse to philosophy. And, the analysis of the doppelgänger offered in this chapter agrees in many respects with Webber's argument, especially in his emphasis on the doppelgänger's dialectic being non-teleological, which leads to a narrative of interruptions and "frozen moments."[74] On the other hand, however, Webber places too much emphasis on the loss suffered by the doppelgänger subject. For instance, Webber's reading of Hoffmann's *Sandman* through Freud is mediated by a pervasive notion of loss.[75] The ontological precondition for such a notion of loss is a rift between reality and fantasy: In the *Sandman*, the "reader remains split between the lure of a fantasy world [seen] through the looking-glass and more realist inclinations."[76] This split between reality and fantasy in the discussion of the *Sandman* is, according to Webber, indebted to Hélène Cixous.[77] However, while Cixous uses the distinction between reality and fantasy that Freud himself draws in "The 'Uncanny'" only in order to deconstruct Freud's attempts to sustain such a distinction, Webber on the contrary makes it the linchpin of his extrapolation of the doppelgänger. As it is stated in the opening paragraph of Webber's book, the doppelgänger "represents the subject as more or less pathologically divided between reality and fantasy."[78] The problem is that such a distinction in criticism simply begs the question: a fictional character is always already both real and fantastic. And the upshot of this problematic assumption is that the loss of reality ascribed to the pathology of the doppelgänger is then given an ontological twist: the subject now becomes "profoundly relative."[79] It is too easy to speak about loss vis-à-vis the doppelgänger, and criticism cannot gain much by insisting on the distinction between reality and fantasy. The dialectic of loss can be overcome with an insistence on the ontology of the subject that the doppelgänger presents, an ontology based on the relations established by and with the subject. The possibility of such a positive articulation of the doppelgänger can be retained; and it has to be retained if criticism is not to become a lament.

The crucial point for deriving from Freud an ontology of the subject that adheres to Jean Paul's doppelgänger is to insist on the formal relationality of this ontology. The subject cannot be given in terms of content—it can neither be reduced to pure content nor be divorced from content. Relationality is able to provide the conditions of the possibility of thinking the subject without recourse to content. And, at first blush, Freud would seem to be moving away from the forms of absolutism that content gives rise to. After quoting Freud's own summary in "The 'Uncanny'" of *Beyond the Pleasure Principle,* which concludes by saying that "whatever reminds us of this inner 'compulsion to repeat' is perceived as uncanny," Neil Hertz observes: "The feeling of the uncanny would seem to be generated by being reminded of the repetition compulsion, not by being reminded of whatever it is that is repeated. The becoming aware of the process is felt as eerie, not the becoming aware of some particular item in the unconscious."[80] The uncanny, then, is a feeling in its becoming and it is not reducible to the *what*, to some specific content. Freud has also explicitly said as much by denying that the uncanny is a "positive feeling," or a feeling that arises from objects, and hence it is not to be related to aesthetic beauty.[81]

It is important, at least for historical reasons, to consider Freud's understanding of the doppelgänger, despite the fact that it would be precipitous to conclude that the Freudian structure of subjectivity and its uncanny feeling can be unproblematically squared with the critique of loneliness. Indeed, turning precisely to *Beyond the Pleasure Principle* one is faced with Freud's efforts to equate the compulsion to repeat with biological causes and thus to derive an empirical teleology. This return to content is attested in the essay on "The 'Uncanny'" as well: "The fact that an agency of this kind [conscience, *Gewissen*] exists, which is able to treat the rest of the ego like an object—the fact, that is, that man is capable of self-observation—renders it possible to invest the old idea of a 'double' with a new meaning and to ascribe a number of things to it—

above all those things which seem to self-criticism to belong to the old surmounted narcissism of earliest times."[82] Remarkably, despite having avoided the idealist abstraction of the ego, the ego is still absolutized. Conscience has an immediate access to the self, including the repressed and thus the region governed by negation. The difference with transcendentalism is that, while feeling for it is unlocalizable, the loneliness of a nonplace, on the contrary the uncanny for Freud is too localized, confined to specific feelings that arise out of narcissistic relations. Yet the upshot is the same to the extent that there is a part of the self that supervenes every other function. Relationality has lost its formalism; absolutism has ensued.

It is not the place here to analyze the absolute subject as it is given by the positing and negation of the empirical, that is, the obverse of the opposite from transcendental idealism—this task will be taken up in the next chapter. Suffice it to indicate here how this absolutization develops. The ideal self is at the center of an infinite regress generated by an endless mirroring of scientific fact and fantasy.[83] A single quality, empirical content, is attributable both to the ego's observation of itself, and to the ego's connection to the outside. But if there is to be a supervening part of the ego such as conscience, then it can neither be solely enclosed in the inside, making a figment of the subject, nor can it be solely fastened on the outside, since such an observing subject would lack conscience. Conscience has to include an apprehension both of the outside and the inside. However, conscience cannot distinguish between the two different contents in a single moment or act without producing more content, a further self-apprehension. Which, in its turn would require a further observing ego to supervene on it, a further self-apprehension—and so on and on. The upshot is an infinite number of consciences, not a "double" but a multiple ego. It is not possible to circumvent this regress of self-reflection, so long as content is the common denominator of all subjective functions. Leaving aside the tenability of such a conception, the fact remains that the doppelgänger, as it has been explicated thus far, is incommensurable with it. The numerical value of the characters or the splits within one character (or however one wants to indicate such a number) is totally irrelevant to Jean Paul's conception of the doppelgänger. Instead, what matters is the type of subjective relationality established. The "return of negation" cannot be a return of content—the doppelgänger is not a genetic explanation of the self. However, Freud's insistence on narcissism as the mechanism of what provides the self with its subjectivity in terms of the outside/inside distinction does precisely that: it derives the doppelgänger from a causal or teleological explanation; it generates a narrative of origin.[84]

There are clearly two contrary forces in the essay on "The 'Uncanny,'" and it would be reductive to privilege either. There are at least two reasons—ultimately interrelated—that demand this. First, what is played out here are the different Freudian versions of repression and the role that the castration complex and feeling play in it. Second, the genetic explanation is still useful insofar as it provides a linear narrative that gives the self its singularity. However, such a singularity must be related to a site of plurality—to repetition—in order to avoid a regressive infinity based on subjective identity. What the genetic explanation necessitates, by the very threat that imposes on the subject, is precisely a reinscription of the terms involved here—one that is akin to Jean Paul's reversal, an infinity of subjective difference. Moreover, it is precisely the threat felt by the subject as the process of its differentiation that is the uncanny.

Attending to the second point first—that is, the issue of retaining a subjective singularity alongside an infinity that is not regressive—requires attention to the movement of Freud's argument, and the way it is interrupted, even reworked, in a long, dense, and enigmatic footnote. And to do so, it is crucial to show the context within which the footnote appears in "The 'Uncanny.'" Freud starts his article by identifying the uncanny as a feeling of repulsion and distress that is not, however, aroused by intellectual or cognitive uncertainty.[85] Freud then moves on to a lexical investigation that provides a definition from Schelling: the uncanny is that which ought to have remained secret but has nevertheless come up. This is accompanied by the observation that the uncanny is characterized by an inherent ambiguity so that it can coincide with its opposite. Then follows a paraphrase of the Hoffmann tale of the "Sandman," which leads Freud to the conclusion that the ocular anxiety that Nathaniel exhibits is in reality castration anxiety. The mechanism of repression has been set in motion, and Nathaniel's object cathexis is infinitely displaced so that anyone he loves is being destroyed. At this point Freud introduces a "complication," namely that the object that has produced the uncanny must not be merely something feared but also related to an infantile wish. Thus primary narcissism mediates between repulsion and appeal—in the coincidence of the opposites canny and uncanny. From here on Freud adds details and examples to his argument of the narcissistic origin of the uncanny. Thus, he invokes the doppelgänger, primitive narcissism, the split between conscience and the rest of the ego, the compulsion to repeat, and the animistic belief in the omnipotence of thoughts. The final section of the essay questions whether the uncanny is a category proper to fiction or reality.

This précis shows the pivotal position that narcissism occupies in Freud's account. Narcissism is what facilitates the movement from infantile or primitive wish to repression and fear, from the canny to the uncanny. It is the sufficient and necessary cause that makes the genetic account possible. It is the organizing principle of Freud's linear paraphrase of the Hoffmann tale. Finally, it gives the subject its subjectivity, a subjectivity governed by a notion of identity between the subject and its ideational content or inner representations.

At a crucial point, however, just as he has drawn his conclusions from the "Sandman," Freud inserts a long footnote whose force destabilizes the teleological paraphrase of the tale. The footnote opens with a crucial remark: "The material elements in the poet's work of fantasy are not in fact so wildly twisted, so that one could not reconstruct their original arrangement [or, as the last clause can also be translated: so that one could not repeat their original construct]."[86] Attention to the detail of Freud's expression is crucial. Freud does not claim that there is a foundation on which Hoffmann has built, like a mechanic, a story and that an arrangement of the material would render the foundation visible. Not only would this deprive the uncanny of its quality as a secret, since a secret cancels itself out the moment that an iterative foundation is found for it. More important, the grammar and syntax of the phrase do not permit such a reading. Three points will suffice: First, there is a startling evasiveness in Freud's formulation. The absence of proper names in the main clause and the impersonal construct of the subordinate clause are linked by a double negative. The moment that extrication is called for and even seems to be announced in advance, Freud has recourse to a circumlocution that itself is in need of extrication. This is not merely a remark about Freud's intention, rather it indicates precisely what Freud does not intend: the secret that organizes, but does not found, the extrication to come and which is betrayed in the linguistic formulation. That this extrication is unfounded in the context of the essay's argument is made clear by the final remarks of the footnote, which seek, on the one hand, to relate the extrication to the narcissism that hovers in the text above the footnote and, on the other hand, to relate the genetic explanation offered by that narcissism to Hoffmann's biography. Freud initially hesitates before a risk and then at the end seeks to deny that he has taken any risk at all. Second, the subjunctive of the subordinate clause places the reconstruction in the realm of the possible. It would be possible to perform such a repetition of what is original. This in turn leads to the third point: the original arrangement is a potential, and not something performed conclusively. The originality of the arrangement consists precisely in the possibilities that it opens up and which function as the conditions of the construction of materiality—but not solely of the material elements of the "Sandman." The emphasis is on the constructability, and not on the construct. These three observations already indicate that Freud's reconstruction will be articulated within a structure that passes from the material to the origin but without equating the latter with content. The implications for the Freudian system are enormous, and it is not here the place to present them. Rather, what is relevant is that Freud secures a conception of infinity given through finitude.

In this setup, repetition and subjectivity acquire a meaning that is neither dependent on a logic of identity, as will be shown forthwith, nor, as will be shown later, on the notion of narcissism that is operative in the paper on "The 'Uncanny.'" Repetition and subjectivity are codetermined through a chiastic form of relationality. According to the footnote, the split in Nathaniel's father-imago generates a series of oppositions. In his childhood, there is his "good" father and the "bad" one who is the Sandman or Coppelius. At university, Professor Spalanzani corresponds to the former, while the optician Coppola corresponds to the latter. Now, since the professor created the automaton Olympia, it follows that there is an identity between Olympia and Nathaniel. In actuality, Olympia is, in Freud's terms, a "dissociated complex of Nathaniel's which confronts him as a person." However, there is a crucial complication. The father image is not split merely in terms of "good" and "bad" father, or from the perspective of Nathaniel's castration anxiety, his feminine and masculine attitude toward his father. In addition to this, the imago is also split between the mechanical and the ocular. In childhood, the mechanical is represented by the "bad" Coppelius who "has screwed off his [Nathaniel's] arms and legs as an experiment," while the "good" father, who intervenes to save Nathaniel's eyes, represents the ocular. At university, Coppola is the bad optician, while the professor is the mechanician who created Olympia/Nathaniel. Surely, Freud is correct to say that "both the mechanician and the optician were the father of Nathaniel (and of Olympia as well)." However, what this chiasmus has produced is a destabilization of identity.[87]

Freud does not seem to be aware of the destabilizing force of the chiasmus. Or, if he is aware, he strives, at the end of the footnote, to reduce that force by an appeal to Hoffmann's own life. Freud attempts to accommodate the notion of subjective identity in the short story to its author's own identity. However, if such a move to biography is resisted, then the full implications of Freud's chiasmus will come to the fore. Repetition will be shown to be a function of the chiasmus, having decisive implications for the origin of identity. The chiasmus undermines the originator of identity. The identity of the "good"/ocular father as opposed to the "bad"/mechanical one in the first series is refashioned in the second series as "good"/mechanical and "bad"/ocular fathers. This refashioning is mediated by what the father creates: Nathaniel in the first series and Nathaniel/Olympia in the second. The father in the first series privileges sight and its representations in consciousness. Conversely, the second series privileges determinism over representation. The identity of the father, regardless of whether he is the "good" or the "bad" one, is always given vis-à-vis the offspring's privileging either the deterministic or the representational genesis. However, no strict causality is thereby established, since it would be equally valid to conceive of the offspring's identity as given by the father. The "good"/ocular father generates Nathaniel in the first series, and the "good"/mechanical father generates Nathaniel/Olympia in the second series. The father generates the son's identity, but, in an anachronism that eschews teleology, the son also creates the father. Freud's equivocations in the footnote about how the identity is generated stem from an impetus to stabilize identity in the face of the vertiginous movements in Hoffmann's story. However, whereas the given identity is in each case secured, the identity of the giver of identity remains unstable. Thus, if the giving of identity is viewed from the perspective of its being given by the offspring, then it is easy to deduce who the "good" and who the "bad" father is. Simultaneously, the identity of the offspring remains an open question, a slide from one position to the next, from the "real" Nathaniel to the "fantastic" Nathaniel, from the "sane" Nathaniel to the "insane" Nathaniel, and from Nathaniel to Olympia. The same effect can be observed if the father is taken to be the giver of identity. In this case, the offspring's given identity is secured in both series—in the first series it is Nathaniel, and in the second series it is Nathaniel/Olympia. But the identity of the father remains unstable, sliding from "real" father to "fantastic" Coppelius, from the "rational mechanic" Spalanzani to the "optical sorcerer" Coppola, from the benign to the nefarious father. Therefore, the origin of identity creates a chiasmus that undermines the origin's claim to be the source of a causality that secures identity. A teleology that can only secure its effects, but not its causes, is no teleology at all.[88]

While Freud is attuned to the complexities that arise from the "divisions of the father-imago," as he calls them in the footnote, and while he is also aware of the complexities that arise from the identity of Nathaniel and Olympia, Freud nevertheless has not fully grasped the implications of the chiasmus that he has suggested. The logic of the chiasmus dictates that, since neither conception of a single origin can be given priority in the genesis of identity qua identity, the conception of identity includes both. Or, more accurately, it does not include either, since any single origin has been denied. What this denial does is to reintroduce negation. However, negation is now transformed. It is no longer a negation of something, a drawing of a line of exclusion. Rather, negation becomes a region—the nothing region, the formal region of relationality—within which subjectivity unfolds. Thus, the logic of the identity of the same has been replaced by a logic that locates identity in terms of relational differentiation. The meaning of repetition radically changes within the new conception of identity. Repetition is no longer that material element that is inherent in a cause, only to come to the fore in the effect. When Freud said in the first sentence of the footnote that the material elements presented in a fictional manner can be reconstructed or repeated (Freud's word was *wiederherstellen*), this should not be understood as saying that identity can be recovered from something suppressed, that it can be reconstituted or recuperated. Rather, the repetition that subjective identity demands is a productive one, a *wieder*-herstellen. The product is new—singularity is retained—but this new product is a repetition to the extent that it springs forth from an "original arrangement." Origin is thus both formal, the relational differentiality that allows for repetition, and productive, since the repetition is a product.

The contention here is that this differential origin is what gives the identity of the doppelgänger. Further, it gives an ontology of the subject. This has definite implications for conceptions of the doppelgänger that emphasize loss as its essential feature. The logic that would have ascribed a notion of loss in the chiasmus of subjective relations in the "Sandman" would have operated somewhat as follows: as already indicated, in the two series of the divided father-imago the identity that remains unstable is that of the giver, the identity of the origin. The first move in the logic of loss would have been to point out that this instability is impossible to erase, given that the move from cause to effect would forever be lacking. The lack resides in the fact that the connection between the exteriority of the mechanical and the interiority of the representational ocular can never be fully reconciled. The second move would be to explicate this abysmal loss as an endless reflexivity, a subject standing in-between mirrors, in a *mise-en-abîme* that destabilizes any meaning given to, or given by, the subject. Finally, it would have been concluded that the doppelgänger subject is pathologically relative. What this logic of loss is relying on is precisely the identitary logic of the same. The irrecuperability of meaning or subjectivity assumes that such a recuperation is possible. However, this can only be asserted by assuming an identity of what has been lost. Contrary to this dialectic of loss, the chiasmic logic retains causality and teleology as a *productive impossibility*. The infinity that the impossibility of causality creates is here the organization of the original relations. Those relations need no definite content and thus are not dependent on sameness. And they are productive because, as already shown, they allow for repetition. When this productive impossibility is articulated in terms of the ontology of the subject, the result is the doppelgänger, the product of the repetition. The doppelgänger's subjective ontology is generated by a chiastic or differential identity. What persists on the site of relationality as the site of identity is an asymmetry—the chiasmus—that resists any attempt to be stabilized or foreclosed.

Perhaps the best characterization of this identity is as "unsinnig zwanghaft," the words that Freud uses to characterize Nathaniel's love for his unleashed complex.[89] Identity is a senseless necessary connection, a compulsion to create an image of oneself, which, however, is both nonsensical and impossible to contemplate (*unsinnig*). This compulsive identity, more of a repetition really or a compulsion to repeat (*Wiederholungszwang*), is forever moving and unable to fix onto a single image or object. It is the very structure of iterative identity, not its object or content, that is designated in the footnote as the castration complex—the structure that Freud introduced at the beginning of the footnote as the "original arrangement" of the "material elements" of the story. Within this structure there is no conclusive metonymic substitution of proper names. Instead, the proper names function as the metaphors that make the unfolding of the structure possible. Castration, as that structure, is the name that subjective identity has taken when it is no longer possible to construe it as a correspondence, but when identity is understood as the relations that persist within the structure itself.

In the footnote, the image and its signification have indeed attained a structure in which they are infinitely rearrangeable. And, the expression of this structure gives the subject its identity. The uncanny then is not the product of the object, but the threat that the subject experiences within that structure, as the subject surmounts genetic teleology. Further, the uncanny, insofar as it is a feeling that already participates in the continuous becoming of the self, produces one's own self-identity in language. An identity, moreover, that is differential, given by relationality, or, as Freud has put it early on in the essay, "wir selbst Fremdsprachige sind," our self-identity is given by a language that is foreign, differentiating our own subject.[90] In Freud's discussion of the doppelgänger, which immediately follows his explication of the "Sandman," there is also a nexus between identity and repetition. All that is needed for Freud's doppelgänger to be accommodated within the structure introduced by the footnote, is to understand the "limitless self-love [*uneingeschränkten Selbstliebe*]"[91] not in terms of primary narcissism but in terms of the "original arrangement" of the castration complex. The self-identity, with its "splittings, divisions and substitutions [*Ich-Verdopplung, Ich-Teilung, Ich-Vertauschung*],"[92] produced by self-love is impossible to restrict, precisely because its origin is in a universal arrangement that can never be fully encountered *en face*, it is in a state of perpetual becoming and incompletion.

Having shown that it is possible to retain both singularity and infinity in an extrapolation of Freud's notion of the subject, a return can now be made to a point alluded to regarding the different versions of repression in Freud's work. Discovering an articulation of the doppelgänger in Freud that is compatible with Jean Paul's is anachronistic in two respects. On the one hand, it affirms the nonlinear chronological—that is, nonoriginary—arrangement of castration in the footnote, and, on the other, it reads "The 'Uncanny'" through Freud's late understanding of repression, anxiety, and the castration complex. Having already looked at the former, a brief glance at the latter is now called for. At this juncture, it should be noted that Samuel Weber has demonstrated that it is possible to read "The 'Uncanny'" through the theory of castration published from 1926 onward. The key to such a reading is to view anxiety as that which produces repression. Thus it is related to the castration complex, which is the paradigmatic anxiety. "The castration complex now appears as the *nucleus* of the Freudian theory of the uncanny."[93] Not only is this a move beyond the primacy of narcissism on which the earliest theory that derived anxiety from repression had to insist. Further, it precludes a conception of subjectivity as "fully self-conscious."[94] And, therefore, it leads beyond a repetition of narcissism based on identity and to repetition as "the articulation of difference, which is equally a dis-articulation, dis-locating and even dis-membering."[95] The subject produced by the structure of castration cannot be pinned down to either the mechanical or the ocular. Instead, it is articulated by the relation of the two as they unfold in the subject's materiality. There is no steadfast identity, but only regulative difference. Castration becomes the infinite, the original arrangement, toward which the subject strives in its singularity.

Although Weber does not pursue his analysis explicitly in terms of the absolute self, it can easily be reinscribed in that register. The crucial point of Weber's reworking of the uncanny is that as a feeling it can never be given absolutely. As such, it is antirepresentational, something that always exceeds a specific subjective feeling: the uncanny as implicated in the structure of castration exceeds affect on the phenomenal level. This structure finds expression in language or, more precisely, a certain type of linguistic expression, which Weber explicitly associates with Walter Benjamin's extrapolation of the allegory in the *Trauerspiel* book. The nothing—the negation, the "No"—within this structure of subjectivity then figures in a double gesture: as the repression of the structure of castration that, however, is only ever present in its very repression, that is, in its allegorical expression (Benjamin) or ambivalent opposition (Freud).[96]

The nothing, in this construal, is allowed to return, but it is a nothing akin to Jean Paul's nothing of the doppelgänger. Its exceeding of subjective affect is a function of the excess in language over mere signification. This excess transgresses all the limits that are established in relation to the subject and that create a topography of the self that allows for interpretation. Further, this is an excess over the absolute subject, that is, the subject that can posit its immediate self-identity only when its parameters are strictly defined. In this setup, the negation returns, but now the nothing is the region of excess that the subject transverses, mindfully walking on the thin line between the blinding light of immediate self-consciousness and the blind negation of repression. It was stated earlier that this subject's compulsion is its insistence on transgression. But perhaps this is not a proper transgression, since, if the doppelgänger's normal state is the overcoming and undoing of the limits, then what there is here is a transgression of transgression; a redoing of the limit, not as a fixed line, but as the liminal zone of transgression.

The limit is the nothing zone of the subject—the doppelgänger. The doppelgänger is this liminal subject that allows for the relation between image and signification to be infinitely repeated, while that repetition, in turn, allows for the subject's differential identity.

"DOUBLE ACTS" AND TRANSFORMATION

The liminality of the doppelgänger can be expressed by saying that the subject has a dual relation to openness. There is a formal openness that is insubordinate to content and thus infinite. And, the material manifestations of this openness are of necessity finite and to that extent limited. By holding these two types of openness together, the critique of loneliness can give a place to the subject. And it is in this place that the reversal enacted by the doppelgänger makes sense, as the necessity of the finite for the infinite. The relations established there are precisely what the liminality of the doppelgänger denotes.

However, an aspect of the relationality at the heart of the definition of the doppelgänger remains obscure: namely, whether the very notion of relationality demands a process of delimitation of the two areas between which relations develop. In other words, is a demarcation required between the infinite and the finite? Are these two separate realms, with different laws and established borders? Or, are these two realms, to the extent that they are delimited at all, merely delimited by each other? This is an important question since it pertains to the ontological constitution of the doppelgänger. At the beginning of the previous section it was claimed that formal openness takes precedence over empirical content. Such a claim might be construed to imply that ontological relationality presupposes two distinct realms. This is not the case. If the differential identity of the doppelgänger is to be adhered to, it has to be the unfolding of the relation between infinite and finite in such a way that both the relation itself, as well the infinite and the finite, are presented in the event of their relationality, that is, the interplay between singularity and repetition. This is what is meant by the liminality of the subject. What the liminal precludes is the positing of a negativity that points to a presupposed transcendence governing the subject. There is no transcendence established by, or establishing a, hierarchical ontology.

The precedence of "form" over "content" in regard to the doppelgänger was meant to indicate that a genetic, causal, or teleological narrative is unable to attain to the "white nothing" and the narrative structure implied therein. This is a structure that is not shackled by content but rather unfolds as a gesture in the event of the relation between the limitless and the limited. However, what has to be resisted is any attempt to completely deny the genetic any access to that event.[97] As has already been intimated, the reversal of the "white nothing" is made possible only by the appropriation of the nothingness that is overcome. A genetic narrative still has a function to play. It is just that this function is not the dominant one—precisely because openness, not domination, is originary: that is what the precedence of the formal aspect of the ontology of the doppelgänger indicates.

A clearer delineation of the infinite-finite relation is needed. However, this task is not to be pursued by examining the differential aspect between the two. This formal difference has already been pursued in the previous section. Rather, what is required is to look more closely at the relation from the point of view of finitude or negativity. What has to be shown is that there is still a residual transcendence in the finite. However, this is a transcendence only to the extent that it allows for the crossing over from the finite to the infinite: a transcendence as porosity that makes liminality possible—and hence a transcendence as the condition of the possibility of transformation. (Here, the emphasis is on the allowing. The crossing should not be assumed to have been completed or that it can be completed. Instead, what is allowed is that gray area that attains to both finitude and infinitude where the doppelgänger subsists.) What was previously described as uncanny is this porous transcendence—transcendence as the overlapping of the limits and as the threat that this overlapping poses to the subject. There is an assertion here of the untenability of absolute feelings, too. As such, the liminality in question is part of the ontological explication of the doppelgänger. However, the ontology is not exhausted here but is further determined by a close examination of the finite elements. These are the elements that constitute the narrative. Their link to ontology manifests itself in two ways: first, as the issue of technique and, second, as the question of disciplinary differentiation. As it will be shown, Fichte seeks to deny transformation through the operation of a transcendence. This transcendence from the infinite to the finite will be premised on an "alien element" that will not properly belong to either. This will lead Jean Paul to conclude that a sharp opposition between infinite and finite is untenable. Even when such an opposition is posited, as is the case with Fichte, still the opposition undoes itself. And this self-undoing, this transformation, always takes place in materiality. This is the import of technique: being or form is transformation.

In the very first sentence of the *Clavis*, in the prologue that precedes the presentation of the doppelgänger's letter, Jean Paul seeks to explain the way that the *Clavis* differs from *Titan*—the novel to which it is an appendix to the appendix. From the very beginning, the differentiation between literature and philosophy is posed: "The Clavis is primarily the last part in the *comic appendix* to Titan; but it is detached from the old nais in order to move freely and over limits, where the corpulent Titan can never follow it."[98] The metaphor of the "old nais" is crucial in understanding what Jean Paul claims here. As the editor of the *Sämtliche Werke* explains, "nais proboscidea" is a kind of snail whose hind part is sometimes detached and continues to live on its own.[99] Therefore, if the *Clavis Fichtiana*, as its placement and name indicate, is indeed a cipher to the novel and to Fichte, this is not to be taken as a rupture between philosophy and literature. The "cipher" to the philosophy of Fichte is a transformative process, so that philosophy and literature are not hermetically separated, but rather the latter turns into the former—the snail/literature lives on as philosophy. And, given that the *Clavis* does not pretend to be philosophy either—or, at least, to be what Jean Paul refers to as "pure" philosophy,[100] and today is referred to as representational philosophy—the former can also turn into the latter. Thus, what the metaphor of the snail asserts is transformability itself. There are no clear lines separating literature and philosophy. Just as the doppelgänger is liminal in character, so also the link between literature and philosophy that is posed through the doppelgänger is also liminal, a link on the margins of both literature and philosophy where the margin that belongs to one is spontaneously transformable into the margin that belongs to the other. It is as if the novel *Titan* cannot follow the *Clavis*, because the *Clavis* "deconstructs" the novel, no less than it also "deconstructs" the philosophy of Fichte.

To disclose the implications of this move, it is necessary to follow closely the text. The very next point raised in the *Clavis*, which Jean Paul esteems to be the finest achievement of the *Clavis*, is to have shown the untenability of Fichtean philosophy. This is done in a way that extrapolates technique with reference to the transformation introduced by the snail metaphor. The argument is that technique can be understood either as a trick, or as the process of transformation. Both conceptions hinge on the way completeness and liminality are understood, which in their turn are linked to Jacobi's polemic on the nothing and negativity in Fichte. Therefore, for Jean Paul, technique has clear implications for ontology. Now, technique as trick designates Fichte's assertion of the independence of philosophy, that is, philosophy as a realm that is governed by reason and sharply delimited from other discourses, such as literature; however, this assertion is premised on the assumption of the existence of the other discourses, from within reason itself, despite the fact that the very independence of reason makes such an assumption illegitimate. It transgresses its self-imposed limits, forgetting the independence of reason—and therein, precisely, consists the trick. In other words, the infinite cannot separate itself from the finite without presupposing the latter in such a way that the finite is entangled in the infinite and the latter's independence is shattered.

Conversely, transformative technique does not simply assert liminality and hence eschew the independence of philosophy. This kind of technique has to be understood as a form of ironic appropriation of the other kind of technique. In a passage quoted above, Jean Paul explained that as soon as the doppelgänger tries to present "something stylistically difficult" it reverts to "comedy." The same point is also made in the prologue, but there it is given an additional quality. Jean Paul proclaims his respect for Fichte and idealism, but then he indicates that he also makes use of the "Belgian mischief" of ironic praise.[101] Now, however, Jean Paul adds that this does not merely raise the issue of interpretation; it also shows that the doppelgänger's "confluence [*Zusammenschütten*] of comedy and seriousness" demands that each reader or reviewer separate the different ingredients and thereby arrive at the conclusion that "he can only grasp what is serious *through* what is comic."[102] In other words, it is a particular type of interpretation: an interpretation that calls for an understanding of the serious through the comic, but without the rejection of either of the two ingredients. This interpretation is generated by the ironic narrative that is amenable to it.[103] It is precisely the narrative that overcomes the demand for a causal explanation.

Caution is necessary here. This ironic narrative that makes up the *Clavis* is not to be understood in a sense of dialectical usurpation. What is praised, and thereby ironized, is not overcome in the sense that the irony becomes part of a progress toward a specific telos. This would require a detached subject that observes and supervenes over such a progress. This would turn irony into a mere rejection that seeks to substitute one position for another, and thus eminently ironizable itself. Instead, what matters to Jean Paul is a nondialectical type of irony.[104] Thus, the doppelgänger in the letter that forms the main part of the *Clavis* continually *affirms* the nonliminality of the subject by persistently taking up the Fichtean position. But this very affirmation is equally and simultaneously a *denial*—a denial not only of what has been affirmed but also a denial of what is being denied, a denial of absolute denial, which only turns it in the affirmation of the original affirmation. However, this new affirmation is transformed by being implicated in the movement of ironic whirl, for it can no longer be identified squarely with the philosophy of Fichte but has now become part of the process of the reversal that divests content and makes identity differential. In other words, transformative technique presents the full consequences of the other's position, but only if that position is capable of being completed and thereby occluded.

To recapitulate, the finitude that gives the doppelgänger its liminality is explicable in terms of narrative. This appears in two respects: as the nonpriority of literature over philosophy and vice versa, and as technique. Further, technique is also split between trick and transformation, and the split is dependent on the way that completeness features in technique. Technique as trick starts with incompleteness, as the independent realm of reason, and then poses a separate area of completion. The narrative that features in this kind of technique is inherently teleological, a causal narrative that seeks to deduce the genesis of the finite from the infinite. Transformative technique, on the contrary, is the manner in which completion is achieved only by reverting to incompleteness. Transformation's narrative structure is markedly different. Although there is an appropriation of the teleological narrative, this appropriation should not be seen as a form of dialectical process. Rather, it is a *narrative in crisis*. The word "crisis" retains here its full denotative force. It indicates, on the one hand, the threat that transformation raises to a linear narrative, which is the condition for the transformation to take place. On the other hand, "crisis" harks back to its Greek etymon, denoting the moment that *krisis*, or judgment, is possible. This latter aspect of crisis, as already shown, is responsible for the genuine political motive in the critique of loneliness.

Yet, despite this explication of technique and the status of disciplines, the link between the two remains opaque. How does technique lead to a nonhierarchical relation between philosophy and literature? Or, how does the reciprocity between literature and philosophy demand a certain narrative technique? A short answer will assert the ineliminability of crisis, both as the kind of narrative that cannot be eliminated and as the ineluctable presence of the political. The latter has already been demonstrated as the critique of the absolute feeling of loneliness, but the former needs to be further examined in Jean Paul and specifically in the way that the Fichtean subject is ironized by the doppelgänger. The point has to be made by explicating further the dependence of subjectivity to variant narrative structures. Crucially, a teleological narrative presupposes a subject divided between subjectivity as the actor in the independent realm of reason *and* an acting agent, either as doer or narrator, in the finite realm where finitude unfolds. This division lies at the heart of the metaphysics of self-reflection that legitimates teleological narrative—a metaphysics that is exemplified by Fichte's idealism. To the contrary, given its formal difference, such a division is incommensurate with the ontological structure of the doppelgänger, as it has been explicated with reference to the uncanny. It is precisely by asserting this difference and the force of denial embedded in it that Jean Paul turns to technique and shows the trickery in Fichte's system.

After introducing transformation as the snail metaphor in the opening paragraph of the *Clavis*, Jean Paul claims that his major achievement is one of technique. This achievement, however, figures as a critique of the Fichtean technique. In Jean Paul's formulation, the *Clavis*'s, and hence the doppelgänger's, greatest achievement is "to break down the Fichtean idealism with the apodictic existence of the alien with-I [*fremder Mit-Ichs*] on which it supposedly rests."[105] It is crucial to understand what Jean Paul means by the expression "alien with-I." Such a term does not appear in the *Wissenschaftslehre*. Indeed, there is a derogatory tone; the very collapse of the Fichtean system depends on this alien element. The meaning will be become clear by moving into the next paragraph. "Fichte's so-called idealistic idealism lives in the absolute to the extent that ... there is just no other access into the finitude and existence (easily reversing from them to the absolute) without the unmeasurable dogmatic leaps, flights and misconceptions, which were exactly what called for explanation, but which want to be the explanation themselves."[106] Jean Paul has absorbed Jacobi's criticism that, insofar as there is a division between spontaneity and receptivity that derives from an absolute I, the division posits either a god or a deified subject. There is no way to bridge the gap, except with a leap, Jacobi's *salto mortale*, that merely assumes what it is meant to prove. From this perspective, it is evident that the "alien with-I" is but *der Ich*, the corporealization of the Fichtean *das Ich,* which led to the demise of the doppelgänger in the *Titan*. Jean Paul is well aware that, strictly speaking, *der Ich*, or the "alien with-I," is not to be found in, and cannot be assimilated to, the *Wissenschaftslehre*. Jean Paul's point is that *der Ich* or the "alien with-I" is nevertheless assumed in the Fichtean system. So long as the I is absolute, it can never be reconciled with existence, unless a sleight of hands occurs—and it always, and of necessity, does occur. A philosophy that seeks to achieve the completion of knowledge and to eliminate deception by absolutizing the categorical functions of the I is nevertheless destined to include a deception—and this is a trick, a technical manipulation. As Jean Paul puts it: "Philosophy best deceives us by double acts."[107] And he adds a footnote to explain what a "double act," or *Steftenstück*, is: "Thus calls the conjurer those tricks for which he requires a second person."[108] The conjurer is Fichte.

Nonetheless, why is this *mere* trickery? Why does the "double act" compel the move to transformative technique and reciprocity between literature and philosophy? The reason is to be discerned in the nothing and negation in the Fichtean system. First, the absolute loneliness and nothingness critiqued by the "white nothing" require the trickery of the *Steftenstück* in order to operate. As the doppelgänger expresses it in the concluding words of the *Clavis*, cited at the beginning of this chapter: "There is consciousness in me only of my highest Not-Consciousness. Inside me the mute, blind, concealed and labouring demogorgon, and I am he himself." The "demogorgon" at work within the self is indeed the same as what Jean Paul calls the "alien with-I" at the opening of the *Clavis*. This citation from the end of the *Clavis* further highlights that, through the critique of loneliness, the doppelgänger has appropriated the Fichtean position. There is no distanced and independent subjectivity posed by the doppelgänger; instead of a dialectical sublation, the doppelgänger is denying what it has affirmed. The argument here is that this denial is not merely a rejection of the adversary's position. Rather, the denial is the demonstration that that position is already implied in the denier's positions. In other words, Jean Paul seeks to show that the critique of loneliness is already implicit in Fichte's philosophy.

To demonstrate that, Jean Paul has to offer not merely a refutation, but also to proffer a positive presentation of the relation between the two positions. This is precisely the transformative aspect of technique. After identifying the "double act," or *Steftenstück*, in Fichte's technique, Jean Paul observes:

> [T]his absolute I-ness, so far as it is the ground of its ground, I would certainly deny, as well as its grounding; so that eventually not only *nothing* is left over—that would be too much and already *determined*,

because nothing already excludes the *All*—but also *infinitely* less than nothing and *infinitely* more than all, in short, the groundlessness of the groundlessness.[109]

It will be recalled that, according to the first principle of the *Science of Knowledge*, the I posits itself absolutely, that is, subjectivity becomes the "ground of its ground" in the pursuit of cognition. To escape this pure self-grounding, the I also posits a not-I, the negation of itself, as its second principle. Through the interaction of I and not-I, or their limitations, the absolute I will access objectual reality, according to the third principle. Jacobi's criticism pivots around the second principle. If the negation of the I, the nothing, is measured in comparison to the absolute I, then the nothing is "infinitely less" than the absolute I implied in the not-I. And, if the negation of the I is measured in comparison with the rest of the world, then the not-I is "infinitely more" than what is outside the absolute I already implied in the not-I. Jacobi observed that, by taking the nothing as a substance, then the "infinitely less" merely defines God, while the "infinitely more" deifies the subject. The self-grounding has been undermined and the whole edifice is crumbling. But this is not all. Jean Paul makes the additional point that this double nothing indicates "the groundlessness of the groundlessness." This is precisely the liminal space that Jean Paul extrapolates later in the text as the "white nothing." The point, however, is that the very grounding leads to groundlessness. The two different nothings, requiring a *das Ich* and a *der Ich*, ultimately assert only one nothing that is rearticulated as the liminality of "the groundlessness of groundlessness."

A philosopher might object that Jean Paul is doing considerable violence to Fichte's formulation, given that the distinction between the two nothings is absent from the three principles of the *Wissenschaftslehre*. Nonetheless, the objection is unfounded. Jean Paul is a very close reader of Fichte, so much so that he follows Fichte's argument all the way, only to distill from the conclusions the consequences that Fichte himself is unwilling to extract—as if Jean Paul pretends to have been duped by the conjurer, only to point out at the last moment the hidden person who has made the trick of the "double act" work. In fact, the distinction between the two nothings is drawn later, at a crucial point in the first version of the *Science of Knowledge*, and it is a distinction at the heart of the division between subjectivity and the subject that the doppelgänger seeks to overcome. To understand why Fichte has to assume a second nothing, it has be remembered that the opposition between the absolute I and the not-I is enacted within independent reason itself. It is not a dialectical opposition in the Hegelian sense; rather, it is a pure opposition. This compels Fichte to demonstrate the manner in which cognition of objects is made possible. Fichte's argument is twofold, and it rests on the conception of the action of a divided subject.[110] The first move is made within the theoretical part of the *Wissenschaftslehre*, that is, the part that is still within the independent reason. The pure opposition between absolute I and not-I, as it is enacted by the reproductive imagination, is continually taking place. Nevertheless, this indefinite occurrence will never determine the self, unless there can be something external to it. In other words, from within reason, an obstacle or check, what Fichte calls the *Anstoß*, compels the absolute I to assume that there can be something outside itself. But this is not to arrive at the object yet. Instead, the very opposition between absolute I and not-I relies on the possibility that the opposition will be carried out outside the self. In Fichte's formulation: "The objective to be excluded has no need at all to be present; all that is required . . . is the presence of a check on the self, that is, for some reason that lies merely outside the self's activity, the subjective must be extensible no further. Such an impossibility of further extension would then . . . give it [the I] the task of setting bounds to itself." But this is not to place the not-I in the world, apart from the absolute I. Rather, this task is "merely the requirement for a determination to be undertaken within it by the self as such, or the *mere determinability* of the self."[111] From the perspective of theoretical consciousness, all that is possible is mere determinability, or the realization that the external is possible.

It becomes clear at this point why the concept of action is so crucial for Fichte. His coinage of the term *Tathandlung* was meant to include both the pure subjective element, the *Handlung*, as well as the objective element, the *Tatsache*.[112] The subject is divided between intelligence and freedom.[113] The check forces the subject to this realization, and thus the distinction between subject and object arises, which facilitates the transition to the practical part of the *Wissenschaftslehre*. Even so, what is still needed is a transition from mere determinability to real determination. Herewith comes the second move to Fichte's transcendental argument, which is also the moment when the distinction between the two nothings is made. The argument proceeds with an examination of the absolute positing activity of the I. There is an infinite and unlimited pure positing I that "*apart from* it there is nothing." But this also means that "the self includes everything, that is, an infinite, unbounded reality."[114] This latter act of positing can no longer be pure, since it refers to the world, encounters resistance, and thus is an "*objective* activity [objective *Thätigkeit*]."¹¹⁵ Now, from the point of view of the practical, the conclusion that determination requires an object is reinscribed as the necessity of an object for determination to take place at all. This reinscription is accomplished by the infinite "striving [*Streben*]" of objective activity, so that now it appears that striving is the condition of the possibility of pure activity: the practical is the foundation of the theoretical.¹¹⁶ Fichte summarizes his argument as follows:

> The absolute self is absolutely identical with itself . . . nothing therein is distinguishable, nothing manifold; the self is everything and nothing, since it is nothing *for itself*, and can distinguish no positing or posited within itself.—In virtue of its nature it *strives* . . . to maintain itself in this condition.—There emerges in it a disparity, and hence something alien to itself. (*That* this happens, can in no sense be proved a priori, but everyone can confirm it only in his own experience. . . .) This alien element [*Dieses fremdartige*] necessarily stands in conflict with the self's striving to be absolutely identical; and if we fancy some intelligent being outside the self, observing the latter in these two different situations, then *for such a being*, the self will appear restricted, its forces rebuffed. . . . But the intelligence positing this restriction is not to be some being outside the self, but the latter itself.¹¹⁷

It is this "alien intelligence," which cannot be proved but that does all the proving, that Jean Paul has termed the "alien with-I," the "mute, blind, concealed and labouring demogorgon." In the passage from the *Wissenschaftslehre* quoted above, Fichte is acutely aware of the distinction between the logical nothing in intelligence and the ontological nothing vis-à-vis reality. Elsewhere, he is even aware of the deification of the I due to the substantiation of the nothing that Jacobi was to accuse him of.¹¹⁸ His argument is that, by starting with the ontological nothing, the self has the capacity to *observe* both these acts—the pure and the objective activities—and to distinguish them, whereby self-limitation becomes an act of freedom; the self is given a world. Transcendentally, the two nothings are interdependent, determinable by each other. All that is needed for this to work is the presence of the "alien element" within the self.

The trickery of this maneuver is that it leads to the conclusion that ultimately both these nothings are *nothing*. They cancel each other out through the mediation of the "alien intelligence," which Fichte would later call the philosopher. In section 1 of the "Second Introduction to the Science of Knowledge," Fichte says: "In the Science of Knowledge there are two very different sequences of mental acts: that of the self, which the philosopher observes, and that of the philosopher's observations."[119] The subject is divided between intelligence and will by assigning different qualities to the nothing and to the negations of the self. While this self persists in its division, the philosophical I—unprovable, yet part of everyone's experience, according to Fichte—assumes a privileged point of view that is supposed to unify the self. Yet, this unification is premised on forgetting that the structure of the divided subject had already given specific qualities to the nothing. By hiding the philosophical I, the "alien intelligence," behind the absolute I, Fichte makes the two nothings lose their metaphysical qualities; he annuls them and instead turns them into quantities of this hidden self. "If the self did more than strive, if it had an infinite causality, it would not be a self: it would not posit itself, and would therefore be nothing. But if it did not endlessly strive in this fashion, again it could not posit itself, for it could oppose nothing to itself; accordingly it would be no self, and would therefore be nothing."[120] This more and less than nothing, which Jean Paul referred to in order to indicate the trickery in Fichte's argument, disrupts the forward movement of Fichte's exposition. There is a perfidious shuffle in Fichte's argument. Whereas the negation of the second principle signified the logical nothing, and the nothing introduced with the objective activity of practical consciousness indicated the ontological nothing, now the nothings suddenly lose any metaphysical valence. The two nothings at this juncture are no longer philosophical concepts, since they could not be any more determinable than the unprovable "alien intelligence," the "alien with-I" or *der Ich*, which they quantify. The nothing has become a turn of phrase, a lexical expediency, an instance of literature at a pivotal point of the *Wissenschaftslehre*. The consequences are dramatic: for what is now substantiated in language as well as philosophically substantialized is the "alien intelligence" that legitimates the two nothings. The Fichtean progression from the center of the absolute I's universe to the objective word is dependent on that alien I. The argument that supposedly leads to the world is premised on a linguistic arbitrariness that seeks to conceal itself as the story of the triumphant genesis of the world through the I—that is, it conceals itself using the guise of teleology. Whereas this construal of nothingness provides for Fichte the foundation of this system on practical consciousness since it becomes the condition of the possibility of the "alien intelligence," what it proves for Jean Paul is the "groundlessness of the groundlessness."

It is critical to realize the full impact of the disagreement between Fichte and Jean Paul. The force of Jean Paul's objection is to have granted everything to Fichte, to have accompanied him all the way to section 5 of the *Wissenschaftslehre* where the priority of practical consciousness over theoretical consciousness is established with recourse to striving. And to have even accepted that priority. Yet, while Fichte concludes here that the I has now found and founded its world, Jean Paul on the contrary observes that the only thing that the I has found is the absence of foundation. The progression of the I is not merely stemmed or curtailed; rather, it is retroactively shown to be no progression at all. Although this progression is expedient in that it has brought philosophy to the fore, the retroactive reworking that irony allows has a destructive force that undoes progression and teleology. Thus, through irony, *literature is installed at the edge of philosophy*.[121] The two cannot be wrested apart—and yet each holds it own part, its own narrative. The trick in Fichte's technique has been to install literature where there was supposedly only philosophy. A trick that was premised on a divided subject that was to be united by what was "alien" to it. However, the trickster is found out, and what he had sought to construct is transformed—not to its opposite—just merely transformed to a state where transformation is possible. In other words, what follows from Fichte's argument is transformation—not transcendence. But this is also a transformation of Fichte's own argument, since transformation takes place in the particular, not in the pure realm of reason where the I posits itself absolutely. Transformation is formation.

The full impact of Jean Paul's irony, then, if it is rigorously pursued to its logical conclusion, can only be that Fichte himself had also arrived at the doppelgänger's conception of subjectivity—with all the implications that this entails: the formal differentiality of the subject and the narrative of crisis that belongs to transformative technique. *The philosopher is the doppelgänger who affirms the independence of philosophy with the use of literature, and thus in the same stroke denies that independence.* Thus, it is not only the *Clavis* that asserts the reciprocity between literature and philosophy, but also the *Wissenschaftslehre* itself— and despite itself. Jean Paul's conclusion, then, articulated in the guise of a "definition" of the doppelgänger, is this: *the doppelgänger is the subject that cannot be denied*. Sure enough, the doppelgänger can have different manifestations, each with its own unique characteristics, as what follows attempts to demonstrate. Yet these characteristics are given by what attempts to deny them. They are given by the linear, teleological narrative to which the doppelgänger responds by transforming it. And they are also given through philosophy's attempt to secure the identity of the self-reflexive subject, that is, to deny literature by making it an "alien element"—that "alien element" can always return at the end in the guise of the doppelgänger.

The liminality of the doppelgänger and its dual relation to openness is reflected in the transformations introduced by the doppelgänger. Transformation figures as difference and separation. The former indicates the presence of the transformability of the doppelgänger, the differential relations that are its ontological constitution. The latter is the doppelgänger's narrative that criticizes and thereby transforms what seeks to deny it. From the point of view of difference, the doppelgänger cannot be denied, since it is an ontological structure of relationality. From the point of view of separation, the doppelgänger itself cannot deny but can only assimilate through technical transformation what it criticizes. This is, then, the liminal place that resists absolute denial—the place created by the reversal of the "white nothing." What matters for an understanding of the doppelgänger is the staging of this liminality.

CHAPTER TWO

The Subject of Modernity

*Law and Temporality in
Alexandros Papadiamantes*

Out of the dull strength and power of the animal the human spirit tries to push itself forward, without coming to a perfect portrayal of its own freedom and animated shape, because it must still remain confused and associated with what is other than itself. This pressure for self-conscious spirituality... is the symbolic as such which at this peak becomes a riddle. It is in this sense that the Sphinx in the Greek myth, which we ourselves may interpret again symbolically, appears as a monster asking a riddle. The Sphinx pronounced the well-known conundrum: What is it that in the morning goes on four legs, at mid-day on two, and in the evening on three? Oedipus found the simple answer: a man, and he tumbled the Sphinx from the rock. The explanation of the symbol lies in the absolute meaning, in the spirit.

HEGEL, *Lectures on Aesthetics*

... AND ... : THE DOPPELGÄNGER AS THE SUBJECT OF MODERNITY

A reworking of denial so that it can never be absolute is the linchpin of Jean Paul's doppelgänger. Fichte, as it has just been shown, needed an "alien element" within the absolute I which, however, had to, but could not, be denied. Jean Paul highlighted that that alien part, the "demogorgon" inside the subject, is like a conjurer's trick. In addition, the unraveling of the trick is also the debunking of absolute denial, and hence the elimination of absolute loneliness. The lament about loneliness at the end of the *Clavis* paradoxically implies that there is no last man. Hegel, who had been a student of Fichte's, also objected to the positing of this "alien element." The introduction to his *Phenomenology* concludes with the following programmatic statement: "The experience of itself which consciousness goes through can, in accordance with its Notion, comprehend nothing less than the entire ... realm of the truth of the Spirit. . . . In pressing forward to its true existence, consciousness will arrive at a point at which it gets rid of its semblance of being burdened with something alien, with what is only for it, and with some sort of 'other,' at a point where appearance becomes identical with essence."[1] The coincidence of essence and appearance is the truth of the Hegelian Spirit. This coincidence is a form of infinitude through "true existence," that is, particularity. What Hegel explicitly denies is the Fichtean move, whereby the philosophical I can start from within its own ratiocination in order to discern the "alien" element that will lead it to praxis. Hegel inverts this schema by starting with praxis, while arguing that the truth of the Spirit in a sense follows or accompanies the acting consciousness in all its actions so that any action, in its truth, is an unfolding of the Spirit. However, while Hegel, like Jean Paul, also attacks the "alien element," the issue for Hegel is about the "first man," identified as Oedipus in his lectures on aesthetics, because Oedipus solved the riddle of reality. The secret of the enigma is in man himself, the coincidence in Spirit of essence and appearance. Thus, whereas Fichte sought to conceal the secret, Hegel insists precisely on the revelation of the secret. The question, now, arises: Is the structure of the first man who reveals the secret amenable to the subjectivity of the doppelgänger who unravels the trick? In other words, how does a turn from a last to a first man nuance an understanding of the doppelgänger?

The problematic that this turn bequeaths to the doppelgänger can be summarized thus: particularity, in its truth, is infinite. Or, rather, a particular consciousness has to be negated in order to sublate into spirit. There are two good reasons for the negation of particular consciousness. First, if particularity is equated with the transitoriness of passing experience, then arbitrariness can be avoided by offering the kind of holistic synthesis promised by an eternal consciousness. In other words, the absolute uniqueness of experience needs to be tamed—if everything is unique, then everything will also be novel and ungraspable. Second, even if particularity is sublated, the dialectic still seeks to retain it to the extent that each stage of the dialectic incorporates the earlier ones. These two moves mean that, on the one hand, there is no absolute denial here. Nothing is denied; it is just that the earlier stages are negated. On the other hand, this operation of negation still eliminates the subject's reality—a murder of the subject's particularity of, in, and as itself. Loneliness returns here, but it will not be the loneliness of the last man stranded in reason's kingdom and unable to reach reality. Rather, here is the *loneliness of the first man*, the one who solves the riddle of reality, the one who discovers the secret of particularity and of the human with the use of his reason, only for reason to take over his consciousness. It is with the death of phenomenal consciousness that the Spirit of reason is born. Thus, the first time, the time of the birth of a new framing of the law as well as the law's new framing of the subject, is also the last time, the end of time. Hence the loneliness of the first man. The loneliness of the first man, then, differs from the loneliness of the last because of the different relation between infinite and finite. With the last man, the direction was from the infinity of reason to the particularity of praxis—from subjectivity to the subject. With the first man it is the opposite direction, from the finite to the infinite, from the particular whose enigma is negated in totalizing reason. Here, the finite has to be negated; its particularity has to be killed; the singular subject is murdered so that the enigma of its experience can be resolved in the institution of a higher legal order. This law is eternal, and it coincides with Spirit, that is, the reflection of the subject into subjectivity. With this self-reflection, absolutism returns in the guise of eternality and loneliness.

The doppelgänger will arise, again, with the denial of the first man's loneliness. Because of the effective presence of the doppelgänger, man will not be allowed to reflect himself eternally. The progression toward the eternity of reason will be curtailed. This will be precipitated by the reversal of the doppelgänger, that is, by the disruption of the one-directional movement from the finite to the infinite. But the reversal, as it was presented in the previous chapter, is inadequate to address the issue of the first man: whereas the "white nothing" effectuated a placing, the infinite unfolding allowed at this place still does not preclude that the loneliness of eternal reason will not return. While Jean Paul's reversal of Fichte's dialectic consisted in showing the impossibility of moving from the finite to the infinite because the infinite is in the finite, the reversal here will consist in the impossibility of moving from the finite to the infinite because the two cannot be separated. It is an illusion that the negation of the particular—*the act of murder*—will solve any enigma. This is not to suggest that the reversal pertaining to the first man is ontologically distinct from the reversal of the last man. Rather, the reversal has to be nuanced further to account for time and, specifically, the way that the particularity of the present and the future of the universal are intertwined. However, the project again consists in debunking absolutism—this is the imperative of the doppelgänger. With the reversal of the first man, time also becomes an issue. Yet to interrogate time is also to interrogate the law. How could the law of negation not lead to the eternal? How could the death of *a* particular consciousness not lead to the birth of *the* first man? In other words, how can the laws of negation *and* loneliness be retained without being opposed and thus canceling each other out?

After Jean Paul, this death—the negation of particular consciousness in favor of a higher one—will accompany the doppelgänger in its every step. This is attested from the nineteenth-century doppelgänger stories, for instance by E. T. A. Hoffmann, to contemporary doppelgänger novels, such as Saramago's.[2] The doppelgänger's curriculum vitae is blood-stained: recall Edgar Allan Poe's "William Wilson" or Dostoevsky's *The Double*, the *fin-de-siècle* tale of Dorian Gray by Oscar Wilde, and R. L. Stevenson's *The Strange Case of Dr Jekyll and Mr Hyde*. Death is also accorded prominence in Otto Rank's first influential monograph on the doppelgänger. The argument here is not that death in the doppelgänger narrative is necessarily a direct or indirect emanation from, reference to, or development of the Hegelian dialectic. Rather than see death solely within the problems raised by Hegel and their solution in his system, death presents in fact a problematic that is crucial for posttranscendental idealist thought.[3] This is the attempt to move from the real, particular, or finite to the fantastic, universal, or infinite. It is precisely this move that Hoffmann designates in the preface to *Die Serapionsbrüder* as the Serapionic principle: narrating the real as if it were fantastic.[4]

Associated with death is the figure of following, accosting, or pursuing. The doppelgänger very often will pursue its other, or be pursued by it, or both, which would usually be a prelude to a murder. This ineliminable pursuit is attested in the word "Doppelgänger," since the compound name means literally a "double-walker." It is further attested in prevalent motifs of the doppelgänger, such as the pursuit by the shadow. Yet its motive power will not come to the fore, unless the legislative force of the follower or the shadow is acknowledged. What is installed here is a primary injunction, a foundational demand, which does not merely usher in the law, but even more emphatically should be seen as the opening legislative move for subjectivity. Autonomous subjectivity cannot deny the law, because the subject is always already within the law; there is no denial of the law. This idea is succinctly expressed in one of the most influential jurisprudence treatises of the Enlightenment, Cesare Beccaria's *On Crimes and Punishments*: "Within a country's borders there should be no place which is outside the law. Its power should follow every citizen like a shadow."⁵ This does not merely mean that within a sovereign entity the law is omnipresent. It also means that the very omnipresence or undeniability of the law constitutes sovereignty as such. Consequently, it is the placing of the subject after this act of constitution and within the region thereby constituted that is defined as individual autonomy. Finally, omnipresence or undeniability is an injunction for the perpetuity of the law. Each subject, every individual citizen, can follow or break specific laws; but the law as such, of necessity and without exception, follows subjectivity and the citizen. The law is the eternal mirror of subjectivity. The doppelgänger's act of murder comes precisely at this juncture: it signifies its resistance to the assimilation within strict legislative borders instituted by a single foundational origin. This is an affirmation of the doppelgänger's liminality. Such a subject lives on the limits; it persists aside or beside the law, or in *paranomia*, as Stathis Gourgouris puts it, to designate the subject of modernity.⁶

The act of murder, therefore, will be thoroughly misconceived if it is taken as merely illegal, or even somehow immoral. Rather, murder's intervention challenges the perpetuity of the legal borders and the eternality of values. The challenge, then, is a thoroughly *political* act. But this challenge is not primarily directed to the borders or values as such, but rather to their perpetuity or eternality. The challenge is mediated by time—the temporality of the perpetual pursuit instigated by death. The subject of modernity has to go through time but without rescinding the temporality of the infinite—this would inevitably annul its liminality. The subject's shadow remains the law—law as that which allows for both finitude *and* infinitude. However, this "and" is not to be taken as a mere additive, something extra. Or, in temporal terms, the "and" signifies that which disperses the infinite in the finite and thereby subdues any antagonism between them. The "and" specifically does not signify something that comes after, or before, or synchronically with the finite—in other words, the "and" does not signify an origin. The "and" conjoining finitude and infinitude points to something more primary in the distinction between particularity and universality: it points to *singularity*. The subject in modernity gains its singularity.

Michel Foucault explores the relation between particularity and universality and the subject of modernity in the chapter "Man and His Doubles" in *The Order of Things*. The sovereign, as the one who institutes the law, "has no place" in the finitude of human nature, according to premodernity.⁷ The overcoming of this exclusion ushers in modernity: "For the threshold of modernity is situated . . . by the constitution of an empirico-transcendental doublet which was called *man*."⁸ This implies that the law is no longer constituted by a foundational act giving birth to a first man, but rather there is in the modern subject "an imperative that haunts thought from within."⁹ However, this internalization should not be taken as a new attempt to negotiate the space of the inside and the outside; rather, the internalization reworks the relations so that the originary distinction between inside and outside is inoperative. And this reworking has a temporal register: "The original, in man, does not herald the time of his birth . . . it links him to that which does not have the same time as him."¹⁰

Such a contretemps will appear later to indicate, strictly speaking, the realm of justice rather than that of the law. Justice counteracts absolutism by disrupting the one-directionality in the relation between infinite and finite. Yet this disjunction is also a conjunction—that is, the operative presence of the "and" in the mingling of the empirical and the transcendental by the doppelgänger. With the reversal of the contretemps the origin is never stable, never given, but always in a movement of return and retreat. And it is that movement of singularity which, for Foucault, designates the subject of modernity as the doppelgänger:

> Calling to one another and answering one another throughout modern thought and throughout its history, we find a dialectical interplay and an ontology without metaphysics: for modern thought is one that moves no longer towards the never-completed formation of Difference, but towards the ever-to-be-accomplished unveiling of the Same. Now, such an unveiling is not accomplished without the simultaneous appearance of the Double, and that hiatus, minuscule and yet invincible, which resides in the "and" of retreat *and* return, of thought *and* the unthought, of the empirical *and* the transcendental, of what belongs to the order of positivity *and* what belongs to the order of foundations.¹¹

The opening up of modernity is located in the interstices of the "and" which lead to the disappearance of the sovereign subject and to the emergence of the doppelgänger. The infinite is no longer something that is excluded from man, but rather that whose imperative is to remain incomplete, in a state of perpetual completion. The internalization of this project of incompletion is also the internalization of time. This opening up is a new type of subjective autonomy, the modernity of the doppelgänger.

What is necessary for this contretemps to be staged is, in Foucault's formulation, the "calling to one another and answering one another." There must be an enunciation, an address to another, a call to the "you." For this address to retain its "invincibility" there must be no supplication. The "you" can never be allowed to introduce a process of futural completion of the "I." In other words, the negative must remain "restless" and never lead to a reconciliation in the whole.[12] The appearance of the doppelgänger introduces an infinite distantiation and an infinite proximation between the "I" and the "you" which is always enacted on the finite plane. The distance between the "I" and the "you" is the "hiatus" of the *and*. This hiatus will be broached here with reference to the work of Alexandros Papadiamantes. Modern Greek prose is indelibly marked by the writings of Papadiamantes. Yet despite the modernism of his writings and regardless of his contribution to the institution of Greek letters, Papadiamantes will be crucial here because of his modernity. That is, Papadiamantes' writing will be shown to lead to the emergence of the doppelgänger. The claim to such a modernity is made by the final clause of his novella Ἡ φόνισσα (*The Murderess*): the subject dies "between human and divine justice." And a moment earlier that same subject had called out: "Here is my dowry"—to which no reply was either expected or forthcoming.[13] In the interstices of this "between" the idea of a just time, a time of justice, will arise. And in the nonresponse of the call the subject will persist alone—albeit not in place, but alone in relation to the infinitude of time, in loneliness as the negation of a fixed future, but a negation that is perpetual and hence futural.

It might be asked here: Why Papadiamantes? Why this name which is not just obscure but absent from the historical accounts of Western modernism? And why that body of work signed by Papadiamantes that does not seem, at first sight, to bear any resemblance to the well-known doppelgänger narratives? An answer to those questions has to be given in three stages. First, the idea of the modernity of the subject, as it has been sketched above, should not be confused with modernism. The notion of modernism—or the various regional modernisms, be they European or American, Asian or African, and so on—is usually secured with recourse to certain stylistic characteristics: the breaking of narrative rules and boundaries, epistemological insecurity, the disappearance of the author, and so on. Conversely, the notion of modernity resides in the rupture between specific stylist features and their appearance.[14] A project of modernity does not focus on the characteristics that can be gleaned from the narrative but rather on the operation of the text itself. For example, then, the disappearance of the subject is not merely a characteristic or feature of modernity; moreover, it is indissoluble from the project of modernity as it is enacted in each particular instance. That project, as already intimated, can be viewed within a particular setting of a contretemps of justice—the laws or rules or style are interrupted by their use or unfolding. If the primary aspect is the unfolding of the project of modernity, then the absence, up to now, of the name Papadiamantes does not indicate anything about the work signed by Papadiamantes; all it indicates is the pragmatic horizon of the histories of modernity written thus far—a horizon, needless to say, which, if it is constructed with adherence to modernity's own project, should remain in a process of return and retreat, of expansion and contraction, and thus inherently open to the signatory "Alexandros Papadiamantes."

Second, Papadiamantes' *The Murderess* is linked to the literature of the post-Jean Paul doppelgänger. Papadiamantes had steeped himself in that tradition. Working as a translator, Papadiamantes came into active contact with the European literature of the nineteenth century and even was responsible for the introduction of several European authors into Greece. Specifically in relation to the doppelgänger, *The Murderess* was written after his translation of Dostoevsky's *Crime and Punishment* and in a sense directly derives its plot from the Russian novel.[15] Now, the doppelgänger, at least as a motif, figures in *Crime and Punishment* in various ways. Very synoptically, not only can the notion of death be linked to Dostoevsky's earlier novel *The Double* and through that to the doppelgänger stories of Gogol, but, in addition, the name of the murderer, Raskolnikov, means the "split one"; thus the subject presents an internal rupture.[16]

Third, *The Murderess* presents clearly the conceptual issues of the first man. The problematic of the posttranscendental doppelgänger—namely, the entrapment of the subject in the infinite when it is given its finitude, what Foucault calls the "enslaved sovereign"[17]—is a central problematic of Papadiamantes' oeuvre. The infinite, the time of the future, is represented by God. Papadiamantes remained a self-avowed believer in the Orthodox doctrine. Yet at the same time Papadiamantes practiced the secular activity of modernist writing. And in this practice, the figure of God came to be repeatedly disrupted. The staging of those disruptions, which open up the time between the finite time of the human and the infinite time of the divinity, are intimately related to the doppelgänger as the subject of modernity. Such disruptions, which are subdued in Papadiamantes' earlier work, intensify in his later production, especially *The Murderess*, which is thus instructive in the presentation of the problematic of the doppelgänger's temporality.

This operative presence of the doppelgänger will be broached through the figure of confession. With confession, there is a secret to be disclosed and thus canceled out. The relation between the secret and the disclosure is structured by the assumption of an authority, God, who is eternal. Thus, the disclosed secret can institute a first man, such as Hegel's Oedipus, who negates reality in favor of a higher legal order. The subject of modernity, the doppelgänger, disrupts the temporality of confession. *The Murderess* ends with Hadoula or Frankojannou drowning, pursued by the police while she is trying to cross over to the church on a small island in order to confess to Father Akakios.[18] Papadiamantes explicitly states that Hadoula perished "between divine and human justice."[19] This space of the "and" between the human and the divine is linked to the contretemps or internalization of temporality by the subject of modernity. This is highlighted when no one responds to the call of confession, when the subject is confined to the "and" and cannot align itself absolutely either with the divine or with the human.

Significantly, confession also figures in stories that have been traditionally interpreted as doppelgänger narratives. Moreover, it figures in such a way as to raise the issues of temporality and the pursuit, the law and death. The work that immediately springs to mind is James Hogg's *The Private Memoirs and Confessions of a Justified Sinner*.[20] Hogg's novel presents the problematic of a killing that is justified from the perspective of a person who is elected by God. Not only is the murderer the brother of the murdered, and thus in a sense a self-murderer (the narrator's story ends with the disappearance of the murderer), but also what mediates the relation between the two brothers is a ghostly figure, presumed to be the devil. Thus, the breaking of the moral code is instigated by someone who is positioned outside that code. As Linda Bayliss has demonstrated with reference to Hogg's *Confessions*, to assume such an outside is to posit ab initio the Christian paradigm. Whereas the devil for Christianity is the absolute evil, the ancient Greek god "Hermes from whom the devil derives so many of his attributes was neither evil nor good, but apparently symbolized an order outside these ordinary dualistic concepts." To remove the devil "from the sinister side of Christian dogma" is to restore Hermes' "mediating aspect."[21] As the messenger of the gods, Hermes delivers sayings that are not of the order of the true or false. The gods cannot lie—their sayings *can never be denied*.[22] Simultaneously, nonetheless, the gods' message is never straightforward, they "speak with forked tongues."[23] Thus, the message of the gods—a message that speaks of the future and comes from the future—has to be continuously interpreted; it has to be reformulated in human language and its divine nature restlessly negated. The liminality, then, posed by the distinction between an absence of absolute denial and a perpetual negation is the liminality introduced by the call of the confessant. And it is this liminality, the *and* between denial and negation, that will be shown to stage for the doppelgänger the *and* in the return and retreat of Foucault's man of modernity and his double.

Finally, the "forked tongues" of the gods have a significant political import. As Derrida has argued, it is a characteristic of lying that it has to be intentional. Conversely, to move outside the opposition of true and false entails that such sayings should not be taken as pure, intentional acts—as malicious, egocentric acts. Instead, they should be taken as acts that undo the pure maliciousness and egocentricism of intentionality, and hence they constitute the political element par excellence.[24] For the political to be highlighted, it is paramount to pay attention to the reversibility that permeates the scene of lying.[25] The subject who operates through the reversal is precisely the doppelgänger. The political, then, comes to the fore with the doppelgänger obeying the laws of reversibility, such as the one expressed in *The Murderess*: "Nothing is exactly what it appears to be, anything but, in fact rather the opposite."[26] Such *apophatic sayings* establish a double legal demand. On the one hand, the operation of this law of unintentionality is unstoppable—this is what can be understood as the uneffacement of justice. And, on the other, such a justice allows for the questions "Who gives this law? Who authorizes this justice?" to be effective without being occluded. These issues are addressed in *The Murderess* so long as the setting of Hadoula's death "between divine and human justice" is recognized as central to the narrative.

COMMUNITY WITH THE DEAD: SELF-CONFESSION IN *THE MURDERESS*

The story of Papadiamantes' novella *The Murderess* is simple. Hadoula is a grandmother who despairs about the fate of villagers in her small island community. The plight of the families is accentuated by the customary requirement of providing a dowry for the marriage of the females. This leads Hadoula to take the matter in her own hands, and to embark on a killing spree of young girls, starting with her own infant granddaughter. When suspicions start arising, Hadoula escapes in the mountains of the islands, with the police in pursuit. At the end, Hadoula tries to find sanctuary in the chapel of a small off-shore island, in order to confess to Father Akakios. As the tide comes in, she drowns "between divine and human justice."

Hadoula's recollections of her hard life interrupt the linear narration of the murders and Hadoula's flight. These recollections are a kind of confession. In the first chapter, Hadoula spends her nights attending to her infant, sickly granddaughter, while her own life is relayed in her mind. She "goes 'crazy' [εἶχε 'παραλογίσει']" reliving the extreme hardships of her past, which are due to the plight of women of the Greek island societies in the nineteenth century.[27] The women's power is limited, and they are a burden to their family because of the customary dowry. This relay of her personal past, like a confession to herself, provides her with a justification to strangle her own granddaughter, since the murder will unburden the family. Afterward Hadoula visits the church of St. John in Hiding, whose name signifies that it is the place to go to relieve oneself from a hidden sin, that is, to confess what under normal circumstances could not be confessed.[28] This visit to the place of confession reaffirms the justification for the strangulation of her granddaughter and precipitates the killing of other young girls. Finally, even though in the last sequence Hadoula is aiming to confess, it was not her idea to go to Father Akakios, but it was suggested to her by someone who was warning her that the police were closing in on her. Thus, Hadoula is running to the church in search for a sanctuary.[29] It is an attempt to choose the law that will pursue her.[30] Whereas the human laws promised incarceration for life, Hadoula still hoped that after the confession Akakios could assist her to escape on a passing boat.[31] There are clearly ulterior motives, which presumably were never going to be confessed to Akakios. The figure of confession, then, runs throughout the novella, justifies the murders and does so through a disjunction between human and religious customs that govern society as well as Hadoula's subjectivity. The argument here will be that the figure of confession in *The Murderess* poses a rapprochement between divine and human law, a region that mediates between them.[32]

Before stating that Hadoula died "between divine and human justice," the narrative has Hadoula look up and see the arid lot that she had received as her dowry, upon which she exclaimed "Here is my dowry!" Who is the witness to this call? Whence is its authority derived? Is this a call to humankind pointing out the injustices associated with women's dowries and which lead Hadoula to murder? Or is it a call to a higher authority that has the power to redeem in the heavens any injustices and sins perpetrated on earth? The absence of a witness to the call means that there is no proper religious confession. As suggested, the ushering in of the subject of modernity—the doppelgänger—is also precipitated by a "calling to one another and answering one another," as Foucault puts it. Hadoula's call makes it appear that the subject in *The Murderess* has an affinity with the subject of modernity. Yet it cannot be the same, for Hadoula does not expect a response. Her call is not directed to anyone in particular, and yet at the same time it has the potential to be directed to every man and god. It sets the caller apart, only in order to make her part of the largest possible community. This is a call that excludes in order to include—a paradoxical, maybe even an impossible call. What it brings forth is not so much a direct response, as a *responsibility* to sustain the disjunction–conjunction between divine and human law. Besides the call *to* another subject, there is a call *of* the call, something that is in the calling itself. And it is in the calling as the law that regulates its legal protocols. Ultimately, it will be the interplay between the *of* and the *to* of the call—the call *of* the divine and the call *to* the human—that will unravel the impossible possibility of this call. However, this relation between the *of* and the *to*, the divine and the human, can be construed in two ways: either as a revelation, in which case a secret is disclosed; or as revealability that is the presentation of the relation between the two laws. The argument here will be that revelation and the disclosure of the secret are always premised on a unified subjectivity and hence seek to deny the doppelgänger. The secret leads ineluctably to the paradox of how to disclose it without thereby annulling it, and hence grounding subjectivity in a groundlessness, a lawlessness—in madness. Conversely, revealability brings forth the relationality proper to the doppelgänger—it presents the doppelgänger's law. For these two different alternatives to come to the fore, attention must be paid to the call of responsibility and its impossible possibility in *The Murderess*.

This is the call of self-confession—the call that is not directed to anyone in particular but which contains a responsibility pertaining to both the divine and the human law. The passage in *The Murderess* in which Papadiamantes explicitly writes about self-confession narrates how Hadoula had stolen money from her mother but never managed to acknowledge it:

> So she had built her little house with her economies. But what was the first foundation of that small capital sum? At that moment in the sleep-

less night she confessed it to herself [τὸ ἐξωμολογεῖτο καθ' ἑαυτήν] for the first time. She had never mentioned it even to her confessor [πνευματικόν], where anyway she used to confess only very small things, just the usual sins that the priest knew before she said them: malicious gossip, anger, women's bad language and so on. She had never admitted [ὁμολογήσει] it to her mother in her mother's lifetime, though she was the only person to suspect and to know it without even being told of it. It was true she had thought about it and she had decided to tell her in her last moments. But unhappily, before her death the old woman became deaf, dumb and unconscious, "like an object," as her daughter described her position, so Hadoula had had not opportunity to admit her misdemeanour [νὰ τῆς ὁμολογήση τὸ πταῖσμά της].[33]

The reason for the theft was that Hadoula's mother had swindled her betrothed by offering too meager a dowry, such as the arid field that Hadoula noticed just before drowning. What is striking about this passage is the distinction drawn between different types of confession. Hadoula's self-confession (ἐξωμολογεῖτο καθ' ἑαυτήν) is differentiated from the confessions to her confessor when she was seeking forgiveness. It is further differentiated from the admission (ὁμολογήσει) of the theft. Forcing a differentiation between both divine and human laws, at the same time self-confession becomes the site where the two laws face each other and interact. Now, there is a further differentiation within admission. The admission can be of a "misdemeanour" and thus subject to civil law. The admission to her mother, however, is altogether different. The money Hadoula stole had not in fact belonged to her mother because the mother herself had surreptitiously appropriated it from Hadoula's father and hidden it in the house.[34] Thus Hadoula's intended admission to her mother would also have been an admission of her mother's misdemeanor. And if an admission is an address to a *living person*, Hadoula's self-confession is mediated with the figure of death. It is only possible because of the dying mother, "deaf, dumb and unconscious, 'like an object.'" The call of self-confession is inseparable from the figure of death. The absence of a direct addressee only demonstrates that the region with a particular disjunctive–conjunctive legal framework inaugurated by self-confession also constitutes a *community with the dead*. However, how could such a community serve both the divine and the human imperatives?

This question requires an examination of the temporality of self-confession. Past, present, and future are intertwined. In self-confession the secret to be confessed is already known. The mother knew that

Hadoula had stolen the money. There is in advance a secret communion between mother and daughter, both of which are part of the surreptitious stealing that is being conducted. The secret thus becomes a constitutive element of the community established here. This is a practical element. Hadoula is a peasant woman, anchored in particularity, and concerned with her earthly troubles. She is, to use an expression from *The Murderess*, "torn by the claws of reality."[35]

Self-confession, then, starts from the particular. The present has a synthesizing power, which pulls together the human and the divine. The paradox is that the synthesis of the laws also pulls the subject together reconstituting individuality. It is a paradox, because self-confession ab initio undermines the distinctness of the individual. Self-confession is a call directed back to the self. The intentionality toward the external is lacking—it is as if the external has been negated. This movement back to the self and the erasure of intentionality can be interpreted in two ways. One interpretation is of the self-institution of a first man whose negation of reality is the establishing of a new legal framework—as if the individual has been murdered in favor of individuality. The other interpretation is that the operative presence of the doppelgänger establishes a political project that leads to modernity by challenging the sovereignty of the subject and the authority of the law. In both cases there is a secret as an element of the community. But whereas the first man seeks to usurp the secret, the doppelgänger on the contrary seeks to sustain it. Yet if the usurping is in fact a denial of the doppelgänger, this can only be done by emphasizing the content of the secret. Conversely, the differential ontology of the doppelgänger, as it was presented in the preceding chapter, has a formal relationality. As it will be argued, this formality cannot be denied without lapsing into self-contradiction. Certain rules or laws can be set to counteract that formality—therein consists the positing of a law-instituting subjectivity—but the doppelgänger will always return because, as will be shown in the next section, it pertains of a justice that is not reducible to the law.

Everything, then, depends on how the secret is conceived in relation to the community. Both a disclosure and a suspension of the secret refer to the future. It is necessary, then, to look at the temporality of self-confession. Three characteristics schematically present the temporality of self-confession: First, in relation to the past, self-confession is the making of a secret community in which there are no secrets: the conjunction through a secretive a-secrecy. Secret *and* nonsecret: only ever a secret because without it there will be no confession, but also always already known. The community of self-confession, then, is like a sect or a secret society in which one must be initiated and into which one is admitted by calling out a password. Second, in relation to the time of the present, self-confession entails an incessant labor. There is an infinite movement of exclusion and inclusion, which is registered in the novella as the task of killing young girls. There is no end to that labor, the membership in the community of the dead can be expanded indefinitely; there is no quota on the number of its members. Third, the future is registered as the possibility of assimilation in the future to a community that already exists. The future is created by entering the community. This means that the future has a particular structure; it is a future anterior. Yet to allow the future to be created means giving content to the future—that is, solving the secret. The initial entry into that community, that is, the way that Hadoula became member of it, already reveals to her in advance her fate. This initial act sets her apart just as it makes her part of that community. And the only way that this counter-directional movement could lead to initiation is through a revelation. Something is revealed to Hadoula to make her a member of that community. Revelation makes Hadoula the initiator of that community, its first member and sovereign. It is possible to read Hadoula's murders in such a way and to see Hadoula as a first man. There is, however, another way, which consists in seeing the future as creative, that is, as that part of the present that allows for creating. With a contentless future, the doppelgänger is at work. What the doppelgänger resists is a reduction of the subject to an authority that regulates temporality.

Self-confession marks a particular problematic in Papadiamantes—the relation between divine and human law—which is not be confused with mere motifs. For instance, Hadoula is not be to confused with the motif of the "evil old woman." In the short story that inaugurates Papadiamantes' mature work after the early historical novels, "The Christmas Cake" (1887), an old woman tries to poison her daughter-in-law, only to inadvertently kill her own son.[36] This first filicide is still a morality tale, and the tripartite structure of self-consciousness is absent from it. The problematic of self-confession points precisely at the impossible conjunction-disjunction between divine and human law, and it shows the influence of Dostoevsky.

Fourteen years before writing *The Murderess*, Papadiamantes had anonymously translated *Crime and Punishment*, a work that also has the tripartite structure of self-confession.[37] The operation of a nonsecret asecrecy and its secret society is very much at the heart of *Crime and*

Punishment. It is not only that Raskolnikov justifies his action through his arguments, whose extreme rationalism set him apart from the Russian customs. In addition, the idea of a figure who sets himself apart and commits a crime is derived from Pushkin's "The Queen of Spades." In Pushkin's short story, Hermann becomes privy to a secret sequence of card numbers that would allow him to win in the game of faro. These numbers—three, seven, and one—are precisely the amount of rubles that Raskolnikov stole from the murdered pawnbroker.[38] And, these numbers are the key to reading "The Queen of Spades" as an allegory of the Decembrist uprising, the failed attempt of a secret society for reform, which was suppressed by the tsar and led to the execution of Pushkin's close friends.[39] There is, then, in Dostoevsky's novel a pervasive operation of the secret that binds an elect community in the quest of social reform. In terms of the unfolding of labor, it is instructive to note the meticulous registration of the "real" St. Petersburg in *Crime and Punishment*: Raskolnikov moves between actual buildings; the extreme heat of July 1865—the time of the murder—is verifiable through weather records; and the political debates of the time, particularly Alexander II's judiciary reforms, are represented with the progressivist investigator Porfiry.[40] The subject struggles within a network of relations that are particular. Finally, it is not only in the guise of the ratiocinations that Raskolnikov publishes as his article that revelation is operative in *Crime and Punishment*; it is also in the apocalyptic dream in prison through which Raskolnikov achieves redemption.[41] The fact that the tripartite structure of self-confession is to be found in *Crime and Punishment* is not to overlook important differences with *The Murderess*.[42] Nevertheless, this tripartite structure effectuates a region between divine and human justice in which the subject moves. In a letter to Katkov, the editor of the *Russian Messenger* that serialized *Crime and Punishment*, Dostoevsky provided a synopsis of the novel: "Divine truth and human law take their toll, and he [Raskolnikov, the murder] ends up by been *driven* to give himself up."[43] The temporal structure of self-confession makes possible a fissure between divine and human law mediated by death. Or, more accurately, it is murder that makes possible the contact between the two laws.

The problematic of the relation between divine and human law necessitates tracing the relation between the temporal structure and the law in *The Murderess*. First, then, how is the secretive asecrecy registered? This is the past that creates the possibility of a secret society or sect. Women in Hadoula's family possess special powers whose provenance is unknown and which pass from one generation to the next. Hadoula's recollections in the first chapter begin with her mother, Delcharo, being pursed by men who want to punish her because she had cast a spell on them. After Delcharo, the magical powers pass over to her daughter, since Hadoula was able to cure with secret herbs and to perform abortions. Like her mother, she also controlled the people around her. For instance, Hadoula uses the idiomatic expression "σκαρώνω πρωιμάδι" (literally, to build an early one, that is, to become pregnant before wedlock). Delcharo had used this expression as a scare tactic to prevent contact between Hadoula and her betrothed fearing that Hadoula will alert him to the meager dowry.[44] Hadoula, on the contrary, conspires for her daughter to "build an early one" so that the marriage would have to be carried out despite the prospective husband's requests for a larger dowry.[45] In both case, the same idiomatic expression indicates at least three things: on a literal level impregnation, on a linguistic level the use of a phrase as a spell, and on a communal level the manipulation of others for financial ends. Finally, Hadoula's second daughter, Amersa, is also endowed with supernatural powers: Amersa's two main métiers are her auguring powers and her spinning skills on the loom.[46] Her craftsmanship in the loom coupled with her mantic propensity depicts the three women like the fates, deposed from the ancient world of myth where they were revered and feared, and implanted into the hard reality of nineteenth-century Greece where their womanhood makes them socially inferior. At the same time, their gender also allows them to be like the fates, the female semigoddesses who control the destiny of others. Thus, it is those special powers, as they are registered in the millennial movement of a myth and in the present reality of their actions, which both exclude and include them from power. Hadoula, then, is a member of a familial disposition located in this inside-outside zone, whose roots are both mythical and denominational. This is a mythical kinship—and thus known since it transverses a filial line, but also unknown since the supernatural is not subject to cognition.

Yet, despite this secrecy, what is also made obvious from the pursuits of Delcharo and Hadoula is that the powers with which the women are endowed do not make them immune from persecution. On the contrary, one is always already under communal laws. It is precisely those powers that make them subject to relentless pursuit. The community is inherently suspicious of that which transcends its habits—a suspicion that will contribute to Hadoula herself being chased by the police. After the accidental drowning of a girl in a well—which did *not* take place through Hadoula's acts, the girl was *not* murdered—the public prosecutor suspects Hadoula. From then on, from chapter 11 to the end, which is more or less the same length as the first ten chapters, Hadoula is pursued by the law.[47] This indicates that the supernatural secret powers of the women are still situated within a preestablished network of legislative relations to which the women are subjected. This subjection will determine their subject. And it is a subject that carries a secret—the secret powers of the women—which from the very beginning separates those who are subject to it from the customs of the people and the laws of the state, and, as will be seen, gives them a different future.

The special powers also give Hadoula the obligation to act—right here, now, in the present. This action that cannot be analyzed solely with recourse to its particular telos; it is also an action that perpetuates the secret that passes from mother to daughter. The secret is the condition of the possibility for the act. Papadiamantes addresses this issue in the most condensed chapter of the novella, chapter 5, in which Hadoula murders her granddaughter. The chapter starts with the story about how Hadoula managed to marry off her daughter without conceding to the groom's demands for a large dowry. Hadoula, as noted above, used her mother's idiomatic expression—or, even, magical spell—"σκαρώνω πρωιμάδι," illustrating her membership in the secret group. Three months after the wedding the first child was born, a girl. Three years later there was a boy, and two years after that another girl, the sickly infant nursed by Hadoula. At this early hour Hadoula again considers the burden that girls place on their families. Hadoula sees that, and therefore she feels happy after the funerals of young girls:

> Whenever she returned to the house of the dead girl to attend to the ceremony of *consolation* in the evening, old Hadoula could find no words of consolation to say, but she was all joy and she blessed the innocent infant and her parents. And the grief was joy and the death was life and everything was inside-out.
> Ah, look... Nothing is exactly what it appears to be, anything but, in fact rather the opposite.
> Given that the grief is joy and the death is life and resurrection, then the disaster is happiness and the disease is health.[48]

Hadoula will obey the imperative according to which "nothing is exactly what it appears to be, anything but, in fact rather the opposite." This gives her the obligation to turn from murderess to healer, to heal by murdering.[49] And it is an obligation assumed in the name of the people and for their own redemption. Moreover, it is sanctioned by Hadoula's confessor.

> And the poor parents lose their mind [χάνουν τὸν νοῦν], and pay so much for quacks and threepenny drugs, to save the child. They never suspect that it is when they are thinking of "saving" that they are really "losing" ["χάνουν"] the offspring. And Christ had said, as Frankojannou had heard her confessor explain to her, that he that loves his soul shall lose it [θὰ τὴν χάσῃ], and he that hates his soul shall keep it unto life everlasting.[50]

Thus both the church and social conditions—synthesizing in the present their different legislative protocols—demand this loss which is in fact a salvation. To not see this—to be "blind" to the work of death spread by the wings of the angels[51]—can lead only to madness. The parents lose their minds after they have failed to save their children. It is only by not losing their children, which is in fact denying the child's salvation, that the parents will not lose their minds. Losing their minds is a symptom of their not realizing what real salvation is. Hadoula is ready to assume her psyche-iatric obligation—the healing (iasis) of the souls (psyche) as well as the minds of the people. This responsibility entails that she heals—that is, kills—the children herself.

Hadoula thus becomes the healer in this community of the dead—the dead who are killed in order to be saved, *truly* saved, from the hacks and destitution and into the kingdom of God. The community of the dead, then, will be a community that is in-between this world and the heavens, a threshold to paradise. This threshold contains the imperative that "nothing is exactly what it appears to be, anything but, in fact rather the opposite." Every action, be it a deed or a speech act, has to obey this command. The world of particularity is never to be revealed directly. Only the ones chosen to be part of the group could possibly have the right to gain access. And they can only gain access by adhering to this incessant apophasis, the negativity that propels appearances into a perpetual dissimulation. In effect, the command says: act *because* you know the secret law that turns everything to its opposite, but act *in such a manner* so that the secret will not become common knowledge, for it is too powerful and it can drive people to lose their minds. And, given that the manner or technique which dispenses the secret is always apophatic, there is no way of stopping at any point. The movement is beyond a thesis (θέσις) and an antithesis (αντίθεσις), it is a movement

The Subject of Modernity 85

that does not offer any guarantee of security or rest—there is not stable "putting down" (θέσις); the task is endless.

> Would it not really be right, if only humans were not so blind to assist the scourge that fluttered in the angels' wings, instead of trying to pray it away? But look, the angels take no sides and make no favors. They take away boys and girls alike into Paradise. In fact all the more boys. So many precious only sons who died untimely [ἄωρα]. Girls have seven lives, the old woman reflected. Not much makes them ill and they seldom die. Should we as good Christians not help in the work of the angels? Oh how many boys, and how many little princesses are snatched away untimely [ἄωρα]! And even little princesses die more easily than the infinite multitude of female children of the poor. The only ones with seven lives are the girl children of the poor! They seem to have been multiplied on purpose, to punish their parents with a foretaste of hell in this world. Ah, while one thinks about this the "mind is on a high" ["ψηλώνει ὁ νοῦς του"]!⁵²

The expression "the mind is on a high," used at the end of this paragraph is not synonymous to the expression "the poor parents lose their minds," which opened the previous paragraph. It is not synonymous because Hadoula's thought process does not "lose" sight of where salvation lies—she is not blind like the parents. Rather, her thought process has the luminosity of a clear perception seeing things unhidden, as they really are, in their truth. In the present everything has turned "untimely [ἄωρα]." The task, then, is to turn time "inside-out" in order to correct time, to unravel that which appearances hide and oppose. A task, in other words, of standing above time, higher than the present, and seeing that present panoptically, "from a height," and thus to give time (ὥρα) to the people, to give them a time which is the present. However, this task is also enormous, veritably endless given the multitude of girls.

This giving of the present, then, is a law different from divine and human law, a law above the dialectic, and thus a lawless law. The lawlessness of the subject's endless task is hard to determine, because it is almost aberrant, mad:

> In reality, Frankojannou's "mind had started being on a high" ["νὰ ψηλώνῃ ὁ νοῦς της"]. She had gone "crazy" ["παραλογίσει"]. It was the consequence of proceeding to higher matters. She leant over the cradle, She pushed two long, tough fingers into the baby's mouth to "shut it up."

She knew it was not all that usual for very small children to "shut up." But she was now "crazy." She did not know very clearly what she was doing, nor did she admit to herself what she wanted to do.

She kept her fingers there for a long time. Then she withdrew them from the little mouth, which had ceased to breathe, and pulled at the baby's throat, and squeezed it for a few seconds.

That was all.[53]

The colloquial expression "the mind is on a high" means "to lose one's marbles," to go insane.[54] It is the madness of incessant labor—the madness of the endlessness of the apophatic task. But it is also a madness because it puts the subject in a detour that is "higher" than the present, already transgressing the law that it sought to institute and protect with its apophatic movement. With the killing of the girl, Hadoula has indeed instituted a community with the dead, but she herself can never commune with them; she cannot address them. She has "gone crazy," she is παρά-λογη (*para-loge*): meaning, she is not reasonable, she does not operate within *logos*, she is a-logos. She is at a place apart because the customary laws, human and divine, do not apply to her. She is, then, also παρά-νομη (*para-nome*): meaning, she is illegal; she does not operate within the law; she is without the customary laws. Hadoula's endless task, the apophatic madness of her psyche-iatric healing, repeats, then, a separation like that already noted in regard to her past: the prefix *para-* is the border between her and the reason, legality, and madness of the others. However, at the same time, this lawlessness can also be the institution of a new law, a law above normal laws and the dialectic, a law of the end of the law.

Yet the institution of a higher law already points to the future, not simply in that it discloses the salvation promised by Hadoula's healing-killing, but also in that it institutes a community under the sign of this new law. In which case, Hadoula's madness will be the loneliness of the first man of that community of the dead, the one who holds the secret of reason and the dialectic and promises salvation. The subject can only uncover the future through a revelation that wrenches it apart. This loneliness is a symptom of Hadoula's madness that threatens even the secret bond that binds her with Amersa, her daughter with mantic powers. In chapter 4, Amersa had run in the middle of the night to her mother attending to the sick granddaughter, because Amersa has had a nightmare: "I saw the infant girl was dead and that you [Hadoula] had a black smear [or, sign, σημάδι] in your hand."[55] Chapter 4 concludes by reaffirming Amersa's prognosticating predilection, since her dreams were signs (σημαίνωσιν).⁵⁶ After the description of the strangulation of the granddaughter, chapter 5 ends by remarking that "Frankojannou failed to recollect her daughter's [Amersa's] dream.... Her mind had gone 'high'! [Εἶχε 'ψηλώσει' ὁ νοῦς της!]"⁵⁷ Thus, madness also separates Hadoula from her kin. Hadoula has gone "high" above her daughter with whom she was bound by the secret supernatural powers. The text indicates this separation with the use of quotation marks: while the whole idiomatic expression "the mind is on a high" was placed in quotation marks in the previous two instances, in the third instance only the "high" (ψηλώσει, which is actually a verb, indicating an action) is in quotation marks. And this heightening effectuated by the sign is further accentuated. After the first murder, Hadoula goes to St. John in Hiding, the church where people go to confess their deepest secrets. Yet Hadoula does not seek to confess, she does not ask for forgiveness. Instead, she asks the saint for a sign (σημεῖο) to tell her whether she was indeed justified.⁵⁸ Only after Hadoula thinks that she has received that sign, does she commit her next murder.⁵⁹ The following murder is not even properly perpetrated by Hadoula, because she just makes a *wish* for a young girl to fall in a well, and her wish comes true.⁶⁰ More important, this signposting also functions as a signal or password of the future. On her way to murder more girls, people greet Hadoula by saying that "God has sent you!"⁶¹ The sign reveals the future in that it reaffirms the past. The sign justifies what has already been revealed to the subject. The temporality of the sign is a future anterior.

However, this future anteriority can be interpreted in two different ways: either as a revelation or as revealability.⁶² Hadoula, as she reaches out to her granddaughter's throat and commits a murder, at that very moment she assumes that something specific has been revealed to her. This revelation is the apex of self-confession as well as its undoing. It is the apex of self-confession in precisely revealing the secret law of the law, the law beyond the dialectic that has been apophatically pursued. But this revelation is an apophasis, a negation of the future that becomes a corrective of the negativity of the present. This law of the future, which gives the obligation for an endless present task, holds the whole temporal structure of self-confession together—it is the transcendental temporality of self-confession that results in revelation. It is what already and always is given in self-confession: the law that transcends the segmentation of part, present, and future in order to reveal their structural unity. This is the unity reflected in the unitary subjectivity of the law, that is, in the first man. The anterior-future becomes a meta-time which gives a meta-language: higher than, but still part of, the present; an endless present, but still outside that present and its endlessness; giving articulations that are not only secretive but that also present a secrecy as the foundation of subjectivity. This is a revelation of what self-confession calls *of*, a revelation of its secret, an expression of the inexpressible. Nevertheless, for this structure to work, lawlessness has to be preserved. And it is precisely lawlessness that is annulled at the moment that Hadoula strangles the granddaughter: the secret has been reinscribed in a higher authority that institutes a new law. This precipitates the undoing of self-confession. The past, which bound Hadoula to her daughter, Amersa, is immediately suspended and superseded, giving way to the law of a higher community, the community of the dead. The task of the present is not endless any longer. A criterion of its reinscription is found in the act of killing. The carrying out of the murder transfers the acting in the present to an act that is always already futural. More important, the relation between the divine and the human laws is itself suspended and superseded. Self-confession as revelation fails at the point that it synthesizes the human and the divine in an act that negates them and transfers them to a plane where any difference between them is inoperative. Finally, with the expression of the inexpressible secret, Hadoula has forged for herself a new total individual identity. She has become the sovereign in that region between divine and human law; thus, she is the sole one who has executive power in this region. Instead of the political openness of the doppelgänger, she has installed a despotic rule.

Conversely, revealability sustains the inexpressible. To read *The Murderess* as sustaining such a possibility—a possibility which shows the impossibility of denying the doppelgänger—is to read the structure of self-confession in a different way. This way avoids any conciliation of opposition within a higher authority, and hence finds conciliation only as the unfolding of the oppositions endlessly enacted by the power of the negative. This is to persist, also, with the repetition of the two laws—or, more accurately, with the repetitive enactment in the two laws, an enactment that cannot escape from them and achieve a specific content under a different rule. The sign does not need to reveal as such. It can be the structure of the possibility of revelation, that is, revealability. It need not reveal any content. The sign is a revelation *as such*. And, as God's envoy, the one who always responds to the call "God has sent you!" Hadoula is linked with the god Hermes, the Olympian gods' messenger. As it was argued earlier, Hermes was the bearer of the divine messages, but the messages, as signs, were never self-evident. In the language of *The Murderess*, "nothing is exactly what it appears to be, anything but, in fact rather the opposite." This negativity illustrates the obligatory lying of the doppelgänger, whose "hypocritical" pronouncements are outside the binary true-or-false.[63] The future anterior, then, that Hadoula becomes privy to is neither true nor false. Rather, it is a future that discloses a law that cannot be reduced to this or that, a law that is incessant and constantly revealing itself by making revelation possible. As such, it also becomes the transcendental condition of the possibility of self-confession. But in this case, self-confession does not pertain only to the future—the *of* in the call. Rather, the double inscription is maintained: self-confession retains both a *to* and an *of*. The negativity pertains to both the human and the divine; it persists on the threshold that links and separates, conjoins and disjoins them. After all, Hermes was not only a messenger but also the one who escorted the dead to Hades. Thus, to stay with the revealability of the sign is also to descend to the underworld, to make a community with the underworld. But at this place no sovereign power can be usurped by the subject. The subject is not allowed to act in order to precipitate the passage to the community of the dead.

And yet, how is it possible to sustain the obligation of this "not allowed to"? How could this prohibition be obeyed without revelation, without a new and higher legal framework? This is the limit of negativity, the limit of self-confession. Having reached this limit, its threshold must not be transgressed if the liminality of the doppelgänger is to be maintained. But this calls for an investigation of this limit, an investigation on the limit (a limit that, it will be argued, pertains to how madness is conceived in *The Murderess*). And it is an investigation that needs to highlight precisely the connection that this threshold and limit *allow*. In other words, it needs to show the transcendental condition of the lawlessness of negativity, without sublating this lawlessness in a revealed law. It is a lawlessness that will turn out to place an obligation that comes from justice itself. But because it will not be a justice revealed, the obligation will be a call to a subject outside the confines of individuality, a call to the doppelgänger. But this is also a call that can be uttered only by following a specific critical protocol. This is a protocol that does not equate *The Murderess* with a revelatory self-confession. Thus, the justice of the doppelgänger also places demands on criticism—the demand against a future with a content, that is, against reading the novella as a secret.

THE PENUMBRA: OBLIGATIONS

Hadoula's self-confession made possible a double framing of the call. The call is inscribed twice, first as the address to someone and then as its transcendental temporality. Further, within both framings there is the demand for apophasis, stated in chapter 5 of *The Murderess* as "nothing is exactly what it appears to be, anything but, in fact rather the opposite." Such a demand places an obligation that both subjects the subject to an endless task and because of that subjection discloses the structure of its subjectivity. So far, only the possibility of this double framing or inscription has been examined. What needs further elucidation is the way that the two different elements are combined. How is the address of the call connected with its transcendental content? This question has far-reaching implications for the notion of subjective law in *The Murderess*. On the one hand, the demand of negativity and apophasis obliges the subject to secrecy, to never directly expressing what underlies its actions. On the other hand, the metatime and metalanguage of the calling *of* of self-confession are always expressible; they have already been revealed; or, they are always already *revealable*. It appears, then, that the suspension of the addressee entails two contradictory laws: a law of the secret and a law of the nonsecret; a law that can never be expressed and a law that has been expressible even before its actual expression. To inquire, then, into the connection between the two different inscriptions of the call is to ask whether it is possible to have a complete inexpressibility separated from a complete expressibility. Or, conversely, whether such a bifurcation is impossible and hence the expressible always implies the inexpressible and vice versa.

This is a dilemma that leads back to the region between divine and human law, in which Hadoula drowns at the end of *The Murderess*. The connection between the two framings is the connection between the two laws. What will be argued here is that the connection is a threshold where both obligations interpenetrate and intertwine, an ante-region to both laws but reducible to neither. The iterability of the laws in this region casts a different shadow—a penumbra—from the shadows of either. It is a penumbra, because the origins of the shadows of the laws in the human and the divine can be glimpsed, but it is a shadow outside the shadow proper in the sense that by effectuating a connection between the two it can be reduced to neither and yet it cannot be separated from them. Thus the penumbra is never completely visible, never completely expressible—rather, it is what makes expression possible. It is the law of fiction that, by not being commensurate with any law, must remain lawless.

The penumbra, then, is doubly enigmatic, the secret of the secret. But can there be a secret of the secret? How is one to discern it? How can one hear its call? Its history of reception shows that the criticism of *The Murderess* to date, so far as it has been possible to ascertain, takes it upon itself, as a kind of obligation, to demonstrate what can be discerned and heard. In other words, it has always been assumed that the inexpressible can be separated from the expressible, the divine from the human. And the way that this separation is facilitated has always been said to reveal the inner meaning, or the secretive secret, of *The Murderess*—or, rather, not so much the text itself, as the meaning hidden in the text by its author.[64] Such interpretations would always posit a separation in the secret, which in one move both unravels the mystery of the secret and places the author as the detached source of that unraveling.[65] It is through the author that the revelation of the inexpressible is always carried out. An example is Guy Saunier, who argues for a type of psychoanalytic interpretation of Papadiamantes' oeuvre. This interpretation revolves around "Papadiamantes' personal myth," that is, his oedipal complex. Saunier constantly places upon the critic the obligation of cryptography, that is, to decipher that encrypted myth. Papadiamantes "has created a complex cipher" in narrating his oedipal complex, but he thereby "managed to express the inexpressible—to say the unsayable."[66] The apex of this myth is, according to Saunier, *The Murderess*, which is a "cryptographic admission" of Papadiamantes' identification with Hadoula, whose murders represent the oedipal drama.[67] The insistence of secrecy has given rise to a number of psychoanalytic interpretations of *The Murderess*.[68] The secret ineluctably refers to the repressed, and the temptation to see the sublimation of repression into art is one that criticism has often succumbed to. However, is not the cryptogram of the secret a cancellation of that secret? And, if that is so, then is not art also canceled out, replaced by a crypto-graphico-psyche-iatric machine? On the contrary, to insist with art is to insist with the secret: this is not to resist its cancellation but to "diagnose" the "return of negation" that both suspends any negation of the secret and, as argued in the preceding chapter, allows for a differential ontology of subjectivity—that is, for the doppelgänger.

Despite reservations that arise from the beginning, the supposition of the authorial obligation to reveal the secret cannot be dispensed with until an examination of the temporality that underlies it has been examined. To put the issue in terms of the temporal structure of self-confession, the issue in each case will be whether the endless task of the present could be separated from the future anterior. This separation is always mediated by something external to the text, the author. In the two most prominent lines of interpretation of *The Murderess*, the sociological and the theological—which reproduce the demands of a human and a divine law respectively—it will become clear that this separation has the effect of turning revealability into revelation. In each case, a content is revealed. This could not allow the reversal. To find the logic of the reversal—that is, the doppelgänger—in *The Murderess*, will entail a different approach, a different connection between the endlessness of the present and the future.

The first emphatic articulation of a sociological reading of *The Murderess* was conducted by Valetas in his monumental biography of Papadiamantes. Valetas argues that *The Murderess* is a "vehement protestation" against the poverty of the people by the "ideologue" Hadoula who "is not murderous by nature." In the Sporades islands "filicide due to dowry obligations was a universal but unadmitted [ανομολόγητο] phenomenon, known to all but kept secret [κρυφό] by all." Thus, Valetas continues, although Papadiamantes morally condemned the killings, "as a man he saw the other side of the coin, the aim of the murderess, and he praises that . . . because by presenting and condemning the crime Papadiamantes wants to eliminate its cause."[69] Thus, Valetas is committed to the absolute present of the novella: "There are no influences by Dostoevsky here, nor is there any imagination (we know the author's sources); there is the [unbearable] Greek reality."[70] This is a very clear statement of two elements that are indispensable in any consistent sociological reading. First, there is a rupture between creation, on the one hand, and nature, on the other. What Papadiamantes *creates* by representing Hadoula's murders is never reducible to nature and its causes. Hadoula was not murderous, but it was the social hardship that caused her insanity, which in turn caused the murders.[71] However, the upshot of the separation between creation and nature is that it necessitates a teleology.[72] Any sociological reading would have to assume such a teleology. Second, the insistence on the present reality as the author's sole source of inspiration has the effect of destabilizing generic determinations. Denying Dostoevsky's influence on the writing of *The Murderess* in effect says that Papadiamantes' creation negates any generic categories or a periodization. In a sense, then, Papadiamantes creates his own genre.[73]

Both the telos, which results from the separation between creation and nature, and the development of the genre are futural: they both present a diachronic historical evolution. However, it could be asked at this point: How is the future of social theory related to the future of literary production? This is not merely an arbitrary question but a question that sociological criticism has to confront, since it pertains to the placement of the subject, the author, in relation to the future. The question quickly turns into an aporia: How could the author negate the genre, if the author is really part of the irresistible telos inherent in his society? Inversely, how could individual creation occur, unless the author is outside the movement of common development? The uniqueness of the creation demands the author to be part of the social, while the uniqueness of the genre's development itself demands the author's segregation. The former presents the author as a lone genius who grasps "reality" as a whole, whereas the latter presents the author as the madman who is apart. Loneliness, at this point, would eliminate the distance between the genius and the madman. Furthermore, a sociological critique will of necessity revert to a symptomatology of the author. Unable to decide what the primary cause is, the outside world or the internal spirit of the author, the only recourse is to annul art by setting the crypto-graphico-psyche-iatric machine in motion, which is obliged to interpret the work as the author's *self-confession*, as Papadiamantes encrypted *revelation* of the present.[74] Effectively, all that is thereby disclosed is the pedestrian fact that there is a link between the present of the author and the future, but nothing more can be said about the nature of the relation between the two—which is precisely what had called for explanation. So much for the sociological approach.

For theological interpretations of *The Murderess*, Hadoula is the embodiment of absolute evil to the extent that her murders are against the law of God—that is, she is the devil. Stelios Ramfos also argues that Papadiamantes was above any influences such as from Dostoevsky in order to indicate the absolute uniqueness of his creation.[75] However, this uniqueness here is not due to an extraordinary development of the individual author, as was the case with the sociological interpretation. Rather, Ramfos is compelled to argue that, because of Hadoula's absolute evil, she "can be a representative of every epoch and every society," that is, she incarnates a universal value.[76] This universal value, as the image of God, is attached to a notion of a singular time—above and beyond past, present, and future. This "achrony [αχρονία]" entails the "transcending of the sovereignty of instinct and law."[77] This time, then, is posited beyond the teleology entailed in a sociological interpretation. As such, the laws of logic are inoperative in that time: A law that poses divine creation at the beginning "entails the incompatibility of that creation with the bifurcation between good and evil as higher powers," and the thought embracing that creation is "beyond logic."[78] This time, further, necessitates the "priority of content" in that the image of God is revealed in every detail of reality, in every creation.[79] However, if this content presents "a whole and self-governed world that is reflected by [Papadiamantes'] writing, nevertheless it also automatically transmits a time that is not continuous with the present and foreign to it."[80] This cosmic time, the time of God, "is the secret of his [Papadiamantes'] art, the element that governs his descriptions and stories, but without ever appearing, without even its being unraveled in the course of the events."[81] The present's being is "its never happening in itself" because the "work is the moment of eternity, the synopsis of time in the event of the reception of the divine [by the author]."[82] Denying this time causes the insanity of Hadoula whose ideological will to change only leads to absolute evil.[83] Ramfos's moral of the story is unequivocal: "The end of negation is catastrophe.... Only one who has nothing to overcome ... can partake of eternal life."[84] And this can only be done by "the silent suffering of the world's hardships,"[85] which "restores in the miracle of creation [that is, the world], the primal unity" of eternal time.[86]

Notwithstanding the political implications of revelation, it can still be pointed out that negation—and thus the dialectic—is far from eliminated here.[87] What the primal unity of a cosmic temporality has to negate is precisely the political.[88] This negation is never carried out directly, but only through the author who reflects the purported cancellation of the dialectic in this world—a fact that guarantees his absolute uniqueness and thereby also negates the work's genre. If negation does persist, however, is not Papadiamantes, then, still trapped in "the sovereignty of instinct and law"? Maybe Ramfos seeks no negation of negation, but an a-negation or de-negation: a suspension of negation in the apophasis of Papadiamantes' art, what Ramfos calls "the secret of his art." The individual, however, is still present as the author of this unique secret. And if this author, Papadiamantes, cannot be identified with the creator of this world, then this is only because as a mortal Papadiamantes is a reflection and transmission of the supreme Author, just like his writing reflects the whole world and transmits eternal time. This mechanism of representation is governed through the sameness to the "primal unity." The now and the I are an infinite reflection of that primordiality, a *mise-en-abîme*, or, to use a phrase from Papadiamantes' early novel *The Merchants of the Nations*, "we are nothing but Echo."[89] But from the moment that that mechanism is operative, the authorial enunciation does not secure any eternal values, as Ramfos proclaims, but instead shows, in the words of *The Merchants of the Nations* again, that "in vain would an answer from you be expected. It could not be final."[90] Transcending the bifurcation of natural instinct and man-made legal systems was meant to affirm a separate temporality in which laws, and hence dialectics, were inoperative, that is, a divine law beyond natural determinism and individual will. And yet, the individual remains; he has signed *The Murderess*, and if that signature is to be turned into a divinely inspired mission, then the words become a *confession*. They confess an unfinality of answers, an unbroachable cosmic achrony, the pervasive ambiguity of mythical echoes cut off from their source and destiny. And rigor would demand that the same ambiguity will be echoed in the distinction between divine and human law. The distinction must—as an obligation—remain a revelation only of the content of divine and human law, but never of its image. The law of law, the law that governs the relation and which has been calling for explanation, must also remain undecidable. In other words, the theological interpretation cannot assert the universality of a revealed content without its being implicated in negativity and thereby losing its universality.

Despite their seeming incompatibility, time is registered in both the sociological and the theological reading in terms of a gap or a complete rupture. A part of time, either the diachrony of evolution or the achrony of universal value, is excluded. This exclusion can be recorded only because of the mediating figure of the author. Further, despite the completely different conclusions that both approaches draw in describing the content of *The Murderess*, they both identify an analogous rupture in the character of Hadoula: her mind was "heightened"; she had gone mad; she was completely separated from everyone. For both interpretations, these two exclusions are the negation of something as well as the way of canceling negation as such: an end of negation as the telos of human history or the eschaton of divine nature. Furthermore, both strategies entrust this end of negation to the time of the future. And, this future is contained in a moment of the present, the moment when Hadoula goes mad: the future, be it social or divine law, is represented in this caesura of the present. At this point, the human and the divine touch—they are put into contact and they interact. However, the problem in both approaches is that the caesura is foreclosed. The moment of madness is complete; there is an absolute exclusion, and the event of contact or interaction is occluded. To put it in terms of the temporal structure of self-confession, according to both a sociology and a theology of *The Murderess*, when Hadoula goes on a "high," the anterior future becomes present, and in such a manner as to dissipate any mystery. The secret of self-confession is expressed as the "message." This may be given different contents—either the revelation of a revolution or a paradise—but the structure of ascribing this message is always inscribed within the same framework that isolates a moment of absolute exclusion. Accordingly, the secret of the secret for both procedures is precisely this absolutely other time. That is what the call of self-confession as revelation consists in: the transcendental signifier that governs both discourses and regulates their juridical protocols. Ultimately, however, what both discourses seek to hide in their attempted revelations is that they have been unable to provide any explanation of the way that the human and the divine come into contact only to exclude each other. In other words, the call's "of" is merely posited as outside the oppositions that regulate the discourses, and is broached only in the reflections, representations, and mirrorings of the oppositions themselves. It is broached only in this endless detour of analogy—a detour that does not fail to fall back upon itself, to return to its source, but is still unable to say anything decisive about it. This point was also reached in Kant's description of madness as analogy, as shown in Chapter 1. The detour, then, is aberrant. Following the rigor of its logic—that is, according to the obligation placed upon it by its own laws—both discourses are mad. And not just "mildly" mad; they are completely mad, with a completeness that reiterates the moment of eternal exclusion.

There is, however, a different way to approach the moment of exclusion. Because it is a way that denies the *absoluteness* of exclusion, it is not amenable to the constitutions of the divine and the human laws. Since this different way would insist on the iterability of the moment of exclusion, the denial of absolute exclusion is not a negation of exclusion. There is no absolute novelty, there is no revelation; rather, all that is present at that moment is the formal structure of revealability or iterability. Negativity is preserved—albeit transformed, a negativity that would remain negative rather than be sublated into an end. The negative as it unfolds in both approaches will be retained, even if changed, reversed. This reversal has already been alluded to as the endless labor of Hadoula and as the limitless apophasis of enunciation. This is a reversal that takes place in particularity and at the time of the present. And yet, the reversal is not a pure and simple making present—it does not point to particularity. On the contrary, what effectuates the reversal is precisely the future anterior—which has been described as the revealability of self-confession. What this reversal sets in motion is a double trajectory: destroying or negating any vestige of autonomous or complete individuality, while also denying that there is a notion of subjectivity which, as a transcendental signifier, has secured the destruction or negation. This reversal ushers in the singularity of the doppelgänger.

This ushering entails that repetition will be operative in *The Murderess*—in other words, that the doppelgänger is operative. For repetition to take place, the self-confession's call has to have both a *to* and an *of*. There must be both an address to someone and an address of and as something. The call can neither exclude other subjects nor exclude a legislative region. And, more generally, the call of self-confession *has to* retain both the subject shadowed by the laws *and* an I that is not reducible solely to the divine or the human law. This "has to" of self-confession shows the obligation entailed in the threshold between the divine and the human law, between the particular and the universal, the diachronic and the achronic. Further, this obligation cannot be analogical, which means that it cannot conduct a detour to the outside and then back to the inside of the law. It is the obligation to deny the absolute exclusions entailed in interiority and exteriority and to allow for the threshold to operate as the site and the temporality (*chronos*) of the repetitive and aberrant exclusions. Two questions, then, have to be raised: First, how is analogy to be reconfigured? Or, to put it differently, how could madness not be absolute? And, second, how can the subject avoid becoming a self-standing mirror of the transcendental relation between the laws? In other words, how does the authorial voice register the *to* and *of* of its address without privileging either? Answering these questions will not only show the doppelgänger in *The Murderess* but will, in addition, show the kind of shadow, the kind of law—or, rather, *lawlessness*—that follows the figure of the doppelgänger as a subject of modernity.

What is raised with the question of madness is the issue of whether its principle of interruption is contained in it. How is it possible to understand Hadoula's madness in such a way as not to need to circumscribe it within a legal system that is founded through an exclusion, by something external to it? And, more broadly, how can a self-confession, which institutes a community of the dead and thus a call that has no addressee, still not be completely aberrant? To pose this question necessitates a further scrutiny of the idiomatic expression that describes Hadoula's condition: her mind was on a "high," ὁ νοῦς της ψήλωσε.

This expression, it will be recalled, appears three times in the crucial chapter 5 of *The Murderess*. First, Hadoula contemplates the endless task of healing poor families by killing their young girls. Thinking all that, one's mind goes on a 'high.' Papadiamantes inserts at that point an ellipsis in the narration, after which the description of thoughts ends and a description of the situation at hand ensues: Hadoula *really* acts and strangles her granddaughter. Here, however, it is not just anyone who could go on a "high," but it is specifically Hadoula who goes on a "high"; she goes mad (παραλογίσει). Thus, whereas the first use of the expression is a general statement, the second is a specific one. And, whereas the first still indicates a state of mind that responds to the endless apophatic task, the second effectuates a particular break between Hadoula and the laws or customs of the community. The third use intensifies this break, since Hadoula's mind being on a "high" resulted in her forgetting the auguring dream that Amersa, her daughter, had told her about. Thus, Hadoula is apart not only from the larger community but from her closest kin as well. Clearly, then, there is a differentiation of usage of the expression ὁ νοῦς της ψήλωσε. And what has to be resisted at this point is to give a foreclosed meaning to each usage. If that were to happen, then Hadoula's apartness would have been already placed within a mechanism of exclusion. What has to be put into question, and in such a manner that the question will be sustained, is an "inside-out" movement. It will be recalled, though, that the thoughts that led to the first usage were instigated by Hadoula's realization that "the grief was joy and the death was life and everything was inside-out. Ah, look... Nothing is exactly what it appears to be, anything but, in fact rather the opposite." There is an impossibility of fixing a telos to singular human relations, and happiness, as the completion of human well-being, can be achieved only through disaster. Thus, the second and third usages pull the different legislative frameworks apart in the same movement that pull the subject apart from the others, whereas the first usage seems to point toward a logic of reversibility. It is only through the repetition of joy in sadness, of life in death, that the subjectivity of the "heightening" or ὕψος is possible. This is the law that obliges Hadoula to her endless task, a task that puts one's mind on a "high." But does the "high" here indicate madness pure and simple? There does not seem to be an analogical structure that bifurcates between something real and its representation mediated by a subject. What seems to take place with this "heightening" of the mind is more like an allegorical procedure, whose protocols precisely indicate the destruction of the referent through the use of its other (ἄλλο), the mutual destructibility of opposing and foreclosed laws. These are the allegorical protocols of reversibility. Remarkably, the noun ὕψος, heightening or the sublime—a cognate of the verb ψηλώνω of the expression "the mind goes on a high"—has been used by Longinus in precisely this allegorical sense. Moreover, Longinus' use is carried out in terms of a distinction between the divine and the human such that the two spheres interact and intertwine.

The passage in question is chapter 9, paragraph 7 of *Peri Hypsous* (On the Sublime). It reads:

> Meanwhile everything, sky and Hades, mortal and immortal alike, shares in the conflict and danger [συμπολεμεῖ καὶ συγκινδυνεύει] of the battle. These conceptions are of course terrifying, and from a different perspective, if they are not taken as allegorical [κατ' ἀλληγορίαν], they would be completely ungodly [ἄθεια] and improper [οὐ σῴζοντα τὸ πρέπον]. It seems to me that Homer, in recording the woundings, quarrels, vengeances, tears, imprisonments, and manifold passions of the gods, has done his best to make in the *Iliad* the men gods and the gods men. For us unhappy men [δυσδαιμονοῦσιν] death is the harbour of our troubles [λιμὴν κακῶν], whereas he made everlasting not the gods' nature [φύσιν] but their misfortune [ἀτυχίαν].[91]

What is most remarkable here is the participle δυσδαιμονοῦσιν. It not only contains and repeats the chiasmus between men and gods of the preceding sentence; it does so by complicating it in terms of the law and time. Longinus has just cited in §9.6 the famous theomachy, or battle of the gods, from the *Iliad*, and here in §9.7 comments on its sublimity (ὕψος).[92] This must follow an allegorical procedure (κατ' ἀλληγορίαν), which is summarized in the chiasmus that Homer makes "the men gods and the gods men." The participle δυσδαιμονοῦσιν in a sense reiterates the chiasmus. However, the difficulty is not only that the verb δυσδαιμονῶ is absent from the Greek corpus and that the participle δυσδαιμονοῦσιν in Longinus §9.7 is the only surviving verbal cognate, but also that the participle's verbal provenance and hence the actative in it make it difficult to understand what the word means. The noun δυσδαιμονία and especially the adjective δυσδαίμων are common enough, and they are usually taken to indicate unhappiness or misery; hence, the translation of δυσδαιμονοῦσιν offered above has been "unhappy men." Yet, the reiteration of the chiasmus of men and gods in the participle δυσδαιμονοῦσιν entails that the second compound, δαίμων, meaning god, has to be retained. And it has to be retained in a manner that brings the action in the participle to the fore. From one point of view, this makes the participle impossible to translate. And yet, simultaneously, it makes the participle a very accurate description of the ὕψος that characterizes the subject as it becomes involved in the divine but without rescinding the human. From this latter perspective, the subject becomes an allegorical function. What differentiates the subject from the gods, as the presence of the prefix δυσ- indicates, is the presence of unhappiness, unfulfillment, incompletion. However, this "disaster" for humankind may not be so disastrous after all: for it is the absence of such a prefix that banishes the gods from good fortune, so that their misfortune (ἀτυχίαν) is everlasting. For humans, on the other hand, there is an end point that can redeem them: the harbor of death. This point provides the interruption between the eternity of godly misfortune and the particularity of human unhappiness.

However, what the allegory demands, what it places as an obligation upon the human, is that this interruption is not exclusionary. The first point raised by Longinus in the description of the theomachy is that there is a participation of sharing in that battle of the gods: the sublimity (ὕψος) of Homer's battle description consists in that in the poem the mortals fight with and are in danger alongside (συμπολεμεῖ καὶ συγκινδυνεύει) the gods. Longinus then goes on to indicate that the way that sharing is carried out provokes certain legislative obligations. Thus, the participation of the human in the divine has to be carried out allegorically. Denying this would also be a denial of both the godly and the proper. Allegory, then, demands that both the demands of the divine laws and the human customs are exercised. The fact that this demand is allegorical entails that there is no stable measure; there is no *logos* according to which (*ana*) there will be a distribution of the two laws. There is no analogy. Rather, what pertains is a perpetual turning and counterturning between the human and the divine. They are both destroyed as self-consistent entities. It is this turning and destruction that is the principle of allegory and that is contained in the participle δυσδαιμονοῦσιν. The subject is the reversibility between human and divine, but in such a way that, even though the particularity of human misery is endless and hence divine, it still retains the possibility of redemption through its interruption.[93]

This allegorical procedure is precisely what leads one's thoughts on a "high." And it is grasped by Hadoula when she realizes that nothing is what it appears to be. The endless task is the infinite unfolding of allegory's destructions. These are the destructions that bring the future and the eternal to the present. They do so through the reversal of the particular, through its allegorization. But this allegorization must resist being reduced to a revelation. Allegory is the destruction of law; it is the lawlessness of fiction. The moment Hadoula forgets that—with a forgetting that is an improper heightening and thus a reinscription of the law, an actualization of the law in the present—the structure falls apart. Therefore, murdering her granddaughter is not mad because it follows lawlessness, but it is mad because it forgets lawlessness and takes the law in her own hands. This is the hubris of her heightening. All the same, it is a hubris that retains in its first moment the allegory of incessant labor and thus is inscribed within its lawless forgetting. This inscription places Hadoula both in the divine *and* the human law. The power of this "and" is the obscure part of the shadow of the two laws, the penumbra, that presents Hadoula's as a subject of modernity, a doppelgänger.

This is not to argue, however, that the allegory and the penumbra are forever unrealized. The converse is the case. At every instance of their presentation, what is disclosed is the political. To put this differently, the allegorical demands—with a demand that is the obligation inscribed in allegory's lawlessness—that its call retains both a *direction* and a *formality* proper to it. Always someone is called and something is said, even though *who* is called and *what* is said must remain forever undecidable. In other words, the rhetoric of the text itself retains allegory—allegory is not reducible to this or that character of the story. This rhetoricity enters the public arena with the work's publication. The author, then, carries the obligation placed on him by the penumbra. This obligation, the lawlessness of fiction, precludes an understanding of the author as the bearer of a true message, such that a theological or a sociological approach would contend. Instead, the obligation places the author as the guarantor of the destruction of absoluteness in the subject. If the author bears any message at all about the subject, that would be the singularity of the doppelgänger. This consists in the retention of both the divine and the human law *and* the infinite hesitation and undecidability between the two. This infinite hesitation allows for the threshold between divine and human law, but without being reducible to either. This threshold, the penumbra, is the condition of the possibility of the shadow of both laws, the *justice* of fiction.

This justice also follows the temporality of allegory. It uses the apophasis that interrupts the present with an anterior future. One example from *The Murderess* will show its operation in the text. It has already been mentioned, when discussing the revealability of self-confession, that the third episode of a girl dying is not a murder. Hadoula merely makes a wish that a girl fall into the well: "'Eh, my God, and if you fell in, Xenoula!' said Frankojannou with an uncanny laugh."⁹⁴ A moment later, the girl falls in. Papadiamantes describes the time that it took her to drown:

> With an instinctive movement, Frankojannou wanted to shout out and to run for help. But she drowned [ἔπνιξεν] her own shout in her throat before it was uttered, her movements were paralysed and her body froze. An eerie thought came into her mind. She had just uttered the prayer, more or less as a joke, that the child should fall into the well, and look it happened! So God (did she dare [ἐτόλμα] to think this?) had heard her prayer, and there was no need to move her hands any more, and her prayer was answered.⁹⁵

The "drowning" of Hadoula's shout not only erases any clear demarcation between herself and the drowning girl; it also anticipates Hadoula's own drowning "between divine and human justice"—a drowning that will take place later but whose trajectory is already in place since Hadoula has committed murder. The word "drowned" in this context effects allegory.

While Hadoula's voice drowned, her mind kept on thinking. At the threshold between the drowning of the voice and the thought that God has heard her prayer is inserted the parenthetical remark "(did she dare to think this?)"—a threshold that allows for allegory's temporality to unfold. Whereas as a phrase it is clearly a narratorial apostrophe and is even bracketed out of the direct description of the events, this question also has the effect of de-framing the whole description. For, what does the question really mean? What is its rhetorical import? It can be neither a genuine question about something unknown, since it has already been divulged that Hadoula had thought that her wish had been carried out, nor can it be a question that implies a negation (a rhetorical question), because there is nothing that it can obviously be a negation of. What is peculiar about this question that addresses the reader is the verb "to dare." What could this mean, given that this daring deed has already been announced, it has already been carried out? Perhaps what is daring is Hadoula's apophatic labor, which works with magical spells and wishes, and which effectuates a fissure between divine will and the human obligation to help someone who is drowning. But if the question does point to the fissure between the divine and the human, the "perhaps" still persists. For the statement of this fissure still does not explain why the narrator had to wonder about it. After all, Papadiamantes has been describing this fissure in Hadoula's actions all along.

Perhaps—and here the perhaps is to be taken very seriously, as the inscription of a futurity to the question—perhaps, then, the question is what is called a figure of praeteritio in rhetoric. A praeteritio is when one says "I will say nothing about something" only to go on and say it. It is a figure that shows preterition, a neglect or omission on the part of the person speaking. This is a neglect to keep a promise but also to keep what was meant to be a secret. An omission that relates to the preteritive, the past, which was to be kept secret, as well as the future, in which the secret is going to be revealed. The praeteritio, then, is a figure that purports to create a rupture in the present, an absolute exclusion. But in its figurative structure, and the futurity of it, that exclusion has already collapsed. The narrator pretends to exclude, only to make inclusion possible. And this pretense is a lie, an apophasis that is registered on the edge of a double obligation: both divine and human. The praeteritio, then, is the aberrant and lawless—the mad—voice of the narrator, perhaps even the author as such (the signatory of the text), who attempts to contain the call within certain limits or laws that are instantly and incessantly transgressed. But they are transgressed so that the lawlessness of fiction can be reinstated—and, therefore, they are affirmed in their being transgressed. This affirmation, which presents an anterior future, is the justice of narration. It can take place only within the sphere in which the narration will reach another, that is, within a polity (the call's *to*). And it can take place only as an allegory or apophasis that ushers in with it the political (the call's *of*).

The subject that emerges from this double inscription of the call is the doppelgänger. As mentioned at the beginning of this chapter, restating the conclusion of the preceding chapter, the doppelgänger is the subject that eschews absolute denial. What has been shown in this chapter is a distinction between negation and denial. Negation is the form taken by the subject's participation in the particular. As such, negation is operative; it consistently returns and reinscribes itself. But all these repetitions of negation are related to the law, which follows the subject in all its movements in particularity. Further, those are negations of the law; they destroy any protocol that is either exclusively human or exclusively divine, either only empirical or solely transcendental. As those laws follow subjectivity, they make their presence felt in any of the subject's enunciations, such as the calls of self-confession that have been described. They are presented through their destruction. Thus negation becomes the way that legal systematicity as such is made possible. The negation of the laws is the negation of the individual and self-subsistent subject, the individual subjected to a sovereign entity. And, thereby, the doppelgänger comes to the fore.

The negations on their own, however, cannot contain that which allows for their operation. At this point the distinction between denial and negation becomes crucial. Whereas negations are particularized and endless, an incessant task directed as a double demand upon the subject, denial is the affirmation of a temporality that allows for the retention of the future in the present—an affirmation of singularity. This is not a retention that holds the future as a visage with a clear contour. This is the anterior future that comes to puncture the endless task of negation. Interruption is made possible not through a specific revelation. Rather, it is made possible through the revealability allowed by the process of allegorization. Denial is the retention of everything destroyed by negation, albeit in a different form, as an allegory or as an apophasis—"inside-out," reversed. Further, this reversal attributed to denial's retention of negations must also retain the human and divine laws. The laws are no longer foreclosed systems but function as the reversibility of that foreclosure, the lawlessness or *paranomia* of their endless obligation. This places a different obligation upon the subject that denies without ever denying absolutely—upon the doppelgänger: it is the obligation to see not only the law that follows the I like a shadow but also that obscure part of the shadow, the penumbra, which precedes the shadow as its condition of possibility and which can be called the justice of fiction. At the same time, the fact that justice is meaningless without the laws entails that the obligation of the penumbra is inherently political. The political is whatever has been demanded by the penumbra.

This penumbra, "minuscule and yet invincible," to use Foucault's phrase, resides in the *and* that binds the doppelgänger in a movement of "retreat *and* return," the secret and the nonsecret, the expressible and inexpressible, the human and the divine. The penumbra partakes of both simultaneously, and yet this partaking is never complete, constantly in progress. As such, the doppelgänger becomes the medium of this progress, the element that gives the binding power to the *and*. This is not to say that the doppelgänger is an I plus a spectral image or spirit of it. This would be a mysticism, akin to the ambiguity of mythic laws.⁹⁶ Nor is the doppelgänger the statute and custom that, as Beccaria has contended, follows the I everywhere. This would place strict borders on the subject outside of which it would not be allowed to venture. The doppelgänger is the liminal subject, the subject that walks on the zone of the penumbra between the shadows of the laws. There, the doppelgänger becomes the medium that resists the closure of both shadows. There will always be a puncture in them, and that's where the doppelgänger is to be found. This puncture, as the analysis of Papadiamantes' works has demonstrated, is a temporal structure, not a specific time, this or that past, present, or future. Even less is it time as a whole, regardless of whether that whole is taken as a diachrony or an achrony. Rather, it is the making present of the future anterior. The moment that this future anterior arises, such as in the heightening described in chapter 5 of *The Murderess*, the doppelgänger is present. Its presence is not opposed to absence but emerges as that which made possible—the medium of—the presentation of that temporality. That medium is the subject of modernity.

CHAPTER THREE

The Task of the Doppelgänger

Jean Paul as Collocutor of Maurice Blanchot

> ... *friends to the point of this state of profound friendship in which a forsaken man, forsaken by all his friends, meets in life he who will accompany him beyond life, himself lifeless, capable of free friendship, detached from all bonds.*
>
> GEORGES BATAILLE

The distinction between denial and negation in the preceding chapter allowed for a figuration of the subject as the doppelgänger. At the same time, this figuration entailed that the doppelgänger is operative not only in the literary work but also in the criticism addressing that work. The doppelgänger becomes the medium to interpret the work. However, two issues remain. The first raises the questions: To whom is the dissolution of the autonomous individual and the appearance of the doppelgänger to be attributed? Is it solely to the characters of a narrative or is it also to its signatory, the author? Asking these questions raises the task of criticism as a problem. For if there is a clear border between the text and the author such that the doppelgänger can be located only in the former, then does not this border pull apart the subjectivity of the author that can never be reconciled with the doppelgänger? And when this happens, as demonstrated with the theological and the sociological readings of Papadiamantes' *The Murderess*, the critical process treats the author as the source of the secret of the work, while the work is treated as a revelation. Conversely, to treat the doppelgänger as the medium of interpreting a work entails that criticism will have to deal also with the author under the rubric of the doppelgänger. The critical task that takes the lawlessness and justice of the doppelgänger seriously will have to also look at the author as a doppelgänger.[1] The first issue, then, has to do with the protocols of a critical procedure working through the doppelgänger. Although this issue will have to include notions such as genre and canonicity in terms of the subject, there is a second issue that is implied therein and that extends the inquiry even further: this is the issue of the philosophical task. For since the doppelgänger has escaped from the confines of the printed page and has entered into the realm of a historical development, then it is not just the subject as character and/or as author that is put into question; it is also subjectivity as such. Thus the expansion of the doppelgänger ineluctably leads from literature, to criticism, to philosophy.

These two issues, which amount to a double demand, emulate and dissimulate the twofold injunction of the law that was presented in the preceding chapter: private *and* public, human *and* divine. Therefore, what will have to be retained is the future anterior—as the temporality of the doppelgänger that disrupts the occlusion of legislative protocols, as it was argued in the preceding chapter. However, the path that *will* lead to this future will also have inflected the *and* of the subject of modernity in a different way. The staging of the relation between negation *and* denial both within criticism *and* within philosophy means that the second step will be an *and and*. This repetition will not be only the effective presence of repetition in the double bind between the two laws, as explicated in the section on the "Penumbra." It will also be a plural repetition and one that unbinds, a justice that can be neither contextualized nor legalized and as such a futural justice, always to come—but also a justice that has always also arrived, one that is already here even though its mode of presence will be one of disappearance; this indicates the doppelgänger's ability to dissolve both the general and the particular. This is the operative presence of the doppelgänger that cannot be reduced to mere presence.

In other words, at issue are literature, criticism, and philosophy—three tasks, practices, and institutions that are to be approached through their disappearance, or, rather with the disappearance of presence effected by the doppelgänger. There is no better place to demonstrate this approach than in the work of the French author, critic, and philosopher Maurice Blanchot. His writings enact a dissolution of established boundaries between genres and discourses, but they do so by meditating on the boundary, that is, on the legitimacy of separation to which each individual legal framework would always aspire. Blanchot's work enacts the liminality of the doppelgänger and does so by precisely breaking the borders between literature, criticism, and philosophy. However, given Blanchot's professional position as a critic, philosophy is often hidden in his text. His writings stage an encounter between literature and criticism in which philosophy is present despite the absence of its name and protocols. This is the kind of writing that does not look for answers, insisting instead on the power of the question.

> To write as a question of writing, question that bears the writing that bears the question, no longer allows you this relation to the being—understood in the first place as tradition, order, certainty, truth, any form of taking root—that you received one day from the past of the world, domain that you had been called upon to govern in order to strengthen your "Self [*Moi*]," although this was as if fissured, since the day when the sky opened upon its void. I will try in vain to represent him to myself, he who I was not and who, without wanting to, began to write, writing (and knowing it then) in such a way that the pure product of doing nothing was introduced into the world and into his world. That happened "at night." During the day there were the daytime acts, the day to day words, the day to day writing, affirmations, values, habits, nothing that counted and yet something that one had confusedly to call life. The certainty that in writing he was putting between parentheses precisely this certainty, including the certainty of himself as the subject of writing, led him slowly, though right away, into an empty space, whose void (the barred zero, heraldic) in no way prevented the turns and detours of a very long process.[2]

Holding the question of writing in abeyance, resisting an answer, entails a fissure in the self. This is a fissure that pervades the self's activities, which are on the one hand the law-following occupations of the day, while on the other hand they are of the night and of a heralding void that breaks the self apart only to give it another part: "he who I was not and who, without wanting to, began to write" but to write in such a way as to sustain the desire contained in the act of writing. The contradictory demands placed on the self in the realm of the "night" are the demands of the doppelgänger; because they are demands that can never be configured within a program, they are not commensurable with the operation of any law. Yet this is not to say that the law is not necessary for the emergence of the doppelgänger. Writing, as Blanchot makes clear, needs—although this need will not be all-encompassing— "tradition, order, certainty, truth, any form of taking root."

Blanchot's point will be misconstrued if it is read as positing an obscure enigma of the artwork versus a transparency of daytime occupations such as newspaper reviewing. It is not merely that the "he" accompanying the "I" cannot be put on and off at will like a piece of clothing. Rather, it is to insist on the I's "heraldic" nature: that is, the ineluctable accompanying that sustains the subject as a question. This sustaining of the question is the operation of the doppelgänger, and as such it is related to writing qua writing "as a question of writing, question that bears the writing that bears the question," in other words, a writing that responds to the law and thus to the doppelgänger. From the perspective of the law a distinction can be drawn about the different genres or protocols of writing activities, but as writing confronts itself as a question and as individuality dissolves, writing—just as the self—loses any foundational legitimation.³ This disappearance, effectuated by and in writing, is indispensable for broaching first the question of literature and criticism, and subsequently the question of philosophy.

The question of criticism comes first. In 1959, and as part of a response to a questionnaire published in the journal *Arguments*, Blanchot wrote "The Task of Criticism Today" (republished as the introduction to his *Lautréamont et Sade* four years later, but with a few minor, but significant, modifications, which will be discussed later). The opening sentence of this piece reads: "There are many aspects to this question [the question of criticism] that I cannot deal with here."⁴ This is a *captatio benevolentiae* that seeks to capture the audience's favor by purporting humility before a subject matter that exceeds the addresser.⁵ Given this seemingly conventional opening admission of defeat in the face of something that has a breadth and gravity that is ungraspable (such as God or a king), the second sentence comes as a surprise: "One of these has to do with the insignificance of criticism itself."⁶ What constitutes the greatness of criticism such that it necessitates an opening apologetic turns out not to be greatness at all, but rather insignificance. However, Blanchot's paradoxical trajectory does not end here. Not only does he implicate the movement of criticism, ab initio, in a spiral of transvaluation, but the second sentence turns out to be a lie—or, more accurately, the hypocrisy of praeteritio, since the whole article is going to address precisely what it says that it cannot deal with, namely, criticism's insignificance. Not only then do the two opening sentences transfer the value of the divinity and sovereignty to the critic; this value is also devalued, deemed worthless, insignificant. Yet this insignificance, because of the rhetoricity of its presentation, still partakes of the future anterior that, as demonstrated in the preceding chapter, characterizes praeteritio. Thus from the first few words of the article, Blanchot's notion of the critic is in accord with the doppelgänger, which is implicated in the future anterior of lying.

The notion of insignificance is configured twice in "The Task of Criticism Today." First, criticism is insignificant because it derives its importance from the existence of the "two weighty institutions" of journalism and the academy. Between the contextual and expeditious activities of the former and the "solid and permanent" ones of the latter, criticism's role is merely "mediating." Criticism eschews the great rigor and ambition of the institutions of journalism and academia; it cannot aspire to their historically determined protocols, since criticism renounces the right to power, "realising that it has no authority [*titre*] to speak seriously in the name of history."[7] The second form of criticism's insignificance is related to its uncontainable object, the work of literature. Criticism amounts almost to nothing next to the work. However, this does not entail the obsequiousness of a servant in front of a king or a god, since, as already affirmed in the first two sentences of "The Task of Criticism Today," such figures have been devalued and their power subverted. Rather, the criticism's "movement of disappearance" in front of literature "is the very sense of its accomplishment which means that, in realizing itself, it disappears."[8] However, this affirmative disappearance establishes a complicity between literature and criticism: "Criticism is nothing, but this nothing is precisely that in which the work, silent, invisible, lets itself be what it is."[9] Blanchot, then, correlates the inexpressibility and revealability of the work, the disappearance of the work's call in a *praeteritio*, to the procedure of criticism. Thus, criticism not only "ceases to distinguish itself from the work," but even more emphatically, criticism is the work's "epiphany [*l'épiphanie*],"[10] it is responsible for the futural anteriority of the work. One is, briefly, in the other, because the transformations and unfoldings of the work in the future are part of criticism's operation. The insignificance of criticism, therefore, is the insignificance of literature itself. They are insignificant because they have renounced the power dialectic that sustains institutions such as journalism or the academy; moreover, their insignificance seems prior and more fundamental than the weighty significance of institutions—although this is a point that will not be discussed for the moment, because it introduces, perhaps, a third configuration of insignificance, which will be addressed later.

Given that the criticizability of the work is contained in the work itself, what needs further elucidation at this juncture is the way that the doppelgänger is part of this correlation of the work and criticism—and, moreover, a part in such a way as to include the author himself. The author also has to be part of this affirmative disappearance that makes the work criticizable and that is responsible for the dissolution of subjectivity through the operative presence of the doppelgänger. In other words, how is the author himself to pertain to transformability vis-à-vis the work? How can the author disappear in a future anterior? This problematic will be pursued through a reading of Blanchot's récit *L'arrêt de mort* (*Death Sentence*).

| | |

It is not proper to begin writing about *Death Sentence* with a plea about the difficulty of the text, for this récit attains such a simplicity of plot and description that it is anything but difficult.[11] Nor is it proper to begin with the anxiety of addressing a text that has been dealt with by so many critics, despite the fact that *Death Sentence* is perhaps singular in the fascination that it has exercised over the readers of Blanchot. The reason that any *captatio benevolentiae* is inappropriate has more to do with what J. Hillis Miller has referred to as the "double bind."[12] For, if the "double bind" is an injunction whose very articulation is simultaneously its transgression, it would be inappropriate to approach a text that points out something—the terrifying complicity ("*quelle complicité pleine d'horreur*")—that seeks to outdo the "double bind." Not by denying the double bind. A denial will always be inadequate, because, as Blanchot wrote in 1948, it will only provoke the return to what has been denied. Rather, the complicity has to do with a "third" element, always unnamed and unnameable, never to be beheld, like the secret hidden away in the narrator's closet (*armoire*).[13] An element of "nocturnal obscurity [*obscurité nocturne*],"[14] since it responds to an absence that, although in itself can never become present, is nevertheless linked to a kind of presence, the writing hand—of which Blanchot did not see fit to remind his reader in 1971.[15] This disappearance, effectuated by and in writing, will be shown to be the inexpressible element in the subject. As a disappearance it sets in motion a movement of devaluation that a traditional *captatio benevolentiae* could not tolerate, while by setting up the inexpressible it also points to the future's anteriority that cannot be captured unless the declarative statement effaces intentionality in a movement of preteritive pretension.

The question for criticism is: How can one address such absence? If something is completely absent, there can be no reference to it. The quandary is even more prominent for the critic: How is writing about something that is not "on the page" possible? The force of the secret in the closet is shown at the beginning of the récit, when an unnamed woman "made a move to open it [the closet], but at that moment she was overcome by a strange attack."[16] She fell helpless on the bed, breathing hoarsely, like a death rattle (*à râler*). The secret is dangerous. In a reaction that recalls the unnamed woman's reaction, Nathalie "began to tremble, her teeth chattered, and for a moment she shivered so violently that she lost control of her body." At this point Blanchot distinguishes between law and justice: "I could do nothing to help her; by approaching her, by talking to her, I was disobeying the law; by touching her I could have killed her. To struggle alone, to learn, as she struggled, how through the workings of a profound justice the greatest adverse forces console us and upraise us, at the very moment that they are tearing us apart: that is what she had to do."[17] What is remarkable about the "profound justice" is that it also makes the secret imperative, but without its being related to any content whatsoever. Instead, the only thing that matters is the locus where the adverse forces manifest themselves, in a way such that the subject is torn apart. The critic, then, need *not* posit a *complete* absence. All that is needed is a regulative absence, certainly contentless, moreover threatening and terrifying, but which has nevertheless the capacity to console and upraise. The torn subject and the regulative absence constitute together a "double unbind," a locus where the law cannot hold, but without excluding the law. This place can be called justice—a justice that is registered doubly. First, in the text itself, in the manner in which the characters both follow and are followed by the law. "I had no idea whether I was following her or if she was following me," says Henri about Jeanne, a figure that in large measure stands for the law in *The Most High*.[18] Second, the interpretability and criticizability of the work depend on the "double unbind" of justice. The critical task is broader than an extrapolation of that which is expressed by the legal entity who signs and owns the copyright of the work. The writing hand, as it will be shown, belongs also to a friend, an accomplice, or a collocutor. Yet this accosting presence reconfigures the legally constituted agent, the autonomous individual. Where justice emerges, then, the subject—as a character in the work *and* as the author of the work—will have already been in a process of dissolution. Justice appears at the point—never distinct, constantly negotiated, always here and to come—of subjective disappearance.

Yet the subject remains. There is no absolute disappearance of the subject, nor of the law. Otherwise there will be no consolation, no upraising. The argument here will be that the subject in "an instant of distraction [*un instant de distraction*]"[19] is indeed able to experience this "double unbind." But the experience is one in which self-identity is no longer operative; identity figures in a relation of difference. Justice dispels the self-reflection between subject and subjectivity thereby overturning the logic of sameness. The subject now *is* difference—it has become a doppelgänger. To approach this difference, attention needs to be paid to the relation between the narratorial I (*voix narratrice*) and Nathalie, the two subjects between which there exists the "terrifying complicity." Since not much is actually known of either, it is expedient to start with the one who at least has a name. Nathalie is a name that has a double register, its etymology and its literary precedents. It comes from the Latin verb *nasci*, to originate, to be born, but also to grow, to rise up. Nathalie is a certain origin and an uprising. In addition, there are two famous Natalies in romantic literature, the one in Goethe's *Wilhelm Meister's Apprenticeship* and the other in Jean Paul's *Siebenkäs*.[20] Goethe and Jean Paul, along with Valéry, have been designated by Blanchot as the only nonclassical authors that he was reading as he was taking his first steps in writing.[21] However, as will be shown shortly, Goethe's Natalie does not sit happily next to the Nathalie in *Death Sentence*. Conversely, the Natalie in Jean Paul's novel tallies with a number of motifs and themes that have a compelling resonance in Blanchot's récit.

A tentative approach to the name Nat(h)alie has to start with an exposition of some of these motifs. First, there are remarkable parallels in the first meeting between the narrator and Nathalie in Blanchot's *Death Sentence* and Siebenkäs and Natalie in Jean Paul's *Siebenkäs*.[22] In both texts, the female character appears at night, at a place that is hardly described, and without any explicit reason. The meeting is contingent, accidental, unintended. Both women are clad in black, and both are likened to a statue. They are both shrouded in mystery, not only because they turn their back to the male character, but also because in *Siebenkäs* Natalie wears a veil that hides her face, whereas in *Death Sentence* there is the conspicuous absence of a hat on her head "(which was more uncommon [*plus rare*] than it is now)," as it is proffered in a parenthesis. Further, while in both cases the female is unacquainted with the male, there is nevertheless a moment of déjà vu, a kind of recognition beyond the normative rules of recognition accompanied by the appearance of a very strong feeling within all parties that vacillates between a threatening strangeness and an irresistible appeal. In both scenes there is a glass surface, the window in the hotel room, and the glass door through which Siebenkäs walks and the mirror in which he contemplates the unknown woman. Sight features heavily, as well, since Blanchot's Nathalie cannot see well at night, while the other Natalie cannot discern Siebenkäs's features so that she has to approach him closely and lift her veil. In addition, a number of other motifs are introduced that, although they do not have a direct correspondence in both meeting scenes, are nevertheless related to other themes in the two works. Natalie's veil has already been mentioned, and there are a number of references to veils in *Death Sentence*. And, roses and casts of the dead, which feature throughout *Death Sentence*, are also present in the meeting between Natalie and Siebenkäs. But the most important feature is perhaps Natalie's fiery eyes, a characteristic of Nathalie's as well, underlined after the encounter at the metro, when the narrator enters his hotel room to feel the presence of someone there.[23]

If this register of motifs from the first meetings is incomplete, the whole register of themes common to Natalie and Siebenkäs, on the one hand, and Nathalie and the narrator, on the other, is verily incompletable. It is certainly important to note the autobiographical references in the male characters, since the narrator, like Blanchot, is a journalist, and Siebenkäs is the author of the *Selection from the Devil's Papers*, an early work by Jean Paul.[24] There are several additional similar details, such as the presence of a doctor character who is somewhat derided,[25] and a key of decisive importance.[26] There are also certain stylistic similarities, such as a proclivity for repetitions and the repeated framings of the narrative, for instance, with the use of apostrophe. There is also a preoccupation with the narrative's end in *Siebenkäs*, to the extent that the story spills over into subsequent novels. In addition, Jean Paul significantly revised the text for the 1818 edition. He and Blanchot shared a proclivity for revision. Further, the Siebenkäs character is arguably linked to contemporary political concerns of Jean Paul's,[27] just as the dates in *Death Sentence* give it a strong—even if ambiguous—sense of temporality and topicality.[28] And, considering also other works that were composed in the same period as *Death Sentence*, it can, for instance, be noted, that the first name of the protagonist of *The Most High* is Henri, while Siebenkäs's original name, which he reassumed after his staged death, is Heinrich[29]—as well as the rhyming of Lenette who is Siebenkäs's first wife, and Collete who is the narrator's neighbor in the hotel in *Death Sentence*—as well as Jeanne in *The Most High* echoing Jean Paul's own first name.

The slide here into what may be just arbitrary coincidences is not unintentional. The list of common "motifs" can be expanded furthermore. What is presented here will be only a foretaste to someone who delights in such comparisons and compilations. Ultimately, all these themes and motifs can advance criticism only slightly; they are but a first empirical step. Jean Paul's Natalie might form part of the inspiration for *Death Sentence*, but the theme-based procedure will always be lacking in approaching a récit in which regulative absence holds sway. For a "theme" is, of necessity, dependent on content; there is always a *certain* reference made by way of the theme. And to stay on the thematic level would be precisely to insist on the content such that a solution to the secret of the récit would be called for. Whereas it has already been noted that the regulative function of the secret in *Death Sentence* does not allow for such a revelation—the secret must remain inexpressible. It is not as if *Death Sentence* is a kind of roman à clef, in which the dates, the self-references to Blanchot's journalistic activities, and the references to Blanchot's reading of Jean Paul provide a "key" to unlock the "meaning" of the text. For the dates, as Leslie Hill has shown, are anything but straightforward.[30] And, given that the récit already moves toward an effacement of subjectivity, the autobiographical reference cannot be strictly speaking historical, or even symbolic of a specific historical occurrence. This is not to say that there are no autobiographical elements to the story.[31] Rather, it shows that what has to be resisted is to assume that the empirical aspect is all there is. There is no reduction to the empirical.[32] And it is here that a crucial difference from Goethe's Natalie is encountered. For the crux of the plot of Goethe's novel is that, unbeknown to Wilhelm Meister, he is cultivated by a secret society, to the extent that every chance occurrence can ultimately be attributed to that society's intervention. Natalie is part of this dialectic of concealment and unconcealment, of Wilhelm's journey in an inexplicable world that becomes finally explicated when he is initiated into the sect. The secret, then, pertains to the context of Wilhelm's journey and to his actions. What is excluded is any idea of a regulative and contentless secret. As Walter Benjamin argued in the appendix to his dissertation on German Romanticism, a similar structure is applicable to Goethe's notion of criticism, whereby a work is underwritten by a primordial substance that is forever inaccessible because its content is uncognizable.[33] Goethe's adherence to content in terms of plot and in terms of a presupposition of criticism is never entertained by Blanchot, and it is incommensurable with the inexpressibility of the secret set in motion by the doppelgänger.

Moreover, the inadequacy of staying with the thematic analysis would have had to contend with the plain fact that, despite certain similarities, Blanchot and Jean Paul are separated by significant differences. For instance, the latter's novels unfold in an exuberant and serendipitous meandering that does not accord with the simplicity of a condensed narrative such as *Death Sentence*. Jean Paul's injunction to "Write everything down" seems foreign to Blanchot's universe where silence reigns supreme.[34] Further, Blanchot has taken Jean Paul to task about the relation of death to subjectivity. Thus, in "The *Igitur* Experience" Blanchot observes that the dignity of pure dying does not accord "to the ideal of Jean-Paul Richter, whose heroes, 'lofty men,' die in a pure desire to die, 'their eyes gazing steadfastly beyond the clouds' in response to a call of a dream which disembodies and dissolves them."[35] What Blanchot objects to seems clear enough: the purity of dying is not guaranteed by a beyond that sets the rule. There is no glimpse of any kind of heaven. However, a look at Jean Paul's text will show that this objection is not unambiguous. Blanchot is referring to the chapter "The Dream in a Dream," perhaps the most discussed chapter of *Siebenkäs* along with the preceding chapter, "The Speech of the Dead Christ."[36] The ambiguity of Blanchot's citation is twofold: First, it is doubtful whether the text here represents prima facie Jean Paul's ideas. Not only did Jean Paul relocate these two little chapters in the second edition, but he also ridicules the ideas later on in the novel. In the 1796 edition the two chapters open *Siebenkäs*, but in the 1818 edition they appear in the middle of the novel, at the end of book 2.[37] Both the repositioning and the ridicule of the ideas undermine the notion that there is any straightforward identification of these ideas with Jean Paul's own views.[38] Second, the ambiguity of Blanchot's use of quotation marks should not be overlooked, for what he places within quotation marks are not direct citations. Thus, the "lofty men" who are "heroes," according to Blanchot, are actually, according to Jean Paul, "two sublime friends" who have sacrificed everything, including their lives, but not their country.[39] Maybe this sacrifice makes them heroes—although this is a moot point, not least because of the historical circumstance bracketed by the dates of the two editions of the novel, the years from 1796 to 1818—but nevertheless the word "heroes" is not used by Jean Paul. The case of the second phrase placed in quotation marks by Blanchot, "their eyes gazing steadfastly beyond the clouds," is even more unclear. According to *Siebenkäs*, the two friends are sent clouds by the earth to obscure their views.[40] Blanchot seems to be summarizing the next paragraph, where a series of questions allude to a vision beyond the clouds. But the rhetorical questions in *Siebenkäs* are addressed to Mary, who has been dreaming these "two friends" and the clouds that hide them. As one of the questions puts it, "Are you happy, Mary, because the storm clouds are turning into rainbows?" The answer is, adhering to the logic of the rhetorical question, "No."[41] This may be partly the reason, Jean Paul writes, but the real cause of happiness is that Mary thinks of her child, Christ. And this thought is what precipitates the end of the dream. The vision has dissipated, and Mary embraces her real child. The "resolution" is not provided by something beyond but by the return to the corporeal. Remarkably, then, Blanchot extracts from the passage he misquotes a meaning that is almost antithetical to what Jean Paul seems to suggest.

What is important here has nothing to do with the fact that Blanchot may have made a simple mistake—this would have been the only assertion that a reduction to the empirical could have legitimately made. Instead, what is important is that Blanchot seems here to be citing from memory—he is mis-"quoting." Jean Paul has become part of Blanchot's vocabulary. To the extent that Blanchot is referring to Jean Paul as the real person who authored a specific corpus, then here Blanchot is speaking in Jean Paul's language. And to the extent that this dialogue unfolds in such a particularized language, which apparently Blanchot does not master, the use of that language is irresponsible. However, this irresponsibility should not be seen as a simple mistake, a lack of mastery. Irresponsibility has much more to offer, especially in the way that the subject of the utterance relates to the other subject whose language he has worked with in a way that does not exclude the other and thus operates outside a dialectic of mastery. There is a collusion or complicity between Blanchot and Jean Paul; they become—not merely interlocutors, but—collocutors, each of whose personal identity is inextricably linked, at the moment of the utterance, to the identity of the other. Because of this relation—the relation of the doppelgänger—otherness is no longer a differentiation of attributes, but the very identity as such. There is a forgetting operating here, which results in, among other things, the impossibility of attributing statements directly to one or the other party of this partnership of complicity.

The trajectory of irresponsibility and forgetting, that is, the terms of Blanchot's relation to Jean Paul, are to be found in *Death Sentence*. Thus, the intersubjective relationality which entails the disappearance of the autonomous individual and the appearance of the doppelgänger becomes the medium of approaching the récit. Here the operation and effective presence of the doppelgänger is carried over from the names "Blanchot" and "Jean Paul" to the characters of the récit. However, this is not to posit a syncretism between author and character. Rather, it means that the medium of the interpretation of the work is provided by the doppelgänger's operation. And this operation figures here in terms of irresponsibility. In the episode in the metro, the narrator's use of Nathalie's language, a language he is not fluent in, is characterized precisely as irresponsible. What is asserted here is not merely a motif, a thematic congruity. Rather, the point is broader and touches on Blanchot's conception of criticism and literature. What is enacted here is a rearticulation of the literary canon. So long as the doppelgänger is operative, a canonical author is not whoever has been designated by the academy, the Alexandrian scholar, or even the general history of reception. The canonical author is rather one like Jean Paul, whose name is never mentioned in *Death Sentence* but which nevertheless can be brought into play therein, as the collocational Other who collocutes (in) the text.[42] In addition, precisely because this is not a procedure to fix the identity of the author "Blanchot," this does not allude to any subjectivist extrapolation of the canon. Jean Paul's elided name is not just a manifestation of the fancy of Blanchot, the reader of Jean Paul in the 1930s. If there is a conversation going on here between Blanchot and Jean Paul, it is a conversation without any goal, a silent conversation of gestures, whose effect is to strip the work of both authors from any obvious referential meaning other than the gesture itself. While "personhood and subjectivity are absent, yet a material presence of thought is excessively present. Such a coexistence of the absence of the person and the presence of thought" is what regulates, according to Eleanor Kaufman, the encomia written by French postwar thinkers about their peers.[43] The canonicity that this form of interplay establishes need not be confined to a specific genre of writing. It can be broadened so that the interplay becomes that which defines both canon and genre through a notion of absent subjectivity. This broadening is suggested by Blanchot himself in *The Unavowable Community*. Blanchot cites an anecdote from Bataille, in which Bataille's "interlocutor is not named, but he is shown in such a way that his friends recognize him, without naming him." Blanchot first observes that, through the unnamed interlocutor, Bataille thus "represents friendship as much as a friend." And then Blanchot goes on to suggest that this is a form of "not-doing" that is "one of the aspects of unworking, and friendship, with the reading in darkness."[44] Collocution is taken here to mean precisely this nonnaming of the interlocutor that leads to an interplay of singularity and repetition—an interplay that asserts both the negation of the name as subject and at the same time emphatically affirms the presence of the nonnamed.

Precisely such an interplay emerges in Blanchot's relation to Jean Paul. As it figures in *Death Sentence*, *Siebenkäs* is specifically not the key that will unlock the secrets of the récit, nor will it reveal the contents of the closet, or what dispels the stormy clouds that would have allowed the two friends, Blanchot and Jean Paul, to regard some metaphysical heaven—such a secret would still have asserted presence and the old conception of canonicity. *Siebenkäs* is a key only insofar as it does not unlock anything, a regulative secret that leads reference and representation to failure. It is an absent presence, not present in the form of a "determinate negation" but present only as a collocution. Therefore, the silent presence of Jean Paul in *Death Sentence* is an example of Blanchot at his most rigorous, adhering closely to the law of his own narrative—the "double unbind" that articulates a secret that is no secret at all, since it is absent, without even its very absence being named. Jean Paul, then, is like "the background figure" that Foucault places next to Blanchot, "a companion who always remains hidden but always makes it patently obvious that he is there; a double that keeps his distance, an accosting resemblance."[45] It is especially pertinent to talk about such a doppelgänger of Blanchot when reference is to *Siebenkäs*, the novel in which the word "Doppelgänger" was used for the first time. The same novel in which appellation ceases to designate one character, and instead the identity is given by "this wandering name [*wandernden Namens*],"[46] the anonymity that pertains to the differential relation of otherness.

The impact of the reformulation of the canonical in literature, which allows for the operation of the doppelgänger's lawlessness, finds an additional register, one that is already announced in the Greek word *kanon*, meaning measure, the rule whereby something is measured, the law that generically legitimates literature. However, according to Blanchot, this law is radically different between a novel and a narrative or récit such as *Death Sentence*. Genesis and temporality feature in Blanchot's distinction. Whereas the novel is born out of a chronologically arranged sequence of episodes so that what precedes is the cause of what follows, the récit eschews such a teleology. Thus, the récit is "not the relating of an event but this event itself, the approach of this event, the place where it is called on to unfold, an event still to come."[47] What holds the récit together is not the documentary accuracy of a witness-like account. Instead, the "secret law of narrative" is precisely this "delicate relationship" introduced by the subversion of linear chronology whereby the product, the producing, and the producer of the narrative are co-implicated and are impossible to steadfastly distinguish. This interruption of time and in time introduces a temporality that escapes the hold of presence as a thing to be beheld in the now, and instead installs a presence always "to come," never stabilized, incessantly differential, a future anterior. Hence, it is imprecise to call Blanchot's récits a genre, since the legislating authority is solely ascribed to a futural relation that is never completely fulfilled.[48] Such a relationship is what operates in *Siebenkäs* as well, designated as the "harmonious key [or, the fork, *Stimmpfeife*]" of the narrative.[49] Reminding the reader that his novel is part imaginary and part real, Jean Paul explicates the interplay between the two as the authorial inventions vis-à-vis the temporality of the events due to the lack of documents and witnesses. This interplay as it unfolds in *Siebenkäs* will never find a resolution, as is the case with the different accounts by the four Gospels. Nevertheless, Jean Paul's metaphor continues, this discord is given by the regulative presence of a "harmonious key" that would have resolved the discord of the Gospels. Yet this "key" is only a futural presence, a law of Jean Paul's novel that will never be encountered in the novel itself, only assigned to a harmonized relation that eschews teleological narration. That his key, in turn, will never be able to designate a genre can be shown by a work such as *Clavis Fichtiana* ("the key to Fichte"), which addresses the doppelgänger while treading on the line between literature and philosophy—or, to put it the other way round, a narrative that, because of the doppelgänger, is transformable, as it was shown in the section titled "'Double Acts' and Transformation" in Chapter 1. What takes place, then, between Blanchot and Jean Paul under the rubric of the canon is at least twofold: they both insist on a law about narrative relation that bypasses presence in the present by assigning presence to the future—an absent presence; at the same time, this absent presence is precisely what the companionship of Jean Paul in *Death Sentence* also enacts—Jean Paul as Blanchot's double. Thus, the doppelgänger becomes part of the critical idiom that recalls the name of the author in discussing the text's canonicity.

This twofold aspect of the canon could be expressed by saying that the experience of writing is linked to the experience of reading. The duplicity that underlies Blanchot's reformulation of canonical literature is what pertains between the reader/author and the other author/companion. Linked to this is the dual relation to law, a duality that seeks to capture the just relation of a futural presence in a present absence. This law, the law of narrative given by the "other night," as Blanchot sometimes calls it, or by the neuter—the *he/it* with which *The Step Not Beyond* introduces the question of writing, as mentioned at the beginning of the present chapter—this law, due to its reference to the future, can never be foreclosed. Strictly speaking, then, it can never be formulated or revealed—it is the inexpressibility of the justice made possible by the doppelgänger. This narrative truth, which could never be defined, is, in Christophe Bident's neologism, "*l'absance du sens*," a performance of return *and* retreat from the origin. Thus, the author can no longer be the privileged source of meaning, but "the reader turns into a writer." Bident continues: "The reader no longer receives passively, so to speak, a text addressed to him: he occupies the place of a third person, this third person that Blanchot, with the writer in mind, calls an invisible partner ... [who] also names the lack proper to all language, the appeal to a metalanguage that might supply the measure of all *absance*, that interruption which requires a third, rather than another, in order to manifest itself, between the 'hole-word' ['*mot-trou*'] and the 'word too many' ['*mot de trop*'], which is the neutral foundation of language held in common."[50] The interruption, then, can take place only because of the reversibility between author and reader—a chiasmus which, if it is to be rigorously presented, must be presented in such a way that the relation itself between author and reader is invisible. A relation, therefore, such as the one of Blanchot the reader of Jean Paul. The *invisibility* of the relation is also an intricate balancing act toward the image. This is a relation where, while the image is necessary, it is still found wanting compared to the aural experience of reading. It is the relation extrapolated by Blanchot's Orphic logic of failure.

Yet failure is never an end point. Blanchot in "Orpheus's Gaze" does not construct a dialectic. The opposite is the case, since the emphasis on failure, which affirms that "as if to renounce failure were much graver than to renounce success,"[51] is nondialectical, a movement of suspension. The suspension takes place as the demand of writing, on the one hand, which leads Orpheus to the underworld to rescue Eurydice with his art on condition that he does not turn back to look at her. Yet the work is always already going to disobey this injunction; the work's exigency is the failure to obey the law. Simultaneously, it is in this night of the deep that the origin of the work is located, an origin as uncertain as it is certain that the work will fail. On the other hand, this first "sacred night" that "follows" Orpheus and "binds" his work is not the only night. The other night is given by Orpheus's unbinding gaze, the unintentional turn of the head back toward Eurydice. "It is in this decision that the origin is approached by the force of the gaze that unbinds night's essence, lifts concern, interrupts the incessant by discovering."[52] Thus, Eurydice is the origin of this journey; she is another Nathalie. However, this is not a foundational origin but one that liberates only by a "glad accident," or what Blanchot also calls a "leap"—just as the meeting between the narrator and Nathalie in *Death Sentence* is completely unintentional, their relation not grounded in any teleology. But the leap is not a law, the movement is nondialectical, and thus it is able to hold onto the work and onto the work's lawlessness at the same time, as in a "magic dependence [*dépendance magique*]."[53] This is a logic of disjunction, where the activity of work and writing is always asymmetrical to the gestural language of the deep night, where unworking unfolds at the moment that reference and meaning break down. The same logic is also described in Jean Paul's *Preschool to Aesthetics*. Thus, in section 13 a pure self is said to be creative, productive.[54] But also such a self is always bound to encounter "something dark" that is not created but an origin. This point, or "an instinct," is "the sense of the future." Jean Paul points out that the deficiency in the negation of the presence of the work is not a dialectical one, because "only a true deficiency makes possible the impulse towards it [that dark point]." This is an earthly or worldly something. Yet at the same time it is something infinite that cannot be named. "The common people say simply, 'The *shape*, the *thing* makes itself heard' ['*Die* Gestalt, *das* Ding *lässet sich hören*']. Indeed, to express the infinite, they often simply say: 'It [*es*].'" This neuter cannot be found simply in the day on earth, nor in a "deep heaven [or sky, *in tiefen Himmeln*]"—it is neither something visible nor invisible as such; it is something aural and nocturnal. This poetical instinct takes place in the suspension between the embodied spiritual world and the deified physical world. If the former alludes to the dialectic of the "double bind" and the latter to mythopoetic origin, the point of their mutual suspension—not sublation—is precisely the liberation offered by the instinct. What Jean Paul calls instinct here is precisely the disjunction and asymmetry between the dialectic of clarity and the obscurity of origin.

What holds the disjunct elements together is desire. A desire for writing as a desire for the prohibited image, the image that can never be seen in the deepest night and yet is always seen despite the night, despite the brevity of the gaze. This is the logic of Jean Paul's *Siebenkäs*, a novel about writing, where a series of injunctions are placed so that writing can take place. These are laws against sight, against seeing the most treasured other. Siebenkäs, the aspiring author, is not allowed to see the object of his desire, Natalie. Nor is he allowed to see his *sosie* and best friend, his doppelgänger Leibgeber—the word "Doppelgänger" is used for the first time when this injunction is initially made.[55] This visual prohibition is often described as a journey or a path that leads to the pursuit of the other. The second and final time that Siebenkäs and Leibgeber part company, Siebenkäs is compelled to follow his friend surreptitiously.[56] But Siebenkäs and Natalie follow each other without even knowing it ("not like a shadow, because a shadow disappears sometimes")[57] until, ineluctably, they meet by chance at the very end of the novel in front of Siebenkäs's own empty tomb, his cenotaph whose door opens only by the small key he carries.[58] If the Orphic logic is enacted in *Siebenkäs*, the mannerist sprawl of Jean Paul's novel is nevertheless different from the cold precision with which the Orphic logic is carried out in *Death Sentence*.[59] But what *Siebenkäs* and *Death Sentence* share as an essential aspect of this logic is that desire which prompts a certain type of experience that cannot be extricated from the desire of writing—the author's desire to write, as well as the desire embodied in that writing itself.

Writing this desire and in accordance with it is an interrogation about the limit, because it is faced with the difficulties of beginning and ending. What is the first word, which must presuppose the law of writing in order to begin? What is the last word, which, as a conclusion, must legitimate its operational law? Can writing avoid the aporia between Oedipus as the first man who reveals the secret and Oedipus as the last man confined in a space of infinite loneliness? This is the possible impossibility of writing that does not seek legitimation by securing the law either as a presupposition or as a conclusion. Eschewing the security of an origin and of a telos means that the subject has no more a foundation; individuality is undercut—and thereby the doppelgänger comes to the fore. It is equally the case, simultaneously, that origin and telos are undercut by the operative presence of the doppelgänger. Thus the experience of the doppelgänger unfolds between its being created and its being creative. Writing, as the experience of an activity responsive to the limit, can be generalized. When this happens, action is from the start caught in a circular movement that seeks to establish a law that frames the narrative while the narrative itself is framed to transgress this law. This double movement, as the condition of the possibility of action, is linked in *Death Sentence* with the possibility of singular experience. Singularity, as a unique experience in the now, could be understood as the experience of a personal secret. The effective presence of the doppelgänger demands that the secret will not be revealed but—as shown in Chapter 2—that it will remain *in*visible and *in*expressible. Thus, singularity in *Death Sentence* is linked to *im*possibility. The characters are compelled to act—to begin acting—but they cannot grasp the origin of this compulsion. In the end, this will turn out to be a demand coming from writing itself in its various modalities of disappearance.

This movement of singularity is recorded with precision in *Death Sentence*: The narrator has to go to the theater "for a reason connected to work [*pour une raison de travail*]," and there he unexpectedly catches sight of Nathalie in the company of a young man. This perception is "as if it were behind a window [*comme derrière une vitre*],"[60] framed by a context that circumscribes the parameters of action. Yet the other is not present completely, but present infinitely close and yet infinitely far at the same time. "She remained in my presence with the freedom of a thought . . . and what tacit understanding was therefore established between her and my thought, what terrifying complicity."[61] Action then includes sight, but the sight is as if it comes from "behind the eyes [*une reconnaissance de derrière les yeux*]"; not the recognition of a real person but "a recognition of thought [*une reconnaissance de la pensée*]."[62] The framing of the window experience has put the female object of desire in an extremely precarious position. For the law that allows for the recognition is given by thought, a movement of thought, not an action in the world, and thus in danger of losing her (the female, the thought) in this world. Although there is a complicity of desire, this complicity is terrifying as it installs the danger of the annihilation of the desired other. It is at this point that action is imperative. The next episode unfolds in a very specific time and locale: the metro "at the moment Paris was bombed."[63] However, it remains unclear how much time had lapsed between this moment and the previous moment of the window experience in the theater. Was it the next day? Had the narrator met Nathalie before the descent into the shelter of the metro? Or, was this their first meeting since the narrator's encounter with her as his thought at the theater? These questions are in a sense redundant. What matters is that the entry point into the logic given by the window experience is pursued here with the utmost rigor: the threat of the nonaction of thought gives way here to an imperative to act. And to act in a singular manner. The narrator proposes marriage to Nathalie, using her own language that he hardly knows. And this is an act of complete irresponsibility, not only because he is not fond of wedlock but also because the meaning of the language he has used is elusive. It is an almost meaningless language, but for the same reason all the more meaningful; it has a meaning that can never be translated into any other context. This is the moment of pure action, if such a kind of action exists at all, where words and acts are almost fused. The narrator acknowledges this fusion when he concedes that "inwardly I committed myself to honouring these strange words; the more extreme they were, I mean alien to what might have been expected of me, the more true they seemed to me because they were novel, because they have no precedent."[64] The paradox of this extremity of meaning, of the utterance without "precedent" and without "responsibility" is that, despite the singularity that ensues, the singularity is not one of a subject alone in the world. Rather, the singularity is established between the actor and the other, whose alien language has been used. The only thing that matters in this singular experience is the relation of otherness that persists, even as the narrator reverts back to his familiar French.[65] But even now the French words are strange, exercising a power of madness because the actor "was driven by something wild [*de furieux*], a truth so violent [*une vérité si violente*]" that is unequal to any language.[66] There is surely a failure here, at least of signification. But this failure erases the identity of each party, since the lack of communication turns them into anonymous entities, subjects that cannot utter meaningful names. Nevertheless, this failure is what made it possible to begin, since it was premised on the "complicity" that compelled action.

The singularity of the pure experience of otherness fails, and it is a necessary failure that can achieve much more than any success. Simultaneously, this failure has to be complete, to the extent that success cannot figure in it in any way that reposits the subject. Otherness has to be maintained; success can figure only as the anonymity of the initial complicity in the relation to the other—although this is not a success by intention, since nothing has been accomplished that was not established at that originary moment. However, despite the meaninglessness of the language in the singular experience of otherness, does not the danger still persist that action carries with it a detritus of intentionality? Is not every utterance, even in its nonsensicality, still a "hermeneutical" event that takes place between agents? Blanchot is happy to concede this point. Once action has started, its cessation is problematic.

The narrator is in the full grip of action after the marriage proposal at the metro. He looks for Nathalie without success with a madness that arose "from an impatience [*impatience*] which grew with each passing minute."[67] Accosting this impatience is a series of prohibitions about where Nathalie is allowed to be (she has to be in her loft when her daughter is in town; she is not to go to one of the narrator's hotel rooms). Yet at the same time the prohibitions are transgressed. Everyone acts—and acts madly. Not only has Nathalie gone to the prohibited hotel room; she has also entered the room with a key she has stolen from the narrator's wallet. Yet this "imprudence of desire which forgets the law [*l'imprudence du désir qui oublie la loi*]"[68] leads to the closest possible encounter between the narrator and Nathalie. And the narrator is fully complicit: although he knows that "by touching her, I could have killed her,"[69] and in spite of the fear that she would "break in my hands,"[70] he still touches her, and she touches him back. Their encounter may be a sexual scene remarkable in its nonsensual description. What compensates and makes this one of the most powerful sexual scenes in literature is that every act, every movement, from the silent look to the nontrembling hand, is an act of transgression. As the encounter is prolonged beyond any expectation, it even becomes possible to address the other—and to address her with a command: "Come." A command that is obeyed, even for a moment, since "as I came near her she moved very quickly and drew away (or pushed me back)."[71] Of course, this has already accomplished much more—but also infinitely less—than the nonperception of the gaze of Orpheus. Yet the transgressive desire has still not been satisfied. It persists unabated when Nathalie wakes up cheerful the next morning, and for a whole "week after that day."[72] As the narrator puts it, he endeavors to "remain a little longer in the realm of things,"[73] even by getting involved in the negotiations of a duel. (Is not this reference to a duel proportionally even more anachronistic than Nathalie's not wearing a hat at their first meeting? Or, is it merely an allusion to the duel as a trademark scene of the doppelgänger and by implication a thematic reference to Jean Paul?) Yet as the Orphic logic dictates, "impatience links desire to insouciance."[74] Action is liberated—it is no longer transgressive—so long as it is linked to an instant where care and intention are absent. The narrator is aware of this, as well as of the consequent loss of the "realm of things." "And the most terrible thing is that in those minutes I was aware of the insane price I was going to pay for an instant of distraction."[75] It was an instant of absent-mindedness that brought about the breaking of the law, the madness of action, and the enactment of desire. Lamenting for this instant of distraction—the complicity of the window experience? or, the moment that Nathalie stole his key?—is really a last attempt to intend a prolonged stay in the "realm of things." However, any intention has already been forestalled, the "plan [*projet*]" will have already been carried out: Nathalie has already had a cast made of her hands and face. She is already dead. And yet, upon realizing this, the narrator admits that "I was no longer in the least interested; all that belonged to another world."[76] What has been accomplished by the "plan" is no longer in the realm of things; it concerns a space of complete indifference.

The carelessness and carefree loss of interest, the distracted subject in the midst of dramatic revelation, the experiencing of a joyful abandon in the face of death, this forgetting of the "realm of things," even the forgetting of the instant of distraction itself that brought about thingliness, the forgetting of forgetfulness—this state in which the narrator finds himself is no longer transgressive. It is the very suspension of transgression in the name of justice. The work has taken place; writing has happened. But the only thing that is thereby affirmed is the initial impetus that brought about the work. Unhappiness is no less than happiness at this detour, as the narrator affirms in the final statement of the second part of the récit—the final part of the 1971 edition. Like words and like actions, the passions suffered through things have already been done and undone. There is no sad fate operating here, because the "thought" established at the moment of the "terrifying complicity" between the narrator and Nathalie "if it [or, she] has conquered me, has only conquered through me, and in the end has always been equal to me."[77] It is the origin, then, it is Nathalie, that has given and has been given. This gift and sacrifice is the liberation of the law.

The sacrificial gift should not be seen as something dutiful. There is no categorical imperative established here ("act as if you are distracted all the time"). Not only would this be impossible, since action has long been abandoned; more important, absence has to be maintained. If there is a noncommanding and nonimperative justice that authorizes no laws, it is justice as this absence. This justice can become "visible" as the thought, as Nathalie. But it also has to remain invisible—this is the justice of the secret, justice as the secret. If that was not the case, the whole narrative would have been in the grips of the double bind— in the grips of a command impossible to break and yet impossible to obey. The "unbinding" by the secret is not an ethical or moral command. It is here that the function of writing becomes important: as a prelude to the maddening transgression that takes place between the narrator and Nathalie, an apostrophe installs a prohibition to the narration itself: "I will say very little about what happened then."[78] This prohibition qua law can never be followed and will always be broken.

But this prohibition qua absence can be both followed and broken at the same time—for nothing is there. This absence, this nothingness, is like Nathalie whom the narrator's hands cannot touch and yet touch. Blanchot returns to the hands in the third section of the novel that he saw fit to delete in the 1971 edition of *Death Sentence*. In the form of a command, or even a curse, whoever reads "these pages" is warned not to look for unhappiness in it: "And what is more, let him try to imagine the hand that is writing them: if he saw it, then perhaps reading would have become a serious task for him."[79] Whose are these hands? Are they really Blanchot's? How could Blanchot be so careless as to reinstate the actative of "writing" when all action had given way to absence? Perhaps this third section is not a "mistake" at all, perhaps it is not a coda revealing the secret of *Death Sentence,* in which case the hands are not Blanchot's but belong perhaps to Blanchot's companion, Jean Paul. But if that is really the case, then why did Blanchot delete this third section from the subsequent edition? Maybe he forgot that the hands belonged to Jean Paul. In which case, while Blanchot was rereading *Death Sentence* for the revised edition, he would have thought that the narrative would have been indeed self-canceling. And in a moment of terror and madness Blanchot decided to act: to delete. Or, maybe Blanchot did not forget the absent hands; maybe he chose to forget the very forgetfulness of Jean Paul's name in *Death Sentence*. In which case the deletion of the third part is not an action in any proper sense. Rather, it is the very enactment of the forgetting of forgetfulness, and hence the affirmation of the absent presence, the obscurity, the absence stronger than presence of Jean Paul—the affirmation of a liberating complicity. It is the absence of intention made possibly by writing with the collocutor Jean Paul, an affirmation of the possible and at the same time impossible moment of distraction that sustains the subject as doppelgänger—while the doppelgänger sustains a writing that allows for such a distraction.

| | |

Jean Paul's hands come to interrupt the "persecution" of the writing hand by the nonwriting hand as Blanchot describes it in the first chapter of *The Space of Literature*. If the mastery of the nonwriting hand consists in interrupting the writing hand and restoring primacy to the present, then the absent hand complicates this interruption, infusing the present with the past and the future and thereby undoing mastery.[80] The disappearance of the hands is allowed by the doppelgänger's effective operation in writing. The nothing that it installs at the heart of the work as well as at the complicity characterizing subjective relations recalls the nothingness that pertains to both criticism and literature, according to Blanchot's "The Task of Criticism Today." The most important accomplishment of this failure of visibility is that there is a withdrawal from any dialectic of mastery; both criticism and literature withdraw from evaluation, affirming themselves "in isolation from all value." This release from value, consequently—and these are the concluding words of the version in *Lautréamont et Sade*—opens up history "to that which, within history, is already moving beyond all forms of value and is preparing for a wholly different—and still unpredictable—kind of affirmation."[81] There is here an interplay of at least three elements that deserve attention. First, the overcoming of value entails the devaluation of individual autonomy: there is no secure point from which to pronounce a judgment that will reveal an essence stable in past, present, and future. Nevertheless, the affirmation enacted in the unfolding of this historical development could still be said to posit an autonomy and autoteleia of the practices of literature and criticism. The unpredictability—or revealability—inside every piece of literature and criticism creates its own criteria for its futural unfolding. The historical demand after the devaluation of value through the operative presence of the doppelgänger is that the work remains "within history." This interiority allows for the particular unfolding of the laws presented in each work—just as it has been shown to allow for the transformability of the doppelgänger. The work can transform itself in ways that are unpredictable precisely because of this autonomy and autoteleia. Interiority entails not transformation, but rather transformability, that is, the operative tension of the borderlines or limits of the work itself. The consequence of this move is that literature and criticism, despite their interdependence and intimate complicity, remain as practices distinguishable. The liminality of the one may be related to the liminality of the other, but they do not collapse into each other. They may be within the same history, but they retain their own peculiar historicities. Difference is maintained.

The second element of the devaluation of value by literature's and criticism's insignificance is that, despite their persistent historicities, they are still within history. In other words, highlighting their autonomy and autoteleia not only does not set them apart from politics, it rather makes the political an ineliminable aspect of the way that their lawlessness withdraws from value. The doppelgänger's *hypo*crisy can only be presented within the devaluation enacted in specific works that allow for the doppelgänger, but this also means that the critical task thereby solicited has a "*hypo*," something underlining it, which can never be occluded. This is the work's relation to the political. Leslie Hill insists on the political aspect of the withdrawing of value in "The Task of Criticism Today" by emphasizing that "Blanchot was careful also to evoke the political struggles (against de Gaulle's undemocratic return to power in France in 1958 and France's ongoing colonial war in Algeria, a war that, it is well known, was never *named* as such) occurring at the time at—and accordingly within—literary criticism's own gates."[82] This is made clear, as Hill observes, in a passage excised from the conclusion in 1963—one that came in the 1959 version immediately after the passage cite above:

> Of what, then, does the literary work speak when it rejects all evaluation? Why do we feel ourselves bound by it to the concern for anonymous existence, to being as a neutral and impersonal power, excluding all distinct interest, all determined speech, and calling on the violent equality of becoming? And, if indeed this is the direction it opens up for us, is it not strange that we should then be led to rediscover, in the most superficial kind of criticism, that which in journalistic form is part of the murmur of everyday experience and of life outside, the just continuation of the movement of profound indeterminacy that seeks to communicate in the creation of the work in order to affirm in the work the future of communication and communication as future?[83]

The future that literature and criticism make possible is one that includes in its affirmations the quotidian pursuits of journalism and hence the politics of the day. This is because interpersonal communication has the structure of indeterminacy that characterizes the nothing of literature's and criticism's insignificance. History becomes significant because it necessarily partakes of that insignificance. There are the politics of the everyday *and* the political affirmation of the withdrawal of value attested by literature and criticism.

Moreover, and this is the third element, the conjunction of history *and* the historicities of literature and criticism is one that can be generalized to include writing as a whole. This is not to say that there is an essential experience of writing. Rather, the point is that the temporal structure that yields a notion of futurity that underlies subjectivity need not be confined to a single genre of narrative. More precisely, this means that not only any single genre of literature or criticism but also not even the totality of their genres will be commensurate with the formality that pertains to the futurity of writing as such. This is the futurity that makes possible the formal differentiality of the doppelgänger's ontology. And, as extrapolated in the previous chapter, this futurity is one of the revealability illustrated by the operation of the sign or σημεῖο. Blanchot has addressed precisely this nexus with reference to Heraclitus. The reason for the Platonic preference of oral over written communication, says Blanchot in "The Beast of Lascaux," is that Socrates desires a language that avoids nothingness. Thus, presence guarantees exchange and meaning. Conversely, Blanchot points out that writing, just like sacred language, eschews presence and any stable origin so that "language gives voice to this absence."[84] This is the authority of language recognized by Heraclitus: "The lord whose oracle is in Delphi neither speaks out nor conceals, but points [*n'exprime ni ne dissimule rien, mais indique*; οὔτε λέγει οὔτε κρύπτει ἀλλὰ σημαίνει]."[85] The significance of this authority lies in the fact that the sign is neither a spoken word implying presence, nor a secret that needs to be revealed:

> The language in which the origin speaks is essentially prophetic. This does not mean that it dictates future events; it means that it does not base itself on something that already is, either on a currently held truth, or solely on language which has already been spoken or verified. It announces because it begins. It *points* [*indique*, Blanchot's translation of σημαίνει] towards the future, because it does not yet speak, and is language of the future to the extent that it is like a future language which is always ahead of itself, having its meaning and legitimacy only before it, which is to say that it is fundamentally without justification.[86]

The language of writing, then, allows for singularity, which, as shown in relation to *Death Sentence*, makes possible a beginning and an origin, only to reinscribe this point of departure to something both anterior and posterior. The prophetic quality of writing consists not in revelation, but in the revealability that twists the time of the now in a future anterior. This twisting of time made possible by the power of the σημεῖο necessitates, as shown in relation to self-confession, a dissolution of any steadfast boundaries for subjective individuality; hence it ushers in the doppelgänger. Thus, the doppelgänger is now shown to be implicated in the structure of writing—a structure that determines the autonomy and autoteleia of the work, while sustaining the political in the work. Writing—the writing of disappearance, the writing of the doppelgänger—allows for the conjunction and disjunction between history and the historicity of specific practices.

However, the effective presentation of disappearance in Blanchot's notion of the "unpredictable affirmation" does not exhaust itself in the three elements just indicated. A further question persists, one which points no less to the excising of the reference to the writing hands at the end of the 1971 edition of *Death Sentence* than to the excising of the reference to politics at the end of "The Task of Criticism Today." These are two passages that speak of forms of invisibility, erasure, silence, the withdrawal of presence and value, *and* in a sense enact that withdrawal by their excision after the first publication of each text. Both these procedures are, of course, common enough in Blanchot: his whole work can be viewed as an attempt to address absence and very often he would rework his texts for subsequent publications.[87] Yet in spite of being unable to demonstrate authoritatively (even if a testimony by Blanchot himself about these changes existed) that these two specific excisions are not merely incidental, it does remain curious that Blanchot feels compelled to delete the concluding words that address the absence of which both texts speak. Whence this compulsion? What is the demand that the writer has followed? Is it one of literature or is it one of criticism? Clearly, if it is of literature, it will also have to be of criticism, given that the work of literature, as Blanchot emphasizes, contains its criticism. So it will have to be the conjunction and disjunction of criticism and literature, a movement that like the retreat *and* return of origin indicates the presence of the doppelgänger. Yet this is still only a description of what is made possible with such a disappearance that seeks to avoid authority. The suggestion here is that in the silence and invisibility made possible by the intertwining of literature and visibility there is always a reserve or excess that cannot be reconciled with it. This will be glimpsed in the relation between history and the historicity of literature and criticism that could not claim that nothing is excluded from that interplay. Also, an excess will be glimpsed as the political arises, for neither criticism nor literature would be allowed to claim authority over the contingencies of eventualities—this would turn them into revelations of the future. And, finally, an excess would of necessity also be present in writing, which is caught in the double bind of its impossible beginning and end and the repetition of the negations of different legislative protocols for it to become possible. Besides the stable origin, then, which the practice of literature and criticism have turned into a disappearance, there is still a remainder, a supplement which is even more invisible, darker, further into the shadow than both of them.

This shadow in the shadow was designated in the previous chapter as the penumbra indicating the justice accompanying the doppelgänger. However, what is added here with the complicity between literature and criticism—the author and the reader—and the reinscription of this complicity in terms of writing, is the operation of a third power. This will be called philosophy. It is philosophy that would authorize the absence from the work of that which is not even absent—like the absence of Jean Paul whose name is not mentioned in *Death Sentence*. Philosophy would be able to authorize that not from a position superior or external to literature or criticism. Rather, this is made possible by the repeatability that underlies the repetitions of the *and* which have been shown to characterize the subject of modernity: journalism *and* academia, the private *and* the public, the human *and* the divine—all those conjunctions are repeatedly staged against each other in ways that show their disjunctions—they are negated by their repetitions. However, the repeatability of this process cannot be confined to a literary or critical text and hence cannot be commensurable with the repetitions themselves—even if it was conceivable to have an authoritative figure who could grasp the totality of all those possible repetitions. This is an unbinding whose authority is derived from its lack of authority. This makes it the insignificance of the insignificant, the silence of the silent, the justice of the lawless laws. It is the *andness* of the *and* of the doppelgänger. The relation between the literary, the critical and the philosophical, then, is mediated by the operative presence of the doppelgänger. Is it not just that the links—or reflections—between the literary, the critical, and the philosophical allow for the emergence of the doppelgänger. In addition, and more emphatically, it is the operative presence of the doppelgänger that conjoins and disjoins the literary, the critical, and the philosophical. This double conjunction—the being created *and* creative, on the one hand, as well as, on the other, the reflections on the discursive *and* their interruptions—this is the chiasmus of the doppelgänger. This chiasmus was shown in Chapter 1 to be the ontology of the doppelgänger. However, while the discussion of the uncanny concentrated on the subject, this chapter has expanded the discussion to include the historical. As the kind of genre or canon extrapolated in the present chapter, or as historiography the way it will be presented in the following chapter, the historical is constitutive of the doppelgänger's ontology, it is part of its *andness*.

However, does that *and and* indicate a "double" of the doppelgänger? Such a move must be resisted for philosophy to be retained. The *andness* indicates precisely that which cannot be denied by the negations of the laws. It is the justice that philosophy can address only because it overcomes a foundational exclusion. What this means is that this intimacy, this terrifying complicity, which is located at this minor part of the shadow, is not derived from segregation. It may be what underlies the possibility of conflict and debate, the *polemos* at the core of legality and systematicity, the contestation of politics. But it can never be concomitant with a conflict that excludes the other. To the extent, then, that the doppelgänger is philosophical, it could not possibly have its own "double." This means that the community that such a notion of subjectivity makes possible is not grounded on an exception. Instead, it is what Blanchot calls in *The Unavowable Community* a "community of lovers." Such a community would require a "politics of friendship" or of "hospitality," which can make distinctions without being based on a principle of individual autonomy.[88]

Such a philosophy would have to adhere to its inclusivity—its *and-ness*—also in its relation to literature and criticism. This does not mean that philosophy becomes identical to literature and criticism—they are as different as justice is from law, as well as one law is from another, and from lawlessness as well. What it means is that the historicity of justice is not in opposition to the historicities of literature and criticism. They are not identical, then, but their liminalities are indiscrete. In recounting in *The Unavowable Community* the anecdote, mentioned earlier, about Bataille's unnamed interlocutor who would have been recognized by all this friends, Blanchot had insisted that what was presented by this absence was "friendship as much as a friend." A particular friend partakes of friendship as such, even if they are both present in their absence, present as absence and moreover absent in different ways. The supposition of philosophy at the core of the liminality of the doppelgänger means that literature, criticism, and philosophy are consupponible. It also means that never is an author, critic, or philosopher given the authority to exclude one of the others. Thus, alongside the inclusivity of the political, the subject who practices those different activities, no less than the subjects invoked in and through their practices, are forever immersed in chiasmic relations without a single origin and without a determinable telos. These relations, as well as relationality as such, are the doppelgänger. The task of the doppelgänger is the enactment of those relations in their endless—and hence futural—unfolding.

CHAPTER FOUR

The Politics of the Doppelgänger

Universal History and Cosmopolitanism

> *The realm of history is fertile and comprehensive; it embraces the whole moral world. It accompanies man through everything he experiences, through all the changing forms of thoughts, through his folly and wisdom, his depravity and glory; it must render the account of everything he has given and received.*
>
> FRIEDRICH SCHILLER, "The Nature and Value of Universal History"

AUTOMATISM, AUTONOMY

The doppelgänger, as discussed so far, is the figure that configures both time and place. The doppelgänger undoes *mere* presence; it resists a reduction to a determinate locus as well as to a determinate temporal arrangement. The *effective* presence of the figure of the doppelgänger creates the condition of the possibility of topicality as well as temporality. Whereas the configurations of time and space have been demonstrated separately, an extrapolation of both in conjunction is still lacking. Such an undertaking will involve asking about the time of the past. What is the past of an effective presence? And, also, how is the past referred to and referenced by historiography? There are two ways of approaching this problematic: either a correlation, adequation, or symmetry is posited between history and the writing of history, or alternatively past and historiography are dissymmetrical, ruptured, and relational. On the one hand, then, there is the possibility of a history of historiography, a comprehensive record of recordability itself. On the other hand, there is the seemingly impossible demand to write history without recourse to a predetermined definition of what history itself is. The former may be called the historicist approach, and the latter the materialist approach—although those terms remain provisional until they are further elucidated later in this chapter.

Yet even before an analysis of the different historiographic methods, the argument so far still permits the figure of the doppelgänger to side with materialism. This follows from the recognition that the historicist and the materialist conceptions of the writing of the past are themselves historically determined. In other words, there is a historicity of both the comprehensive history of historiography (historicism) and of the unconditional history of historiography (materialism). This is a historicity that is not to be found solely in the annals of theories of history and in the philosophies about the past. Also, but as importantly, the historicity is part of the way that ideas about memory and the recording of the past have been used by power structures. Any power, be it of politics, theory, and technics, of the law, the religious, or even purely of the individual (supposing, *concesso non dato*, that clear-cut distinctions within as well as between public and private manifestations of power could be sustained), power as such, requires control of memory. Ideology, as the site where precisely the public and the private manifestations of power intertwine, could be understood as gaining control of the most crucial memory of all, that is, the memory of power itself. Therefore, the historicity of historiography is constituted both by the books about history and by the unfolding of the struggle to usurp power. Following the recognition that this historicity is ineliminable from history and historiography, the side taken by the doppelgänger will become obvious as soon as the subject is thought in this setup. Historicism posits a determinate—or at least determinable—connection between the subjects of history and the historical record, while materialism pursues a dissymmetry between the two. In other words, historicism posits a determinate distinction between public and private, whereas materialism affirms their rupture.[1] Because the doppelgänger is the overcoming of a stable origin of subjectivity, the doppelgänger can never be reconciled with the historicist project that seeks such a foundation.[2]

How is it possible, then, to write history without any previous reassurance of what history is? For this question to be pursued through the figure of the doppelgänger, it will be crucial to further explore what it is to be a subject of history. In addition, this pursuit will also have to recognize that the question is not just philosophical but also about literature and criticism. In other words, it is a question about *writing*. Now, from the very beginning the expression "subject of history" appears equivocal. It can mean, on the one hand, the historical individuals *about whom* the historical record speaks—the subject matter of history. On the other hand, it can also mean the subject *who* composes that record, the historian. This will be taken as a productive equivocation, that is, as a suspended undecidability. There is no way of reconciling the subjective and the objective genitives of the expression "the subject of history." This figuration, by denying the subject a reassured position as the source of history, is due to the doppelgänger's elision of a foundational origin.

This gives rise to a series of problematics: First, what is the relation between the historical individual and the historian? Who comes first? And who second? Moreover, if the question of "who comes first and who second"—the first or the last man—could not be answered without recourse to an originary discourse, then is it possible at all to ask it? And, if it is not possible to ask the question about priority, then how would it at all be possible to distinguish between the historical individual and the historian? Second, if the question of priority is impossible, then how could discursive autonomy be guaranteed? In other words, if the historian is not given the right to authorize what constitutes a historical testament or fact, then how could history be distinguished from fiction at all? Third, if the question of priority and hence of discursive boundaries remains in abeyance, then would not history be too loose a concept? In which case, would not historiography, de jure, need to encompass everything, would it not need to include the totality of subjective activity? And, consequently, would not all written histories be de facto failures to aspire to that totality? More emphatically, would not historiography be impossible?

These problematics *convene* the notions of completeness and incompleteness vis-à-vis the subject. First, because a completely autonomous subjectivity is eschewed by the doppelgänger, there can be no foundation for the individual. Second, subjective incompleteness is carried over and inscribed within generic distinctions. Finally, despite the seeming preponderance of incompleteness so far, this only reinstates completeness as a juridical and practical demand. The argument here will be that, as the subject convenes the pugnacious forces of completeness and incompleteness within its own figure, there will be no way of fully reconciling them. Yet, as completeness and incompleteness *converge in* the subject, their polemic can become a productive force for judgment and explanation. In other words, it will become the condition of the possibility of the subject's intervention in history. Thus, the issue about writing history will no longer be one about the struggle of supremacy between completeness and incompleteness, but rather the interruption of this struggle through the subject, which is, moreover, facilitated by and within that struggle itself. Thus, while the agonistic—even antagonistic—element needs to be maintained, this element concomitantly inscribes a field of cooperation and coexistence. This field will be due to the effective presence of the doppelgänger.

Parataxis will be the term used here in order to show the convergence of completeness and incompleteness in the subject of history. The reason is that parataxis does not merely contain completeness as an issue, but it does so by giving rise to the agonistic and the conciliatory without either of them being subsumed to the other. Moreover, parataxis carries the twofold register of meaning that is of interest here, namely it refers to the subject as well as to writing. The reference to the subject is evidenced in that parataxis means an ordered arrangement of individuals—*para-taxis* literally means placing side by side. More specifically, parataxis usually designates the formations of two opposing armies before or during battle. In this meaning, the agonistic is paramount and in such a way that includes political history—the history of the *hypotaxis*, that is, the subordination or conquering (literally, the placing under, *hypo-taxis*) of a people or peoples. But parataxis can refer more generally to any ordered arrangement of individuals. Significantly, such arrangements take place in parades or national celebrations; they may even be the victory parade after the battle or the parade commemorating a victory in subsequent years. Thus, alongside the agonistic, what is also indexed in parataxis is a regular arrangement of time that indicates a progress or progressibility toward an ideal—for instance, the peace and prosperity that ensue after war. Simultaneously, however, the move from the battle to the victory parade to the anniversary celebrations also ineluctably refers to the historical grasping of this movement, to the history that recounts the movement in ways that legitimate its genesis. Highlighting the notion of progress in parataxis turns historiography into "the history of the victorious," as Walter Benjamin puts it in passages that will be discussed in the following section.

If the reference to historiography arises as a consequence of the first meaning of parataxis, its second meaning is explicitly about writing and syntax. The term "parataxis" has a specific use in the technical manuals of grammar and rhetoric. The literal meaning of *para-taxis* as sequential order does not refer here to the subject but to word order. Indeed, parataxis here is the antonym of *hypotaxis* in a technical sense, meaning the placing of something under something else, or, to put it in syntactical terminology, subordinate conjunction. Parataxis is the sequential placing of words that are usually the same part of speech, or even clauses. There is an equality between the terms of such a ligament. Another way of defining parataxis would be to say that it is a simplified syntactical arrangement—an ostensive procedure carried out in the indicative mood. The most obvious example of such a parataxis would be a list, such as shopping list, an inventory, or the credits at the end of a film. More generally, it would be any arrangement that has a technical aspect that can be automated such that it could be recorded in a template (and even automated to such an extent that the recording could be carried out by a machine). However, just as with its previous meaning, this parataxis also cannot remain purely rhetorical or grammatical but of necessity refers to something outside it, namely the subject. Any list stakes a referential claim to the objects it indexes, but the objects are indexed for purposes necessarily linked to human activity. There are no lists or inventories without human intentionality, a listing is always done for a certain reason. Moreover, to the extent that large ordered arrangements of human agents that are recorded have always included the soldiers in an army; and to the extent that such recordings of armies have traditionally been the subject matter of history, then here the two meanings of parataxis become aligned.

The alignment is due to subjection. As Étienne Balibar has demonstrated, subjection is part of the historicity of the subject, from the Latin *subjectus*.[3] (It could also be added here that this meaning is derived from Greek, where the word for subject, *hypokeimenon*, literally means to be placed underneath. Moreover, *hypokeimenon* is the state that results after suffering *hypotaxis*, after being subjected to the act of *hypotassein*, the placing under.) Balibar observes that the emergence from the ancient world entailed a "unified category of subjection"—"the *inner* subject emerges, who confronts a transcendent law, both theological and political."[4] The emancipation from subjection—or at least the project for emancipation—signals for Balibar the placing of the human at the center of the struggle for progress in terms of human rights. The crucial figure here is Kant, who extrapolated the practical or ethical not as a cosmological question, but as a cosmopolitical one, hence giving rise to the idea of a free and autonomous subject.[5] Despite their differences, each understanding of the subject can be viewed as a determination of Foucault's "empirico-transcendental doublet"—which was discussed in Chapter 2. Yet when Balibar explicitly refers to Foucault's subject of modernity, he also remarks that essence and value, and hence subjection, ensue from the equation between the empirical and the transcendental within and by the subject.[6] Thus, a project of *subjecti-*

vation will entail inquiring into the various forms that subjection has taken through time, a historicity of subjection. Yet Balibar concludes from this that inquiring into the dialectic between subjection and subjectivation is endless—"Maybe there is no 'end of history,' no 'end of the story'"[7]—which also implies that subjection is endless. Clearly, this is a legitimate conclusion. However, if the endlessness of subjection is viewed as a finite infinite, and if subjection is examined in relation to *hypotaxis*—and, hence, also to parataxis—then writing will come to intervene in the endlessness of the dialectic. And with writing, and historiography, there will arise another possibility: not of overcoming subjection, but rather of reconfiguring the subject so that *parataxis*, rather than *hypotaxis*, is the determinate term of its finite infinite unfolding.

Consequently, the alignment between the two meanings of parataxis does not indicate that they merge. On the contrary, even if one parataxis is impossible to be sharply distinguished from the other, they still do not collapse into each other. Thus, the relation of the parataxis of subjects and the parataxis in writing is itself paratactic. In other words, and as already indicated, it is not merely the memory of the event that is at issue with parataxis, but more importantly the memory of the nexus of power that allows for memorization. Or, to put the same point in the vocabulary of Walter Benjamin's *Arcades Project*, "politics attains primacy over history."[8]

There is a force of reversibility, then, in the two meanings of parataxis that does not allow them to stagnate in a seemingly impeccable arrangement. One form of parataxis infringes on the other, destabilizing it no less than it destabilizes itself. And yet the fact that that destabilization itself remains paratactic leads to four crucial components for a materialist historiography. Before examining these components in detail, they are presented here schematically. First, the insistence of power effectuates a *rupture between writing and history* understood as past event. The two types of parataxis remain discrete. Second, their discreteness is based on a notion of temporality that conceives time as the accumulation—a synonym for parataxis—of discrete moments of time. Moreover, those moments are homogeneous in their respective totalities. However, as one parataxis infringes on the other, the temporal continuum is itself destabilized and the discreteness of *temporal instantaneity is shattered*. Third, the interplay of completeness and incompleteness arising with parataxis gives rise in turn to the notion of *universal history and cosmopolitanism*—in ways that will be examined in the next two sections of this chapter. Fourth, whereas parataxis appeared in the first meaning to synecdochically render hypotaxis (subjection), still in the second sense parataxis and hypotaxis are antonyms. The contention here will be that as soon as the relation between subjectivity and writing is seen as itself paratactic, then the struggle of usurping power does not so much cease as become reconfigured so that the issue then is *the manner in which the relation unfolds*. This reconfiguration will be shown to be the result of Benjamin's reversal from history to the political.

These components are a result of the figure of the doppelgänger as it configures completeness and incompleteness vis-à-vis the subject through an interplay of automatism and autonomy. To start with the latter, a corollary of historiography has always been the project of individual liberation. The rupture between the thoroughly contingent and hence ungraspable history, on the one hand, and historiography, on the other, has regularly been derived from the premise that the written history is useful for the attainment of human freedom as well as for the polity. This logic is in operation most clearly in the cases where progress is associated both with historiography and the project of freedom. This is the case especially when cosmopolitanism and universal history concur, as in Friedrich Schiller's inaugural address at the University of Jena.[9] Schiller distinguishes sharply between *Weltgeschichte*, which in principle includes everything, even those facts or events for which there is no evidence, and *Universalgeschichte*, which, from the present point of view, harmonizes the totality of knowledge with the use of reason and with the purpose of creating a harmonious society, or at least the institution of a conglomerate of harmonious societies such as Schiller's Europe.[10] Now, even though this history must remain open in order to allow for the capacity for progress inherent in the rupture between *Weltgeschichte* and *Universalgeschichte*, what is indexed under universal history is always necessary, implicated in a scientific concatenation of cause and effect. Thus, an *automatism* is inscribed in the epochal progress toward autonomy.

However, it is also possible to start with an automated discourse—defined as scientific—which can be presupposed as long as subject and object, cause and effect, as well as necessity and freedom, are sharply distinguished. In this case, autonomy will be assumed to be the natural progress of humankind. Yet, as soon as those distinctions become unstable, then autonomy marks the very body of the "automatic" individual, of the automaton. Again, there is no stable rule to distinguish one from the other. And this instability is paramount because of the effective presence of the doppelgänger, which does not allow for the ascription of a cause for action that is either purely automated or purely free.[11] These two complete totalities, as long as they are set side by side, paratactically, contaminate each other, they infringe on each other's domain, and thereby turn their opposite, as well as themselves, into something incomplete.

This process of (self)contamination is evident in the sharp distinction between the historian and the philosopher with which Schiller's inaugural address begins.[12] Schiller asserts that the task (*Studierplan*) of the bread-and-butter historian (*Brotgelehrte*) is permeated with the spirit of slavery (*Sklavenseele*). The reason is that such a historian's ratiocination is limited due to his dependence on occupational protocols and a lack of interest in using reason to contemplate history in its universal aspect; that is, he is trapped in his own purposeless activity, which, however, is not allowed to accommodate a lack of purpose.[13] Conversely, the universal historian is equipped with a philosophical mind (*der philosophische Kopf*) that strives to unify knowledge and to grasp everything in its connection to everything else (*alles ineinander greife*). This mind is evidenced precisely in its advance toward the perfectibility of the spirit (*schreitet der philosophische Geist zu höherer Vortrefflichkeit fort*).[14] However, does not perfectibility aspire to freedom through the mechanical application of rules? In other words, does it not aspire to freedom through the application in the realm of the spirit of the rules of such a mechanical nature as causality? Is not his noble eagerness to work (*seine edle Ungeduld*) toward the completion of his knowledge (*Vollendung seines Wissens*) a symptom of his enslavement in incomplete knowledge? Such a symptom, although it will remain the precondition of autonomy, could never be separated as sharply as Schiller desires from the automatism of the machine or the animal.[15]

Schiller's purposive activity of the philosopher is, mutatis mutandis, Fichte's "conjuring trick," as it was extrapolated in the first chapter. Without intending to efface the significant differences between the two Jena professors, it can still be asserted that the "trick" in both cases consists in an endeavor to secure the real, the practical, the ethical, or the political through a presupposition of systematicity that is, however, only accessible to the philosophical mind. Any phenomenology—in the broadest possible extension of the term, that is, any science of the *phenomenon*—requires a supplementary conceptual element that cannot be reduced to what is perceptible. But it is only a "conjurer's trick"—as Jean Paul puts it in his critique of Fichte—to then try to demonstrate that the phenomenon and its supplement can be completely segregated or distinguished. The trick in Schiller's case unravels in the concept of progress, which is both manifested in the empirical realm and at the same time transcends it. Conversely, to insist on the consupponibility of the automatic and the autonomous is to insist on the regulative necessity of their cooperation in and by the subject of history.

Jean Paul had designated in the *Clavis Fichtiana* that possibility of cooperation with the image of the "silent and labouring demogorgon." This supplementary presence, which can only be reduced to "real" presence through a trick, has been shown in the first chapter to be the effective presence of the doppelgänger. The image of two parts working together—one inside and the other outside, one free and the other mechanical—conjures the image of the chess-playing automaton from the first Thesis of Walter Benjamin's "On the Concept of History." Indeed, as this image will be extrapolated in the following section, it illustrates the cooperation required between automatism and autonomy, between completeness (the theological or messianic drive toward conciliation) and incompleteness (the weak messianism that characterizes reality according to Benjamin's second Thesis, or what might also be called in Derrida's terms "the messianic without messianism").[16] The parataxis of man and puppet in the chess-playing automaton will require a discussion of universal history as it is connected to a conception of materialist historiography. This will lead to an articulation of judgment provided by the interplay between completeness and incompleteness.

Yet the political impetus of parataxis made possible by the figure of the doppelgänger will also require a closer interrogation of cosmopolitanism. The main reference for this task will be Alasdair Gray's novel *Poor Things*. Not only is a cosmopolitan ideal emphatically asserted twice by the main character of the novel—she claims to be "a woman of the world"[17]—but also the question of what constitutes such a woman of the world is presented through the image of a presence inside the body that marks it in a decisive way—a kind of "labouring demogorgon." Thus, due to the doppelgänger's operation, the interplay of automatism and autonomy is presented in the novel. Indeed, the expression "poor thing" in the title can be taken to mean precisely the automatism of the subject who fails to achieve the ideal of freedom at the very moment that that ideal is assumed to have been accomplished. Yet whereas Benjamin adduces ab initio a—messianic—reconciliation of man and puppet, Gray's characters insist on their separation.[18] The way that all their attempts at separation will only affirm the effective presence of that which has been denied—namely, reconciliation—is due to the figure of the doppelgänger. The paratactic in the doppelgänger will be a way of approaching historiography via universal history and the political via cosmopolitanism but without equating either with complete conciliation or total irreconcilability.

THE SUBJECT OF HISTORY IN WALTER BENJAMIN

Focusing on the subject of Walter Benjamin's notion of history conjures up the image of the chess-playing automaton of the first Thesis in "On the Concept of History."[19] In the writing of history, the subject figures both as the hidden chess player inside the mechanism, and as the puppet that moves the pieces on the chessboard outside. There is a mechanism that can potentially be propelled indefinitely, but its operation at each time is determined by the definite stamina of the player crouched in the dark, suffocating compartment. On the board, the continuation of the game is related to the hidden player, while the puppet's jerky movements are incidental to the game's duration. Thus the image of the Turk, as the automaton was known, provides a complex temporality. In terms of movement, the machine can go on forever, while the man only as long as he can cope. Whereas in terms of the game, its perpetuation is dependent on the calculating man, while the puppet is incidental. Thus the complexity of time is created by the juxtaposition—the *parataxis*—of man and puppet. Thereby, the subject becomes an integral part of the act performed by the automaton, but the medium of that act is time itself.

Subjectivity and temporality are not on their own enough to show the import of history. History is not discovered or created immediately, and hence a third term is needed. This third term is writing. Thus, the subject and time are to be examined in conjunction with historiography. However, with the automaton, the doppelgänger is also in play. Because of the doppelgänger, neither of the three terms—the subject, time, writing—will be given a reassuring stability. Rather, the effective presence of the doppelgänger will entail the operation of a productive relationality. It will also be argued that the figure of the automaton—the figure of the doppelgänger—is that which gives history a political significance. The way that the chess-playing automaton, the Turk, configures subjectivity, temporality, and historiography will emerge only after reading Benjamin's texts on history.

As the image of the automaton is refracted through Benjamin's writings the subject as historian *and* as the subject that appears within written history will assume a clearer outline. The coordinates for such an outline can be provided only by Benjamin's writings themselves, and first of all by the unfinished *Arcades Project* to which the Theses were conceived in part as a methodological grid. The fact that the *Arcades* remain unfinished is a problematic element in such an investigation, and one that Benjamin is well aware of: "Outline the history of *The Arcades Project* [*die Geschichte der Passagenarbeit*] in terms of its development. Its properly problematic component: the refusal to renounce anything that would demonstrate the materialist presentation of history as imagistic in a higher sense than in the traditional presentation."[20] Benjamin is not referring simply to the book that was published posthumously as volume 5 of his *Gesammelte Schriften*. Benjamin is also referring to the work (*Arbeit*) of collecting in files a huge volume of material—the enormous list or parataxis of copied citations and written notes.[21] If this material is regarded as constituting the objects of history, then those objects are given through their relation to the subject in the unfolding of time. And since both the object and the subject are given through forms of parataxis, then parataxis becomes the concept that can yield forms of temporality that determine the subject of history.

Parataxis, as the refusal to give anything up, has at least two conceptual aspects: First, to the extent that the parataxis of notes aspires to present a specific place (Paris) in a specific period (nineteenth century), what the refusal announces is the totality of everything that makes up that specificity. Yet this totality was to remain incomplete. A single specific moment is impossible to grasp in its totality, let alone the "complete specificity" of a whole era. The second conceptual aspect is to be discerned in the criterion for collection: the *materialist* historiography. To the extent that materialism, as understood by Benjamin, is a transformative critique, a writing in which the material itself unfolds toward a future happiness, historiography has a "*weak* messianic power" (Thesis II). The past is indexed to something incomplete, the future. Yet this indexing depends on completeness as the past without which the incomplete future is inconceivable. Thus, the two aspects of parataxis show that the subject of history—the historian who writes the history and the subjects for whom the history is written—can only be given through this process of destruction whereby a complete specificity is made incomplete and an incomplete infinity is made complete. The interplay between completeness and incompleteness introduced by parataxis yields forms of temporality that are in each case disruptive.

This disruption is the manner in which the complete gives itself up to the incomplete, and vice versa.

To introduce the notions or concepts of completeness and incompleteness in historiography is to view the writing of history through the prism of universal history. "Universal history" is not an arbitrary choice of term. There are two reasons why universal history is crucial. First, universal history at its most basic introduces the issue of a comprehensive inventory of the course of history. Universal history is a form of list making, the writing down of parataxis. The list has a vital connection to a philosophy of language and hence to narrative, as well as to the condition of the possibility of knowledge. This can be demonstrated with a brief look at list making. On the one hand, from the perspective of the development of different narrative forms, it is important that the earliest examples of different genres use lists in crucial ways: thus, Homer in his epic poem of the Trojan War is not frugal with space in recording each city's contribution to the Greek army or the items on Achilles' shield; and Herodotus in his *Histories* provides detailed inventories of the armies in the Persian wars and of what he saw in his travels; and it should not be forgotten that the earliest European script that has been deciphered, the Minoan Linear II, has been preserved as clay tablets recording the goods produced and stored at the Cretan palaces. The fact that decisively different narrative forms use the same apparatus only proves, as Longinus recognized, that the list is a fertile topos for stylistics to turn into a philosophy of language thereby addressing both the human and the object.[22] On the other hand, the thinkers of the modern era were equally aware of this: Montaigne's use of the list as the only way to record his own experience is a telling example, even if somewhat timid compared with the compulsive list making of a Rabelais or the lists that make up La Popelinière's "perfect history."[23] It is not a coincidence that Foucault starts his history of "words and things" from the seventeenth century to the nineteenth by expounding on the way that a list records not only the objects perceived along with reflection on these objects but also the *épistème* that is sedimented between the individual listed items and that which constitutes the order, or the grammar, of the list.[24] The issues of narrative, subjectivity, and the epistemological status of objects coalesce in the notion of the list so that their relation to history can be examined.[25]

The second reason that universal history is crucial is derived from Benjamin's writings. It is not only that the huge "list" known as *The Arcades Project* can be viewed as a type of universal history. In addition, "universal history" is a term employed by Benjamin himself. Although Benjamin refers to it only once in the Theses, that reference in Thesis XVII is of extreme importance for a discussion of the historiographic method. Further, if "universal history" is taken to mean a "completed history," then contrapuntal to this idea is that universal history is also messianic. "The authentic concept of universal history [*Universalgeschichte*] is a messianic concept."[26] This assertion is significant enough for Benjamin to jot down a number of times in the preparatory notes for the Theses, for instance: "Only in the messianic realm does a universal history exist."[27] Universal history, as the term around which completeness and incompleteness entwine and unfold, is a necessary condition of Benjaminian history. However, it is not a sufficient condition of history. The stress in the last citation from the preparatory notes is on the "only": universal history can be actualized *only* with the coming of a Messiah, on Judgment Day. Moreover, Benjamin warns: "Universal history in the present-day sense is never more than a kind of Esperanto. (It expresses the hope of the human race no more effectively than the name of that universal language)."[28] The utopian vision of universal history in the "present-day sense"—a qualification that will be shown to be of significance for Benjamin—is nothing but wishful daydreaming. If humanity could ever think of pinning its hopes on a universal language such as Esperanto, the historical actuality in which Benjamin was writing the Theses (Nazism, the Stalin pact, etc.) would beg to differ.

Yet, if hope and its language—or the language of hope, the *spero* in the Esperanto—are halted by a pervasive impossibility, Benjamin can still insist that such an impossibility is annexed to a possibility. It is a regulative impossibility. This impossibility could be made productive, so long as it remained regulative. In other words, the aporia about the insufficient necessity of parataxis and messianic temporality for history may yet provide a methodological reorientation or reversal. After all, as the essay on *The Elective Affinities* affirms, hope is for the hopeless, and the hopeless in Benjamin's notion of historiography are the oppressed, in whose name the history that insists on recording the minor detail is constructed. The hopeless are the subjects of written history. The reversal, then, that will reconfigure universal history has to be performed by/through the subject of history. Yet the hapless historian who undertakes the enormous collecting task of a *Passagenarbeit* is no less hopeless. In unfolding the notion of the subject of history, the historian will prove at the end to be as important as the oppressed of the past—although what is ultimately of the most importance is the way that the subjects of written history are related to the figure of the historian. What has to be avoided is placing the oppressed and the historian in a hierarchical structure, that is, to pit them against each other in a power struggle. Such a struggle will inevitably end by privileging either the chess player or the automaton, thus reverting to forms of presence. Conversely, the doppelgänger's effective presence will be manifest in the way that interruption figures as, as well as configures, the automaton—that is, the way that subjectivity, temporality, and historiography are not reduced to forms of subjection or *hypotaxis*.

| | |

To avoid such a power struggle, it is important that the two notions of the historical subject are clearly delineated. Only then would it be possible at the end to indicate what kind of struggle they avoid and what the nature of their alliance is—their complicity. For the moment, the investigation should proceed with the oppressed by asking the question: Who are the oppressed? Who are the hopeless? An answer will reveal that according to Benjamin there is no one identifiable group of people that can be called the oppressed. The question leads to the realization that a philosophy of time is needed. Temporality will yield the historiographic method. Yet this method will require the reshaping of the question: How are the hopeless to figure in a historical narrative? The latter question will lead back to the historian. It will be through the figure of the historian that subjection or hypotaxis will be reconfigured in order to allow for a different notion of community—moreover, a community that is not reducible to the sum of its individual members. Thus, with the destruction of the individual, the doppelgänger will come to the fore.

It may appear self-evident who the oppressed have been. To assume that there is an obvious way of identifying the oppressed and the hopeless, namely as those who have suffered injustice, "the slain [who] are really slain," as Horkheimer put it in a letter of March 1937, would be to miss the crux of Benjamin's thought.[29] When Benjamin transcribed Horkheimer's letter in Konvolut N of the *Arcades*, he appended the corrective that history is not merely science but also a remembrance (*Eingedenken*) that can modify the "facts" of science. "Remembrance can make the incomplete (happiness) into something complete, and the complete (suffering) into something incomplete."[30] Historiography then identifies suffering as the realm of particularity that tends to be viewed as completed. However, this suffering cannot be grasped in toto and thus always remains incomplete. At the same time, the promise of happiness that the oppressed hope to have in the future remains incomplete, since the future cannot be foreclosed; it is always open to possibilities. Yet these possibilities are always already circumscribed by the past, they are dependent on the past and thus complete. This chiasmus between completeness and incompleteness unfolds in remembrance (*Eingedenken*) and, in Benjamin's sense, yields history. Thus, at the heart of history, at the chiasmus of *Eingedenken*, there is an aporia: the hopeless and the oppressed are not merely discovered in the past—they also solicit the discovering of that past. History does not exist without them, no less than that they do not exist without history. This twofold movement is crucial. The response offered to Horkheimer makes it clear that the hopeless and oppressed are not to be discovered directly in a past, "historical" occurrence; rather, they are to be determined by the chiasmus. And the chiasmus is due to the effective presence of the doppelgänger, which eschews the representation of the subject other than as the relationality of its unfolding.

Benjamin's contention is not that the oppressed are in some sense unreal, a kind of simulacrum marching forward from a bygone time. If anything, his point is the opposite. The reality of hopelessness has to be secured through a conception of time that does justice to such a reality. There is a negative part to Benjamin's assertion, when he denies that history is science. This is the rejection of historicism. Although the attack on historicism permeates Benjamin's thought on history, from the *Arcades* to the *Theses on history*, to several published works of the same period such as the Fuchs essay, as well as the preparatory notes for the *Theses*—although, then, the assault on historicism is unrelenting, historicism remains a term never adequately defined by Benjamin. Historicism would indicate at least three distinguishable conceptions of history. First, there is teleological history, which asserts that enlightened man will head toward a cosmopolitan ideal, as Kant argues, or which poses freedom as an end whose attainment in the present would signal history's end, according to Hegel. Second, historicism also includes the attempts to identify independent historical disciplines: a history of art, a history of politics, of economy, of technology, and so on. The problem with autonomous historical inquiries is that they either presuppose a rupture between that discipline and society or they extrapolate inadequate relations between the two, as for instance the psychologism of the Warburg school.[31] Third, historicism includes the practice of adding up facts, while insisting in Rankeian fashion on the self-evidence of these facts—what Benjamin calls "the strongest narcotic of the century."[32] What these different types of historicism have in common is a conception of time as continuous. They presuppose a linear chronological development that is always dependent on empathy with the rulers or the victorious who determine that linearity. Conversely, historical materialism has to blast apart the historical continuum. The doppelgänger cannot tolerate a temporality constituted by the aggregate of discrete moments. Time has to come to a standstill. The dialectical image activates the "emergency brakes" of history. Therefore, who the hopeless are cannot be secured by their being conceived as originating from within a chronological continuum. This would merely be tautological, trying to secure history from within history itself. To say that ultimately "the slain are really slain" is nothing other than reverting to historicism.

Had Horkheimer been presented with the problem of who the hopeless are in this way, he might have retorted that the tautology cuts both ways: Does not dialectical rigor demand that continuity and discontinuity, as its opposite, mutate into each other? Therefore, Benjamin himself would not overcome historicism if he merely imposed a different form—discontinuity—on the already existent material. This line of argument misconstrues Benjamin's rejection of the presupposition of a temporal continuum. The call to blast apart the historical continuum presupposed by historicism is not a call to hypostatize discontinuity. Discontinuity cannot be equated with a generic narrative that identifies a specific group of people as hopeless. This would not make sense, if, as already intimated, the hopeless both make history and are made by it. Discontinuity is not content. History is not self-legitimating. There is no narrative particular to history.[33] There is no narrative particular to the oppressed. Thus, when Benjamin refers to montage in relation to the writing of the *Arcades*, montage is not at all a stylistic device but a methodological procedure.[34] And, when Benjamin talks about historiography in a positive manner, he does not refer to the narration of history, but to its construction: "History is the subject of a construction." The sentence goes on to assert that the site of this construction is filled with "now-time" (*Jetztzeit*).[35] What underlies historiography is an operation of temporal discontinuity. Thus, the philosophy of history has turned into a philosophy of time. This is the inevitable conclusion if discontinuity is not to be reduced to content and if history and historiography are not to be locked in a vicious circle. Further, viewing discontinuity as a temporal category, rather than merely a stylistic mannerism, accords with the development of Benjamin's thought. As

Andrew Benjamin has shown in tracing the meaning of the caesura in Walter Benjamin's work—the caesura in the early critical writings, such as the dissertation and the Goethe essay—is that which stages the contact between particular and absolute. But this interruption works on a formal level and it can be reduced neither to content nor to something transcendental that legitimates that content. The relationality of the elements of this structure makes possible judgments about the truth content (*Wahrheitsgehalt*) of the artwork. The notion of temporal discontinuity in Benjamin's thinking on history transposes the formal structure of the caesura from art to time. Time as the Absolute is "that which allows for interruption; but equally what is evidenced by that interruption."[36]

The extrapolation of the Absolute in relation to time does not only hark back to Benjamin's early writing. It also recalls the extrapolation earlier of the oppressed in relation to history. With the oppressed it was shown that a chiasmus takes place between history and those for whom history is written. The temporal caesura repeats the chiasmic structure. The fullness of time makes incompletion possible, but it is also made by incompleteness. This chiasmus does *not* indicate that the complete and the incomplete, the particular and the absolute, the oppressed and messianic temporality are the same thing. Rather, the point is that the terms of those conjunctions are given within the same structure that has arisen out of Benjamin's philosophy of time. Thus, what is repeated is not solely the complete in the incomplete, and so on, as if they were identical. What is repeated is the constructive principle of history. The paratactically presented information in historiography and the messianic temporality can only be necessary conditions of history. The additional constructive principle indicates that they have a structural connection. This is what makes possible the mutual transformability of the complete and the incomplete, as Benjamin wrote in reply to Horkheimer. It makes possible the little gate of particularity "through which the messiah might enter" every second now.[37] In other words, it is the structural arrangement that makes particularity and the Absolute consupponible and codeterminable. The messiah is not a religious concept; rather, the messiah is the regulative impossibility that allows for interruption as the temporality that pertains to history.

At this juncture, nothing more can be said about who the hopeless are, other than that they are whoever occupies the nexus of particularity in the formal structure of the constructive principle of history. This formulation already discloses at least three points: First, the subjectivity of the hopeless does not conform to historicism's forms of selfhood, such as its identification with a *Geist* or with an autonomous individual I. Second, if the early Benjamin's structural argument about criticism is indeed transportable to the later philosophy of time, then the hopeless will occupy a position akin to that of the material content; and to the extent that the material content is always in a process of ruination, the same process of disintegration of subjectivity will be expected to take place in history.[38] Simultaneously, and this is the third point, specifying the particularity of subjectivity as other than a "fact" of historicism discloses the limit of the question "Who are the hopeless?" For it can provide an answer only in the negative. A positive articulation requires the hopeless to figure in a different question: "How are they to be presented?" This in effect asks for the way that the subject figures in, as well as configures, the chiasmic relations between the complete and the incomplete. In other words, what sort of figure of the subject can make possible Benjamin's philosophy of time? What is the nature of this subjective act that allows for figuration? How does the doppelgänger figure?

Answering these questions requires to focus on the historian and the methodology of historiography. The crucial passage in this respect is Thesis XVII. This Thesis is important enough to be quoted in full here, even though only the first half will be treated immediately, and the other half later:

> Historicism rightly culminates [*gipfelt*] in universal history. It may be that materialist historiography stands out [*sich abhebt*] in method more clearly against universal history than against any other kind. Universal history has no theoretical armature. Its technique [*Verfahren*] is additive: it musters the mass of facts in order to fill the homogeneous and empty time. Materialist historiography, in contrast, is based on a constructive principle. Thinking involves not only the movement of thoughts, but their arrest [*Stillstellung*] as well. Where thinking suddenly comes to a stop in a constellation saturated with tensions, it gives that constellation a shock, through which thinking crystallizes itself into a monad. The historical materialist approaches a historical object only where it confronts him as a monad. In this structure he recognizes the sign of a messianic arrest of happening [*Stillstellung des Geschehens*], or to put it differently, a revolutionary chance in the fight for the oppressed past. He perceives the monad in order to

blast a specific era out of the course of history [*Verlauf der Geschichte*]; thus he blasts a specific life out of the era, a specific work out of the lifework. The product of his technique [*der Ertrag seines Verfahrens*] is that the lifework is both preserved and sublated [*aufbewahrt ist und aufgehoben*] in the work, the era *in* the lifework, and the entire course of history [*der gesamte Geschichtsverlauf*] *in* the era. The nourishing fruit of what is historically understood contains time in its *interior* as a precious but tasteless seed.³⁹

On the one hand, Thesis XVII offers a formulation about the method of historiography. There are two techniques contrasted, universal history and materialist historiography. On the other hand, in order to expand on the latter, Benjamin refers to the historian. The materialist historian is based on a constructive principle. Thus, subjectivity is implicated in method. The latter point will be left unattended for the time being.

Approaching technique entails paying attention to the complexities of this passage. And a complexity emerges from the very beginning in the contrast between materialist historiography and universal history. For if "the *entire* course of history" is something that can be methodologically entertained, as Benjamin suggests in the penultimate sentence, then what is it that really separates it from universal history, taken to mean precisely the aim of representing the entirety of "acts"? The problem will not be solved easily with reference to the precious seed, time. For the very next thesis states that messianic or now-time "comprises the entire history of mankind in a tremendous abbreviation."⁴⁰ Prima facie a moment that comprises "the entire history of mankind" may not appear all that different from the project of a universal history, namely to add up all the "facts." Thesis XVII may indicate why elsewhere Benjamin relates universal history to the messianic.⁴¹ But universal history is thereby, if anything, even more elusive. A closer look at the term "universal history" is called for, yet it should be kept in mind that Thesis XVII explicitly addresses the historiographic method. "Universal history" will become a fruitful concept only if it is viewed in relation to writing and thus in connection to narrativity. This is not to say that there is a specific kind of historical narrative—this has been rejected already. There still is, nonetheless, a method and a technique of writing history.

The issue of what can be recorded in written history—the historical object in general, which includes the oppressed—revolves around the notion of universal history. The reason is that universal history can present most clearly the difference in technique between historical materialism and historicism. What does Benjamin mean with the term "universal history"? The assertion in Thesis XVII that historicism culminates in universal history is not a straightforward identification of historicism and universal history. If the metaphors in the verbs of the first two sentences are heeded, then what is conjured is an image of vertical mobility. Universal history is at the summit (*der Gipfel*) of historicism.[42] And materialist historiography only rises (*heben*) even higher. Thus, universal history is not only the meridian of historicism but also a median between historicism and materialism. Further, the twist in Benjamin's logic has it that universal history as messianic concomitantly functions as a meridian of materialism. The middle point between historicism and historical materialism is, simultaneously, the highest point of each.[43] The fact that the term "universal history" is used only once in the Theses—in Thesis XVII—makes it all the more enticing, given that Benjamin refers to it consistently in the preparatory notes. There, Benjamin strategically draws a qualitative distinction between the "present-day sense" of universal history and a more authentic sense. After repeating the call for the "destructive energies" of materialism to blast apart the temporal continuum, Benjamin observes that this would serve as the precondition to attack "the three most important positions of historicism." Benjamin continues by immediately identifying universal history as the first such position: "The first attack must be aimed at the idea of universal history. Now that the nature of peoples is obscured by their current structural features as much as by their current structural relations to one another, the notion that the history of humanity is composed of peoples is a mere refuge of intellectual laziness."[44] Universal history is unproblematically a historicist category only if the completeness alluded to in it is meant to signify the sum of people. In other words, only the history that sees the victors as those who were really victorious and the slain as those who were "really slain."

Yet this is not the whole story; Benjamin immediately opens a qualifying parenthesis: "(The idea of a universal history stands and falls with the idea of a universal language. As long as the latter had a basis—whether in theology, as in the Middle Ages, or in logic, as more recently in Leibniz—universal history was not wholly inconceivable. By contrast, universal history as practiced since the nineteenth century can never have been more than a kind of Esperanto.)"[45] The universal history of historicism—the universal history in the "present-day sense"—is that of the nineteenth-century positivism. Conversely, universal history is still relevant to a Leibnizian monadology, a monadology reconfigured in Benjamin's philosophy of time as the monad or the dialectical image that, according to Thesis XVII, crystallizes thinking in a constellation in order to make it possible for the historian to approach the object.[46] The distinction, then, between the two notions of universal history hinges on the way that the historian presents an entire record of objects. The question of how the subject of history is presented can be reformulated as how the subjectivity of the historian is to be construed in relation to the writing of the historical object. Universal history coalesces three terms—the subject, the narrative, and the historical object—under the rubric of completeness. The endeavor to record the "entire course of history" recalls what was called at the beginning the paratactic presentation of the specific. A parataxis of "things" is by definition the most emphatic attempt to present those things in their entirety. Such an inventory is a necessity for history. Lists may appear to be simple grammatical structures to the extent that they repeat the same part of speech. This simplicity is deceptive.

The historicist fault is to be deceived by this simple grammar. "Historicism contents itself with establishing a causal nexus among various moments in history."[47] The story that this causal connecting presents is precisely an adding up of facts, an unreflective universal history. The positivist historiographic methodology can be likened to a vast collection of index cards, each card representing a "fact." The historian merely arranges the cards in a way that "makes sense" using the causal methodology of the natural sciences.[48] Such a historian can never question the rhetorical structure of the narrative, because its language is all along assumed to be referential—to be scientific. But this is nothing but the wishful thinking of an Esperanto. Just as positivism's "facts" rely on a metaphysics that pronounces an unproblematic relation between those facts and their interpolations, so also Esperanto relies on a simplified grammar that assumes the unproblematic relation between the name and its referent. And, just as positivism was blind to the grammar of its metaphysics, so was Esperanto blind to the metaphysics of its grammar. This configuration of language's formal properties vis-à-vis its referential power, as well as the metaphysics underlying it, prescribes a narrative dogmatism. It presupposes a grammar that makes language purely referential.

This corresponds to the grammar of the pure language that Benjamin extrapolated as early as 1916 in "On Language as Such and the Language of Man." It is the recognition from within a philosophy of language that universal history not only presupposes a pre-Babel language in which every sentence can be translated, but moreover "that it is that language itself."⁴⁹ A pure concept of universal history requires a pure language. In other words, it requires a narrative devoid of all ambiguity and essentially self-referential. In "On Language as Such" Benjamin identified the essential property of such a language. It is "both creative and the finished creation; it is word and name."⁵⁰ Thus, it is a completely self-enclosed language, the completed language of God that Benjamin distinguishes sharply from the human language of names. Just as a pure language is nonhuman, so also a completely self-referential narrative is impossible for the historian. To the extent that this grammar is presupposed in a way that makes an ontological commitment, it can posit only itself. Starting from the infinity of pure language, it is impossible to reach the particularity of the naming of human language. In this sense, the grammar of positivism turns out to be no grammar at all, but merely a solipsistic onomatopoeia. The movement from the infinite to the finite is always curtailed, never fulfilled. No wonder that the "second fortified position of historicism," which Benjamin attends to straight after the parenthesis that distinguishes between nineteenth-century universal history and the authentic universal history, is "the idea that history is something that can be narrated [*sich erzählen lasse*]."⁵¹ There is no technique of presenting a linear narrative that will lay a claim to present the facts as they really are, no matter how many facts are enumerated. For these facts, derived as they are from an infinite grammar, will always remain incomplete. Both a referential foundation for a philosophy of language and a generic determination of historiography presuppose presence. Conversely, because of the effective presence of the doppelgänger, such a presupposition is not allowed in Benjamin's understanding of subjectivity. Thus, for Benjamin's historian, there can never be an essentially historical narrative.

This is not to say that historiography is impossible. Rather, historiography is to be viewed from the vantage point of a philosophy of time. If incompleteness and infinity are to be retained, then they cannot be constructed like positivism's pure language. Only then will emerge the qualitative difference between "present-day" universal history and universal history as a possibility—or at least as that notion of history that allows for a conception of the possibility of history. For a genuine historiography, Benjamin insists that time cannot be conceived as an accumulation of constitutive moments. Only by overcoming the historical continuum will the grammar of time assume a regulative function. After having singled out the universal history of positivism as the first historicist position to be attacked, Benjamin continues his attack on the second bastion of historicism by elaborating on its narrative form: "In a materialist investigation, the epic moment will always be blown apart in the process of construction."[52] Just like linear time, so also the linear narrative must be blasted apart. The mention of epic narrative, as it comes immediately after Benjamin's discussion of universal history, points to the Leskov essay. "The Storyteller" can be read as an argument about how the temporality of storytelling (*Erzählung*) can produce a notion of particularity as the temporal ground of the infinite.[53] Storytelling presupposes a rich notion of experience, attainable through a slow-paced life. Thus, the audience can achieve the ultimate state of relaxation, that is boredom, so that the story can be retained in memory (*Gedächtnis*). Immediacy also figures as the literal presence of the narrator, whose purpose is to provide practical advice and counsel. The righteous man, as the subject who has the know-how and moral rectitude, is the subject to which storytelling aspires. With death, the immediacy of the telling of a story is referred to the "idea of eternity."[54] Everything that the storyteller can offer refers to this eternity. In which case, "death is the sanction of everything that the storyteller can tell."[55] The movement of storytelling is from the immediate to the infinite. Benjamin illustrates this movement—the technique of storytelling—with the example of a list.

The example, which comes from a story by Hebel titled "Unexpected Reunion," is concerned to show how parataxis—the writing of the historical object—can be allowed to figure in historiography. The story describes the death of a young girl's betrothed in a mine collapse and the subsequent rediscovery of his corpse many years later. What catches Benjamin's attention is the paragraph that bridges the gap between the two distant times. This paragraph is the parataxis of historical events: "In the meantime the city of Lisbon was destroyed in an earthquake, and the Seven Years War came and went, and Emperor Francis I died." and so on.[56] In this list, death is present in every turn of phrase. In the first paragraph of the section that follows, section 12, Benjamin elaborates on the meaning that death assumes in the narrative form of storytelling. This is conducted in terms of historiography, and in such a way that it points directly to the Theses:

> An examination of a given epic form is concerned with the relationship of this form to historiography. . . . The chronicler is the history-

teller [*Geschichts-Erzähler*]. If we think back to the passage from Hebel, which has the tone of a chronicle throughout, it will take no effort to gauge the difference between one who writes history (the historian) and one who narrates it (the chronicler). The historian's task is to *explain* in one way or another the events with which he deals; under no circumstances can he content himself with simply displaying them as models of the course of the world [*Weltlaufs*]. But this is precisely what the chronicler does, especially in his classical avatars, the chroniclers of the Middle Ages, the precursors of today's history. By basing their historical tales [*Geschichtserzählungen*] on a divine—and inscrutable—plan of salvation, at the very outset they have lifted the burden of demonstrable explanation from their shoulders. Its place is taken by interpretation, which is concerned not with an accurate concatenation of definitive events [*Verkettung von bestimmten Ereignissen*], but with the way these are embedded in the great inscrutable course of the world.[57]

The linear narrative of the epic is intricately connected to historiography. But this is not to say that every narrative is properly historical. However, even if the chronicle is not history, nonetheless it still aspires to history in a manner that presents its objects as inscrutable. What this manner precludes is a conception of historiography as a chain of independent events—there is no "concatenation of definitive events," that is, there is no causal narration in the manner practiced by positivism. Such a collection of independent facts can never be fitted into "the great inscrutable course of the world." In contrast to positivism, storytelling makes possible a different form of infinity, and hence a different notion of totality. The difference arises from the immediacy of the presence of the storyteller and the rich experience of storytelling. This is an experience of particularity, an immediate specificity. Whereas the pure language of positivism presupposed an infinite and self-referential grammar, the storyteller starts with the immediacy of the multicolored (*bunte*) worldview.[58] And, whereas positivism is trapped in that infinite grammar, the storyteller, because he starts with particularity, still has access to infinitude. This is Benjamin's point when he evokes the chronicler in Thesis III: "The chronicler who narrates events without distinguishing between major and minor ones acts in accord with the following truth: nothing that has ever happened should be regarded as lost to history. Of course, only a redeemed mankind is granted the fullness [*vollauf*] of its past—which is to say, only for a redeemed mankind has its past become citable in all its moments."[59] The demand of universal history is clear in the chronicle: nothing is to be lost for history. The chronicler can entertain this refusal to let the thing disappear, because his narrative—the *Geschichtserzählung*—is one of immediacy. The chronicle then, in the language of Thesis XVII, stands at the summit of materialist historiography.

Pointing to the road to infinitude from the standpoint of finitude is both the strength of storytelling and the chronicle, and the reason that they are not genuine history. For they pose a bad notion of infinitude. Storytelling has no definite end. In the manner of Scheherazade, the end of a story is only the beginning of a new one.[60] Equally, the chronicle's notion of totality is an impossible one: it is the totality of the Judgment Day (*der jüngste Tag*).[61] The last day is also the first (*jüngste*), and thus completion gives way to incompletion in a movement of eternal return. If the chronicler makes possible the compilation of a list and thus raises the possibility of a record of the historical object and of a universal history, this remains outside the possibilities of historiography. The summit that the chronicle represents is separated from the mountain of historical materialism as if by a bed of clouds. The clouds may always be moving and the demarcation between the two may never be a fixed line. But it is a demarcation nevertheless, because for the materialist that summit is always impossible to scrutinize through the clouds—it is inscrutable. The value of the storytelling narrative is that, despite its impossibility, it still moves history to a region where possibility becomes an issue. This is the region of the particular. Storytelling departs from the particular. Thus, its technique makes immediacy possible. The failure of storytelling only shows that potentiality alone is not enough for Benjamin to guarantee historiography. What is also needed is an act—the very act that the chronicler lacks because he refuses to *distinguish* between events. This is the act of explaining, which, according to the Leskov essay, distinguishes the historian from the chronicler.

Earlier in "The Storyteller," in section 7, Benjamin uses another example that not only includes death and parataxis but also prefigures his distinction between the historian and the storyteller. This story from Herodotus tells of the Egyptian king Psammenitus, who has been defeated in battle, lost his kingdom and, to add insult to injury, he is made to attend the victors' triumphal procession. Psammenitus remains unmoved at his daughter and son passing by—he may not even have recognized them since he stood with "his eyes fixed to the ground."[62] But he was deeply moved at the sight of his old manservant, which prompted him to beat his head and wail. Herodotus, Benjamin argues, is a real storyteller because of the complete lack of explanation. The story is presented in a dry manner, and does not "expend itself"—it reaches a point of incompletion from which it will not budge. Nevertheless Benjamin moves on by offering four different explanations:

> Montaigne referred to this Egyptian king and asked himself why he mourned only when he caught sight of his servant. Montaigne answers: "Since he was already over-full of grief, it took only the smallest increase for it to burst through the dams." Thus Montaigne. But one could also say: "The king is not moved by the fate of those of royal blood, for it is his own fate." Or: "We are moved by much on the stage that does not move us in real life; to the king, this servant is only an actor." Or: "Great grief is pent up and breaks forth only with relaxation; seeing this servant was the relaxation."[63]

These explanations are acts of judgment. The historian differs from the chronicler in that he makes judgments. But here judgment is not understood as any arbitrary ascription of value on a given object. Rather, judgement is the act that intervenes in what is possible. The judgment halts the infinity of potentiality, it intervenes in the perpetual pendulum of completeness and incompleteness. More emphatically, it is the interruption of the movement between infinite and finite.

| | |

Interruption is the act of the technique of materialist historiography and that which makes possible a conception of the infinite and the finite, of the complete and the incomplete. Also, as already intimated, the doppelgänger figures through the operation of the interruption. However, if interruption is also to be linked to judgment, the parataxis of judgments with which Benjamin responds to Herodotus' story does not seem to fix the problem of a bad infinity. For they may appear as individual judgments, pointing toward a notion of infinity as an aggregate of similar judgments—a dialogism between independent and individual "points of view." However, infinity and the finite have to be given by temporality itself. Therefore, time will have to operate in judgment. The time inscribed in the parataxis of judgments in section VII of "The Storyteller" can be presented only when it is distinguished from the temporality of each judgment on its own. The doppelgänger does not figure through a single judgment propagated by a single individual. Rather, the figuration is the enactment of the relationality—the parataxis—set in motion by the temporality of each judgment. Because of the operative presence of the doppelgänger, there is a temporality that is not reducible to either of each of the individual judgments. Rather, the temporality of the doppelgänger arises as the cooperation of the different temporal structures of each judgment—or, more precisely, by what is left out from the sum of those temporalities. The temporalities of the individual judgments indicate a supplementary and interruptive temporality that is the temporality proper to judgment and to the doppelgänger.

The first judgment, which Benjamin copies from Montaigne, emphatically asserts the immediacy of experience. It was at the point that the king was filled up with grief that he had a visceral reaction—as if his body could not help it. This is the temporality of specificity. Conversely, the invocation of fate in the second judgment installs a temporality that eschews specificity, the temporality that knows only of the decisions of the gods and effaces human freedom and ethical responsibility. The image of the world as a theater in the third explanation partly repeats the temporality of fate: the actors act according to a script that cannot be altered. However, here the exclusion of the king from the infinite play on the stage makes it possible that the king could stop being indifferent at the drama and react. The king's reaction is provoked by the eternity of the stage action. The final explanation, with its proverbial nature, has the structure of a storytelling narrative: it offers wisdom. Thus it has the temporality of an immediacy that is directed toward an eternity. None of these construals of time offers a genuine possibility of interruption, since none can offer an interruption of the relation between the infinite and the finite that does not privilege one of the two terms.

The argument here is that for Benjamin none of these judgments on their own in the parataxis could have been a genuine judgment. The possibility of judgment in this passage depends entirely on the figure of the king Psammenitus and the way that he intervenes—interrupts—the parataxis of judgments. As already noted, in Benjamin's retelling of the story, the king stood with "his eyes fixed to the ground" during the parade, hardly noticing his own children. To this parataxis—for parataxis in Greek means precisely the placing side by side, like a parade—of individual catastrophes the king remains impervious, like the bored and distracted spectator of a play. His eyes look at his son, but there is hardly a recognition. Until, that is, he acts himself. Until the moment that his eyes are raised and stop on an image. That this moment is precisely when his old manservant walks in front of him is fortuitous—although one might contend, even more emphatically, that it is entirely gratuitous. All that matters is not what the king sees but how he sees: he recognizes in a frozen moment, in an instant. The angel of history may fix his gaze on the entire course of humankind's catastrophes, but the gaze of the subject is not all-encompassing; rather, it is instantaneous, a rapid adjustment of the eyes. This instant already transports him from the auditorium where he previously sat indifferent into the center stage of the narration where he has to assume his responsibility. This fixing of the eye, the gaze directed to the image of the oppressed confronting him—this hardly perceptible adjustment whose condition of possibility has been parataxis—is all that was missing for a Benjaminian judgment to be made possible.

It is very important that Benjamin has changed Herodotus' story in a crucial respect. While Benjamin claims that Herodotus offers no explanation, in fact paragraph 14 of book 3 concludes with the Persian king sending a messenger to inquire why Psammenitus cried over the old man but not over his own children. Herodotus records Psammenitus' answer: "My private grief [*oikeia*] was too great for weeping; but the misfortune of my companion [*hetairou*] called for tears."[64] Recognition, and hence judgment, can take place only when the other is an *hetairos*, someone who is distinguished from the self, yet also someone who belongs in a community with the self. Judgment is not merely a private affair—it is not an opinion about one's own "house" (*ta oikia*). Rather, judgment takes place on the communal, and hence on the political, space. Just as judgment is distinguished from private opinion, on the same grounds recognition is distinguished from mere looking: recognition involves the political. In recognition, self and other become complicit. In this instant of judgment, the king recognizes in the manner that the historian judges. His tears are the historian's judgment. The complicity that is established between the king and his *hetairon* is the complicity that also pertains between the historian and King Psammenitus at that moment.

The act of judgment is the act whereby a spectator becomes simultaneously an actor. The historian makes, and is also made by, the object of history. This chiasmus corresponds to the chiasmus identified earlier in pursuing the question of who the subject of history is. It will be recalled that then it was shown that the hopeless make and are made by history; and also that time, as the absolute, creates and is created by the interruption of the temporal continuum. These chiastic relations were shown to be the structural principle of historiography. The correspondence of Psammenitus' gaze to the earlier chiasmoi discloses the essential quality of the principle of historiography: it is the act of judgment. The most general answer as to how the subject figures in history is: through this instantaneous act, the act that is performed in such a way that the parataxis is recognized. If it is recognized *as* parataxis, then the historian's gaze cannot be fixed on the whole parade of catastrophes, but it has to concentrate on the "anonymous" old man.⁶⁵ Yet the old man has to be recognized as a paratactic object, that is, as belonging to the structure that unravels the relation between completeness and incompleteness to the infinity of time.

| | |

If this infinity of time is consistently pursued, then the conclusion can only be that a subjective judgment is no longer tenable. It is at this point that the effective presence of the doppelgänger resonates in Benjamin's theory of historiography. The impossibility of subjective judgment means that a subject's judgment can never attain a self-consistent truth. The subjective act is never occlusive. No matter how many individual acts of judgment are possible, they can only be secondary to the possibility of judging as such. This signals the destruction of the subject. The subject cannot fix itself on a stable position from which to pronounce a judgment. The act of judgment destroys the singular individual, because the subject is now dissolved into the I *and* the *hetairon*, the I and the object that looks back at it forming a community that is complicit in judging. The standstill of this judgment is not that of standing on a fixed point. It is, rather, a dispersal, which is crucial to the constructive methodology of materialist historiography, as it is described in Thesis XVII. It will be recalled that Thesis XVII starts with a vertical movement between historicism, universal history, and materialist historiography. The ascent (*abheben*) from historicism to materialism is mediated by universal history. However, by performing a kind of leap, universal history in the form of the chronicle has been shown also to be at the summit of materialism. Benjamin insists in Thesis XVII that this up-and-down movement is not enough: "Thinking involves not only the movement of thoughts, but their arrest [*Stillstellung*] as well." But this *Stillstellung* is not something exhausted within the figure of the historian:

> He [the materialist historian] perceives the monad in order to blast a specific era out of the course of history; thus he blasts a specific life out of the era, a specific work out of the lifework. The product of his technique is that the lifework is both preserved and sublated [*aufgehoben ist*] *in* the work, the era *in* the lifework, and the entire course of history *in* the era.

The historian perceives the monad; he recognizes the historical object. But the product is not up to the historian on his own. Rather, the product is given through his *technique*. In the *aufheben* of Benjaminian sublation the *abheben* from historicism to universal history to historical materialism is halted by erasing the subject from the sublating. The individual I is no more, because historiography can methodologically entertain the "the entire course of history" only through the complicity of the historian with the hopeless. The process of sublation, in Benjamin's sense, is to disperse the historian in the *hetairon*, the *hetairon* in the historian's writing, and then both, as subject of written history, to history's infinite unfolding. Thus, with the operation of the doppelgänger's chiasmic relations, materialist historiography takes as its condition of possibility no longer a subject as individual—but rather the subject as doppelgänger.

This destruction of the subject does not mean that the practice of history does not matter. It does not say that the construction of history destroys the historian as such. Rather, it indicates that destruction is constitutive of historiography. There is no psychological communication between the historian and the historical object—no empathy that mediates their relation. The relation is given through time. On the one hand, this is a full time, one that allows for the entire course of history to parade before the historian; on the other hand, it is a now-time, the instant of recognition that concentrates on one object in the parataxis rupturing its relation to the whole of history. The subject is occupying the position at this point of tension between relationality and nonrelation, between the complete and the incomplete. The subject is given through its occupying. This is another way of saying that the question "who are the subjects of history?" is inadequate. The destruction of the subject demands that only the manner in which the subject acts—that is, only the judgment—can be questioned. And, thus, it is a productive destruction, the condition of the possibility of the historical construction. What is destroyed is history as pure immediacy, understood either as specificity or as a transcendental other. What is constructed is a political community and the possibility of a materialist historiography as political praxis. In the dialectical reversibility between completeness and incompleteness, the finite and the infinite, "politics attains primacy over history."[66] The destruction of the individual subject announces the political in the complicity established between the I and its *hetairon*. This complicity is derived from the effective presence—the figuration—of the doppelgänger.

The Politics of the Doppelgänger

This complicity is captured in the image of the Turk from Thesis I. As shown at the beginning of this chapter, the automaton gives rise to the issue of subjection. Subjection will give a determinate ordering to what is inside and what is outside the automaton. However, such delimitation also de-limits itself—its own limits cannot be sustained and they break down. This happens because of the judgment's interruption—that is, through the interruption that announces the doppelgänger's setting the political in motion. To see how the interruption is acted out by the Turk, it is crucial to follow the movement of the relation between the chess player and the puppet. The parataxis of man and puppet precludes any sharp definition of one independent of the other. They can be independent only in their interdependency. Thus, what matters in the operation of the chess-playing automaton is not who controls the game of chess—the privileging of subjection of hypotaxis must be avoided.[67] Asking this question will inevitably conflate the movement of the pieces and the game itself. In relation to the movement of the pieces, what matters is the cooperation between the hidden chess player and the puppet. And in relation to the game itself, both the player and the puppet as independent entities are secondary compared to the move—the act—on the board. This board is the historian's writing page that, however, is not blank. The black and white pieces are already poised in a parataxis without which historiography is impossible. But historiography is equally impossible without the empty squares that form the space between the pieces. Those squares can be filled to infinity with different moves, but at any given moment each is occupied by a single piece, which is the product of a single move—a single judgment of the complicit man and puppet.

DISPLACEMENT: FIGURING THE COSMOPOLITAN IN ALASDAIR GRAY'S *POOR THINGS*

Alasdair Gray's novel *Poor Things* presents an image that repeats the relation between the different "parts" of the Turk from Walter Benjamin's Theses on history—the image of an entity divided between an inner mind and its outer mobile part. *Poor Things* is a complex novel that resists a straightforward synopsis. It is easier to start by describing it in terms of its structure: In an introduction, Gray announces the discovery of a nineteenth-century memoir detailing the life of young woman, named "Bella Baxter," and written by her husband. The narrator of this book suggests that the young woman was a surgical creation—a kind of Frankenstein creature.[68] This memoir is followed by a letter in which "Bella Baxter" vehemently decries the memoir of her husband as fanciful and denies that she was the product of surgical experimentation. *Poor Things* concludes with Gray's annotations to the previous two narratives.

The image of an entity divided between an inside and an outside is present in *Poor Things* because it relates the revitalization of a young lady's body. However, her original brain is replaced with that of the nine-month-old child in her womb. This *creature*, Bella Baxter, presents the subjugation of a body to a new brain—although, to the extent that the body carries of itself also a memory, it can also be argued that the new brain is subjugated to the old body. As has just been shown in relation to the Turk, in the cases of an actor whose actions are structured by the division between an intelligence inside and an outside mechanical body the doppelgänger prevents the determination of who is in control. The inside-outside problematic is also reflected in the structure of *Poor Things*. Gray claims in the "Introduction" that the main part of the book was discovered in a pile of refuse by the historian Michael Donnelly. The author of the discovered book was Archibald McCandless, who later married the revitalized woman. The found book was accompanied by a letter, in which "Bella Baxter" debunked the assertion that she was a creation, a scientific monstrosity. And, in an appendix of critical and historical notes, the editor tests the veracity of the divergent accounts by providing "factual evidence."[69] Thus, the structure of the novel itself sets in motion a variety of positions, all seeking to supersede the other, all claiming to be true. However, these claims to truth can never be secured by the extrapolation of a neat arrangement of the interior-exterior relations between the various narrators.[70] The parataxis of voices in the novel affirms the effective presence of the doppelgänger that eschews any clear chronological or causal ordering.

The question "Who is 'Bella Baxter'?" would seem to be crucial for *Poor Things*. If the novel is to be read as a detective narrative, then it describes the efforts to determine the identity of the person (or creature) who responds to the name "Bella Baxter."[71] Gray in the "Introduction" explains he had to become a kind of detective of historical facts about her identity. Furthermore, the work of a detective is crucial in chapter 22, when General Blessington appears to claim "Bella Baxter" as his disappeared wife. More generally, if a detective story solves a mystery through the arrangement—the parataxis—of the evidence in the correct chronological sequence, then this is precisely what all the various narrators in *Poor Things* are trying to do: namely, to reconstitute the identity of "Bella Baxter" by determining her past origins—the subjection (hypotaxis) of the identity by the past. Yet all their attempts are in vain. Even the editor's attempt, who in the final sentence is forced to admit that the age of the deceased "Bella Baxter" was either sixty-six or ninety-two, depending on whether an estimate was made of the brain or of the body.[72] Because of the doppelgänger's operative presence, the subjection to and through a chronology that determines the present by securing the past is made impossible. As soon as the subject is divided, bringing the doppelgänger into play, its parts cannot be subjected to a determinate ordering, and the subject is no longer amenable to a secure origin. On the contrary, the divisions multiply, the inside-outside ambiguities proliferate—they cannot be identified as a single, commanding division.[73]

There is a different way in which the detective work can be understood. *Poor Things* contains a portrait of "Bella Baxter" with the caption "Bella Caledonia."[74] Because of her representation as "Beautiful Scotland," the detective work would now have to concentrate on cultural and national origins manifest in the novel. Such detective work would have to unearth all the textual and extratextual references in *Poor Things*—that is, all those elements that make up the cultural and the political, or the public interface. This kind of origin also proves unstable. Just to offer one example: the idea of a discovered manuscript framed by an introduction and "historical sources" echoes Thomas Carlyle's *Sartor Resartus*.[75] However, Carlyle was the greatest exponent of Jean Paul in the English-speaking world, as well as his translator into English. Thus, if *Poor Things* can be said to originate from *Sartor Resartus*, the latter in its turn—but also, consequently the former—could be said to originate in the stylistic experimentations of Jean Paul, who first highlighted the doppelgänger in a footnote to the novel *Siebenkäs* and who offered the doppelgänger's philosophical exposition—through the figure of the "labouring demogorgon"—in the appendix to *Titan* titled *Clavis Fichtiana*, as mentioned earlier.[76] Therefore, a detective work searching for a single origin inevitably leads to multiple origins—an originariness of difference rather than uniqueness.

The solution to the mystery of who "Bella Baxter" is need not assume that the detective novel is its only, or even proper, genre. Maybe the origin is not to be found buried in the past; maybe instead the origin is to be discovered in the future. In which case *Poor Things* would be the story of the formation of the identity "Bella Baxter," a bildungsroman narrative. And "Bella Baxter" herself expresses twice loud and clear what she has become, namely, "a woman of the world."[77] Because of her claim to world citizenship, Bella will become a doctor in order to help, will advocate social change through the Fabian Society, and will publish a militant pamphlet. She will act in the name of personal as well as political freedom—even sexual freedom. "Here is my little Candle, God," says Bella to Godwin Baxter (the scientist who revitalized the body creating "Bella Baxter"—the sexual, the religious, and the scientific are never far apart) referring to McCandless (the author of the found book and her future husband). "Here is my little Candle, God! You were the first man I ever loved after wee Robbie Murdoch, Candle, and now I me Bell Miss Baxter citizen of Glasgow native of Scotland subject of the British Empire have been made a woman of the world!" Yet world citizenship does not refer only to the long list of places that she has visited. After her exclamation mark, Bella presents an inventory of the nationalities—and genders—of her lovers: "French German Italian African Asian American men and some women of the north *and* the south kinds have kissed this hand and other parts but I still dream of the first time though oceans deep between have roared since the auld lang syne."[78] The rapidity and recitational quality of this *jouissance* cannot even tolerate punctuation—syntax as a symptom of freedom. Yet this ineluctable—and paratactical—rapidity of liberation already announces a spectral constraint. The impunctulate is punctuated by its own mechanicity, metamorphosing into automatic speech—the voice of an automaton. Franco Moretti has argued that such an automatism is inscribed in the genre of the bildungsroman itself.[79]

This would mean that the character's attainment of freedom is made impossible by the novel's own genre. In other words, freedom is determined by culture, society, and history—which is precisely Moretti's thesis about the bildungsroman's reflecting the social developments from the end of the eighteenth century until World War I: "In the end, nothing was left of the form of the *Bildungsroman* [after 1914]: a phase of Western socialization had come to an end, a phase the *Bildungsroman* had both represented and contributed to."[80] Thus, following Moretti, *Poor Things* could not be a bildungsroman since it postdates the genre's end. Yet since *Poor Things* is set in the nineteenth century, should not *Poor Things* still be a bildungsroman if it claims to be a "representation" of that society as well as a "contribution" to its understanding?[81] Being a "historical novel," *Poor Things* could still claim to be a bildungsroman. Two pervasive contradictions have arisen: the bildungsroman makes both possible and impossible the representation of the character's attainment of freedom; and, the bildungsroman is and is not a historical narrative. Just as with the detective narrative, the ascription of the bildungsroman genre to *Poor Things* both avows and disavows the narrative. But whereas the impasse in the detective genre was due to the attempt to subjugate the present to the past, the bildungsroman resists the subjugation (or hypotaxis) of the present to the future. Yet given the doppelgänger's effective presence, the subjectifying of *Bildung* still does not entail complete subjection.[82]

As it was argued in the previous section, if the question about the subject is asked through a "who" ("who is the oppressed?"; or, here, "who is 'Bella Baxter'?"; or, more generally, "whose is the 'who' secured through subjection?"), and if the answer to this "who" is sought in a correspondence between a historical, social, or cultural reality and its representation in writing, then that "who" will always have to be given a determinate identity as well as a determinate narrative technique for its representation. Conversely, because of the interlacing between automatism and autonomy in *Poor Things*, that is, because of the doppelgänger, the identity and the narrative cannot be secured as unique and exclusively appropriate. The doppelgänger de-subjects, un-subjects, perverts hypotaxis by affirming parataxis. Because of the chiasmic relations set in motion by the doppelgänger, the question that pertains to the subject is always a "how." *How* do those relations unfold? In what manner or technique are they enacted? Such an inquiry hinges on materialism. But materialism here is understood as the allowing of judgment within this setup of relations. In other words, it is the practice that demonstrates the political significance of any writing that claims to have historical import. This is not to say that politics and history are two discrete spheres that are somehow complete reflections of each other. On the contrary, the effective presence of the doppelgänger is precisely the irreconcilability between history and politics, the essential rupture that constructs their interdependence.

This does not entail that *Poor Things* invalidates both the detective and the bildungsroman narratives. This would only result in the imposition of a new master narrative—that is, yet another subjection. In other words, in order to retain the figure of the doppelgänger, *Poor Things* cannot be an exemplary "doppelgänger narrative," because such exemplarity would create a genre and hence a determinate "doppelgänger presence." On the contrary, because of the doppelgänger's effective presence, the historical aspect of *Poor Things* will be paratactic. While parataxis cannot be confined to a specific character given that the question "Who is 'Bella Baxter'?" cannot contain the doppelgänger, it still pertains to the way that subjection is carried out. Subjection or hypotaxis seeks to be determinative of the subject, all the while failing to do so. The investigation will concentrate on the ways that this failure is enacted—specifically two ways that correspond to the temporality of the detective genre and the bildungsroman. Thus, there will be two concomitant forms of hypotaxis: first, an *antitaxis*, an insistence on retrieving an origin as *genesis*, of finding the past secret in the future (it is called *antitaxis* because it is based on a principle of exclusion, an oppositional or antithetical arrangement); and, second, a *nomotaxis*, an attempt to the *progression toward an ideal*, to create the future based on a past foundation (in *nomotaxis*, *nomos* will retain both its Greek meanings, pasture and the law, which combined give rise to an underlying natural origin). The effective presence of the doppelgänger, and hence the operation of parataxis, will set these relations in a chiasmic movement. In both cases, the past will be in the future no less than the future in the past, and vice versa. (Ultimately, this double movement itself—the movement of the doppelgänger—will not be allowed a diachronic identity but would persist as transformable.) Moreover, the shattering of a temporal continuum that would have guaranteed an origin will be effectuated through the placedness of the subject. But not just any subject—rather, the subject as the cosmopolitan, the man or woman of the world. The cosmopolitan enacts the two forms of hypotaxis, thereby also enacting their self-destruction through the effective presence of the doppelgänger and the chiasmic relations set in motion by it. This dual trajectory will be shown to be intimately linked to cosmopolitanism, with reference to Kant and stoicism. Also, the dual trajectory will be seen to revolve around different inflections of the title *Poor Things*, more specifically, around the understanding of what a "poor thing" is.

The doppelgänger opposes subjection through parataxis. The topography of the doppelgänger gives rise to a movement between the inside and the outside so that neither gains control. Similarly, the doppelgänger sets in motion a temporality for which the past is *in* the future no less than the future is *in* the past. This is the image of the doppelgänger as the Turk and as "Bella Baxter" (henceforth, for brevity's sake, simply rendered as Bella, without the quotation marks). If the Turk revoked and recalled universal history through the judgment made possible in now-time, Bella recalls and revokes cosmopolitanism—and, as it will be argued in the end, parataxis links universal history and cosmopolitanism. "I am a woman of the world!" exclaims Bella. But *how* so? What is it that allows one to claim global citizenship while also being claimed by the world? Whence the *right* to such a claim? According to the first answer, the right comes from the past—although a countermove will show that the direction is reversible. This crossing of paths will not be a double-crossing: the source of the move will not be simply denied. Rather, it will be a productive crossing, a chiasmus that will return to the origin, even repeat the origin, but by a repetition that affirms the origin's transformability through time.

This trajectory gives a specific meaning to what it means to be a "poor thing." What characterizes the first move is an imperative: "Forget nothing." And a page later: "Never forget it, Bella."[83] The person speaking here is Godwin Baxter. Godwin admonishes Bella to remember in order to attain freedom. The first move, then, will be *directed toward liberation* underwritten by a notion of total memory, or at least a memory that creates a totality that excludes something else, namely whatever restrains and ensnares. Freedom is to be achieved by remembering everything that has occurred in the past. Thus the first move also seeks to attain its goal through the past, by using the past, and by adopting a critical attitude toward the past so that the mind can discriminate between freedom and enslavement. The excluded is the "poor thing," that is, an automaton, a mechanical doll, an android (alike, but inferior to, a man, an *andras*) lacking memory and hence lacking the liberating insights afforded by memory. "Forget nothing" instructs to "remember everything" and to use this memory to become a complete and completely free individual (do not be an android; be an *andras*). In other words, do not be a "poor thing"—do not be subjected.

Is there an immediate transition between a lack of forgetting and an effective memory of everything? Is "forget nothing" synonymous with "remember everything"? This question sets in motion the countermove to the attempt to *exclude the "poor thing."* Another way to put this question would be: Will the task of memory result in freedom? Or is remembering itself the enactment of freedom? The ambivalence, then, is whether the past and freedom are created or creative. Significantly, the ambivalence is posed in such a way in *Poor Things*, that the characters must make a decision between the two possibilities. Conversely, as it has already been argued in the previous section, the parataxis of completeness and incompleteness attests to the chiasmic relation between been created and being creative. This is the chiasmus which is effected by the doppelgänger. Thus, the demand to decide between the two in *Poor Things* is also a demand to deny the doppelgänger. What is posited through this denial is a *creature*—the object of creation or the subject of creating. Whereas the admonition to "forget nothing" will seem to demand to decide once and for all in favor of one of the meanings of the *creature*, nevertheless this admonition will turn out to be a prevarication that only highlights the doppelgänger.[84]

The ambivalence within the creature cuts deep into the construal of subjectivity. The gap between everything and nothing, on the one hand, and everyone and no one, on the other, is constantly breached. Explaining in the introduction the decision to retitle the discovered book *Poor Things*, Gray, writing as the editor, explains: "I have also insisted on renaming the whole book POOR THINGS. *Things* are often mentioned in the story and every single character (apart from Mrs Dinwiddie and the two of the General's [Blessington] parasites) is called *poor*."[85] The editor does not justify the title in terms of the meaning of the attribute "poor thing." Rather, he justifies it on the pragmatic ground that the phrase "poor thing" is given as an epithet to almost everyone in the novel, that is, "poor thing" signifies the totality of individual presence. Yet the exceptions are curious. If the meaning of a "poor thing" is someone enslaved by the past, then it would be merely incidental that the *housekeeper* Mrs. Dinwiddie has not been called "poor thing." Is she not a house servant? Similarly with "the General's parasites," such as detective Grimes, whose idiosyncrasy of leaving out personal pronouns is a symptom of there being "nothing personal in him"; his speech as well as his personality are those of an automaton obeying orders.[86] Now, if, following the editor, the "poor thing" is understood as the listing of the instances of its attachment to specific persons, then the past is something that has already been created. Whereas if the meaning of the expression "poor thing" is given its full extension, then it becomes creative. In other words, just like freedom, and precisely as the other side of freedom, to be a "poor thing" can be both created and creative. Because this ambivalence between created and creating is mirrored between freedom and its opposite, the way that memory facilitates a passage to freedom is codetermined by its opposite passage leading to subjection.

At this juncture, the meaning of the "poor thing" is given a philosophical import. Securing the "poor thing" would entail the securing of freedom. What has to be discovered is the exact point at which subjection is excluded from freedom, assuming all along that such an exact point exists and can be grasped. This is an indispensable assumption in the imperative to "forget nothing" as a passage to freedom. There can be no *passage* from remembrance to freedom or from forgetting to enslavement without such a point of complete rupture. The paths to memory and freedom, on the one hand, and to forgetting and subjection, on the other, are heading in diametrically opposed directions. Thus, the relation between the two pairs is *antitactic*—that is, they are mutually exclusive. However, a closer look at the passage in which the imperative to "forget nothing" is articulated not only does not unearth that point of exclusion, but it further undermines the assumption of its existence. The "poor thing" is the automaton. Starting by the positing of freedom, the attempt is made to exclude the automaton. However, because of the subject's configuration as a doppelgänger, the automaton will always return to inflect—to infect—the autonomous subjectivity. The doppelgänger disturbs the *antitaxis*—the mutual exclusivity—between autonomy and automaticity.

This can be demonstrated initially by examining the status of Bella's "letter to posterity" that accompanies her husband's book—the letter in which the imperative to "forget nothing" is expressed twice. Its positioning in the structure of *Poor Things* is of a second-degree interiority. The "letter to posterity" is contained in McCandless's book, which is contained in the volume edited by Gray—there is a voice inside another voice, as well as a voice inside the other two. Yet this arrangement is mobile. All these interior distinctions would collapse if it were assumed that the sole author is Gray himself; and yet, at the moment of their collapse they would also be displaced—transferred—to a distinction between Gray-the-fictional-editor inside Gray-the-real-author. This process of displacement and transference could be further accentuated, always closing the gap between inside and outside while also widening it. However, assuming for the moment it is possible to distinguish subjects—or characters—within the novel, and simultaneously assuming that the identity of the signatory of the "letter to posterity" is fixed—at least in a legal sense—by the words "Victoria McCandless M.D." at its end, then it might be possible to secure the point at which the exclusion of the "poor thing" is effectuated. For if the exclusion demands that we "forget nothing," it concomitantly demands a recipient of this memory of everything. A memory finds its own ethical security within a subject, only so long as it is also extended toward another subject—nobody can remember anything if they are alone, nor can one be free in isolation. The past requires the future. Now, the addressees will guarantee that

"Victoria McCandless M.D." has both received and practiced (that is, passed on, transmitted, "posted") the task of freedom, the imperative to "forget nothing." Without the addressees there is no freedom and hence no point of exclusion. The first sentence of the "letter to posterity" tries to secure the addressees by accurately specifying them: "By 1974 my three strong, sprouting lads will be dead or senile, so all other surviving members of the McCandless dynasty will have two grandfathers or four great-grandfathers, and will easily laugh at the aberration of one."[87] The recipients, then, are the epigones of the signatory herself, at a specific time and at a determinate generational distance. Yet despite the exactness of the recipients, they did not receive the letter, since they never came into being—the "three strong, sprouting lads" of "Victoria McCandless M.D." were killed childless during World War I.

Maybe it was not despite but rather *because* of the exacting specificity about who the letter was addressed to that there were no recipients. The exact recipient can be determined only by placing a series of restrictions in describing them—by *excluding* those who are not to receive it. However, if Bella's letter really conveys the message about the attainment of freedom through "forgetting nothing," which here also means "remembering everything," then this message is already annulled by the legal restriction—the exclusion—placed on who the recipient is. The recipients are, on the one hand, a product or a construct of a description by "Victoria McCandless M.D.," yet, on the other, they are given the impossible demand to "forget nothing" when this "nothing" must also include "Victoria McCandless M.D." who is a constitutive part of them. In other words, as creatures produced by "Victoria McCandless M.D." they are forever constitutively under the control of her definition of them; they are forever "poor things" in relation to her, even—and *especially*—at the moment that they are admonished to "remember everything" in order to be free. Their freedom is premised on constituting their own individual memory, which must exclude the totality of the memory of "Victoria McCandless M.D." in order for it to be theirs, and yet it cannot exclude "Victoria McCandless M.D." if they are to become the recipients of this message about freedom. Thus, it was not merely the fact that her sons were killed that the letter did not reach its destination, but also because that destination was never free to receive the letter. As soon as Bella exercised her freedom to choose the recipients through an exclusion, which also excluded from any recipient the free choice to receive the letter—that is, as a free subject—then the letter could never arrive at its destination. What is set in motion through the operation of exclusion is a drawing of limits vis-à-vis the subject. But the limits are simultaneously about subjectivity. A subjectivity produced through the imposition of limits, however, can only be a subjected one. Because of the doppelgänger's effective presence, no stable boundary can be drawn. And hence a project to define freedom, as well as to give or communicate that freedom, through the operation of exclusion is entangled in a contradictory logic from the beginning. At the moment such a freedom is its most pronounced, it also recedes the furthest from the horizon of its own self-determination.

Besides the status of the "letter to posterity," the same movement (the move that posits freedom and the countermove that shows the persistence of the "poor thing") is described in the two pages of the letter in which the expression "forget nothing" occurs twice. Godwin admonishes Bella to remember the poverty of her youth in Manchester, her repressive education in a convent and her miserable marriage to General Blessington. As Bella explains, "Baxter taught me freedom by surrounding me with toys I had never known as a child."[88] The toy referred to here is a doll's house, and Baxter uses it to demonstrate that subjugation permeates all levels: from the servants to the young daughter of the master—"another little female doll"—whose position is hardly better than the scullery maid's. The young mistress and the scullery maid "'both are used by other people,'" Bella is taught to observe, "'they are allowed to decide nothing for themselves.' 'You see?' cried Baxter delightedly. 'You know that at once because you remember your early education. Never forget it, Bella. Most people in England, and Scotland too, are taught not to know it at all—are *taught* to be tools."[89] The imperative to total memory and freedom has to exorcise those who are taught to be tools, who are trained to be utility instruments, like an animal or an android. They are excluded from freedom because individual freedom must exclude them if it is to exist at all. Just as the microcosm of the doll's house is a representation of the whole cosmos, so also the individual call of emancipation is a call for the emancipation of the whole of humanity. The lesson on freedom does not pertain only to a singular individual but to individuality as such. Humanity, then, will be free as long as it excludes the animal, as long as it overcomes mechanicity. It has already been shown how the position of the "letter to posterity" within *Poor Things* undermines the clear distinction between humanity and automatism. However, the whole novel is permeated with examples of the automaton's persistence—of how the erasure of the automaton and the animal only reinscribes automaticity and animality in an even more central position. Two examples from the "letter to posterity" will demonstrate the point: First, a few pages earlier Bella noted her younger son's "imitating the stiff movement of a clockwork doll" as part of his military training.[90] The date on the letter—"1st August, 1914"—makes a mockery of Bella's optimism that this emulation is an isolated phenomenon. Second, just a couple of pages after the lesson on freedom, Godwin, the teacher, describes himself as "a big intelligent dog," and Bella states that she wants to "convert him to humanity."[91] Thus, there are no independent observers of the doll's house who are not simultaneously—and *because* of their observing—also displaced inside it.

Bella, then, calls herself a "woman of the world," supposing that she is a free individual; however, at the same time the automaton claims its *right* to be inscribed in her autonomy. The automaton claims such a right because of the logic of exclusion sustaining the project of autonomy. The doppelgänger's prerogative is that automatism and autonomy are interlaced, in spite of the characters' insistent efforts to hold the two apart. However, such an effort is symptomatic of the tradition of Enlightenment cosmopolitanism. Kant, for instance, in his paper "Idea of a Universal History with a Cosmopolitan Purpose," draws this distinction clearly in the strategic paragraph that summarizes his position before the nine propositions:

> Since men neither pursue their aims purely by instinct, as the animals do, nor in accordance with any integral, prearranged plan like rational cosmopolitans, it would appear that no law-governed history of mankind is possible (as it would be, for example, with bees or beavers). We can scarcely help feeling a certain distaste on observing their [the men's or mankind's, *Menschen*] activities as enacted in the great world-drama, for we find that, despite the apparent wisdom of individual actions here and there, everything as a whole is made up of folly and childish vanity, and often of childish malice and destructiveness.... The only way out for the philosopher, since he cannot assume that mankind follows any rational *purpose of its own* in its collective actions, is for him to attempt to discover a *purpose in nature* behind this senseless course of human events, and decide whether it is after all possible to formulate in terms of a definite plan of nature a history of creatures who act without a plan of their own.[92]

There are several distinctions drawn here, all of them exclusory: First, mankind is separated from the animal because the latter's history is already foreclosed: the animal's behavior is predetermined, hence a total or "law-governed" history of the animal is possible. Second, mankind—or men, the multitude—is separated from the rational citizen of the world, from the philosopher, because from the history of the irregular folly of the simple man it would be impossible to produce any rational historical record. Out of these two exclusions, an elite of humanity is isolated; yet despite their small number, those philosophers relate to humanity as such much more intimately than everyday men or animals. Because of their privileged access to rationality and thus to human nature, the philosophers and the cosmopolitans are the representatives of the political ideal. However, while this political ideal is premised on the exclusion of the slaves of instincts, still the rational cosmopolitan cannot separate himself completely from mechanism. When in the seventh proposition Kant explains how a commonwealth will be established (*Anordnung eines gemeinen Wesens*), he argues that there can be an "optimal internal arrangement" of the commonwealth. However, the perpetuation of this communal living, this *gemeine Wesen*, is, Kant argues, modeled on the automaton. It "can maintain itself like an automaton [*so wie ein* Automat *sich selbst erhalten kann*]."[93]

The attempt to establish a project for freedom with the positing of an individual who is free to the exclusion of the animal or the automaton is a chimera. The automaton and the animal return; their spectral remains give motility to the limbs of the enlightened individual. As it has been shown with the similar logics in Fichte (who, as demonstrated in Chapter 1, attempted to show the passage to praxis through the operation of the philosophical mind) and with Schiller (who, as argued in the beginning of this chapter, posited a philosopher who can grasp universal history), the operation of the doppelgänger resists the subject's equation with a subjective completeness—it resists subjection. However, in *Poor Things* another possibility arises. Instead of reading the proclamation "I am a woman of the world" as the call of an emancipated person standing apart, it could also be read by starting from the animal and the automaton—that is, by using the opposite direction, by starting from natural suppression in order to arrive at the goal of freedom.

|||

This opposite direction of the first move also aims at establishing a political subject who enjoys freedom. Here, however, the animal and the automaton are presupposed. Freedom will be sought by working through them, or by referring them to a higher register. Thus a new meaning to the title of the novel emerges: a "poor thing" is not the excluded, but rather that which has to be raised higher in conformity with a prototype. Both the human and the prototype are related to the natural—to "poor thingliness"—yet while the human's prerogative is to rise above it, the prototype's relation is solely due to providing the rule or method whereby the human rising will be measured. In any case, the "poor thing" becomes the basis upon which a projected autonomy is built.[94] The autonomous self is the subject who is based on "poor thingliness." If something is excluded here, that is exclusion itself, which is mediated solely by the prototype. The countermove here will contest not only whether the absence of exclusion is possible at all, but also the premise of that absence, namely the criterion that makes the "poor thing" possible. Yet regardless of what seems a radically different departure, this move will also turn out to be involved in an inescapable aporia, and it still implicates the issue of the cosmopolitan subject—moreover, in ways that are determinative of the aporia. Cosmopolitanism persists as an issue because Bella is "a woman of the world," in accord with the imperative to "forget nothing." However, since the meaning of world citizen is changed, the memory it is based on will also have to be changed. Thus, to "forget nothing" will actually mean here to "remember nothing."

Besides the exegesis of *Poor Things*, the issue of the "poor thing" as the animal on which a cosmopolitanism can be based is embedded in the cosmopolitan tradition itself. This is evident in Plutarch's famous description of Alexander's cosmopolitanism:[95]

> The much-admired Republic of Zeno . . . may be summed up in this one principle: that all the inhabitants of this world of ours should not live differentiated by their respective rules of justice into separate cities and communities, but that we should consider all men to be of one community and one polity, and that we should have a common life and an order common to us all, even as a herd that feeds together and shares the pasturage [ὥσπερ ἀγέλης συννόμου νομῷ κοινῷ] of a common field. . . . It was Alexander who gave effect to the idea. . . . As he believed that he came as a heaven-sent governor [θεόθεν ἁρμοστὴς] to all, and as a mediator for the whole world, those whom he could not persuade to unite with him, he conquered by force of arms, and he brought together into one body all men everywhere, uniting and mixing in one great loving-cup, as it were, men's lives, their characters, their marriages, their very habits of life. He bade them all consider as their fatherland the whole inhabited earth, as their stronghold and protection his camp, as akin to them all good men, and as foreigners only the wicked; they should not distinguish between Grecian and foreigner

by Grecian cloak and targe, or scimitar and jacket; but the distinguishing mark of the Grecian should be seen in virtue, and that of the foreigner in iniquity; clothing and food, marriage and manner of life they should regard as common to all.⁹⁶

This passage exhibits a decisive twofold argumentative maneuver. Initially, there is an analogy between the commonwealth and the animal herd. Consequently, this leads to a distinction between the Greek and the foreigner. However, the lead-up to the second step and Alexander's role in it will be obfuscated unless the analogy's ambiguity in the word νομῷ in the expression ὥσπερ ἀγέλης συννόμου νομῷ κοινῷ is held in abeyance.

The word νομῷ is translated above as "the pastures," as the dative of the noun νομός, meaning "place of pasture" or, more generally, "a place of habitation." However, a different rendering may be suggested because of the tautology "as a herd that feeds together and shares the pasturage [ὥσπερ ἀγέλης συννόμου νομῷ κοινῷ]." The tautology is more pronounced in Greek, since συννόμου (feed together) and νομῷ are almost homophonous if the prefix is ignored. According to Babbitt's critical apparatus, Helmbold suggests νόμῳ, the dative of νόμος, meaning "habit or law, habitual action, custom." In that case the translation would be "as a herd that feeds together and has common laws (or habits)." This is not merely a matter of stylistics, or even debating the accuracy of the manuscript. Although the shift of the accent produces radically different renderings, Plutarch's understanding of Alexander's cosmopolitanism in fact requires both meanings—that is, a nomotaxis, the placing side by side the two meanings of nomos. This is not as capricious as it might appear, given that both "pasture" and "law" in Greek share a common root in the verb νέμω, which indicates spatial arrangement or distribution, as well as pasture.⁹⁷ However, the accommodation of both meanings has far-reaching implications for the analogy between the commonwealth and the herd. For what is entailed is no less than understanding the law and the habits of the community—everything that constitutes the organizational matrix of people and peoples living under a common justice—in such a way as to be inseparable from natural necessities such as nutrition. Moreover, that natural necessity is given a particular topicality—the pasture, the site of the habits' unfolding. Whereas Kant had sought to emphasize the foreclosed possibilities offered by animal behavior and hence to distinguish the liberated cosmopolitan, the analogy offered by Plutarch offers the obverse formulation: the ideal polity is based on a spatial arrangement that differs little from that of the herd. To put the same point in a vocabulary that is not Plutarch's but which nevertheless generalizes his analogy: the regularity of the law, the foundation of legality and hence of the polity, the lawfulness of the lawful, has as its condition of possibility a state of nature, a political arrangement that is analogous to animal community.

Now, retaining the effective presence of both the law and the pasture runs the risk of turning the commonwealth into an oxymoron. Despite their foundational proximity, the herd and the polity must be separated. Not every creature can be admitted to world citizenship. At this point the contribution of Alexander is crucial. Given their nature, the citizens cannot separate themselves from the animal. But the separation can be effectuated by that which can never be given to them, namely the power of the king, the legal authority of the sovereign. Alexander admonishes the citizens under his rule—his subjects—to distinguish themselves from the foreigners. This distinction is based not on language or customs but on virtue. The foreigner is the one who lacks virtue. The violence of Alexander's definition consists in abolishing the nexus upon which the ambiguity between pasture and law existed. Now, both citizenship and virtue are guaranteed by the emperor's decision, by the exclusion that he effectuates. To be subject to that decision, to be subject to the cosmo-polity of the great Macedonian empire, entails rising above the basis upon which citizenship as such is guaranteed and approximating instead the "heaven-sent" decision making of the sovereign. Thus, it is not the subject that can draw distinctions and exclusions constitutive of the body politic. The process of exclusion is solely reserved for Alexander himself. If this inability of the citizen to effectuate exclusions remains a guarantee of a continual link with animality, Alexander's divine right to decide sets him apart not only from habitual behavior but also from natural exigencies. Moreover, that only the sovereign can exclude forever and decisively is what separates the citizen from the sovereign. In addition, the sovereign simply has the right—it has never been given to him.

The sovereign cannot be a subject. The presence of the divine in the king effaces the parataxis of autonomy and automatism. What this means for the citizen, however, is that hypotaxis, or subjection, has gained sway. This can be discerned in relation both to the king and to the citizen, and in particular in the way that corporeality figures in both. The king's body encompasses both the corporeal and the body politic.[98] The whole polity is constituted through him, while his flesh-and-blood body is separated from the herd. As for the citizen, while his personal memory may be inscribed in his body—the animal part of his nature—nevertheless corporeality and memory as such are given only by and through the king. In the hypotactic cosmopolitanism of Alexander's empire the citizen always approximates the king, who, like a god, is forever inaccessible and yet remains the prototype on which citizenship is premised. All future development of the polity as well as any single citizen is conditioned by that divine prototype. The citizen may "forget nothing" of his or her personal identity, but the civic identity is provided by the king, and hence the citizen is barred from political memory—hence the demand to "forget nothing" is synonymous with the demand to "remember nothing." Thus development, the opening up of the future, as it is referred to the king, is always a partaking of the king and the divine, which is barred to the animal. For the subject to be a citizen, the subject has to rise above the animal in order to partake of the body politic, but it can never reach the divine body of the king that is constitutive of the body politic. Moreover, this curtailed rise is not a choice of the subject—rather, the subject is subjected to it by the sovereign. Yet parataxis persists in the subject—parataxis is operative so long as the subject remains responsive to the doppelgänger. Hypotaxis in the construal above would have to insist that the past is transfixed to the future, that the past is *in* the future, that is, that the animality is ameliorated in the development toward the divine. On the contrary, parataxis will keep the future *in* the past: animality will become inscribed in the body of the subject *and* of the king, thus directing development back to the previous time of nature. Resisting a necessitation of the rights of the human as emanating from the king's divine right to make the initial constituting decision will entail the deconstitution of the process of development toward the divine, showing it to be nothing but the reinscription of animality and automaticity.

    The body resists. The body's history resists. The history of and on the body resists. *Poor Things* demonstrates how the constitution of the political through the divinely ordained exclusion made by the king cannot evade the reinscription of traces of the body's history. This corporeal memory's operation puts into question the equation between the "forget nothing" and the "remember nothing," thereby curtailing the smooth progress from the "poor thing"—the animal or the automaton—toward the divine prototype. This is the work of the effective presence of the doppelgänger in *Poor Things*—more precisely, the effective presence of the undecidability between an inner self within an outer body. The corporeal memory traces the past *in* the future, no less than the future *in* the past. The latter—the future *in* the past—erodes the king's appropriation of the body politic as well as counterdirects the citizens' approximation to that ideal. This move and countermove appear throughout *Poor Things*, but they are nowhere more pronounced than in the relationship between Godwin Baxter and Bella. Godwin is, according to one account, the genius scientist who put together the body of a woman and the brain of the fetus in her womb, thereby creating Bella. According to Bella's own account in the "letter to posterity," Godwin saved her from being a tool by teaching her the politics of "forgetting nothing." However, are these two Godwins all that different? Either because of surgery or education (training), Bella's change amounts to a form of amnesia. The purported causes of this amnesia might be different—either the implantation of a nine-month-old brain, or the forgetting of how to be used by others. Yet the result is the same: Bella forgets nothing—which means that she gains access to the history of oppression. But also she remembers nothing—her body has relinquished the function of *being* a tool; she no longer remembers how to *act* as a tool. Her political action is premised on the handing over of her decision-making memory to something outside—namely, to the person who caused that amnesia, either by educating (training) her or by operating on her. That person is Godwin Baxter, whom Bella wants to "convert to humanity" all along calling him "God." However, "God" is not merely a nickname if that appellation is taken as a symptom of Bella's amnesia. Or, to put this the other way around, if "God" provides the aetiology for Bella's amnesia, then the cause is to be sought at the point of wavering between natural instinct and habitual or legal organization—between νομός and νόμος.[99]

Bodies resist. The bodies of Bella and Godwin—so different and yet so similar—resist their subjection through nomotaxis. The resistance is due to the doppelgänger's parataxis, which retains the corporeal memory of the "poor thing." Thus, the result of Bella's amnesia is a state of transience or passing away.[100] Her happiness, evident in her sexual liberation and linguistic proclivity, never exhibits itself by an attempt to arrest the moment but rather by always being carried away by immediate experience. Thus, for instance, a few days after her engagement to McCandless she elopes with Wedderburn. This happiness, however, is not the result of the absence of inhibition as such but rather of the absence of unconscious inhibitions, the lack of repression, even the lack of an unconscious. This state is diagnosed by none other than Charcot, the head of the Salpêtrière and the teacher of Freud. According to a medical report obtained by Godwin, "Charcot daringly suggests the amnesia has enlarged her intelligence.... Charcot said that she was unusually free of the insane prejudices of her compatriots.... Bella Baxter's most striking abnormality is her lack of it."[101] And when Bella visits Charcot in Paris, the doctor greets her as "the only completely sane English!"[102] Complete sanity equals complete happiness, the happiness that only an animal could achieve. The obverse side of Bella's lack of an unconscious, however, does not entail that she is utterly uninhibited. Prohibitions in the guise of rules and laws, the habits that bind people together, persist. She is completely sane—and not an animal—because of being subject to those rules. But this further implies that Bella is completely subjected to those communal rules. She forgets nothing because there is nothing repressed to remember—and this also means that there is no resistance to be offered to the rules. Their institution is beyond her control and intervention.[103]

The second time that Bella proclaims "I am a woman of the world" takes place precisely as she insists her *presence* in places all over the world and her *happiness* or direct experience in those places qualifies her to be a cosmopolitan woman.[104] Her "political conscience," soon to be formed, effects the transition to unhappiness. Crucially, unhappiness is constituted by, as well as constitutes, the marks on her body—the corporeal memory that cannot be erased.[105] The next day, Bella witnesses beggars fighting for a few coins in the street of Alexandria. At that point, the unconscious returns: remembering the marks on her body indicating that she had been pregnant, Bella thinks that she recognizes her own daughter among the beggars: "a thin girl blind in one eye carrying a baby with a big head who was blind in both she is held tight in one arm held the other straight out swaying the empty clutching hand from side to side mechanically as if *in a trance in a trance* I stood and walked to her ... she was my daughter perhaps."[106] The interstice in the repetition "in a trance in a trance" marks the transversal to unhappiness. Bella recognizes her kinship to the oppressed, the mechanical, the depraved—the animality of the "poor thing." Moreover, at this instant, and despite herself—in a trance—Bella remembers: or rather, her body remembers. Her body tells her that the future, the epigones, have been in the past. Bella can no longer carry herself in the transience of the moment and according to the ideal of complete happiness. The return of the unconscious signifies the possibility of resisting the law and the rules that institute human communality. This return, in a state of trance, also signifies that the body does not allow one to "remember nothing." The subject as doppelgänger can never be premised on a pure automaton or animal. There is never pure passivity nor pure passing away. From that point onward, the trajectory of Bella's life is as an effort to reinstate corporeal memory as the foundation of the political. Her body's memory has nothing to do with "an animal instinct that lacks its proper object," as Mr. Astley asserts.[107] After the incident in Alexandria, Bella knows that there is no way of disentangling the private memory of transience ("forget nothing") and an inaccessible public memory ("remember nothing")—the distinction Mr. Astley insists on. Such an insistence can be premised only on the animal instinct that can find satisfaction only in response to an immediate object—only in transience and passing away.[108]

And what about Godwin—that body so different from and yet so alike Bella's? Godwin is God so long as he guarantees the constitution of the nomotactic. This means that he must be separated from it. God must not be commensurate with the animality and automaticity underlying the political movement, because he is the one who sets that movement in motion. He has created the subject called Bella, regardless of whether the creation is through surgery or training. And yet his body is not unlike Bella's. Indeed, it can be suggested that Bella is made in his image—but whereas he is a bungled experiment, Bella is a successful one. The creation turns out better than the creator, one might say, although this is a precipitous judgment, for who or what would give the measure of comparison? In any case, God is also an automaton: Godwin relates how his father and a nurse "managed to produce him" and that he was "big from the start," but he was affected with a "chemical imbalance" that necessitated the strictest diet and medical vigilance.[109] Having been taught the secret medical knowledge by his father, Godwin was then able to produce Bella.[110] At the scene in which Godwin dies, the parts of his body are described as falling apart, and the moment of death is described as the sound of "a sudden sharp snap," as if a cable broke.[111] So God is also an automaton. Therefore, "poor thingliness" will also have to pertain to that prototype, which not only constitutes but is also constituted by it. The sovereign of a nomotaxis is not only like Alexander a "heaven-sent governor [θεόθεν ἁρμοστὴς]," but also a creature gobbled together like an animal (ζωόθεν ἁρμοσμένος). God-win has won over God not because he is an evil genius but rather because he is an ingenious automaton, and hence never merely an automaton—never purely subjected. Rather, even Godwin is subject to the doppelgänger—he is made a subject by the doppelgänger, as he himself admits: "I cannot remember a day I did not feel inside me a woman-shaped emptiness."[112] As the inside-outside distinctions proliferate, and as the origins of what one feels and the motivations for action are displaced, the doppelgänger is effective. And it is even effecting the one who was supposed to have the ultimate distinction-making power gathered in his own body.

| | |

So if both attempts to secure Bella's right to call herself "a woman of the world" have failed, does this entail a failure of the cosmopolitan project in *Poor Things*? An answer to this question will be forthcoming as soon as the notion of the "right" is itself questioned. Both attempts exhibited a logic that was attentive to hypotaxis, in terms of both personal subjection and a subjection of meaning within writing itself. The notion of the "right" was always reduced to a form of presence—either the presence of an exclusion made by the subject as its passage to subjectification or the presence of the prototype, which was to be approximated for the subjectification to be effectuated. Conversely, to retain cosmopolitanism would necessitate a different articulation of the "right." Moreover, such a notion will have to be secured by parataxis.

The first thing that should be noted is that hypotaxis cannot be simply expunged. An exclusory polemic between parataxis and hypotaxis serves only the latter and results in articulations of mere presence. Parataxis will have to be derived from the various failures of cosmopolitanism outlined above. In other words, cosmopolitanism will be secured by embracing the various contradictions that seemed to make it impossible—that is, by working through the impossibility of freedom within subjection. Embracing the impossible is not only cosmopolitanism's condition of possibility but also effective due to the doppelgänger. Because of the doppelgänger the attempts to secure a stable point failed—stability, either within the subject itself or in the nonsubject (the sovereign), is undermined in a movement of displacement by the doppelgänger. With the doppelgänger, *this movement of displacement constitutes the ineliminable right of the subject.*

The subject of such a right can never be a heroic individual who, like Bella the Fabian activist, expects a utopian future "because we are actively creating it."[113] There are no heroes in *Poor Things*. Bella's activism turns out to be nothing but an atavistic longing for the "poor thing" that she used to be before the incident in Alexandria, the messianic belief that happiness is possible so long as the "animal" is taken care of. Thus, in her pamphlet *A Loving Economy*, "she blames herself for the Great War because she bore too many sons and did not *cuddle* them enough. She asks working-class parents to reduce future armies by having only one child. She wants to make it feel infinitely precious by having it share their bed where it will learn all about love-making and birth control by practical example. In this way (she thinks) it will grow free of the Oedipus complex, penis envy and other diseases discovered or invented by Doctor Freud."[114] Before the formation of her political conscience, Bella did not know of repression, and she lived in the transience and passing away of the "poor thing." Now, in the *Loving Economy*, she advocates a repression of repression, a new "remember nothing" as a return to that past happiness. The epigraph on the cover of *Poor Things*, "Work as if you live in the early days of a better nation," is here given an ironic twist: the "as if" is conflated with existence and the past is discovered in a future catching up with the present.[115]

Yet, even if Bella's essentializing of the epigraph to "Work as if you live in the early days of a better nation" results in its perversion, this does not mean that its relevance to the issue of rights has completely disappeared. In the same year as *Poor Things*, Gray published the political pamphlet *Why Scots Should Rule Scotland*.[116] There, the defense of the rights of the citizens is made abundantly clear. The issue of Scottish independence is conflated in Gray with the issue of a defense of democracy. Gray's claim is not a nationalistic one. Rather, democracy is defended along lines that recall Enlightenment's insistence on the universality of humanity as the basis of the political constitution; moreover, in this concept of humanity, as with Plutarch's cosmopolitanism, basic rights include such necessities as food and clothing.[117] Furthermore, such a democratic project has to keep in sight local particularity—hence the claim for Scottish independence.[118] Therefore, the rights of the citizens on a legal level have to be defended. They have to be defended in order to allow for action and progress. It is the progress indicated by the "as if" of labor in the epigraph. If the "as if" is not to be essentialized, then it has to be retained on a pragmatic level. The "as if" is the gesture toward the ideal—not that ideal itself, nor its representation. Therefore, the "as if" is given a task guaranteed by the present, not by the future. And this is the task to work toward improving the life of citizens—a task derived from the notion of natural justice and enshrined in the legislation protecting human rights.

However, the question remains: How plausible is the securing of these rights through a universal humanity, when the very notion of a universal human essence has been put into question? As it has been demonstrated, both the claim to a humanity based on the individual and a humanity based on a natural or "animal" basis but guaranteed by the sovereign are imbued with self-contradiction. How to defend humanity, and a project of cosmopolitanism, while traditional humanism is crumbling?

The answer to this question has been provided implicitly already: the animal and the automaton have to be incorporated into the notion of the human subject. Thus, Kant was correct to say that an ideal commonwealth would be related to the automaton; although *pace* Kant, this does not mean the automatic dispensation of reason, but rather the inclusion in the rational process of an element of excess that can never be reconciled with it. Moreover, Plutarch was also correct to point out the nexus of the body politic and the herd; although this nexus should not be allowed to resolve itself in an essentialization of the animal guaranteed by a person who is apart from the subject. These two distinct movements both have to be retained and in such a way as to be interactive in a definition of subjective autonomy. Such an interaction creates a chiasmus between the automaton/individual and the animal/subject. The chiasmus operates by an infinite process of displacement, a perpetual instability and negotiation of borders between autonomy and automaticity. To secure a notion of human rights, then, is to be infinitely responsive to the porosity and transformability of the autonomous automaton. However, the infinity of negotiation and responsiveness cannot be allowed a reconciliation either in the subject or in the nonsubject. This is not to posit a state of "perpetual war" but rather to adhere to the infinite complexity of the particular. Infinity is not given by something external to it; rather, the gift itself is what is infinite. This finite infinite is what has been called here the doppelgänger. By refusing to disentangle the inside-outside distinction, the subject as doppelgänger acts out the chiasmic relations of the autonomous automaton. This acting out is never stabilized but is always in a movement of transformability. To be allowed to partake of this movement, as well as to claim responsibility for it—this is the *right* of the autonomous automaton, of the doppelgänger.

For such a right to arise, then, at least three elements need to be in play: first, a movement of displacement enacting the chiasmus; second, an open ontology of the subject that will allow for the movement; and, third, a certain spatiotemporal positioning of the subject so that the process of displacement is configured without being reduced to mere presence. All three elements coalesce in a single sentence of *Poor Things*. This sentence could be called the "caesura of the work" to the extent that it undoes any ambition to achieve completeness, conciliation, or a messianic happiness. When Bella visits Charcot for the second time in the Salpêtrière, she tells him of her trips around the world. Delighted by Bella's adventures as well as by the way she relates them, Charcot asks her to participate in one of his hypnosis exhibitions, although he knows from the previous visit that Bella is not amenable to hypnosis. In other words, Charcot asks Bella, the "completely sane" woman, to help him impress the eminent spectators in the Salpêtrière. Alluding to the arising of her political conscience, Bella observes: "I suppose you will tell them that my pity for poor people is caused by a displaced sense of motherhood."[119] This single sentence presents the three elements adduced above, because it brings into play the doppelgänger—no less than it can only be uttered because the doppelgänger is effective. Moreover, it does so through a complicitous hypocrisy, which is itself constitutive of the theatrical arrangement—the *hypokrisis*—proposed by Charcot. Therefore, the three elements that allow for the doppelgänger's notion of right can be examined under the rubric of the hypocritical and its displacing activity. The doppelgänger is in play because lying erodes all metaphysical security about, as well as emanating from, the subject.

The first element, which pertains to remaining open to truth by allowing for chiasmic displacement, has already been raised in Chapter 2. There, the hypocrite was the lying subject. However, lying was not the intentional deceit of someone else, but rather the lying that puts intentionality into question. In other words, the hypocritical questions the hegemony of a truth understood as eternal or permanent. The hypocritical subject—the doppelgänger—allows for the political process by remaining open to negotiation and by refusing to rest on a notion of revealed truth. When Bella says that her "pity for poor people is caused by a displaced sense of motherhood," she repeats Mr. Astley's assertion that her reaction in Alexandria was caused by "an animal instinct that lacks its proper object." Pity or animal instinct, any notion of empathy or sympathy, cannot allow for the openness of the hypocritical, because they are always based on an aetiology that discovers causes in immediate experience. What is needed, on the contrary, as it was argued in the previous section on Benjamin, is for the temporal continuum to be blasted apart. Only by the recognition made possible in now-time is judgment—and hence the political—possible. Thus, Bella's lying by designating her "displaced motherhood" as the "cause" of her emotions is a moment of self-recognition, which moreover further displaces the displacement it refers to. If Astley's extrapolation of the displacement is the movement from the outside (the emotion's cause) to the inside (the emotion), Bella's displacing of the displacement is the countermove from inside back into the outside. But this new inside is not the same as the old one. The repetition of displacement creates a hypocritical interiority as the positioning where the true is not given a resting place. In this interior, truth itself is displaced from its eternal predominance.

The second element, which pertains to a subjective ontology that resists essentialism and the reduction of the subject to mere presence, has also been discussed earlier, as the multiplicity of origin made possible by the chiasmic relations set in motion by Freud in his reading of Hoffmann's "The Sandman." This is another possible sense of "displaced motherhood," that is, an origin that is infinitely destabilized. It is, of course, not accidental that Bella is addressing Charcot, Freud's master—Charcot who, as George Didi-Huberman has demonstrated, was not only a master of displacement himself but also the psychiatrist whose work on hypnosis not only gave rise to an automaticity of the subject but also, despite his best efforts, did not manage to secure a scientific extrapolation of, or complete mastery over, that automaticity.[120] But here the displacement of originariness has also to be taken literally: the parataxis of the mind inside an external body as in Benjamin's Turk, or the displacing of the fetal brain into her mother's cranium as with Bella. Parataxis, as it has been extrapolated in this chapter, describes the displacement of the inside to the outside, so that the subject will not yield to subjection. This displacement in *Poor Things* has been presented as the resistance to the hypotaxis, which takes the guise of either an autonomous individual or an animal foundation. Thus, a text such as *Poor Things* does not reveal an ontology of the subject, but rather figures the process of revealability—as it was called in Chapters 2 and 3—which is the condition of the possibility of the doppelgänger's ontology.

However, this is not all. The open ontology of revealability does not exclude revelation. This is not a reversion to the position rejected previously—the position that holds onto an eternal truth. On the contrary, it is to insist that revealability does not become foreclosed solidifying the open ontology in an image of complete liberation. Losing the power to say "I," that is, losing the power to be a sovereign deciding upon subjection, and hence allowing for the operative presence of the doppelgänger, entails that subjection can never be completely overcome. The autonomous subject reverses to the automaton while the animal reverts to the individual. But although this process counteracts subjection, it does not do so in a realm—a utopia—where subjection has been eliminated; rather, this enactment takes places alongside subjection. Thus, Bella is subjected to Charcot just as she is projecting her "displaced motherhood": "'You recognize that? Then you are a psychologist!' he [Charcot] cried laughing [in response to Bella's assertion]. 'But you do not say so tonight! Society is based upon division of labour. I am the lecturer, you are my subject. Our august audience will be disconcerted if anyone but the great Charcot passes opinions.'"[121] Yet this does not entail either complete subjection—a dystopia of resignation. Subjection persists so that subjection will not be allowed to hold sway. And it persists precisely as the parataxis of autonomy and automaticity unfold. Subjection is the threat to parataxis, the uncanny resistance that sets it in motion. However, this further implies that, besides the particular manifestations of parataxis that counteract any foreclosure of the relation between autonomy and automaticity, there must be an additional substratum upon which the threat will be exercised. This can be called the paratactical, which is to be distinguished from the particular application of parataxis. However, the paratactical is not simply a foundation, since it is the condition of the possibility for undoing the inside-outside arrangement. Nor is the paratactical something to be discovered merely in the past, since it has already been argued that the past is in the future and vice versa. Rather, the paratactical is *hypo*-critical in the sense that underlies *krisis* or judgment. It is the condition of the possibility of judgment. Such a judgment is effectuated—as it was shown in relation to Benjamin—through the rupture of the relation between particular and universal, between infinite and finite, or between the spatiotemporal relations of parataxis which oscillate between completeness and incompleteness. Thus, the paratactical not only is irreducible to presence, but it is rather the very rupture that presence retains in itself as an ineliminable excess that turns it into an absence.[122]

Finally, the third element—the spatiotemporal positioning of the subject—pertains to the figure of the doppelgänger that cannot be reduced to a specific locus or to a determinate chronology. As it was argued in Chapter 1, this sustains the distinction between the political and politics. Moreover, given that the doppelgänger cannot be reduced to a single person—there is neither a last nor a first man—and because autonomy is in play, a certain complicity or at least interaction has to be inscribed in the notion of the subject. This again recalls a notion of the hypocritical—the space and time of the theater, the theatricality (*hypokritikoteta*) that pertains to human relations. With her reference to displaced motherhood Bella agrees to become part of the playacting proposed by Charcot. This theatricality remains open to subjective interaction so that the actors are not occluded by being assigned roles that encompass their identity. Although the theatricality of the figure of the doppelgänger has been alluded to, certain aspects of its problematic have not been addressed yet: What is the law that determines the action on the stage? Or, are there no laws? But does not the absence of law become a law in turn? And, if it comes a law, would it then lead to a cessation of happening—of being? These questions will be pursued in the next chapter, through a reading of Walter Benjamin's work on Franz Kafka. All that can be stated at the present juncture is that theatricality holds identity in abeyance, refusing to reduce it to the sum of specific features or essential characteristics.

By putting forth the figure of displacement, then, Bella claims the right made possible by the doppelgänger. This is a right that is not given merely by legislation—be that a statute or a metaphysical precept of truth. Rather, it is a right that remains responsive to the parataxis of the autonomous and the automatic, while also carrying the responsibility for enacting the infinite displacements that autonomy and automaticity bring into play. In this sense, the cosmopolitan is the doppelgänger. It is the politics of an automatic cosmopolitan.[123] The political made possible by the doppelgänger is open to the completeness of time (universal history) and place (cosmos), while remaining constantly vigilant to imbue them with incompleteness. The displacement of conciliation to irreconcilability and vice versa is a task undertaken only with a sense of infinite responsibility. It is a responsibility toward the finite—and hence toward praxis and politics, or rather, cosmopolitics.

CHAPTER FIVE

Self-Inscriptions

Failing Kafka and Benjamin

Σκηνῖται τῆς γραφίδος καὶ τῆς ζωῆς, ξένοι εἰς τὰ ξένα, μὴ ἔχοντες ἐδῶ μένουσαν πόλιν, δὲν ἐπαύσαμεν να πλανώμεθα.*

ALEXANDROS PAPADIAMANTES

THE PURE MACHINE'S GAMBIT: BENJAMIN'S "THESIS I"

The doppelgänger is operative in a notion of theatricality that undoes simple presence. The staging suggested by theatricality—the place of the actors and the audience—complicates the distinction between what is on the stage and what is outside the stage. But this does not entail the outright rejection of the inside-outside distinction. Rather, it will

---

* A straightforward translation of this epigraph is: "Tent-dwellers of the pen and life, foreigners in foreign lands, without a city, we did not cease wandering." However, the first word, σκηνίτης, translated above as "tent-dwellers," resists a single meaning. To the extent that it is derived from the noun σκηνή, meaning "tent," it can also synecdochically signify the particular group that lives in tents, namely the nomads or the gypsies. However, the biblical reference "without a city" (Hebrews 13.14) also makes it possible to identify that group as the Jews. Thus, Papadiamantes, a Greek and a self-avowed Orthodox Christian, identifies himself with other national and religious groups. But this is only an initial instability in the meaning of σκηνίτης. For σκηνή also means "stage." In the thought expressed here, it is a stage that combines both writing and life. Papadiamantes describes the staging of life and work. But this scene is not merely a creation; it is also creative. It is, namely, the creative ambivalence of the nomad who destroys any attempt at direct subjective identification, be it in terms of race or religion. And it is an ambivalence between being created and being creative that cuts through the conjunction of life and writing, interrupting their relation. "Σκηνῖται" then becomes a void word, a word that means nothing. But not because of an absence of meaning—for the word is meaningful, as the above extrapolation indicates. Rather, the word means nothing in the sense that the "nothing" stages a constitutive structural relation of the subject. But not of all subjects, not of subjectivity as such. Rather, it is a constitutive relation of a singular subject, the one who has pronounced this nothing-word "σκηνίτης." The citation comes from an unfinished manuscript and it can be found in Δ. Α. Δημητρακόπουλος and Γ. Α. Χριστοδούλου, eds., *"Φύλλα εσκορπισμένα": Τα παπαδιαμαντικά αυτόγραφα (γνωστά και άγνωστα κείμενα)* (Athens: Kastaniotis, 1994), 192.

Self-Inscriptions 193

be argued that the staging becomes a fruitful concept when it allows a self-inscription so that the life and work of the actors are neither permanently ruptured nor eternally reconciled. Walter Benjamin's essay on Kafka is crucial to this undertaking for two reasons: First, theatricality is central to the Kafka essay. It will be argued that there are three kinds of theater in the Kafka essay, the world theater, the Nature Theater of Oklahoma, and a theater characterized by what Benjamin calls the "lost gesture [*der verlorene Gestus*]."¹ Thus, the Kafka essay thematizes in a unique and expedient way Benjamin's notion of theatricality.² Second, it is precisely through the third kind of theater, the theater of the "lost gesture," that Benjamin refers to a doppelgänger story. However, what the "lost gesture" discloses need not be confined to a specific story or motif; it also configures the subject. Thus, the doppelgänger will turn out to be the subject of the "lost gesture." But this would not be an essentialist definition of subjectivity. Rather, the doppelgänger will arise precisely at the point of suspension of the world theater and the Nature theater. This will be shown to be instrumental for a philosophical understanding of Kafka's literary project and of Benjamin's critical project.

Before turning to Benjamin's essay on Kafka, it is important to outline the issues related to theatricality and the way the doppelgänger becomes operative. To this end, the first thesis of "On the Concept of History" is again crucial. Thesis I in its entirety reads:

> It is generally known that there was once an automaton constructed in such a way that it could respond to every move by a chess player with a countermove that would ensure the winning of the game. A puppet wearing Turkish attire and with a hookah in its mouth sat before a chessboard placed on a large table. A system of mirrors created the illusion that this table was transparent on all sides. Actually, a hunchbacked dwarf—a master at chess—sat inside and guided the puppet's hand by means of strings. One can imagine a philosophic counterpart to this apparatus. The puppet, called "historical materialism," is to win all the time. It can easily be a match for anyone if it enlists the services of theology, which today, as is generally known, is small and ugly and has to keep out of sight.³

It will be recalled that at the end of the section "The Subject of History in Walter Benjamin" in Chapter 4 it was argued that the relation enacted by the Turk should not be resolved in favor of either the dwarf or the puppet. Rather, it is a relation of complicity—a paratactic relation. Such a relation allows for the movement of the chess pieces on the board and hence for the interruptions effected in the game of chess. And since the dwarf stands for the "small and ugly" image of theology and the puppet stands for historical materialism, this means that, as Rebecca Comay puts it, "in insisting on the co-implication of 'historical materialism' and 'theology,' Benjamin is neither *proposing* nor *exposing* their final unity."[4] It is precisely this eschewal of unity that indicates the doppelgänger effect, as it has been discussed thus far. Comay also incisively comments: "If the large puppet's overt manipulation of the chess-pieces would seem to repeat or reflect (in inverting) the dwarf's covert manipulation of the puppet, it is perhaps less a question of exposing, theatricalizing or expressing the latter's secret than of subverting our habitual assumptions regarding exposure or theatricality as such."[5] In other words, by holding the secret parataxis of dwarf and puppet—of theology and materialism—in abeyance, then "theatricality as such" becomes the issue. Comay's insight will be misconstrued if the expression "theatricality as such" is either equated with a specific theatrical performance or with a universal and essentialized notion of the theater. Rather, the theatricality made possible by the doppelgänger is that positioning that *exposes* the subject to a concrete situation and to its universalized counterpart but *fails* to reconcile the two. This failure is what is at issue, because it signifies the impossibility of reducing the subject to either the empirical or the transcendental, thereby giving rise to Foucault's "empirico-transcendental doublet"—to the doppelgänger. By insisting that the relation "has to keep out of sight," Benjamin indicates an interruption of the metaphysical presence that seeks to retain the image in the guise of self-reflection. Thus, failure is constitutively linked to theatricality as such.

The theatricality of the Turk gives rise to the political in at least two ways derived from the failure of the subject's unity—from the doppelgänger. First, it is clear from Konvolut Z of *The Arcades Project*,[6] titled "Die Puppe, der Automat," that Benjamin ascribes a political significance to the automaton. What holds Benjamin's attention in this Konvolut is not only that puppets and automata acquire a "sociocritical significance" (Z1, 5), not only that they are linked to the Marxist concern for the means of production (Z2), and not only that are they thereby linked to a conception of experience that is psychoanalytically nuanced (Z2a, 1), but also, and more importantly, that they are linked to the Aristotelian prediction that slavery will be abolished through the use of automated machinery (Z3). Thus, the automaton indexes the history of the oppressed. This is a history made possible by the Aristotelian recognition that it is not merely necessity but also contingency, and hence history and politics, that characterizes the automaton.[7] Second, in relation to the subject, it is important that the dwarf is hidden by a "system of mirrors." The mirroring effect is, as already intimated, the effect of ideology: reflection positions the subject as either in a state of complete hiddenness or in a state of complete transparency. Thus, the subject is either in the complete isolation required by immediate knowledge of itself, or alternatively the subject presents the future by instituting the law in its own image, that is, the two forms of self-reflection. With mirroring, the secrecy of the last or the first man respectively is to be maintained at any cost. Conversely, because that secrecy is untenable, as it has already been argued, then the mirroring trick is bound to fail. The upshot of both these aspects is that, when Benjamin says that the imaginary "philosophic counterpart" to the Turk "is to win all the time" in chess, then the emphasis should not be on the winning, but rather on the failure of this formula—as it was manifest to Benjamin in 1940. It is a failure of a specific conception of the "philosophic," a conception that manifests itself in the necessary and eternal conclusion of the expression "all the time." A certain kind of philosophy promised that the automaton will abolish slavery and class division with the cooperation of a learned—a doctored—mind. But the mind is doctored also in the sense of "tampered with" or impure, a mind infected with automaticity, contaminated with the doctored propaganda of power politics. The doppelgänger critiques the "doctored subject," which is thereby shown to be unitary only as a result of a mendacity about its own disjunctions. Thus, the Turk may "win all the time," but only in a realm of absolute loneliness, bereft of others, and hence a realm in which its only opponent would be a self-reflection in the mirror. This is a win resulting in complete failure.

The fact that Benjamin does not lament this complete failure—he does not even seem to dwell on it at all—should not be seen as an inconsistency or defect. The reason is that with the first few words of Thesis I such a complete failure has been forestalled. "Bekanntlich soll es." These are the first words of the thesis: "It is generally known." It is not the content of what is known that matters but that it is commonly known. The first phrase of the Theses opens up a community of listeners to which it is addressed, as if to an audience at a performance. This gesture acknowledging, even creating, an audience for himself is the gesture of the storyteller as described by Benjamin. Storytelling, as it was shown in the preceding chapter, depends on the presence of the audience and hence it is a narration that is premised on particularity. This particularity counteracts a certain philosophic tradition that insists on a chimeric "all the time." In effect, this locates the unfolding of the political in the gaps created between the eternal and the specific, the automatic and the autonomous, the conceptual and the contingent. Such gaps can never be closed with appeals to eternity so long as the starting point is particularity. The failure to bridge this gap reinscribes the concept of failure so that it can no longer be complete. It is the failure of the unitary subject, which is due to the operation of the doppelgänger. However, as it was also noted in the preceding chapter, storytelling still does not adequately outline the operative presence of the doppelgänger. The multifariousness as such of the particular can be guaranteed only by something transcendent. Because of its infinite regress, potentiality is not enough for the doppelgänger; what is also needed is potentiality's arrest in an act of judgment. While the temporality of the historical judgment has been presented with recourse to the episode of King Psammenitus in the Leskov essay, the way that temporality is imbued with theatricality remains unclear. As it will be shown, this is a crucial issue about the language—or the failure of language, language as failure—in which the doppelgänger can effect its operative presence. Moreover, it will provide a link between Thesis I and the Kafka essay.

To show this link, it is necessary to turn to the source of Benjamin's description of the Turk, Edgar Allan Poe's article "Maelzel's Chess-Player."[8] Failure features in two distinct yet related ways in Poe's article. First, Maelzel's theatrical presentation of the automaton during the exhibition games is an indication for Poe that the automaton is not what he calls a "pure machine."[9] That is, Poe argues that the Turk's operation requires "immediate human agency."[10] A pure machine would always win. Poe describes in meticulous detail the performance: "At the hour appointed for exhibition, a curtain is withdrawn . . . and the machine rolled to within twelve feet of the nearest spectators."[11] Then Maelzel "informs the company that he will disclose to their view the mechanism of the machine."[12] Maelzel opens up all the different compartments and drawers of the automaton, so that "every spectator is now thoroughly satisfied of having beheld and completely scrutinized, at one and the same time, every individual portion of the Automaton, and the idea of any person being concealed in the interior . . . is immediately dismissed as preposterous."[13] During the exhibition, Maelzel also performs various antics. For instance, when "the Automaton hesitates in relation to its move . . . he [Maelzel] has also a peculiar shuffle with his feet, calculated to induce suspicion of collusion with the machine in minds which are more cunning than sagacious." But these "mere mannerisms" are merely a trick, because it is clear that Maelzel could not have intervened in the operation of the machine and "he puts them in practice with a view of exciting in the spectators a false idea of pure mechanism."[14] In other words, Maelzel tries to throw the suspicious observers off the track of what is really the case, namely that there is a hidden chess player and that the identical manner in which the inners of the Turk are always displayed before the commencement of a performance is designed to conceal that chess player.[15] The performative presence of the exhibitor, then, is part of a conjuring trick to disguise the fact that the automaton is no "pure machine."[16] And, with this conjuring trick, which seeks to deny a corporeal presence, the figure of the doppelgänger is already in operation: the showcasing also denies, in general terms, the failure to demarcate a sharp boundary between mind and body, human and machine, inside and outside, and so on—all the divisions whose mirrorings have been shown to structure those notions of subjectivity that remain blind to the doppelgänger.

Yet no matter how hard one endeavors to leave the doppelgänger out of sight, to consign it to the unthought and the unknowable, the doppelgänger always returns. And, as it has already been argued, its return is registered in language, and particularly in those expressions that specifically attempt to negate or deny it. Here, the second feature of failure in Poe's article becomes apparent: namely, in the linguistic apparatus of what Comay calls "theatricality as such." Poe meticulously records that "When the question is demanded explicitly of Maelzel—'Is the Automaton a pure machine or not?' his reply is invariably the same—'I will say nothing about it.'"[17] This silence, encapsulated in the word "nothing," can acquire three meanings: First, it is a non-ostensive silence, a silence that does not point to anything in the environment or to the stage on which it is uttered. Thus, it is a silence that guards a portion of that stage—a portion that is to remain invisible and inaccessible, and yet, for that very reason, all the more indispensable. Second, it could be construed as a garrulous silence, a denial that in fact says something about what seeks to remain hidden in the stage, a muteness that reveals the hidden element and hence the performative totality. This is Poe's interpretation, according to whom Maelzel's "nothing" merely reveals that the automaton is not "a pure machine." However, there is a third possibility. Silence and the word "nothing" here are to be taken literally, so to speak, that is, as elements of the theater itself—elements that are neither to be hidden nor to be revealed. Thus, the utterance "I will say nothing about it" is not primarily an indicative sentence; rather, it is part of the script of the show; it is a gesture of the performance.[18]

The importance of distinguishing the three types of silence—the three nothings—is due to the different ways they allow for the connections between failure, action, and language to be conceived. Failure is part of all three versions of silence, but its figuration differs according to how acting and speaking are construed. In any case, there is a connection between actions and words on the stage. This is obvious also from the fact that Maelzel's announcement "I will say nothing about it" is similar in certain respects to his mannerisms during the performance, such as the "shuffle with his feet" whenever the automaton hesitated before a move. Both the actions and the expression are gestures related to the possibility or impossibility of the "pure machine." Now, the first nothing's construing of the silence as absolute merely means that every gesture contains within it an element that belongs to it insofar as it is ambiguous—with an ambiguity that turns it into a secret. Consequently, this ambiguity results in the *failure* of distinguishing between words and actions. On the contrary, the second alternative distinguishes actions and words, but such distinctions are ultimately reconciled in the eventual revelation of the secret. In other words, actions and words *fail* to conceal a higher realm of reconciliation—their failure being precisely the inauguration of that pure realm where they coincide. As opposed to the first alternative, the third one insists on the distinction between actions and words, since the literal and material aspect of each gesture is to be maintained; in addition, as opposed to the second alternative, here no final conciliation is forthcoming, since what matters is the gesture as such. Thus, the third alternative includes both the other two, but not completely—it *fails* the protocols of both the ubiquitous ambiguity and the permanent conciliation of actions and words.

The third type of failure, nonetheless, succeeds in rupturing the relation between action and speech. This rupture is instrumental if the political is to be understood as the interruptive presence of judgment—judgment as the mediation between the particular and the general, the specific and the abstract, the finite and the infinite, or, in the vocabulary used above, between a victorious and a defeated silence. Thus, the nothing in this third type of silence is configured by the doppelgänger, whose effective presence cannot be denied—but also in such a way that the efforts to deny it become part of it. In other words, the failures of subjectivity—failures to hide or reveal the secret, or to achieve immediate self-cognition, or to attain autonomy, and so on—only point to the figuration of the doppelgänger. Can this failure that is allowed by, as well as allows, the doppelgänger be called a success? Maybe it can, but only in a qualified manner: a success that fails to determine what it is a success of. A success that never knows where it is passive or active—a subject that persists between the allowing and the allowance. In other words, a success that is endless, and hence a subject—the doppelgänger—that is always under way, in a process of formation, figuring—configuring no less than disfiguring—itself.

It may be countered that such a "successive failure" is in effect a failure, for it has achieved nothing. And such a counter would be gladly conceded, so long as the "nothing" is of the third kind discussed above. The reason for such a concession would not be that it would win the argument: for its winning strategy is clear in the gambit that concedes everything to the opponent, so long as the "everything" is inscribed in a process of endless formation and transformation—which is precisely the import of the third nothing as it has been explicated above. However, the win is merely a secondary aftereffect; what matters is the movement of self-inscription—the kind of inscription that counteracts any attempt at self-reflection as a foundation of subjectivity. It was observed earlier that, if according to Benjamin's Thesis I, the "philosophic counterpart" to the Turk wins every time, then the emphasis should not be on the winning, but rather on the manifest failure of such a philosophic strategy at the time the Theses were written. This is not merely to say that "reality" somehow superimposed itself onto the Theses. Rather, the point is that, in Poe's formulation, the automaton "would always win" if it were a "pure machine."[19] The failure to always win, then, is the failure of the machine because it is not a pure machine. However, this also does not entail the failure of machinery tout court. Indeed, the machine persists—it persists as the maneuver of self-inscription. It was observed that with the opening words of Thesis I—"Bekanntlich soll es"—Benjamin conjured a community of listeners. But also, those same listeners, and by the very same maneuver, conjure Benjamin as the writer of the Theses. This double gesture, the *allowing cum allowance*, is the effective presence of the doppelgänger. And theatricality is incumbent upon this gesture—theatricality as the staging of this dual relation, as well as its suspension in the nonrelations of the nothing. Benjamin, then, when he says in Thesis I that the dwarf/puppet will always win, repeats (or rehearses) Maelzel's expression of "I will say nothing about it": while the winning formula is being affirmed, that formula is premised on the pure automaton—that is, it is premised on the very notion undercut by the opening of the thesis. What fails, then, is not merely the dwarf, not merely the puppet. There is an *alliance* between complete hiddenness and absolute revelation premised on their mutual reliance on the "eternally the same." Self-inscription is the failure of this alliance—the failure of eternality and sameness.

Another way of describing the self-inscription that characterizes the third kind of nothing would be to say that the giving away of self-reflection—the pure machine's gambit—places the demand on the subject to remain endlessly open. The word "gambit" here retains its dual meaning: a gambit in chess is both a sacrifice and an opening strategy—for instance, the "king's gambit" or the "queen's gambit." Thus, a gambit is like the third strategy of the nothing described above: it sacrifices something—there is a failure—but this is only part of the game because it solicits a response by leaving the game open. This is not an openness of either ambiguity or conciliation, but rather the openness of an infinite responsiveness to the other. The doppelgänger demands this responsibility in the subject. The pure machine's gambit is a responsibility also to the first kind of nothing—the nothing of indistinction and ambiguity, which for Benjamin is a mythic quality indicative of the "world theater" of the Kafka essay; as well as a responsibility to the second nothing—the nothing of conciliation, a nothing that coincides with the arrival of the Messiah and the subject's redemption, which Benjamin describes in the Kafka essay as the Nature Theater of Oklahoma; finally, because the third nothing's infinity is premised on finitude, it recalls Jean Paul's "black nothing"—the nothing of the doppelgänger.[20] (As it will be shown, this nothing also arises in Benjamin's Kafka essay, and it is linked to the "lost gesture"—a gesture that will open up a stage altogether distinct from that of the world and the Nature theaters.) Thus, the political project of the doppelgänger is not construed in terms of concealment and revelation, but rather in terms of responsiveness and responsibility. However, for that responsibility to come into effect, the subject's self-inscription is indispensable. Such a self-inscription, on the one hand, configures the subject in terms of its words and actions, and, on the other hand, disfigures those words and actions, consigning them to a trajectory of a failure to totalize intention and meaning. What persists, however, is the figuration of self-inscription. What persists is the subject, the doppelgänger.

From this persistence follows that in the critical project the author cannot be eliminated. So long as the author is infracted through self-inscription, then the author is instrumental in the critical project. In other words, so long as the author has performed the self-inscriptive gesture, thereby remaining open and responsive to otherness as well as to the failures of subjective unity, then criticism has to respond to this inscription. This point is at the crux of Benjamin's reading of Kafka, as is made clear in a passage of utmost importance from Benjamin's essay.

> Kafka could understand things only in the form of a *gestus*, and this *gestus* which he did not understand forms the cloudy spot of the parables. Kafka's writings emanate from it. The way he withheld them is well known. His will orders their destruction. This document, which no one interested in Kafka can disregard, says that the writings did not satisfy their author, that he regarded his efforts as failures, that he counted himself among those who were bound to fail. He did fail in his grandiose attempt to convert poetry into doctrine, to turn it into a parable and restore to it that stability and unpretentiousness which, in the face of reason, seemed to him to be the only appropriate thing for it. No other writer has obeyed the commandment "Thou shalt not make unto thee a graven image" so faithfully.[21]

For such a critical task, "gesture" is a crucial term, since, as the quotation shows, gesture in Benjamin's essay on Kafka becomes the locus where actions and words—or, in the vocabulary of Benjamin in the Kafka essay, life and work—as well as the law unfold and are articulated.[22] The gesture is linked to a logic of failure.[23] The fact that Kafka himself could not comprehend his own writings constitutes both his cunning and his pretentiousness. It constitutes the doppelgänger's *hypocrisy* in the threefold sense outlined at the end of the preceding chapter: as a political program that resists utopian visions or mythical occlusions; as a subject whose operative presence does not reduce it to mere presence but indicates that which underlies judgment; and as the theatricality that is a self-inscriptive gesture. Thus, Kafka's writings are presented as an "untrammelled journey," which escapes his own grasp and results in failure: that is the reason why "no one interested in Kafka can disregard" his will to have them destroyed. Yet, at the same time, this failure is a fulfillment of his wish in advance—even in the absence of its being carried out—to the extent that failure succeeds in keeping Kafka's most central imperative, the prohibition of images.[24]

The second section of this chapter addresses the distinction between the world theater and the nature theater in Benjamin's essay on Kafka, in order to show how they ultimately lead to a third type of theatricality, which is discussed in the third section. However, one question will remain: Is it possible to present an author's self-inscription—to present an author as a doppelgänger—without the critic self-inscribing himself? Would not the absence of such a self-inscription be self-contradictory, because the critic himself will be providing the image—a self-reflection—in relation to which the work will have to be measured? If the self-image is not to be installed as an idol, that is, if the world is to be successfully disenchanted and demythified, there can be no complete failure of the image. For then the *absence* of the image, a nothing, will be reinstated, and the power of an empty pedestal can be as strong, or even stronger, than the power of what it may bear on it. Thus, it will have to be shown that, alongside Kafka's doppelgänger, the critic himself—Benjamin—must also respond to the doppelgänger. This is addressed in the final section.

WORLD THEATER AND NATURE THEATER

In a letter to Gerhard Scholem dated 12 June 1938, Benjamin undertook a review of Max Brod's biography of Kafka, which had been published the previous year.[25] Benjamin's caustic remarks revolve around Brod's justification for ignoring Kafka's instructions for his writings to be destroyed following his death.[26] This justification took the guise of a theological interpretation of Kafka's opus, no less than Kafka himself as a "saintly" person. While objecting to this, Benjamin underscores that Kafka's instructions are "the ideal place to broach fundamental aspects of Kafka's existence."[27] According such a privileged position to Kafka's will introduces a twofold problematic. On the one hand, one's work is not simply related to one's biography, but even more emphatically writing and life confront each other in a way that informs the critical process. On the other hand, this nexus of life and work is closely related to the law: the subject is determined by the way that injunctions and imperatives unfold in life and writing. This twofold problematic was prefigured four years earlier, in Benjamin's essay "Franz Kafka: On the Tenth Anniversary of His Death," as is made clear in the passage from the essay cited above. Even though the essay predates and hence could not have explicitly referred to Brod's biography, the insistence therein that Kafka obeyed the law against the "graven image" broaches the same problematic.

This is not at all to suggest that a collision between two different theologies is played out between Benjamin and Brod. Rather, the prohibition of images will also be an argument against theological interpretations of Kafka. The argument will show how a topology is interarticulated with the subject. Whereas the theological mode is dependent on what is internal and what is external to the subject, Benjamin rejects such a spatial arrangement. The subject figures in a different topography, one not governed by the lure of appearances—a subject that confronts the allure of myth. Thus the subject's perceptions "fail," but that failure—the doppelgänger's operative presence—only signifies the collapse of the individual—or rather, the individual as unifying the subject's appearances. Benjamin's insistence on the gesture in Kafka is inseparable from the rejection of the individual in favor of the actor of what he calls the nature theater—the Theater of Oklahoma from Kafka's last chapter in *America*. Thus a different kind of subject, a gestic actor, replaces the individual. To demonstrate this movement from the individual to the actor recourse will be sought in Kafka's works, especially the *Metamorphosis*. Further, given that the discussion of the doppelgänger has all along insisted that the doppelgänger is the dismantling of the individual's preponderance, then it will be expected that the doppelgänger will be operative in this problematic. Indeed, as it will be shown, the doppelgänger will be that residue of subjectivity in the individual that remains unthought and unknown and that will compel the move toward the actor of the nature theater. However, as it will be made clearer later, the nature theater actor and the doppelgänger cannot be equated. Instrumental in these distinctions will be the conjunctions and disjunctions between action and word, between life and writing.

The confrontation of life and work within a problematic of the subjective imperative—"Thou shalt not make unto thee a graven image"—is essentially the question of the subject's freedom. How can the subject be free and at the same time adhere to a law? To pursue this question it is necessary to investigate the way that the subject figures in the law. However, the law, and hence the subject's freedom, function very differently in a theological mode, as opposed to a mode that implicates the subject in a logic of failure. The difference can be discerned in their respective conceptions of space. The theater—as the space wherein the gesture is enacted—can be approached by distinguishing it from a space that is governed by the theological economy of interiority and exteriority. Even if the theological economy of place poses a remainder that will be inaccessible—because sacred or holy—still that remainder will be none other than the doppelgänger's effective presence. Because the doppelgänger reconfigures the economy of space, the remainder will no longer be amenable to a purely theological understanding but will of necessity acquire a political significance as well.

Brod's theological interpretation in the biography of Kafka address the issue of the link between life and work precisely when Brod provides a justification for ignoring Kafka's instructions to have his writings destroyed.

> The category of sacredness (and not really that of literature), is the only right category under which Kafka's life and work can be viewed. By this I do not wish to suggest that he was a perfect saint.... But... Franz Kafka was on the road to becoming one. The explanation of his charming shyness and reserve, which seemed nothing less than supernatural—and yet so natural—and of his dismayingly severe self-criticism, lies in the fact that he measured himself... up against the ultimate goal of human existence. Here, too, we can find one of his motives that held him back from publishing his works. A characteristic that places him in the realm of the sacred was his absolute faith. He believed in a world of Rightness, he believed in "The Indestructible" of which so many of his aphorisms speak. We are too weak always to recognize this real world. But it is there. Truth is visible everywhere. It glints through the mesh of what we call "reality." This explains Kafka's deep interest in every detail, every wrinkle of reality.[28]

Kafka's promotion to holiness is used to explain his severe self-criticism, which prompted his order for the destruction of his manuscripts, and, simultaneously, justifies Brod's disregard of the instructions, as well as his editorial decisions. The "Indestructible," another name for God, remains forever present yet ineffable, in a sense immanent but at the same time separate from the human world of contingency by an unbridgeable chasm. This "Indestructible" announces Brod's spatial and exegetical economy. Kafka's absolute faith can perceive the divine presence in the minute details of accidental relations. However, man cannot immediately perceive this presence. Brod discerned in many of Kafka's manuscripts contemplations of this theological nature, for instance, in the diary entries of 1920, which Brod expunged from the edition of Kafka's diaries and published separately as a collection of aphorisms under the title *He* (*Er*). Kafka's writings belong to the category of sacredness because they posit two distinct spheres. On the inside there is the person whose moral purity affords him an endless freedom to perceive external appearances. Kafka qua this moral personage is self-contained. Whereas the sainthood of his inside is a whole, the external perceptions remain contingent, accidental, impossible to accommodate in the ambit of moral imperatives. From the vantage point of Kafka's absolute faith, the outside has also to be posited as truth, as a whole. There was nothing vulgar in Kafka's perception of the external world, Brod contends, since what may appear as such in its contingency is essentially a divine manifestation. Kafka is depicted as a Job from Prague.[29] He never struggles with himself; he measures himself only against the ultimate goal of existence: he struggles only and exclusively with God. His sacred writings transcend the everyday plane. They are the representations of Divine Will in "every wrinkle of reality." Starting from an impeccable ethical sphere, Kafka's struggle aims to represent the contingent in the eternal. The result of this exegetical and spatial economy is that, although life and work are initially posited as separate, they nevertheless reach a point of utter indistinction. However, that point can be reached only in the saint—or, at least, in Brod's qualification, in a person who is on the way to sainthood. Saintliness is necessary because indistinction and ambiguity are a mark of the sacred. Now, this ambiguity is regulated only by the "Indestructible," therefore a remainder of the unthought or unknown in the subject itself remains impermissible. In other words, such an economy seeks to deny the doppelgänger—it *has to* deny the doppelgänger, because the unthought can be given only via God and hence through an operation of transcendence.

Kafka's struggle for transcendence is attested, according to Brod, in the ending of the *Metamorphosis*, when the possibility of happiness in marriage is afforded to Grete after the demise of her vermin-brother. Brod insists that the *Metamorphosis* is not based on the decadent principle of horror writing. Instead, in it "the whole of the free world is revealed" because it is based on a principle that is "healthy, positive, inclined to everything that desires to live, everything gentle and good, the blooming girlish body that shines over the hero," in other words on the principle that the morality of the personage achieves the representation of the good Divine Will.[30] It is instructive to juxtapose Brod's healthy image of Grete to Blanchot's reaction to the same image. For Blanchot the blossomed girl (*aufgeblüht Mädchen*, as Kafka puts it), ripe for a good man after Gregor's death, is the height of horror. Kafka's work is here a struggle with existence: writing becomes an affirmation of the contingent plane, but at the same time affirms itself upon it. Affirmation is different from Brod's conception of struggle. This affirmation is also a kind of transcendence, but one that is predicated on God's death; it is, as Blanchot calls it, a "dead transcendence" but because of that all the more terrible since it is stripped of any moral certitude guaranteeing a true outside (an unmoving "Indestructible").[31] The whole theme of the *Metamorphosis* is an illustration of the torment of the literature of "dead transcendence." For Gregor, "to exist is to be condemned to continually fall back into existence," that is, he is forced to reckon perpetually with the accidental—in particular, the accident of his transformation. There is still hope that the struggle will end, as indeed it does in Gregor's death, an "almost happy death by the feeling of deliverance it represents, by the new hope of an end that is final now." There is a release from the endlessness of the particular. Yet this is shuttered by the full-of-life Grete (*immer lebhafter werdenden*), whose sensual awakening is the "height of horror; there is nothing more frightening in the entire story."[32] The world of Kafka according to Blanchot, very much like Benjamin's, is faithful to the Mosaic Law warning against setting oneself up as an idol. The "law" in the affirmation of existence cannot pretend to rest on the individual's confirmation of, or by, an immediate divine imperative. This is the opposite of Brod's conception of a happy ending to the *Metamorphosis* as an effect of the good Divine Will. Paradoxically, it is Brod's "Saint Kafka" who breaks the Law whereas the secular Kafka remains faithful to it.[33] But the law of "dead transcendence" or the law against the image should not be taken merely as a specific prescription. Rather, these laws indicate the subject's resistance to being reduced to prescription and transcendence. Thus, they are not rules but rather the penumbra within the law that opens up a realm of justice. Such a justice is allowed by the doppelgänger, as it was argued in Chapter 2.

What needs to be shown here is how the ineliminability of the doppelgänger is a functional element that operates within, and allows for the operation of, a theological interpretation, all the while without the doppelgänger being commensurable with it. To this end, imitation plays a crucial role. The economy of transcendence is regulated by imitation. Imitation demands that one acts as if the transcendence toward the image is possible. Of course, a complete transcendence is ab initio presumed to be impossible—by definition, one cannot be God. This means that the divine becomes the measure of imitation. Consequently, because the measure is incommensurable with both the life and the work of a person, then life and work become ambiguous terms. The imitation allowed by the economy of "dead transcendence" is completely different. Here, God is dead, and hence the measure of the imitative activity is lacking. Thus, the person is in constant lack; there is a perpetual debt to be paid. The affinity of Blanchot's to Benjamin's Kafka is discernible at this point. It is a small step to move from the economy of *debt* to the laws that procure *guilt*—an even smaller step in German, whose

Schuld encompasses both meanings. For instance, in the *Metamorphosis*, Gregor sacrifices his freedom in order to repay his parents' debt to the director (*um die Schuld der Eltern an ihn [den Chef] abzuzahlen*). However, the family remains innocent (*unschuldig*) in relation to the office. In the eyes of the director, it is Gregor who is guilty because of a recently entrusted money collection. Soon after, Gregor is happy to overhear that the father has a hidden hoard that could have settled the debt of the father, yet the joy is unjustified, since it is the hidden surplus that precipitates Gregor's ultimate defeat by his father.[34] There is a nexus of lack and sacrifice, guilt and atonement that cuts through Gregor's milieu. Traversing the distance from debt to guilt offers a sight of that nexus in Kafka's world as it is conceived by Benjamin.

This is the nexus of fate, and fate, for Benjamin, denotes an enchanted world in the grip of myth. "Kafka's world is a world theater [*Welttheater*]," notes Benjamin, and the "law of this theater is contained in the tucked away sentence that 'A Report to an Academy' contains: 'I imitated because I was looking for an exit [*Ausweg*], and for no other reason.'"[35] Imitation functions here between two spheres, the internal and the external, which are, on the one hand, spatially separated, and, on the other, conceptually interrelated. Benjamin's expression that discloses the law of this theater already makes a double—and seemingly contradictory—gesture: on the one hand, the law is said to be contained in the ape's pronouncement, which in its turn is contained within "A Report to an Academy." However, this double containing—the verb in each case is the same, *enthalten*—is unbalanced by an additional description of the law's placement: the law is tucked away, or, more emphatically, it is a secret law, it is pronounced in a sentence that itself is encrypted: *ist in dem versteckten Satz enthalten*. The participle *versteckten* creates an ambivalence in the spacing: if this tucked away, secret, encrypted sentence is indeed contained within Kafka's text titled "A Report to an Academy," still its secrecy and hiddenness as such remain to be deciphered and presented in full light. But it is a moot point whether that secrecy itself is also contained in the container, or whether in matter of fact it exceeds the container, escaping the inside-outside dichotomy. Or, a third alternative would be that, if that secrecy is a gambit, like the one presented in Thesis I of "On the Concept of History," then it would not matter at all whether that sentence prescribes the law or whether it proscribes the law that it prescribes; for in that case, the effective presence of the doppelgänger will have already made possible the subject's reinscription within a different matrix, a matrix, moreover, which is not deducible within the ambit of containment but only forms the movement of inscription itself. Thus, it is a matrix of inscribability—an allowing of, and a being allowed by, inscription, and in such a way that even the noninscription of imitation is made possible. Or, to put this the other way around, the doppelgänger is that which destroys imitation all the while itself allowing, and being allowed by, imitation. The exit (*Ausweg*), then, as the operative presence of the doppelgänger, is not a stepping outside the law of imitation, but rather its structural rearrangement.

Yet, if Benjamin's sentence, which designates the law of the world theater, preempts—prompts—the subversion of that law's power, the fact that the law is still permissible within a certain ambit is crucial. Moreover, to the extent that that ambit is repeatedly broached by Kafka—it is Kafka's world theater—the characteristics of the world theater's stage must be carefully outlined. As already noted, its main characteristic is that it is fated. The law of the world theater is that of the court officials and the holders of power, of the persecuted like K. and the *Kreaturen* like the Cat Lamb, Odradek, and Gregor Samsa, of the fathers and the sons. Moreover, these surreptitious laws are not only unwritten, but also—or, more precisely, therefore—impossible to avoid, they are fated: "A man can transgress them without suspecting it and then must strive for atonement [*Sühne*]. But no matter how hard it may hit the unsuspecting, the transgression in the sense of the law is not accidental but fated, a destiny which appears here in all its ambiguity."[36] Benjamin elaborates on this fated law with reference to the inherited sin (*Erbsünde*) that pits the father against the son and the son against the father. This sin does not consist in the father's bringing the son to the fallen world. On the contrary, the sin is the son's complaint. The sides of the table have turned: guilty is not the doer, but the one who is compelled to an interpretation of the deed; and the persecutor is also the executor of the punishment. The description of ambiguity in the mythic laws evokes formulations Benjamin had used thirteen years earlier in his essay on law and justice, "Critique of Violence": "Laws and circumscribed frontiers remain, at least in primeval times, unwritten laws. A man can unwittingly infringe upon them and thus incur their retribution [*Sühne*]. For each intervention of law that is provoked by an offense against unwritten and unknown law is called 'retribution' (in contradistinction to 'punishment'). But however unluckily it may befall its unsuspecting victim, its occurrence is, in the understanding of the law, not chance, but fate showing itself once again in its deliberate ambiguity."[37] As it

Self-Inscriptions 209

will be shown, there is a strong link between Benjamin's early writings on law and fate and the later essay on Kafka—a link precisely on the way that life and work are conceived.

Fate makes the structural arrangement between life and work ambiguous. This ambiguity is registered on the body. It paralyzes the subject—or at least makes it impossible for the subject to act. Such intractable action manifests itself as the loss of speech or language. But this loss will be thoroughly misconstrued if it is taken to be a psychosomatic symptom; rather it is a manifestation of the psychical and physical powers that pervade the existence of the subject with ambiguity. Benjamin recounts the Talmudic legend about a princess who "languish[es] in exile in a village whose language she does not understand" while she waits for her fiancé.[38] According to the rabbinical interpretation, the princess is the soul who does not understand the language of the body, the village she lives in. This explains her preparation of the Friday meal: preparing a meal for the absent fiancé is the only way to "express her joy in a village whose language she does not know."[39] Speechlessness, therefore, implies the return to the dependence upon the somatic, to the mythic direction toward what is termed in "Critique of Violence" "mere life [*des bloßen Lebens*]."[40] However, this "mere life" or the exilic body are not simply opposed or countered, they are not something that can be simply expunged:

> This village of the Talmud is right in Kafka's world. For just as K. lives in the village of Castle Hill, modern man lives in his own body: the body slips away from him, is hostile towards him. It may happen that a man wakes up one day and finds himself transformed into vermin. Strangeness—his own strangeness—has gained control over him. The air of this village blows about Kafka, and that is why he was not tempted to found a religion.[41]

The first sentence of this quotation is straightforward: the village, the body, is center stage in Kafka's world theater. However, the movement of Benjamin's thought must be traced with care, so that it does not lapse into an all too quick and customary lament about, or tirade against, the hostility of the body toward the subject on that center stage. Rather, if that hostile body "slips away" from the subject, this only indicates the predicament of "modern man." According to this predicament, man's "*own* strangeness" has overpowered him. Strangeness, then, and the body and hostility themselves, belong to the interiority of the subject. However, this interiority is articulated only as exteriority, as existence in the village or on the world stage. Thus, on the one hand, the overpowering is not a force purely external—as if it were an injunction emanating from a sovereign subject, or a declaration of war, or the declaration of a resumption of hostilities that founds a notion of politics. The predicament of the modern man cannot be squared with that outside which assumes the name of politics, because it also exemplifies writing—Kafka's novel *The Castle* and the novella *The Metamorphosis*. Moreover, on the other hand, the overpowering is not a force purely internal. There is no "Saint Kafka" who was separated from his world through a communication with the "Indestructible," as Benjamin makes clear: "The air in this village is permeated with . . . a putrid mixture. This is the air that Kafka had to breathe throughout his life. He was neither mantic nor the founder of a religion."[42] Kafka's world theater is a theater that includes Kafka not only as a spectator but also as an actor.

Instead of seeing the exilic body and "mere life" as an effect of a strangeness that is controlled by the spatial economy of interiority and exteriority, they can better be understood by comparing them to what was called in the preceding chapter "poor thingliness." In which case, the transience of experience, the strange experience of the hostile body, is not only something merely experienced but also the estrangement on which experience itself rests. This estrangement is different from that which is strange, in the same way that the mythic nothing, which was shown in the preceding section to hold onto a secret by surrounding it with ambiguity, is different from the nothing that responds to this ambiguity. A response is Kafka's predicament, since he "had to breathe throughout his life" the air of mythic ambiguity. Such a response is made possible by the ineliminability of the doppelgänger, since the doppelgänger is not containable within the protocols of any law, even if that law is unwritten. The doppelgänger is in a process of formation. But this formation is not only about life; it is also about writing. Kafka's breathing of the "putrid air" in his life is the reason that such an air is also contained in his writings. But the fact that life and writing are both apart and yet also part of each other means that they partake of a subject that does not permit the separation of a law of imitation from life and work. Rather, the operative presence of the doppelgänger is precisely the strangeness as such—the uncanniness—that characterizes the subject as lifework. This strangeness manifests itself, among other things, in a double impossibility: the reduction of the subject to a mere presence as a postulate of the political and the complete reduction of the somatic in the name of an "Indestructible." The strangeness of the doppelgänger destroys—leads to failure—such reductions.

However, besides the spatiality disclosed by the exilic body and its strangeness, the Talmudic legend also speaks of another dimension: the legend about the princess further intimates that the exile—existence—carries a futural promise. Its fulfillment will coincide with the coming of the messiah. Thus, the way that the body—and hence the subject—is conceived hinges on how existence *in the present* is related to the future. Will the present always have to wait for the future? This is a question that leads to a radically different notion of the theater in Benjamin's essay. This is the Nature Theater of Oklahoma in the final chapter of Kafka's *America*. The distinction between the world theater and the nature theater is drawn clearly in a note from the beginning of 1935, when Benjamin had started reworking his essay on Kafka. The note recalls the law of imitation of the world theater: "'I imitated because I was looking for an exit, and for no other reason,' said the ape in his 'Report to an Academy.' This sentence also holds the key for the place of the actors of the Nature Theatre 'Right here' they must be congratulated, since they are allowed to play *themselves*, they are freed from imitation. If there is in Kafka something like a contrast between damnation and salvation, it has to be searched for entirely on the contrast between the world theatre and the Nature Theatre [*allein in dem Gegensatz zwischen Welt- und Naturtheater*]."[43] What is striking about the relation between the nature theater and the imitative paradigm is that the sentence that discloses the imitation pertaining to it is no longer couched in a spatial arrangement of a double container and its hidden element, as was the case with the world theater in the Kafka essay. Rather, here what is contained in the sentence is unambiguously named: it is a cipher that places the actors of the nature theater in the here and now. The hidden or encrypted element has been disclosed, the future is being fulfilled in the present. There is no imitation here, no sharp dichotomies that characterize its imperative. The actors do not assume any roles; they actually play themselves: "all that is expected of the applicants [for the nature theater] is the ability to play themselves."[44] In the nature theater life and work are reconciled. Imitation does not operate here, because the actors play themselves. This also means that their gestures cannot be copied; they are inimitable. This coincidence of life and work further means that when Karl Rossmann enters the nature theater troupe, he becomes "pure, transparent, entirely without character [*durchsichtig, lauter, geradezu charakterlos*]."[45] Such a purity, says Benjamin, using Rosenzweig's words, corresponds to the actors' "elemental purity of feeling [*elementaren Reinheit des Gefühls*]."⁴⁶ The actors' pure gestures distinguish the nature theater from the world theater.

The purity of the actors on the nature theater of Oklahoma means that the ambiguity of the law of the world theater has now been resolved: life and work are reconciled. Thus, those on the stage of the nature theater "have been redeemed."⁴⁷ Where mythic laws hold sway, there is damnation; on the nature theater, there is salvation—not a putative or potential salvaging, but the presentation of an already redeemed subject. Redemption is the breaking loose from the fetters of the interior-exterior causality: on the stage, there is no imitative paradigm dependent on an economy of space. The stage becomes the actor's world in which life takes place, and there is nothing outside this state. The enormous importance accorded to the nature theater in Benjamin's reading of Kafka is manifest in anachronistically designating it as coming after *The Trial* and *The Castle*. "The reader of this announcement [of the Oklahoma Theater] is Karl Rossmann, the third and happiest incarnation of K., the hero of Kafka's novels."⁴⁸ There is here a move away from the spatial organization that the laws of fate give rise to. The unfettered and transparent actor has entered a space whose economy is no longer primarily spatial. This uneconomy of space, however, poses a problem. If, as explicated above, the doppelgänger's effective presence manifests itself as the strangeness of formative relations, then does the actor's elemental purity entail the denial of the doppelgänger? Or, to put the same point in the language that was used in the first chapter: if the nothing designates a region of complete inclusion, then the nothing indicates a substance, and hence a determinate presence—which does not square with the doppelgänger's undoing of presence.⁴⁹ Precisely because of the peril of lapsing into the substantialism of mere presence, Benjamin provides a crucial distinction in his discussion of the nature theater. Here, the ineliminability of the doppelgänger is designated as that which is "mysterious": "The mysterious place and the entirely unmysterious, transparent figure of Karl Rossmann are congruous."⁵⁰ The subject has attained transparency and purity, but these characteristics can be taken up only on a stage that itself remains mysterious. Thus, the precondition of purity—that which makes the staging of purity and redemption possible—remains in itself strangely impure and untransparent.

The impurity and untransparency that constitute the mysteriousness of the nature theater's stage should not be confused with the mythic ambiguity of the world theater. While fate ensnared unsuspecting victims because its laws were hidden, each gesture of the actors on the nature theater is unique and hence cannot be framed within a law: "What Kafka could fathom least of all was the *gestus*. Each gesture is an event—one might even say a drama—in itself. The stage on which the drama takes place is the world theater[51] which opens up toward heaven. On the other hand, this heaven is only background; to explore it according to its own laws would be like framing the painted backdrop of the stage and hanging it in a picture gallery. Like El Greco, Kafka tears open the sky behind every gesture."[52] There are no laws proper to the staging of the gesture. The only certainty is that, if one attempts to provide an image of the sky—to give the law of the sky—then the framing of this image will be destroyed along with the image's being torn apart. However, this does not entail a complete absence of the law. With the nature theater there is no "definite symbolic meaning" for the gestures or a rule whereby an imitative correspondence can be established.[53] Nevertheless, Benjamin underscores, "such a meaning from them [the gestures] is approached in ever-changing contexts and experimental groupings [*in immer wieder anderen Zusammenhängen und Versuchsanordnungen*]."[54] The law is not separate from the gesture, but constitutive of it. Each gesture constitutes the law and the process of constitution is ever changing—it coincides with the enacting of the gesture. There is here no falling silent as an effect of the law; rather, each gesture articulates the law anew and fully. The articulation characteristic of the nature theater is opposed to the silence of the world theater. But articulation is not a verbal expression but rather the gesture of the actor.

How is the doppelgänger to figure within such a setup? Clearly, the resistances and strangeness due to the effective presence of the doppelgänger cannot be reconciled with the actors whose law-constituting gestures reconcile their life and work. The doppelgänger, as already intimated, arises at the gap between life and work, in which case, the doppelgänger will not be equated with the gestic actor, but rather will arise due to the mysterious element in the staging of the gesture that sustains such a gap. The persistence of such a gap means that the relation between world theater and nature theater is not one of complete exclusion. The operative presence of the doppelgänger in both entails that, despite their being distinct, they are still interconnected. In other words, the gap will be sustained by that which the nature theater seeks to deny: the mythic that completely ruptures the relation between life and work. However, this is not to revert to the ambiguity of the law.

Rather, by juxtaposing the redemptive reconciliation of life and work in the nature theater and their aberrant ambiguity in the world theater, the relation between the two theaters will come to the fore. Then it will be obvious why the relation that both the world theater and the nature theater sought to sustain is still necessary: because of their alliance in both seeking to deny the doppelgänger. Benjamin had broached that relation as early as his 1919 essay "Fate and Character."

In "Fate and Character" it may appear at first that myth and redemption are, or should be, segregated. Nevertheless, an attentive reading of "Fate and Character" shows that such a segregation is untenable. Moreover, this untenability will be due to the functional operation of the doppelgänger. To demonstrate that untenability, a parallel reading of Kafka's *Metamorphosis* through the concepts of fate and character will be provided.

At the opening of "Fate and Character," Benjamin contends that the traditional understanding of fate and character conceives them as causally connected. Fate is equated with external events, while character is located in the body of the person. The external signs that accompany fate are "placed [*eingestellt*]" in a religious context, whereas the internal ones in an ethical context.[55] If the character of a person is known, and if the situations that the person enters are also known, then the future is "accessible [*zur Stelle*]."[56] At this place, fate and character "coincide [*zusammenfallen*]," and it is impossible to decide to what measure an individual is determined by fate or character.[57] Such coincidence undermines the causal relation between fate and character and, consequently, the concepts themselves. As a result, Benjamin argues, the concepts need to be defined as separate: "On the basis of this definition, the two concepts will become wholly divergent; where there is character there will, with certainty, not be fate, and in the area of fate character will not be found."[58] Such a separation entails the mistaken identification of fate with a religious aspect and of character with a moral aspect. Therefore, the religious and the ethical must be disentangled from fate and character respectively.

Guilt is said to be the main feature of the law of fate: "Law condemns not to punishment but to guilt. Fate is the guilt context of the living."[59] The balance between the inside and the outside of a fated subject is undecidable. "The fated subject is indeterminable. The judge can perceive fate whenever he pleases; with every judgment he must blindly dictate fate."[60] (This recalls the law of the father: "The fathers punish, but they are at the same time the accusers.")[61] The person is ensnared in the tight net that fate throws around it. The judge is the master of both the past and the future of the character. These laws function not on a level of reality, but rather on a level of semblance (*Schein*)—that is, on the level that Benjamin in the "Critique of Violence" identifies with myth, or in the Kafka essay with the world theater.[62] This collapse to semblance or appearances condemns the person to silence, as it has already been argued. Thus, for instance, Gregor Samsa in *Metamorphosis* cannot be understood by anyone—they no longer speak his language.

Character dismantles the "weft" (*Gewebe*) of fate. But only a "weak understanding [*ein schwacher Verstand*]" would recognize the operation of moral valuations in this tearing.[63] Morality is dissolved in character. Extricating character from the net of the fates and divesting its traits from any moral valuations gives birth to the comic hero. The valuation of character traits such as "clever" or "stupid" is retained, but this valuation is now separated from moral imperatives. This separation is an apophasis on the part of the character. The comic hero assumes a singular trait; his feelings are pure and transparent, just like the actors of the nature theater: "The sublimity of character comedy rests on this anonymity of man and his morality, alongside the utmost development of individuality through its exclusive character trait. While fate brings to light the immense complexity of the guilty person, the complication and bonds of this guilt, character gives this mythical enslavement of the person to the guilty context the answer of genius. Complication becomes simplicity, fate freedom."[64] This single character trait of the comic character can be illustrated again with an example from the *Metamorphosis*. Gregor is a verminish character through and through. His bodily movements are articulations of his pure verminishness. Whether Gregor approaches the chief clerk who retreats horrified to the staircase, or he is chased around the room by his father or he is mesmerized the violin—these "dances" have no symbolic meaning. They simply make up the single most literal trait of the vermin: its uncontrollable movement, unmediated and hence lacking reason. This simplicity—Gregor as a character—gives the *Metamorphosis* a pervasive comic aspect.[65]

However, as soon as Benjamin insists that the concepts of fate and character must be defined as "wholly divergent," he also notes a caveat: "In addition, care must be taken to assign both concepts to spheres in which they do not, as happens in common speech, usurp the rank of higher spheres and concepts [*Hoheit oberer Sphären und Begriffe*]."[66] Although Benjamin seems to be indicating a sphere that is more noble

(*Hoheit*) and higher (*oberer*), nevertheless the example that he provides places that sphere in between fate and character. (This recalls the way universal history, as it was shown in the preceding chapter, is the meridian of historicism and materialist historiography as well as their median. On the one hand, this prevents the reversion to the causal relation between fate and character rejected by Benjamin at the beginning of the essay. On the other hand, as it will be argued, it indicates the structural rearrangement characteristic of the doppelgänger.) Benjamin refers to the tragic hero as the person who aspires both to innocence—as opposed to fate's guilt—and to happiness—as opposed to the moral neutrality of character:

> It was not in law but in tragedy that the head of genius lifted itself [*erhob*] for the first time from the mist of guilt, for in tragedy the demonic fate is breached. But not by having the endless pagan chain of guilt and atonement superseded by the purity of the man who has expiated his sins. Rather, in tragedy pagan man becomes aware that he is better than his god, but the realization robs him of speech, remains unspoken. Without declaring itself, it seeks secretly to gather its forces. It does not just put guilt and atonement into the scales, but mixes them indiscriminately. There is no question of the "moral world order" being restored; instead, the moral hero, still dumb, not yet of age—as such he is called a hero—wishes to raise himself by shaking that tormented world. The paradox of the birth of genius in moral speechlessness, in moral infantility, is the sublimity [*Erhabene*] of tragedy.[67]

In relation to the discussion above, it is striking that the movement toward a nobler and higher order is identified with the birth of the tragic hero. Simultaneously, the tragic is distinguished from fate's dialectic of guilt and atonement as well as from the character's purity. However, what distinguishes the tragic hero also places him in contact with both fate and character. The characteristic of rising up resembles the trait of a character, although in tragedy it is still connected to the ethical. Thus, in *Metamorphosis*, Gregor makes several attempts to rise up: rising up from his bed or rising on his hind feet—maybe because rising up is what distinguishes the human (*anthropos*, man, is derived from the verb meaning "to rise"). These often frantic attempts place Gregor within the sphere of action, and hence of ethics. As the tragic hero lifts his head, the image of the gods remains powerful, and man is dumbfounded in regarding it. The "paradox" of the tragic hero is that he is still impelled to contemplate fate and hence to absorb its effect: he becomes speechless.⁶⁸ However, it is a "moral speechlessness." Speechlessness is a prerogative of the moral valuations that the hero cannot master because of his "moral infantility" or his innocence. Thus Gregor is anything but speechless at the beginning of the *Metamorphosis*, when he garrulously tries to explain his leave from work. The others' inability to understand him, premised on Gregor's assumption of guilt—guilty of lustful thoughts, as the framed photograph of the lady with the fur in his room indicates to his family, or guilty of embezzlement, as his boss assumes—demonstrates the context of fate that silences Gregor. These moral judgments condemn Gregor to speechlessness. Therefore, there is a region opened up by the tragic here which is higher than, but also between, the fate of the world theater and the redemption of comedy.

At this point, it becomes possible to schematize the way the doppelgänger operates within the setup established by the relation between the world theater and the nature theater. Such a schematization responds to the problematic posed by the nexus of life and work. The world theater conceives the relation between life and work as already created—which also means that the relation is being allowed by laws external to it. These laws are inaccessible to the subject, and hence their invidious ambiguity makes the subject indeterminate and entangled in the web of fate. Nonetheless, life and work on the stage of the nature theater are creative. The gestures of the actor are permitted by the law, which is being constituted in the process. The actor is redeemed—completely liberated. However, the doppelgänger transforms and deforms both mythic enslavement and redemptive liberation. The doppelgänger persists as the strange or mysterious element that reinscribes fate and redemption from within. Thus, the law of imitation characteristic of fate remains hidden within a complex of containment; yet the ambiguity of the complex of containment, as it was argued, makes it possible to understand the hidden not as a secret prohibition, but rather as the prohibition that has to remain hidden for the law to retain its ambiguity. And with this realization—which is ushered in by the functional presence of the doppelgänger—the net of fate has started to unravel. A similar unraveling occurs on the stage of the nature theater, which has to remain mysterious for the purity and transparency of the gestic actor to be maintained. But, as it was argued, this mysteriousness of the stage already inscribes the strangeness that characterizes and is characterized by the doppelgänger. The doppelgänger is, then, operative in both the world theater and the nature theater. Its operation is felt at the point where their respective configurations of life and work are disfigured but also configured. This movement of destruction and transformation is the figuration of the subject as doppelgänger.

If this discussion of the doppelgänger appears dependent on the world theater and the nature theater, then this only indicates that there is no immediate representation of the doppelgänger. The doppelgänger persists in its being absent—or, to put it the other way round, it persists in the necessary oscillation and instability between world theater and nature theater. However, this is not merely to define the relation between life and work in a negative manner—that is, in opposition to fate and redemption. Rather, as the tragic hero—the "rising up" of the doppelgänger—indicates, there is a staging that is proper to the doppelgänger. Moreover, it is a staging in which life and work attain a particular kind of relation. And it is a relation that will allow for the kind of self-inscription explicated in terms of the chess-playing automaton, the Turk, in the preceding section of this chapter. Thus, if the relation of the chess player and the puppet is a fateful one, then it becomes *indifferent* and either one can be privileged with a slight tipping of the scale. Also, if their relation is reconciled, then neither can be privileged. But then the chess game will be a *pure differentiation*: the moves that constitute the game are concomitantly the positing of its rules.[69] At the end, there is both too much and also not enough to separate these two options: their very segregation suggests that they are dialectically connected by a symmetrical necessity—the necessity of their own sameness, the sameness of their self-reflection. Conversely, the rupture of life and work makes possible both the distinction between man and puppet, and the complicity in the playing of the game. This double movement makes *difference* possible. The destructive aspect of difference only indicates the disfiguration of sameness and self-reflection. At the same time, however, it also indicates the process of self-formation, the endless transformation of the doppelgänger. This is the process made possible by the inscription of difference on the board: the difference attested to by the movement of the pieces in the game of chess. This process also attests to the complicity of the man and the puppet; thus it is a process of self-inscription, of the self-transformation and perpetual unfolding of the doppelgänger.

KAFKA'S "LOST GESTURE"

Benjamin presents Kafka's self-inscription—Kafka's doppelgänger—with recourse to a world distinct from both the world theater and the nature theater. This world pertains to Kafka's failure. Benjamin's insistence on Kafka's failure in relation to the nexus of life and work has already been cited: "[Kafka's] will orders their destruction. This document, which no one interested in Kafka can disregard, says that the writings did not satisfy their author, that he regarded his efforts as failures, that he counted himself among those who were bound to fail. He did fail in his grandiose attempt to convert poetry into doctrine, to turn it into a parable and restore to it that stability and unpretentiousness which, in the face of reason, seemed to him to be the only appropriate thing for it." However, given the operative presence of the doppelgänger, this failure should not be taken as a defeat. Rather, it indicates the failure of the world theater and the nature theater, of fate and messianism, to turn Kafka's life and work into a dispensation of sameness. It is the failure of indifference and of differentiation, giving rise instead to the difference made possible by the "middle world [*Mittelwelt*]" of the doppelgänger.[70] Benjamin insists on the "middle world" in the essay on Kafka. This world is populated by, among others, the "assistants" who, as Benjamin notes, "are outside [the] circle" of the *Kreaturen*, the world theater.[71] "Kafka's assistants are . . . neither members of, not strangers to, any of the other groups of figures, but, rather, messengers busy moving between them."[72] It is for them, "the unfinished and the hapless, that there is hope."[73] Considering a childhood photograph of Kafka, Benjamin also places Kafka in this middle world, "between a torture chamber and a throne room."[74] Benjamin designates forgetting as an essential feature of this middle world: "Oblivion is the container from which the inexhaustible in-between world [*Zwischenwelt*] in Kafka's stories presses toward the light."[75] The actors of the nature theater "resemble [*ähneln*]" Kafka's students, also inhabitants of the middle world, and yet they are different because the "actors have been redeemed. But this is not true of the student."[76] This failure of redemption gives hope to the middle world.

The way failure operates is complex. The demonstration of this operation would amount to a demonstration of how the doppelgänger is operative within Kafka's writings, no less than how Kafka's self-inscription is due to the doppelgänger. The most important aspect of failure is the attainment of difference. Yet difference—the difference of the subject as doppelgänger—sustains itself on at least two levels. First, difference indicates a political project. As Benjamin stresses in the Kafka essay, the "prehistoric forces that dominated Kafka's creativeness . . . may justifiably be regarded as belonging to our world as well."[77] Furthermore, Benjamin observes that Kafka's parables devoid of a doctrine touch on the "question of how life and work are organized in human society." Yet this organization, as it is presented in "The Great Wall of China," "resembles fate."[78] Therefore, Kafka's failure is not a strictly private affair. Rather, through the failure of fate the whole societal organization is challenged. This entails a political project that does not account for the liberation of a private individual, bur rather for the liberation of that subject which puts the individual into question—that is, the doppelgänger. The second element of difference pertains to a refiguration of truth. As Rodolphe Gasché argues in his discussion of "Fate and Character" in "Tearing at the Texture," the birth of the tragic is also the birth of a philosophy of difference: "Through this [the tragic hero's] eye-opening insight into man's distinction from the gods, a difference is made by which boundaries are assigned to myth and nature. Benjamin can, therefore, consider the tragic hero as the prototype of the philosopher who dispels natural and mythical indifference in an act of setting himself apart by raising his head higher. Distinction and difference are rooted in an act of demarcation by which the interlacings of myth are shattered in the name of radical heterogeneity—truth."[79] The terms "philosophy" and "truth" should not be understood as being strictly demarcated. Rather, Gasché's point is that they make demarcation, or difference as such, possible. That is why they entail "radical heterogeneity" as opposed to sameness. These two elements together—the political and the philosophical—constitute a logic of failure that is crucial for understanding both Benjamin's critical essay on Kafka and Kafka's own figuration of life and work within his instruction for his writings to be destroyed. In addition, this logic of failure will be shown to operate by resisting usurpation by any of the terms; rather, it will operate through the reflections and transformations of the terms themselves.

The presentation of this movement of failure will be a discussion of how Benjamin conceives of Kafka's self-inscription. And, given that Kafka's life and work are at stake, then the self-inscription will not be solely the presence of the doppelgänger in Kafka's writings but also of Kafka himself as a doppelgänger. In other words, Kafka's failure will have to be shown to be akin to the rising of the tragic hero. From this perspective, Kafka's instruction for his manuscripts to be destroyed no longer appears surprising: it signifies the tragic hero's "speechlessness." The speechless and cognate categories are of immense importance in Benjamin's thought, no doubt because they mark the link to the silence of fate as well as the rupture from that world. Thus, in the essay on Goethe's *Elective Affinities* Benjamin pays particular attention to the "expressionless." Moreover, as Benjamin makes clear in a note from around 1922, "truth has a [constitutive] relation . . . to silence."[80] If silence is the prerogative of myth, truth must also be related to silence, since myth is not to be overcome by a complete opposition but, as already argued, by facilitating myth's failure. Silence, then, the power to say nothing, presents the complex operation of failure in the Kafka essay.

Whereas the link provided by silence ensures that the failure of myth is not complete and hence oppositional, still the proximity of the two silences means that their distinction is complex. Benjamin approaches this problematic through Kafka's retelling of Ulysses' encounter with the Sirens. According to Kafka, the Sirens' song is actually silent. But the cunning Ulysses counteracts this silence by ignoring the Sirens. Ulysses' gaze "was fixed on the distance, the Sirens disappeared as it were before his determination, and at the very moment when he was closest to them he was not longer aware of them."[81] Benjamin's argument is that Ulysses' gesture vitiates the mythic world of the Sirens. Ulysses is, in the vocabulary of "Fate and Character," the tragic hero. His cunning consists of speechlessness, that is, in the appropriation of myth's own trick. However, this entails a danger. As Gasché puts it in "Kafka's Law," Kafka's world of the laws "is a world in which myth itself has already promised redemption, deliverance from itself. This promise of redemption in Kafka's mythic world is the ultimate mythic category at the service of the perpetuation of myth."[82] Not only is myth inauthentic and distorted, but it also promises a dis-distortion. This promise, however, is a canceling out of the law, which becomes a law in turn. If the Sirens sing nothing, the nothingness of their song can also anticipate Ulysses' own gaze directed at nothing—Ulysses' silent gesture. Thus, the danger is that Ulysses may have avoided the ambiguity of myth; he may have avoided being entrapped all alone in the net of fates; but, this may only lead to Ulysses creating for himself a new law, redeeming himself by being a new Oedipus, another first man. In which case, he would be a thoroughly pure character and his childish measure of blocking his ears would turn his cunning into the trait of a comic character. At this point, the proximity of myth and redemption also betrays their alliance—their conspiracy—in the service of sameness. It is a point where a spontaneous reversion from the one world to the other disguises itself as the spontaneity of freedom.

Conversely, there is actual hope only because of the hopelessness of the law. It is not myth that needs to be distorted; rather, what is required is a distortion of the distortions of myth. "This possibility of a slight adjustment, by way of a dislocation, or displacement of distortion itself . . . in order to turn the distorted world into a redeemed world, is the remainder of transcendence fit for a world of total immanence."[83] And this *double distortion* is a function of reason and cunning, the "Greek way" of Ulysses. With the double distortion, cunning is no longer a character trait. Ulysses, unlike the actors of the nature theater, has not been redeemed—he has not succeeded in the face of the Sirens' failure. Ulysses has also failed. Benjamin cites Kafka's qualification against unequivocally granting victory to Ulysses: "Perhaps he [Ulysses] had really noticed, *although this cannot be grasped by the human understanding*, that the Sirens were silent."[84] Beyond the reach of "human understanding," the combination of reason and cunning takes effect. Beyond understanding, Ulysses gazes at a nothing that is neither already enclosed in a totality nor creating a totality. The nothing is neither appearance nor abstraction. The ambivalence about Ulysses' gaze means that his nothing oscillates between the two possibilities and persists in that irreconcilability. This movement marks, as Benjamin indicates, the "middle world" of Kafka's stories, and it is marked, as it has been argued, by the operative presence of the doppelgänger.

However, here another problem arises—a problem that necessitates a discussion of the author and of authorship. The question is: How can Kafka assert that Ulysses' gesture is beyond human understanding? This does not question whether Kafka's assertion is certain or uncertain, since that would only instate doubt as a methodological principle of epistemology derived from the mind's cognitive capacity. And then Kafka, at the moment he narrates how someone else transcends the limits of myth by bypassing understanding, that very moment Kafka himself would fall back into understanding, and hence myth. (The same problem will also hold for Benjamin, as it will be shown in the following section.) To show how Kafka avoids this double bind is to show *how* he did not understand the *gestus* that constitutes the "cloudy spot" of his parables. It is to explain why what "Kafka could fathom least of all was the *gestus*." The urgency of this problematic explains Benjamin's insistence on Kafka's instructions for his writings to be destroyed. It shows that liberation cannot be achieved only through one's work. In addition, liberation has to be indexed within one's life. Kafka's will is a gesture within the nexus of life and writing. Thus, it effects not only the assistants and students of the middle world of his stories but also the author of these stories and the stories' authority as statements about the world. In other words, at issue is not only how the gestures of a character in a story enact the oscillation between myth and redemption, but even more pressingly how Kafka inscribes himself within gesture as such. It is this self-inscriptive and oscillating gesture that Benjamin calls a "lost gesture." The implications for a theory of the doppelgänger are far-reaching. For in that case, the doppelgänger escapes the confines of the page and its absent presence is instilled within the author and his authority. Through this infinite reflection of author and authority the literary work attains both a philosophical and a political significance.

An approach to this problematic has to start with the movement characteristic of the middle world, namely oscillation. Benjamin observes that "Kafka does not tire of describing these fluctuating experiences. Each one gives way, each one mingles with its opposite."[85] This "fluctuating" or swinging experience that distorts itself and distorts its own distortion is Ulysses' trick. It opens up a staging of both myth and the messianic but without being reducible to either. This new staging is distinguishable from the world theater and the nature theater.[86] Further, this experience is infused with an anxiety described in terms of forgetting. The individual has forgotten the laws of myth, but this means that they are contained within him. Significantly, the pure autonomy of the individual is excluded from this sphere: "What has been forgotten ... is never something only individual."[87] This overcoming of individuality is inevitable at the point of contact between philosophy and the political. The operative presence of the doppelgänger as forgetting in the experience of oscillation is not premised on either a dichotomy of life and work, or on their reconciliation. Moreover, it is the reason why Benjamin explicitly rejects psychological explications of Kafka's work. This can best be demonstrated with recourse to Kurt J. Fickert's study of the doppelgänger in Kafka. In *Kafka's Doubles*, Fickert argues that "literature [was for Kafka] a vehicle of self-examination," made possible by specific kinds of experience, namely "autoscopy, and ... multiple personality."[88] Through this symptomatology of selfhood, and hence of his own self, Kafka managed to discern the "dichotomy [producing] the conflict-ridden man and the artist observing himself."[89] This double life of everyday activity and authorship is what Fickert identifies as Kafka's doppelgänger. But this abject duplicity is also said to produce a unity with the use of the doppelgänger: "Kafka is portraying himself and his *Doppelgänger*" in stories such as the *Metamorphosis*.[90] Thus, while the doppelgänger is said to be a symptom of a "double life," one aspect of this double life, namely writing, usurps the other. Kafka then becomes a symbol of humanity as such because he has managed to overcome the divisions that mark human psychopathology. That Fickert's extrapolation is nothing but a form of mythic thinking is demonstrated by the fact that Kafka's own self-reflections, as manifestations of a redeemed humanity, annul the premise on which those very self-reflections were based: namely, the "double life" of Kafka the individual. (It will be recalled that this syncretic circle was shown in the Introduction to be prevalent in many psychological approaches to the doppelgänger.) Consequently, Kafka's writings are based on an imitation of his life and hence effectuate a transcendence. But this only highlights the secret alliance of myth and redemption. The doppelgänger, as discussed in this book, is emphatically not the doppelgänger as outlined by Fickert. Whereas Fickert still requires the individual in order for the experience of the "double life" to be enacted, Kafka's subject of the fluctuating experience, as it is described by Benjamin, is a forgetting of individuality.

To discern the figuration of this nonindividual subject—the doppelgänger—in Benjamin's essay on Kafka, it is important to hold onto the fluctuating experience that will bring Kafka's self-inscription to the fore. And this means that the refiguration of the individual is a process of configuration and disfiguration that does not find rest at any point. For this process, "reversal" is a crucial term, as attested by one of the most important sentences in the Kafka essay: "Reversal is the direction of study which transforms existence into script [*Umkehr ist die Richtung des Studiums, die das Dasein in Schrift verwandelt*]."[91] This reversal is staged differently from the staging in the nature theater. While the pure gesture promises a complete forgetting of the law of imitation, forgetting in terms of the reversal is the incompletion of a struggle. There "is a tempest that blows from the land of oblivion, and learning is a cavalry attack against it."[92] This struggle is against not only the distortions of mythic law but also against the pure forgetting by the characterless actor of the nature theater. Reversal, then, is two things at once: First, it is a staging of transformability. There is neither pure destruction nor a pure resignation to existence: "Whether the students have lost their script [writing, Holy Writ, *Schrift*], or whether they cannot decipher it, comes down to the same thing, because the script without the key [cipher, *Schlüssel*] that belongs to it is not script, it is, rather, life. I see in the immediate transformation of life into script the meaning of the 'reversal' [*Umkehr*], which presses forward in certain Kafka parables."[93] Transformation is the literary effect of Kafka's writings—transformation is an effect of technique and hence linked to particularity, as intimated in Chapter 1: Benjamin emphasizes that Kafka's parables unfold "the way a bud turns into blossom. That is why their effect is literary."[94] The staging of transformability does not provide a cipher, and hence it is endless. Second, this endlessness, far from being redemptive, is in matter of fact distorting. The scribes and students who struggle against oblivion, this "fanatical mien," are frenetic and "out of breath; they fairly race along," preoccupied as they are with the brevity of life.[95] Because of this incessant struggle they are still not liberated,. The struggle has left its mark on their bodies: they hunch over the script. This mark, which Benjamin calls an *Urbild*, is indicative of the individual who seeks self-presentation only to find its individuality distorted.

The reversal in the Kafka essay is akin to the dialectical reversal noted by Benjamin in Konvolut K of *The Arcades Project*: "politics attains primacy over history." When this reversal from history to politics was discussed in the preceding chapter, it was shown to be precipitated by the doppelgänger. This entailed an understanding of the doppelgänger as a relationality yielding a notion of subjective ontology. This relationality has three aspects: a destruction of autonomous individuality, which leads to commonality; a retention of the subject as the capacity to interrupt the movement between completion and incompletion; and the responsibility to retain relationality as the exigency of the political. These three aspects are also present in Benjamin's essay and notes on Kafka. However, the emphasis on the reversal here is nuanced in a different way, namely on a kind of writing that has been voided. There is nothing supporting this writing from the outside; it exists as its own movement of reversibility. At the same time, the assertion that there is no support for writing brings to the fore the nothing that constitutes and is constituted by that writing. The nothing operates by enacting the relations between destruction, interruption, and responsibility. Thus, its operation indicates the effective presence of the doppelgänger—the freedom made possible by the doppelgänger. At this juncture, it becomes clear why it has been necessary to distinguish between the characters of Kafka's stories and Kafka as an author. The voiding of writing, the nothing, describes the type of relationality between life and work. Because of this the doppelgänger prevents the author of the parables from staking a mythical or theological claim of knowledge. Thus, Kafka's writings will no longer be a biographical cognition but rather an enactment of the demands put forward by life. Moreover, their failure will be the enactment of the relationality between commonality and interruption. And to the extent that this relationality is undertaken with responsibility, it will also be undertaken with the doppelgänger. To demonstrate this, the three aspects of the reversal—commonality, interruption, and responsibility—have to be traced in Benjamin's writings on Kafka. This will amount to demonstrating how the nothing in Kafka is akin to Ulysses' nothing as described above, as well as how the nothing leads to self-inscription, as was outlined in the first section.

There must be a nothing, then, which de-constitutes the autonomous individual, but in such a way as to be embedded in a community. This means that de-individuation consists in resisting two temptations: the equation of the subject with the life and the laws that constitute the individual, and understanding the subject as independently creating life and the law. Benjamin broached this problematic in a conversation about Kafka with Bertolt Brecht on 6 June 1931, which he recorded in his notebook. According to Brecht, the whole of Kafka's work consists of variations on the single theme of the author. This theme is the interaction of the individual with its environment, and Kafka's variation is a constant astonishment in the face of this interaction. "The astonishment of a man who senses the appearance of enormous shifts in all relations but without being able to accommodate himself in the new organizations. For the new organizations ... are defined by the dialectical laws which dictate the existence of the masses as well as of the individual." Benjamin's understanding of the setup between the individual and dialectical laws attests an overcoming of individuality. Kafka's kind of writing, the way that it consists of a certain kind of statement, makes possible the inclusion of the other, the community, but in an agonistic manner.

> But with his astonishment, in which he mixes liberally panic and horror, the individual as such must reply to the almost incomprehensible dislocations [or distortions, *Entstellungen*] of existence which give away the emergence of these laws.—It seems to me that Kafka is so under the influence of it / them [*davon*] that he cannot at all present undistorted anything in our sense. In other words, everything that he describes is a statement about something other than itself. The lasting visionary present of the distorted things reciprocates the inconsolable gravity, the despair in the gaze of the author himself.[96]

In the author's statements the individual enacts the description of its existence (his struggle against the laws and the way the laws are communally constituted) only as a distortion. What is described is never the actual object. *Nothing* is named. A description only describes the opposite of what it refers to (a point which will be taken up in more detail in the following section). It remains unclear—and therefore untranslatable—what the "davon" refers to. Is it the astonishment that overpowers Kafka? Or, perhaps, the dialectical laws? Or the shifts in the communal relations? Maybe it is the individual as individual who only finds itself out of place because of the preceding factors. In which case the individual will have ceded its place to the doppelgänger, to the subject who is not permitted to ever say "I am I." Kafka's utterances have the structure: "Nothing that I describe names anything"; with the addendum: "Including this description." This subject does not have apperception—it can never have a self-presentation accompanying its perceptions. However, this would not mean that it is doomed to be divorced from the world since it no longer has a hold on its appearances. Rather, the opposite is the case: the subject does not have apperception because it has totally distorted—destroyed—its appearances.[97] This entails the doppelgänger's undercutting of a transcendental subjectivity that underwrites the operation of each particular subject—as was the case with the Fichtean project, which postulated the "I am I" as the starting principle of philosophy. In other words, this entails the absence of an authority to protect or secure the author. The destruction of the individual announces the collapse of the attempt to guarantee the subject in its own image or self-reflection. The nothing operating here does not pertain to knowledge of the objectual world—the world in which the subject of subjectivity subsists. The subject's gaze is turned around. Its perceptions are not of things but of scripts of things. The reversal transforms existence into writing. "Nothing" is named. The act of non-naming protects the subject from self-representation, from making a law and an image of itself. Kafka's subject inscribes itself by this "original act."[98] This original act is only possible if the subject is not alone in the world. Its necessary condition is another for the statement to be communicated to. Hence, the necessity of the elimination of a pure or autonomous subject.

The second aspect, interruption, indicates the maneuver whereby a decision can be made in the process of naming. Again, the particularity of the author is indispensable. The author makes decisions that are premised on particular situations. Writing—the author's existence—is not an indefinite act. The particularity of the act of writing offers the—impossible—possibility of ending. The perpetuity of existence is punctuated by the putting down of the pen. With this, the original act of naming can be actualized. Even if the author's statements mean nothing, still this nothing is not absolute. Nothing *is* named—if only obliquely, circuitously. Benjamin addresses this "nothing" when he refers to the frenetic activities of the students, who, like the fools (*Narren*) never tire or sleep; but also, "perhaps these studies had amounted to nothing. But they are very close to that nothing which alone makes it possible for something to be useful."[99] Benjamin then cites from the collection titled *Er* the aphorism that describes hammering as a real and painstaking craftsmanship and simultaneously as a nothing. Studying and hammering indicate the interruption that names nothing. Thus, the interruption, as act, is also self-destruction. These two processes are concomitant. The reversal is not simply the destruction of subjective autonomy *plus* the interruption. Rather, the reversal is *both* in simultaneity, in their consupponibility.

There is another aphorism from the same period as *Er*, which Brod might have titled "The Cossack Dance" if he had selected it for publication, and which captures the consupponibility of the interruptive act and self-destruction under the rubric of writing.

> Writing refuses itself to me. Thus the plan of the autobiographical investigations. No biography, but investigation and discovery of the smallest possible integral elements. From this I want to build myself up just like somebody whose house is unsafe and who wants to build next to it a safe one, wherever possible using the material of the old house. Though it turns bad when his strength ceases in the middle of the construction and so now, instead of an unsafe but at least standing house, he has a half-destroyed and a half-ready house—therefore nothing. What follows is madness, something like a Cossack-dance between the two houses, whereby the Cossack scratches and digs out the earth with his boot-heels for so long, until his grave is formed beneath him.[100]

Autobiography is an investigation and discovery of existence. Or rather, existence is the writing that builds oneself up. This building starts from an experience that is distorted like a decrepit house. The distortion provides the hope that the house can be relocated (or dislocated) and constructed anew. However, the process cannot complete itself; one gets exhausted. In the experience that fluctuates between two distortions, there is frenetic movement, the dance of the Cossack; but, also, there is the stillness and silence of the nothing, the grave formed by the dance. Yet the nothing is distorted as well: the writing, perhaps incomplete and inaccurate, has nevertheless been enacted. Something has been written despite—or, because of—the refusal of writing. Kafka's self-inscription is circuitous, it never builds a domus, a stable center; in its whirling dance, the individual cannot stand on a fixed point. There is no individual auto-nomy—that is, there is no transcendental law that functions as a pure self-presentation (*Selbständigkeit*) for individuality. Thus, writing makes possible the destruction of subjectivity while being made possible by it. This consupponibility prevents mere presence—it prevents the individual or subjectivity from mastering possibility as such.

The consupponibility of self-destruction and interruption has a twofold consequence: by not being commensurate with mastery, it is an enactment of freedom; at the same time, nonmastery also entails that the subject is in a process of formation, always there and always to be further elaborated. Both of these characteristics have been shown to arise out of the operative presence of the doppelgänger; however, what is important here is their interdependence. Freedom is no longer a "thing" in the world; nor is it given through the objectual world, but rather through their destruction. The Cossack dance is enacted on ruins, on a field of destruction—of nothing. Writing stands in this field of destruction—or, perhaps, it is more accurate to say, in this field of catastrophe, of the turning around itself (*kata-strephein*), the reversal. Kafka, the individual scribe, is like the Cossack. Benjamin's argument—that Kafka's parables fail to achieve "unpretentiousness [*Unscheinbarkeit*]" because the instructions for their destruction were connected to Kafka's failure to attain a doctrine—here achieves a specific meaning. From the present vantage point, Kafka can be seen to feign (*scheinbar sein*) to address objective reality. By bypassing the objective reality of appearance (*Schein*), by destroying apperception, Kafka has gained his freedom. Here, the realm of myth subsists, but its appearances can never overpower the subject—the doppelgänger. Freedom is premised on a realm—the nothing—that cannot be equated with the phenomenal. At the same time, particularity is maintained through the act of writing—the writing that names the nothing. This double movement of reversibility is due to the doppelgänger. Benjamin alludes to the doppelgänger in the final section of his Kafka essay, titled "Sancho Panza," showing that the consupponibility of self-destruction and interruption entails a politics of responsibility.

At this point, "lost gesture" is crucial. Significantly, the discussion shifts from the inhabitants of the middle world to Kafka himself.

> Experiments have proved that a man does not recognize his own walk on the screen or his own voice on the phonograph. The situation of the subject in such experiments is Kafka's situation; this is what leads

him to study, where he may encounter fragments of his own existence—fragments that are still within the context of the role. He might catch hold of the lost gesture [*Er würde den verlorenen Gestus zu fassen bekommen*] the way Peter Schlemihl caught hold of the shadow he had sold. He might understand himself, but what an enormous effort would be required!¹⁰¹

The invocation of Adelbert von Chamisso's *Peter Schlemihl* links the experience of the lost gesture to the doppelgänger. For instance, Otto Rank refers to *Peter Schlemihl* as a prime illustration of the doppelgänger.¹⁰² Yet besides the invocation of the doppelgänger as a literary motif, Benjamin's reference to the "lost gesture" traces the movement of Kafka's self-inscription—the doppelgänger as a figuration of the subject. The subjunctive in the sentence (*er würde . . . zu fassen bekommen*) is crucial. It denotes a possibility—or, even more emphatically, the condition that allows for the possible. Unlike Schlemihl in Chamisso's novella, Kafka's lost gesture is not striving toward a restitution of a unity. The lost gesture is that which allows for the effort to take place, but Benjamin does not posit a reclaiming of the shadow as an endpoint. What this means could be further explicated if the shadow, as it was argued at the beginning of Chapter 2, is taken to be the law that follows the subject. Thus, Benjamin is not arguing that Kafka's lost gesture reconstitutes either his individual subject or subjectivity as such. Instead, the effort to catch the shadow, enormous and endless as it is, signifies the permanent rupture between the subject and its transcendental legal securing. But Benjamin is not concluding from this that the body is sidelined, as if Schlemihl would indicate that the shadow has lost its body—what Marx calls an "inverted Schlemihl."¹⁰³ Then the reality of the subject would have dissipated in the screen and the phonograph. However, this is not the case. If modern technological experience leads to the fragmentation of the subject, this only makes studying all the more urgent. And studying, as an activity of the "middle world," is also an activity in the realm of actuality. Thus, the reference to the possibility of recording experiences with new media does not signify an institution of a new (technological) experience, but the transformability of experience through the subject's persistence in the world—through the actuality of existence.¹⁰⁴

Thus, the gesture is *lost*. Kafka has failed, and his actions amounted to nothing. But this should be taken to mean that Kafka inscribes himself with such a lost gesture. The inscription, however, is not complete; it lacks its law just as it lacks its shadow. It is a lost inscription, beyond the law—and hence closer to a realm of justice, whose gate is the study that characterizes the middle world, as Benjamin observes.¹⁰⁵ That realm which, as argued in Chapter 2, is neither encompassed by law nor segregated from it. Because of this, the subject as doppelgänger enacts lost gestures, gestures of the nothing—where the nothing is the condition of the possibility of gesturing as such. Thus it is a nothing reduced to neither the phenomenal, nor to the transcendental, but rather persisting between the two. Moreover, it is a gesture that, by being lost, also has to remain silent, but then this is the silence that is constitutive of the truth, in Benjamin's formulation noted at the beginning of this section. Maybe this explains why Benjamin regarded "The Truth about Sancho Panza" Kafka's most perfect creation.

> Without ever boasting about it, Sancho Panza succeeds in the course of the years, by supplying a lot of romances of chivalry and adventure for the evening and night hours, in so diverting his demon [*Teufel*], whom he later called Don Quixote, that his demon thereupon freely performed the maddest exploits, which, however, lacking a preordained object, which Sancho Panza himself was supposed to have been, did no one any harm. A free man, Sancho Panza serenely followed Don Quixote on his crusades, perhaps out of a sense of responsibility, and thus enjoyed a great and profitable entertainment to the end of his days.¹⁰⁶

The moment that silence becomes constitutive of truth, responsibility comes to the fore. The imperative that defines Sancho Panza is responsibility. Here, responsibility is precisely the demand to adhere to the dual relationality of the doppelgänger. The imperative neither to reduce the subject to appearance nor to move it to a transcendent realm. Therefore, responsibility is a product of the double bind. The "law" that governs the subject of the lost gesture, the "law" of the doppelgänger, is the concomitant adherence to the irreconcilable laws of particularity and infinity. *Nothing* is named directly, and also nothing *is* named. It is a law, only insofar as it is produced by this impossible reconciliation. And it can only be produced through the responsibility of the subject. Thereby the subject interrupts the vicious circle (*Teufelskreis*) of myth: Sancho Panza's circuitousness diverts his demon (*Teufel*). Freedom is the subject's responsibility to follow its "other half" that has been diverted and resides in books and myths. The lost gestus accomplishes the reversal that turns existence into writing. Kafka's testament, "which no one interested in Kafka can disregard," is also a script, a piece of writing. Therefore, it is also a lost gesture. The Kafka who wrote it was responsive to the doppelgänger.

For that, of course, Kafka needed his demon—the demon that would allow for Kafka's freedom. And he may have found him, if an apocryphon that Benjamin jotted down in preparation for the Kafka essay is correct.

> Kafka and Brod: Laurel sought his Hardy, Pat his Patachon. Offering God such entertainment made Kafka free for his work about which God did not have to care anymore now. But Kafka gave probably free reign to his devil in this friendship. Perhaps he had such a relation to Brod and his deep Jewish philosophemes like the relation between Sancho Panza to Don Quixote and his deeply meaningful chimeras of chivalry. Kafka had several splendid devilish tricks in his own body and Kafka could be happy seeing them romping before him in the form of indecencies, faux pas and unpleasant situations. He probably felt at least as much responsibility for Brod as he felt for himself—or even more.[107]

If Kafka was responsible for Brod, then Kafka's gesture in his instructions for the destruction of his manuscripts was realized after his death, but in the circuitous movement that only the intervention of Brod could have enabled. Yet this is not to separate steadfastly between Kafka and Brod or to assert that their respective demeanors can be fused into a single unity. As Benjamin underscores, Kafka's relation to Brod was one of *responsibility*. The responsibility persists in Kafka's foremost gesture, his instructions to Brod to destroy his manuscripts. Yet that responsibility does not merely make the relation between Kafka and Brod possible to be carried out to infinity, since there is no transcendent image as endpoint. And it does not merely secure, in print, the particularity of the writing act. By the staging of this particular infinite—the doppelgänger naming the nothing—the staging becomes a law outside the interplay of appearances. The law—this law of responsibility—can be actualized only in the dispensation of the doppelgänger's relationality. If that is true, then Kafka is free. A freedom made possible by Brod-Kafka's doppelgänger. Although the expression "Kafka's doppelgänger" is not a possessive; it is rather that which allows for a staging of the doppelgänger relationality, the creation of and the creating of the name "Franz Kafka," while also being allowed by the "nothing" in that name.

LYING WITH BENJAMIN

If the signature "Franz Kafka" is a nothing, while the "nothing" also signs in the name, then the signatory of this thought—that is, Benjamin in his work on Kafka—will also have to be implicated in the same movement. "Walter Benjamin" is related to "Franz Kafka" through the operation of criticism. The doppelgänger makes self-reflection untenable because the name no longer signifies a complete individual, nor is it secured by a transcendental notion of individuality. A twofold movement will show how this untenability figures in the critical task—a movement captured in two different operations of "lying with." First, it will no longer be possible to distinguish "Kafka" and "Benjamin" as distinct individuals whose self-representations achieve completeness—the prohibition against the graven image applies to the critic as well. In other words, the contours of those two proper names will start blurring as a necessary consequence of the effective presence of the doppelgänger. Second, this will also have to lead to the kind of problematic that was encountered in relation to Kafka; namely, if the critic communicates in the gestic manner of the tragic hero, then the full representation of appearances may have been avoided, but its promise of a complete absence would make myth into its obverse image of redemption. Criticism must avoid this progression of self-reflection with a counterturning.

This complicated double maneuvering may lead to an exasperated objection: Why is, after all, a complete self-representation to be avoided? Does not everyone recognize his own image—even if that requires accustoming oneself with the medium in which the image is produced? On a certain pragmatic level, this may be correct. Even an animal may be startled the first time it encounters its reflection in a mirror, yet after some getting used to, the fear disappears, and the animal might even recognize its mirror image as its own self-reflection. However, the example of the animal also shows the deficiency of the pragmatic. For what does "an animal" mean? Is it a cat or a dog, any domestic animal that is likely to encounter a mirror? Or does it also include wild animals, or creatures living in the sea, and so on? Here, two options are open to such a pragmatic view: either to insist on a thorough empirical taxonomy of "modes" of self-representation in different species or to abstract from what is meant by "self-representation" so that it could be applied to only specific examples—preferably only to the human, the animal made in the image of God. Both approaches presuppose a totality that cancels out relation. In a complete taxonomy, a self-image will already have to have been included, whereas in a totalizing abstraction there will never be a self-representation properly speaking. Therefore, both approaches lack a notion of singularity such as uniqueness is finite. In other words, they do not account for singularity such that identity—personal and collective identity, as well as the identity of things—is given through life as a process of temporalization, given in time. Because of this operation of time in singularity, the image can never be timeless—it is never outside life. This time-bound image has been linked to modernity, since, as Sylviane Agacinski puts it, "the idea of modernity refers less to a situation in time than it is itself *a certain way of thinking about time.*"[108] Because a self-representation is the rupture of the subject's relation with time or, even more emphatically, the erasure of relationality as such, then it is nonrelation; it is death. This is why the emphasis throughout this book has all along been on the *relationality* of the doppelgänger. And because of the relationality of the doppelgänger, a self-reflection cannot account for the life of the subject.

This is not to say that nonrelation must be eliminated. On the contrary, death persists; it is inscribed in every image and every photograph. The relationality put forward by the doppelgänger is against totalizing forms of presence, and it would be an equally totalizing endeavor to eliminate the image altogether. Rather, what is important is how the subject related to the image is positioned so that what persists is relation. However, this also entails that the image is never owned; an image of oneself is always an image that implicates another. Eduardo Cadava, in an important book on Benjamin's notions of temporality and the photograph, raises the point about the blurring of the contours of two subjects through the mediation of the image by referring to two photographs, one of Benjamin and one of Kafka. Or, more accurately, Cadava focuses not on the photographs themselves, but rather on how the photographs are described by Benjamin. The first, of Benjamin and his brother, appears in *Berlin Childhood around 1900* (in the 1934 version, that is, the same year as the Kafka essay). The second is of Kafka and is described first in "A Little History of Photography" (1931) and then expanded on in Benjamin's essay on Kafka, in the second section titled "A Childhood Photograph." What is striking in those photographs is not their content—they both are more or less standard studio portraits, showing the young boys surrounded by the extravagant inanimate nature of the photographic studio. Rather, Cadava is interested in the way that Benjamin's description entails a confrontation of the subject with nonrelation. "Benjamin speaks the truth of the self's disappearance in a series of transitions from one double of himself to another."[109] Yet this is not the disappearance of the self; it is not the death of Benjamin. Instead, it means that the signature "Benjamin" is dispersed in the relation that persists between his image and that of Kafka: "The figure he describes is both like Kafka and like Benjamin, since it is in this figure of the other (the photographed double of the little Kafka) as the other (Kafka) that Benjamin encounters himself.... [I]n experiencing the other alterity, in experiencing alterity in the other, he [Benjamin] experiences the alteration that, 'in him,' infinitely displaces and delimits his singularity."[110] Singularity is made possible precisely by the other as doppelgänger—the relation that destroys the individual by showing that the individual's outline, like the outline of the face in a photograph, is never exact, always grainy, trembling.

The important point about the duplicity established in the photographic images of Benjamin and Kafka as well as in the description of them is that singularity is retained by the putting into question of the signature. The signature, that idiosyncratic trace, can be taken as a complete representation of the name, and hence as a complete self-reflection. Cadava shows that just as the inanimate props in the photographic studios blurred the images of Benjamin and Kafka, equally the title of Benjamin's essay on Kafka, another prop, from the very beginning instills a blurring of their signatures: "The very title of the essay, 'Franz Kafka: On the Tenth Anniversary of his Death,' can refer not only to Benjamin's effort to write about Kafka on the anniversary of his death but also to the possibility that Kafka himself has returned from his death in order to write on the topic of this particular return of his death. In this instance, it would be Kafka who, writing from beyond the grave, writes of his death but only after his death—or rather, only after the death of his death. The essay can therefore be said to be written by Kafka in the name of Benjamin or, assuming the first possibility, by Benjamin in the name of Kafka. In either case, what seems to get staged here is the necessity that each sign in the name of the other or of oneself as other."[111] When this movement of countersigning—the doppelgänger's destabilization of any proprietary claim on one's own identity—has been established from the title, Cadava goes on to show that it permeates Benjamin's essay on Kafka. For instance, the essay includes an anecdote about Potemkin who signs documents with the name of the person proffering those documents. Thus, not only the names "Benjamin" and "Kafka" lose their security, but also "Kafka's world is a world in which one never signs in one's own name."[112] The unsigning of the signatory is precipitated by the subject's confrontation with nonrelation, that is, with the death implied in a complete self-reflection. The specter of death impels both the counterfeit of the sign and the emergence of the other. In other words, it ushers in the relationality proper to the doppelgänger.

The blurring of the contours and the signatures is the staging of a theatrical scene in which the subject's image figures its death. The ambiguity of the pronoun "its" in the preceding sentence must be held in abeyance: it is the death of subjectivity no less than the nonrelation—the death—of the image. This petrifaction of the subject, which Cadava calls the "Medusa effect," is a death of the illusion that appearances can provide the constitution of the subject qua subject. Yet this death is of necessity underpinned by relation, by the proximity of the signatories—even in the dismantling of their signatures as complete signifiers. This is a tableau vivant not only of Benjamin and Kafka but also of "Benjamin" and "Kafka" lying side by side as if on their deathbeds—where the inverted commas indicate the suspension of a totalizing relation established by the name, the death of and in the name. In addition, it is a scene in which their relation—their "lying with"— is pushed to the limit and hence dismantled alongside their signatures: a deathbed of Benjamin "and" Kafka, as well as of "Benjamin and Kafka." In other words, nonrelation as the relation proper to the image is not a bypassing of relationality as such, but rather its starkest affirmation. An affirmation made possible by the chiasmoi set in motion in the proper names—the chiasmoi of the doppelgänger.

However, this tableau vivant prompts another scene. And it is a scene at once logically necessary and also enacting the suspension of the comfortable good conscience of deductive logic. This other scene is inscribed in the logical possibilities of the conjunction binding Benjamin and Kafka. For if all the above chiasmoi describe subjectivity's death of and in the signature, then is it not also possible to put the chiasmus itself in quotation marks? In which case, Benjamin's lying with Kafka will be presented in the figure of "Benjamin 'and' Kafka." This suspension of suspension is enacted in relation itself, so that the end will not be allowed to provide a passage to that realm in which the suspension of illusion cedes its place to the illusion of suspension. In other words, the suspension of suspension counteracts the move from the mythic to the messianic. It is not a self-negating, or determinate negation, of suspension, but rather the suspension of the alliance of myth and theology. To recall the vocabulary used in describing Ulysses' trick against the Sirens' silence, it is a double distortion.[113] The upshot of this logical necessity of suspending the "and" is that subjective affirmation as such, the subject's self-inscription, is enacted in particularity.

But the inscription of and in particularity, then, entails a suspension of the certainty afforded by logical abstraction, by the deduction from the rules and laws afforded by transcendental subjectivity—by deducing through the axiom of self-reflection, the "I = I," the doppelgänger precludes the possibility of thinking the subject as a dispensation of its immediate self-cognition.

This second tableau vivant is not a scene from a different play, so to speak, but rather a scene from the same play, maybe from a different act. This is to say that there is a "lying with" in Benjamin's relation to Kafka that is distinct yet interrelated to the "lying with" discussed above as the two figures lying alongside each other on their deathbed. The contention, then, is that the doppelgänger configures the relationship between Benjamin and Kafka in the mutual operation of the two "lying withs." In other words, it is through the distinct—and, hence, related—operation of the second "lying with" that Benjamin enacts a self-inscription which protects his criticism from moving into a realm of pure differentiation. If the first "lying with" was shown to be the dismantling of a totalizing concept of life by the work—the work of and in the image—then the work should not become total as well. This will only lead to the equation of work and life, as in the nature theater. What is needed with the second "lying with" is a suspension of the work in life—a suspension of nonrelation into relation without the latter being a totalizing presence. Self-inscription is enacted in this double failure of presence. However, how could this second "lying with" be approached? Surely, were Benjamin to have included a metanarrative in the Kafka essay that would have deduced his own self-inscription, such a deduction would only have been a self-deduction, that is, a self-reflection. Rather, what is needed is to show that Benjamin's criticism of Kafka contains immanently in itself an inscription that allows for the second "lying with." The second "lying with" must be absent from, yet because of that all the more operative in, Benjamin's essay on Kafka. Moreover, it will have to respond to the middle world of Kafka, the world in which an oscillation or fluctuation prevented the resting on either myth or theology. And it is at this point that the distinction between the silent gesture overcoming myth and the enacted speech of a published essay effectuate a distinction between the two "lying withs." Through the operation of this distinction, the effective presence of the doppelgänger in Benjamin's critical work will be discerned.[114]

As already intimated in the preceding section, truth is, according to Benjamin, constitutive of silence. The contention here is, then, that the first "lying with," the failure of life in work, configures truth in its constitutive relation to silence. However, the sentence that precedes Benjamin's designation of the relation between truth and mythic silence is instrumental for an understanding of the second "lying with." There, Benjamin designates a relation constitutive of speech. Hence, it can be taken as the relation constitutive of the language—the script—that Benjamin's own essay on Kafka is: a relation constitutive of criticism. The passage in question is: "The lie has a constitutive relation to language (so that a lie through silence is immoral). The truth has such a relation not to speech, but to silence."[115] The assertion of the lie's immorality will be entirely misunderstood if taken as a (moralistic) assertion about the "evil" nature of not telling the truth. Benjamin is not interested in such moralizing. Rather, he is interested in describing two kinds of relation that are interconnected to the extent that they ascribe relation as such. Thus, a silent lie is immoral (*unsittlich*) because it is no longer a lie but already speaks the truth. It speaks the truth because silence is a prerogative of the ethical sphere, that is of the sphere of life, the realm of manners (*die Sitten*). Conversely, the kind of speech constitutive of the lie is not an assertion about life, but rather a distortion of life. That is, language is an affirmation ab initio of the operation of the work, the work of lying. What has to be shown is that the operation of the lie relates a subjective gesture—the second "lying with"—which fails to attain a complete life, such as that of the nature theater. Simultaneously, it should be kept in mind that the lie and silence are not apart, but rather both partake of relationality itself.

The paradox that makes the lie fruitful for a criticism that allows for the operative presence of the doppelgänger is the notion of community that it inaugurates. As it has already been argued in Chapters 2 and 4, a lie is of necessity intentional—otherwise it will not be a lie but a factual mistake, an inadvertent slippage. Therefore, it was argued, the political project of lying is based on a notion of the subject that subverts intentionality and hence beyond a transcendental framing of the subject.[116] To inscribe the lie in the political entails that a philosophical ontology of the subject is not ipso facto political; rather, the political and the philosophical are consupponible; they persist at the points of their mutual interpenetration, which are also points of rupture. They persist in judgments and interpretation. The value of the lie for criticism arises at precisely this point and with the following question: Is a complete lie possible? In other words, is it possible to say that a phrase is completely intentional, to the point that it breaks intentionality itself? And, if such absolutism lacks an authority who can ground it, then what are the implications of the political project that has to include in itself also the oxymoron of an inadvertent lie? Or, to put this another way, how is it possible to lie to someone without also lying with someone—how is it possible to say a complete lie without a complicity of the other even to the extent that the other usurps the liar's ownmost intention to lie? This oxymoronic structure of "lying with" pertains to criticism because, as it will be shown, it inaugurates a space in which the subject cedes its position to material actuality. For this, two aspects of lying manifesting the doppelgänger's eschewal of presence are important.[117] The first is the way that lying is related to justice in "Critique of Violence," and the second is how the lie still allows for the singularity of the speaking subject—the critic.[118]

The "Critique of Violence" opens with the following assertion: "The task of a critique of violence circumscribes itself in the presentation of the relation between law and justice. For a cause, however effective, becomes violent, in the precise sense of the word, only when it enters into moral relations."[119] The relation between law and justice can be viewed from the perspective of violence only when the link is provided by moral relations (*sittliche Verhältnisse*). Thus the lie, since it is immoral in the sense outlined above, namely as outside the sphere of intentional action, has no place in a critique of legal violence. This is precisely the point raised by Benjamin in a short discussion of the lie in "Critique of Violence." Violence is structured by a series of oppositions that disclose the legal order. Thus, there is the opposition between the means toward ends versus the ends justifying the means, or the opposition between law-positing and law-preserving violence, and ultimately the opposition between mythic power and pure divine violence. These oppositions are mediated by a politics of pure means, which Benjamin associates with justice.[120] Lying and language are explicitly ascribed to the operation of pure means—an operation in which violence is not constitutive.

> Nonviolent agreement is found wherever a civilized outlook allows the use of pure means of agreement. Legal and illegal means of every kind that are at the same time violent may be confronted with nonviolent ones as pure means. Courtesy, sympathy, peaceableness, trust, and whatever else might here be mentioned are their subjective preconditions. Their objective appearance, however, is determined by the law ... that says pure means are never those of unmediated solutions but always those of mediate solutions. They therefore do not apply to

> the unmediated resolution of conflict between individuals, but always relate to things. In the most emphatic relation to things, the human conflicts about goods open up the realm of pure means. For this reason, technique in the broadest sense of the word is their most particular area. Its profoundest example is perhaps the conversation as a technique of civil agreement. For in it not only is nonviolent unity possible, but also the exclusion of violence in principle is quite explicitly demonstrable by one significant relation: the impunity for the lie. Probably no legislation on earth originally stipulated a punishment for the lie. This bespeaks a sphere of human agreement that is nonviolent to the extent that it is wholly inaccessible to violence: the sphere proper to "understanding," language.[121]

Besides the sphere of violence bespoken by the legal sphere, there is also a nonviolent sphere associated with the lie, understanding and language.[122] It is only in this sphere that pure means are to be encountered—that is, only in the sphere of justice. The implication of ascribing pure means to this sphere is that a teleology is not operative here. And this also means that subjective intentionality is bypassed, to the extent that pure means indicates that there is no conflict between individuals (*zwischen Mensch und Mensch*) intending certain ends, but rather agreement is sought on the utmost objective relations (*in den sachlichsten Beziehung*), that is, in the relations of materiality. Thus, the work of language and understanding does not just resolve itself in subjective activity or in the life of the individual. Rather, the nonviolent lie is the pure means of the operation of negotiation itself, which is always a materialist interpretation, an interpretation of and about things. The political implications of this nonintentional lie—the lie as pure means—are enormous, but they can be summarized in one concise point relevant to the discussion here: the dismantling of individuality as such.

Peter Fenves, in an essay that remains the most significant discussion of lying in Benjamin, expresses the import of the dismantling of the individual in the following terms: "The self and the world are in a peculiar and incomparable manner divorced from one another when the truth has been told. . . . The juridical power that underlies the order to 'tell the truth' . . . owes its origin in a certain critical ability, namely the facility of transcendental subjectivity . . . to represent the world and, concomitantly, to make its representations . . . comprehensible to 'all the world.'" In other words, the law presupposes a subject that tells the truth. Although the subject and its world may be ruptured, the subjectivity or humanity that grounds the subject announces the possibil-

Self-Inscriptions 241

ity that the gap with the world will be closed and that the world will be represented by the subject to the world itself. Because of this presupposed obligation to represent the whole world the law attains to a divine origin—moreover, an origin whose symptom is the split between subject and subjectivity as well as their reflections. But the situation with lying is completely different.

> Mendacity, however, is *in principle* insusceptible to the juridical order in the extremity of its deformation, namely, in "objective mendacity." ... Objectivity should not here be understood as the correlate of subjectivity but rather as a manifestation of the subjectless idea whose "essence" is the presentation of truth. Objective mendacity can be, then, nothing other than the "reversal of an Idea." It is precisely this unrepresentable and nonexemplary mode of mendacity that withdraws from the self-justifying power of subjectivity whereby lying would find its ground and thus a—self-serving or other-serving—reason; this mode likewise withdraws from the legal order while all along putting the legal order ... on trial—precisely *as a lie*, the perversion of the idea.[123]

Mendacity leads to the "subjectless idea" that undoes the self-justifying structure of self-reflection. This is the nonviolent lie, objective mendacity. However, this does not contradict the intentional lie (what Benjamin has called the immoral lie). On the contrary, the intentional lie can put the legal order itself on trial because it has access to it. Representation and subjectivity are not to be dismantled from the outside, but rather pushed to the limit and hence to their own self-dismantling. The lie, as Fenves notes, is a reversal. The realm of understanding, the lie, and language highlighted in the "Critique of Violence," is the realm in which communication becomes a pure means. It becomes a suspension of the suspended intentions expressed by a subject. In this "retarding," as Fenves calls it, the doppelgänger operates as the continual redrawing of the subject's limits, as the undermining of subjectivity's legal order. "If one wants to call this retarding 'justice,' no law can stand in the way."[124]

Lying is the just language. But it is only just when it is no longer counterposed to truth, that is, when the lie is beyond the secrecy of a dialectic of mastery. It is just when it opens up a space—like a theater stage—where interpretation can unfold. The infinity of interpretability, however, is a materialist project, not one based on subjectivity. As stated in the last section of Chapter 1, the formation that takes place in the finite resists occlusion through its infinite transformation. Now, as soon as this just language is related to criticism, then the critical task opens up a community of the lie—a being with that allows interpretation, a lying with. This is a subjectless togetherness, a community of the doppelgänger. Such a community recalls the conjuring of an audience in the opening words of Thesis I in "On the Concept of History," as shown in the first section of this chapter. The expression "it should be generally known" introduced an audience, making possible the staging that has been approached from different directions in this chapter. It will also be recalled that Thesis I provided a self-inscription, such that the Turk's winning would not be eternal. A similar movement of self-inscription must also be allowed in the critical task—the task of the second "lying with." Only then will the critic as doppelgänger come to the fore—or, more accurately, only then will the effective presence of the doppelgänger be demonstrated as inscribed within criticism.

The most important text in this regard is one of the notes on Benjamin's work on lying. Moreover, it is a note that can be allowed to resonate within Benjamin's work on Kafka—in a resonance showing the complicity between the author and the critic. The text in question, titled "Über den 'Kreter,'" refers to "The Paradox of the Cretan," which, according to Benjamin, may be "one of a kind [*das einzige seiner Art*]."[125] The paradox of the Cretan, or the liar paradox, is well known. Epimenides, a Cretan, asserted that "all Cretans are liars." Does this mean that this assertion is true or false? Benjamin argues that in its traditional formulation the paradox is easily resolved, since Epimenides' proposition does not imply that "the liar departs from the truth every time he opens his mouth."[126] However, the paradox becomes "a truly fruitful problem [*wahrhaft fruchtbares Problem*]" when it is reformulated so as to say that "Epimenides maintains that all Cretans, whenever they open their mouths, assert the contrary of what is true," adding the premise that "Epimenides is a Cretan."[127] In its most formulaic, Benjamin adds, this will be expressed in the following manner: "'Every time one of my judgements without exception predicates the contrary of the truth.' From this it would then follow: 'Including this one.' 'Therefore, every one of my judgements, without exception, predicates in accordance with the truth.' 'Including, therefore, the first assertion above.' Which would always revert to the starting point of the circle."[128] Just as with the "win all the time" in Thesis I, the "whenever" and the "every time" are crucial, as it will be shown shortly. At present, it will be recalled that Benjamin designated this structure of a *dissos logos* in the Kafka essay as well as in his notes on Kafka.[129] Thus, for instance, it was shown that in Kafka's middle world each fluctuating experience was canceled out, ceding its position to its opposite, and utterances were said to be distortions always describing something else. To cite again one example, in his 1931 note of a conversation with Brecht, Benjamin had observed that Kafka "cannot at all present undistorted anything in our sense. In other words, everything that he describes is a statement about something other than itself." However, this is not to say that Kafka's *dissoi logoi* are the same as the Cretan paradox, if the latter is taken to be akin to the nonintentional lie of pure means. The difference lies precisely in the direction of the reversal. If the limit disclosed by Kafka's middle world is the reversal from life into writing, the limit in Benjamin's conception of the interpretation made possible by lying is from work into life. Moreover, by its being a counterreversal, so to speak, this will put the relation between life and work in suspension and thus highlight the relationality as such made possible by criticism.

At the same time, the distinct relations established in literature and criticism highlight the difficulty facing the latter. Namely, although the reversal from life to work allows for singularity and nonrelation, how is singularity to be retained in the movement from work to life? This difficulty discloses the importance of the liar paradox. For, as Benjamin has noted, this paradox is "one of a kind." This is not meant to indicate merely a unique problem in logic, but rather to reinscribe logic as well as the subject presupposed by it within a sphere where uniqueness attains a new configuration—one in which the singularity of the critic is effected by the doppelgänger. After the recognition that the liar paradox is "one of its kind" and hence not soluble within logic, a twofold move is required for the singularity of the doppelgänger to come to the fore. Given that the paradox is not "meaningless or nonsensical," it pertains to an "ontological plane [*ontologischen Gebiet*]."[130] At the same time, however, it makes sense as a paradox—it only *is* a lie if uttered by the Cretan in a judgment that claims to be valid.[131] It seems as if Benjamin counters the paradox with another paradox: the lie—a work and not a reference to life—provides an ontology of the subject that leads to its singularity. For this paradox to retain both a certain logic such that the lie will remain a lie, and an ontological import, then two interrelated conclusions must be shown to follow. First, it is only "as appearance [*als Schein*]" that the paradox applies to logic.[132] What must be sought, then, is neither a "logical legal authority," for there is none (*es keine logische Instanz gibt*), nor an alogical one, but rather a reinscription of the logical, a spacing of the antilogical.

Here the solution must be sought in the "I-form" of the judgement, which, as it was shown above, is constitutive to it. Its appearance of logicality is constituted through its conception of subjectivity. Hence the necessity asserts itself not only to conceive of subjectivity as an alogical legal authority [*alogische Instanz*] in contradiction to objectivity and universal validity, but, more precisely, to position the subjectivity's "destructive tendency in validity" as the opposite of the objectivity of validity. According to the metaphysical thesis that would resolve that logical appearance, subjectivity is not alogical but antilogical [*antilogisch*].[133]

Moving to the antilogical means that the singularity of the person who uses language is not given through an operation of validity. This annuls the reflections between the subject and its court of appeal, subjectivity as such. However, Benjamin explicitly allows for a notion of subjectivity that is "antilogical." The contention here is that this subjectivity is the doppelgänger—the subject that persists in the work of language qua language, the lie qua lying, and the paradox qua paradox. But—and this is the second point—this also entails that the lie, language, and paradox cannot be given through the operation of an "always." The Cretan liar is a paradox only if an utterance is inscribed in a "whenever" and an "every time" (I am a Cretan and I lie *whenever / every time* I open my mouth). Conversely, to say that subjectivity as a doppelgänger is inscribed within language and the lie is to insist on the singularity of each utterance. Consequently, the "every time the same" will here mean also "every time different." The suspension of sameness in the work of language is not an erasure of singularity but an answer to the lie of uniqueness. Singularity persists as the lie about oneself. It persists in a lying with oneself in a world where language is also a lying with others.

To locate criticism in this spacing of "lying with" is to avoid locating the work in an independent and autonomous individual. If criticism persists as a lie, this means that the work carries on persisting. If the reflection of the critic is not a self-reflection but rather the reflection of the doppelgänger, then the reflection is no longer essentialized in an atemporal "always the same." The work is always particular, and hence singular. To turn this the other way round, it also means that the doppelgänger that is in the work of the literary writing also persists in the singularity of the critical act. Consequently, the singularity of the critic is plural—in his work the author lives vicariously; his words bespeak another life. This double movement does not merely present one kind of reversal, one kind of relation. Rather, it presents the reversibility

Self-Inscriptions 245

and relationality between literature and criticism that the doppelgänger makes possible. Reversibility and relationality here do not refer to the signatories of the literary and the critical work, unless the signature is a self-inscription outside the bounds of a stable personal identity. There is no rule that determines that outside of self-inscription because it is beyond legal authority—it is the outside as such. Although this nonrule, this antilogical operation, can be given a name: the doppelgänger. A name operative even if—and, especially when—not named explicitly or even denied, attempting to erase its signature: the "doppelgänger."

| | |

A final question presses itself forward at this point. How can one write the name "doppelgänger" without concomitantly being a doppelgänger? Clearly, the writer of the preceding cannot claim a security of opinion and an authority of judgment while writing about the doppelgänger's undoing of such security and authority. However, it will be all too easy to conclude from this that "I am always already a doppelgänger." This would only mean that the discursive parameters of the doppelgänger know of no outside. Whereas, as already intimated, it is the impossible possibility of such an outside that the doppelgänger puts forward. Thus, it may appear that the "I" is faced with the unenviable situation of not simply being unable to assert self-identity, but not even being allowed to assert an identification with that which unsettles self-identity, that is, the doppelgänger. In other words, it may appear that the "I" can never say "I."

The problem in the above thought process does not reside in the formulation of the personal pronoun. Rather, the problem applies to the adverb "never." For with the "never" what is purported is an always the same. Thus, the point is not that "I" can never say *"I"*; rather, the point is that "I" can never say *"never."* With this "never-never," the enunciation inscribes itself, as well as the enunciator, in a movement that includes the subject. But this is the subject given through its particularity, understood as both its work and its activity. The "never-never" always announces the subject, but without recourse to a transcendental security. Consequently, "I" cannot *not* write "I" in every movement that pertains to singularity. The signature persists in the double distortion of the negations of the "I" and the "I"—of the "'I'" and the "'I.'" This nothing is inscribed in the signature no less than it allows for self-inscription. But this does not lead to the absolute loneliness of the "nothing but I," which Jean Paul's doppelgänger showed to be the reduction ad absurdum of apperception. Rather, it leads to a spacing in which the subject is alongside the other: the "I" is always an "I-with."

At the same time, this spacing is not dispensed by itself. The "I" is not essentially political—this would only turn the subject into a determinate presence. The "I" becomes political by allowing for that spacing. In other words, the political is the assumption of the responsibility to create and be created by that spacing. This is an obligation that persists within the subject because of the doppelgänger's ineliminable connection to justice. However, this is not a definition of the doppelgänger in the guise of an identification with justice. Rather, just as justice is a becoming whose end is unknown, similarly the doppelgänger is under way. The doppelgänger as a subject of modernity is under development—it remains to be elaborated.

Thus, the preceding pages have not presented *a* or *the* theory of the doppelgänger. Rather, what has been presented is the operative presence of the doppelgänger in literary, critical, and philosophical writings. The doppelgänger figures as long as literature, criticism, and philosophy reflect each other. And there is no "I" that can claim to put a stop to such a reflection without simultaneously denying the doppelgänger. As demonstrated, such a claim is often made, but in each case the denial of the doppelgänger inscribes it in an even more central position in the discourse that seeks to deny it: the denial shows the blind spot—the unknown, the impossible, the under way, and hence the doppelgänger—operating in an essentialist discourse. Literature, criticism, and philosophy are not a reflection of subjectivity; they provide a reflection of the doppelgänger.

Such a reflection undermines the link between the private and the public, the inner soul and the outer body—all the subjective divisions of metaphysics. To rupture the ruptures that such distinctions seek to establish is the prerogative of the doppelgänger. It is the doppelgänger's political task—a task that persists as nonsubjective reflection. It persists as a materialist reflection. Here, again, another reason is encountered why the doppelgänger does not allow for a prohibition against the first person personal pronoun. Every time that one would claim that "I cannot say 'I,'" what is affirmed is a rupture between the private and the public or the inside and the outside, while concomitantly this rupture will calcify itself in reasons that are either empirical or transcendental. Conversely, the justice of the doppelgänger is a reminder that every utterance is implicated in an ineliminable web of interests and self-serving intentions. And the most insidious manifestations of such pronouncements are those which seek to hide those interests and intentions. To such acts and utterances, the doppelgänger responds with the reminder that there is no subject without subjection, and whoever seeks to deny that is merely seeking to subject another.

The philosophical task is to trace such a dialectic of mastery in its historical manifestations and to reply to it with responsibility. If there is an ontology of the subject as doppelgänger, then such an ontology can be gleaned in the responsibility to history and historiography—a responsibility that cannot be undertaken by presupposing the real presence of subjects. Rather, it can only be undertaken by effectuating ruptures in the divisions of the metaphysical understanding of subjectivity. Those interruptions are acts of judgment. An ontology of the subject is one that allows for the possibility of subjective interruption—an allowing whose precondition persists in the historical. If the historical reflections presented in this book focused on literature and criticism, this is not because a philosophy of the subject is somehow given essentially or primarily in art. Rather, the history of the emergence of the doppelgänger is one in which the literary and the critical have highlighted the resistances proffered against the doppelgänger. The ontological task is to recognize such resistances. Philosophy needs these resistances in order to develop an ontology—which also means that philosophy needs literature and criticism as its others in order to avoid a self-occlusion. Philosophy needs the doppelgänger.

At the same time, the philosophical task is not exclusive—any sphere of thought or activity is amenable to the doppelgänger. However, this is not to proclaim the omnipresence of the doppelgänger, but rather to insist that that philosophical task still remains to be carried out. And it is being carried out precisely by not totalizing it, by avoiding the alibi of its omnipresence. What has to be insisted on is that every sphere of thought and activity has certain limitations. If these limits are not purely subjective, that is because they are inherently interruptive. But this only means that the subject persists, albeit *on* the limit, as the operation of liminality. In other words, the subject is inscribed at the points where transformation, relation, and reversal are possible. This liminal subject is the doppelgänger.

NOTES

PREAMBLE

1. Jean-Joseph Goux, *Oedipus, Philosopher*, trans. Catherine Porter (Stanford: Stanford University Press, 1993).

2. As has often been observed, Sophocles notes this loneliness in the beginning of *Oedipus Rex*, where Oedipus constantly proclaims his standing alone in the disaster that has befallen Thebes. See Sophocles, *Ajax, Electra, Oedipus Tyrannus*, trans. Hugh Lloyd-Jones (Cambridge, Mass.: Harvard University Press, 2001).

3. Henri Lefebvre, *Introduction to Modernity: Twelve Preludes, September 1959–May 1961*, trans. John Moore (London: Verso, 1995), 55.

4. Jacques Derrida, *Of Hospitality: Anne Dufourmantelle Invites Jacques Derrida to Respond*, trans. Rachel Bowlby (Stanford: Stanford University Press).

INTRODUCTION

1. See Roland Barthes, "The Death of Author," in *Image, Music, Text*, trans. Stephen Heath (New York: Hill and Wang, 1977), 142–48.

2. In other words, the doppelgänger in the present book will not be treated as a motif used by Romantic literature, not only because a motif is nothing but an abstraction but also because the doppelgänger, as is argued in Chapter 3, disturbs easy generic designations.

3. Debra Walker King, "Introduction: Body Fictions," in *Body Politics and the Fictional Double*, ed. Debra Walker King (Bloomington: Indiana University Press, 2000), vii–viii.

4. Jean Paul, *Blumen-, Frucht- und Dornenstücke, oder Ehestand, Tod und Hochzeit des Armenadvokaten F. St. Siebenkäs* [1796], in *Sämtliche Werke*, ed. Norbert Miller (Darmstadt: Wissenschaftliche Buchgesellschaft, 2000), 1.2:66. The first time that Jean Paul writes the word, it is spelled with a "t" between the two compounds: Doppel*t*gänger. Later, on page 532, the "t" is elided, and the word is spelled in its customary way: Doppelgänger. However, the passage on page 532 is an addition to the second edition of *Siebenkäs* in 1818, by which time, of course, the

word "Doppelgänger," spelled without the "t" between the two syllables, had been in wide use. Andrew J. Webber, in a remarkable analysis of Heine's famous poem *Doppeltgänger*, shows how the extra "t" "marks a sort of impediment to freedom of speech, a caesura" and the effects that this has to the overall structure of the poem. See Andrew J. Webber, *The Doppelgänger: Double Visions in German Literature* (Oxford: Oxford University Press, 1996), 16. For a useful summary of the historical development of the term "Doppelgänger," see the corresponding entry in Elisabeth Frenzel, *Motive der Weltliteratur: Ein Lexikon Dichtungsgeschichtlicher Längsschnitte* (Stuttgart: Alfred Kröner, 1988).

5. Rodolphe Gasché's *The Tain of the Mirror: Derrida and the Philosophy of Reflection* (Cambridge, Mass.: Harvard University Press, 1986) is not only a study of Derrida's work, but it is also one of the most compelling studies of reflection as a term that organizes discourse.

6. As Ernesto Laclau formulates this point about the politics of the subject, "[T]he particular can only realize itself if it constantly keeps open, and constantly redefines, its relation to the universal" (Ernesto Laclau, "Subject of Politics, Politics of the Subject," in *Emancipation(s)* [London: Verso, 1996], 65). Thomas Keenan, in his remarkable book *Fables of Responsibility: Aberrations and Predicaments in Ethics and Politics* (Stanford: Stanford University Press, 1997), also pays close attention to interruption as that which constitutes the relation between the literary and the political. In a line of argument that will be also be pursued in this book, Keenan argues that such interruptions are manifestations of responsibility. However, this entails that the discourses presupposing a subject based on the security of foundations are divested of political responsibility. "We have politics because we have no grounds, no reliable standpoints—in other words, responsibility and rights, the answers and the claims we make as foundations disintegrate, are constitutive of politics" (3).

7. This alliance shows itself in the figure of Oedipus who, according to the Chapter 1 epigraph from Nietzsche, is the last man and who is also, according to Hegel in the epigraph of Chapter 2, the first man. Oedipus, as the figure who privileges sight and the image, exemplifies the metaphysical drive for presence as an effect of the clarity—or pure light—of reason. See Jean-Joseph Goux, *Oedipus, Philosopher*, trans. Catherine Porter (Stanford: Stanford University Press, 1993).

8. Although the present study agrees with Gordon E. Slethaug in *The Play of the Double in Postmodern American Fiction* (Carbondale: Southern Illinois University Press, 1993) that in the metaphysics of self-reflection the double shows that "the interpretation of experience mirrors our minds" (25), nevertheless the conclusion does not follow that there is a new double whose protocols are radically different. To argue that "the double is really only a linguistic device, a metaphor, authors can demythologize it and ... they can create a metadouble" (27–28) only raises the question of what language is. And if, as Slethaug seems to argue, language is everything, then this merely means that mirroring is displaced from its more traditional carriers (soul, God, or the transcendental subject of Idealism), and placed on an all-encompassing totality called "language."

9. There are three further uses of the term "Doppelgänger that will not be discussed here. The first pertains to a congruity with related literary motifs, such as twins. There is no doubt that twins and the doppelgänger have been related themes, as is shown, for instance, in the useful study by Juliana de Nooy, *Twins in Contemporary Literature and Culture: Look Twice* (Hampshire: Palgrave Macmillan, 2005). However, it is argued in Chapter 3, a thematic analysis in terms of literary motifs is inadequate for an ontology of the doppelgänger. In spite of the congruity, each term has to retain its uniqueness. The second pertains to a nonthematized use of the term "double," or "Doppelgänger." For instance, Maria Aline Selgueiro Seabra Ferreira uses the term to refer to human cloning in *I Am the Other: Literary Negotiations of Human Cloning* (Westport, Conn.: Praeger, 2005); and Uffa Jensen uses it to refer to a specific historical constellation in *Gebildete Doppelgänger: Bürgerliche Juden und Protestanten im 19. Jahrhundert* (Göttingen: Vandenhoeck & Ruprecht, 2005). Third, there is an entirely gratuitous use, unaware of the historical import of the doppelgänger as well as of its philosophical implications—as is the case, for instance, with papers in the field of physics that refer to the doppelgänger in order to designate a relation between particles.

10. This is not to suggest, of course, that every psychoanalytical approach to the doppelgänger is mired in this syncretism. For instance, see the section "The Return of Negation," in Chapter 1, where it is shown that Freud extrapolates an ontology of the doppelgänger that is not caught up in this circle.

11. Ralph Tymms, *Doubles in Literary Psychology* (Cambridge: Bowes and Bowes, 1949), 15.

12. Mesmerism offered to Romantic authors who used the doppelgänger the idea that the occult or the unseen can become manifest. This influence is important for a number of authors, for instance, E. T. A. Hoffmann. And, as Adam Crabtree has shown in *From Mesmer to Freud: Magnetic Sleep and the Roots of Psychological Healing* (New Haven: Yale University Press, 1993), there is a genealogical connection between mesmerism and scientific psychoanalysis. However, this does not entail that the doppelgänger has to be read in terms of a manifestation of the inner self, that is, as a symptomatology of the author. Except in a trivial sense, literature cannot be equated with the genre of biography or with a scene of confession. Although the influence of mesmerism has not been pursued in the present study, it is clear that its influence does not necessarily lead criticism to the syncretism propagated by the psychological reading of the doppelgänger.

13. Tymms, *Doubles in Literary Psychology*, 119.

14. Tzvetan Todorov, *The Fantastic: A Structural Approach to a Literary Genre*, trans. Richard Howard (Ithaca: Cornell University Press, 1975), 160–61. The same disavowal of the doppelgänger qua literature is a standard feature of the majority of the psychological readings of the doppelgänger. Some instances of this will be recorded when they are relevant to the particular discussions in the following chapters. Suffice it here to present only one more example: John Herdman, in *The Double in Nineteenth-Century Fiction: The Shadow of Life* (New York: St. Martin's

Press, 1991), proposes a historical typology of the doppelgänger as a literary motif. However, by the end of the nineteenth century and with the "secularization of the traditional double, its assimilation to a rationalist perspective, the dualistic mainstream is about to move away from fiction into formal psychology. . . . [T]he motif recurs frequently enough in twentieth-century novels and stories, but it seldom occupies the position of centrality that it held in the nineteenth-century works" (151–52). The move "from fiction into formal psychology" can be unproblematic only if the syncretism between the author and the characters of the author's work is presupposed. This book will show that there is no justification for such a syncretism.

There are, of course, variations on this argumentative maneuver. However, what is always required is a positing of an agent whose knowledge or expertise legitimates (that is, mirrors) the process. Thus, to mention one variation, the psychologist can be substituted for the genius-writer. Claire Rosenfield provides her own typology of the doppelgänger in "The Shadow Within: The Conscious and Unconscious Use of the Double," in *Stories of the Double*, ed. Albert J. Guérard (Philadelphia: J. B. Lippincott, 1967), 311–31. What characterizes the unconscious use of the double in Romantic literature, Rosenfield asserts, is that "it was made initially respectable in romance, fairy tale, and mystery story where repressed fantasies asserted themselves with particular vengeance in extravagant plots" (314). Conversely, Rosenfield explains, conscious authors sublimate their symptoms: "Denied an absolute external order . . . he [the author of "the modern *Doppelgänger* novel"] seems forced to create that order in an extreme concern for structure and style" (329). The conscious rising above the symptom through the work of art simultaneously entails a rising above the rest of humanity: "The author's vision of life is his public confession that he is both criminal and persecutor, and that we, as second selves, unconsciously share his guilt" (331). As opposed to Rosenfield's aestheticization of experience, this book will insist on the politicization—always incomplete, provisional, and under way—of the aesthetic owing to the operative presence of the doppelgänger.

15. Hillel Schwartz, *The Culture of the Copy: Striking Likenesses, Unreasonable Facsimiles* (New York: Zone, 1996).

16. Each of these has been treated as a theme in its own right. And entire studies have been written on subthemes of each of these categories. For instance, for a look at how the topos of anagnorisis has been used in stories about going to bed with someone whose identity has been mistaken, see Wendy Doniger, *The Bedtrick: Tales of Sex and Masquerade* (Chicago: University of Chicago Press, 2000). Doniger explicitly links this theme with the doppelgänger (99–101). It will be impossible to treat all these themes and subthemes here. Suffice it to repeat the assertion that a thematic analysis is inadequate for approaching the operative presence of the doppelgänger (see Chap. 3).

17. The most notable example is Karl Miller's *Doubles: Studies in Literary History* (Oxford: Oxford University Press, 1987). Miller is a reader attuned to the complexities of the texts he discusses, yet his monograph lacks a synthesizing prin-

ciple. Just to mention one more example, Aglaja Hildenbrock, in *Das andere Ich: Künstlicher Mensch und Doppelgänger in der deutsch- und englischsprachigen Literatur* (Tübingen: Stauffenburg, 1986), finds an unusual beginning for the "literary motif" of the doppelgänger, namely the prologue to Euripides' tragedy *Helen*, according to which Helen was taken to Egypt and Paris had fallen in love with an illusion (7).

CHAPTER 1: THE CRITIQUE OF LONELINESS

1. See Aristotle *Topics* 104a. Wilhelm Hennis's discussion of "Topik und Politik" is still relevant today for the political significance of *topoi*. See Hennis, *Politik und praktische Philosophie: Eine Studie zur Rekonstruktion der politischen Wissenschaft* (Neuwied am Rhein: Hermann Luchterhand, 1963), chap. 4.

2. Paul Coates, *The Double and the Other: Identity as Ideology in Post-Romantic Fiction* (London: Macmillan, 1988), 5.

3. Ibid. (emphasis added).

4. Slavoj Žižek concurs with this insight. "Ideology must be disengaged from the 'representationalist' problematic: *ideology has nothing to do with 'illusion,'* with a wrong, distorted representation of its social context." Instead, Žižek links ideology to a society's attempt at a "full identity with itself," that is, the interiorizing of identity. Žižek concludes that at this point the critique of ideology seeks to show how the agonistic element undermines "the self-evidence of its [the society's] established identity." Žižek, *Enjoy Your Symptom! Jacques Lacan in Hollywood and Out* (New York: Routledge, 1992), 90–91. Cf. Žižek, "Che Vuoi?" in *The Sublime Object of Ideology* (London: Verso, 1989), 87–129.

5. Jean Paul, *Blumen-, Frucht- und Dornenstücke; oder, Ehestand, Tod und Hochzeit des Armenadvokaten F. St. Siebenkäs* [1796], in *Sämtliche Werke*, 1.2:66. (See note 4 in the Introduction.) Michel Tournier's *Friday* needs to be mentioned here as one of the most significant twentieth-century novels to broach this problematic. Tournier's reworking of Crusoe focuses specifically on the way that the isolation and loneliness of Speranza lead to the encounter with Friday. Gilles Deleuze has shown in *The Logic of Sense* that this isolation leads to a conception of the other as a double or doppelgänger. See Tournier, *Friday*, trans. Norman Denny (Baltimore: Johns Hopkins University Press, 1997), and Deleuze, *The Logic of Sense*, trans. Mark Lester and Charles Stivale (New York: Columbia University Press, 1990). Although the focus in the present chapter will be on Jean Paul, there is a strong link between the German author and Tournier. For it is not a coincidence that in Michel Tournier's *Gemini*, trans. Anne Carter (London: Collins, 1981), the names of the twins are Jean and Paul, invoking the name of the inventor of the word "Doppelgänger."

6. The text in German reads: "Rund um mich eine weite versteinerte Menschheit—In der finstern unbewohnten Stille glüht keine Liebe, keine Bewunderung, kein Gebet, keine Hoffnung, kein Ziel—Ich so ganz allein, nirgends ein Pulsschlag, kein Leben, nichts um mich und ohne mich nichts als nichts—Mir

nur bewußt meines höhern Nicht-Bewußtseins—In mir den stumm, blind, verhüllt fortarbeitenden Dämogorgon, und ich bin er selber—So komm' ich aus der Ewigkeit, so geh' ich in die Ewigkeit——" (Jean Paul, *Clavis Fichtiana seu Leibgeberiana*, in *Sämtliche Werke*, 1.3:1056).

7. The two projects can be related. For instance, Fichte is the bête noire in much of the discussion of subjectivity in Adorno, although after the Kierkegaard book Fichte is hardly ever mentioned by name. However, the allusions to Fichte are unmistakable. E.g., see Theodor W. Adorno, *Negative Dialectics*, trans. E. B. Ashton (London: Routledge, 1990), 200–202. As far as it has been possible to ascertain, the first work on the doppelgänger that highlighted the importance of Fichte and specifically the *Clavis Fichtiana* is Wilhelmine Krauss, *Das Doppelgängermotiv in der Romantik: Studien zum romantischen Idealismus* (Berlin: Verlag von Emil Ebering, 1930). Discussions of the doppelgänger in English tend to either ignore Fichte or mention him only in passing. An exception is Dennis F. Mahoney's engaging article "Double into Doppelgänger: The Genesis of the Doppelgänger-motif in the Novels of Jean Paul and E. T. A. Hoffmann," *Journal of Evolutionary Psychology* 4, no. 1 (1983): 54–63.

8. It may appear here that place is not adequately distinguished from space. But a sharp distinction is not necessary because the two concepts do overlap, although they do not coincide. Jeffrey Malpas is correct to argue that what distinguishes place is that it "is integral to the very structure and possibility of experience," or, in other words, it introduces concerns with historical actuality. See Malpas, *Place and Experience: A Philosophical Topography* (Cambridge: Cambridge University Press, 1999), 32 and chap. 1, passim, where the distinction between place and space is discussed.

9. Michel Foucault, *Madness and Civilization: A History of Insanity in the Age of Reason*, trans. Richard Howard (New York: Vintage, 1988), 95.

10. See Theodore Ziolkowski, *German Romanticism and Its Institutions* (Princeton: Princeton University Press, 1990), chap. 4, for a detailed discussion of madness in the literature of this period.

11. Johann Goethe, *Wilhelm Meister's Apprenticeship*, trans. Eric A. Blackall and Victor Lange, in *Goethe's Collected Works* (New York: Suhrkamp, 1983), 9:267.

12. Jean Paul, *Titan*, in *Sämtliche Werke*, 1.3:772, 775–82. For a comparative study of *Wilhelm Meister* and *Titan*, although not from the perspective of madness, see Lucien Stern, "*Wilhelm Meisters Lehrjahre* und Jean Pauls *Titan*" [1922], in *Jean Paul*, ed. Uwe Schweikert (Darmstadt: Wissenschaftliche Buchgesellschaft, 1974), 33–73.

13. Maurice Blanchot, *The Infinite Conversation*, trans. Susan Hanson (Minneapolis: University of Minnesota Press, 1997), 196, 200.

14. Immanuel Kant, *Anthropology from a Pragmatic Point of View*, trans. Victor Lyle Dowdell, rev. Hans H. Rudnick (Carbondale: Southern Illinois University Press, 1978), 117–18; *Anthropologie in pragmatischer Hinsicht*, in *Gesammelte Schriften*, ed. Königlich Preußischen Akademie der Wissenschaften / Deutsche

Akademie der Wissenschaften zu Berlin (Berlin: Reimer/ De Gruyter, 1910–), 1.7:219. All references in Chapter 1 to Kant's work in German are to the Akademie edition.

15. Kant, *The Critique of Judgement*, trans. James Creed Meredith (Oxford: Oxford University Press, 1952), 82–83; *Kritik der Urtheilskraft*, 1.5:239. This is the case, despite the fact that *Gemeinsinn* sometimes is used to indicate the common understanding (including in the citation from the *Anthropologie*). The German text makes the distinction very unambiguously: "Ein solches Prinzip aber könnte nur als ein Gemeinsinn angesehen werden, welcher vom gemeinen Verstande, den man bisweilen auch Gemeinsinn (*sensus communis*) nennt, wesentlich unterschieden ist: indem letzterer nicht nach Gefühl, sondern jederzeit nach Begriffen, wiewohl gemeinglich nur als nach dunkel vorgestellten Prinzipien, urtheilt." The distinction between *Gemeinsinn* and *sensus communis* has been noted by commentators; see, for instance, Jean-François Lyotard, *Lessons on the Analytic of the Sublime*, trans. Elizabeth Rottenberg (Stanford: Stanford University Press, 1994), 199. Lyotard is in fact much more interested in the "common sense" of the *Critique of Judgement*; see, for instance, his "Sensus Communis," trans. Marian Hobson and Geoff Bennington, *Paragraph* 11, no. 1 (1988): 1–23.

16. This demarcation, before the *Anthropology*, is affirmed already in the *Critique of Judgement*, when, in the Analytic of the Sublime, Kant distinguishes negative presentation (*bloß negative Darstellung*) that does not require intuitions from the case of mental illness (*Wahn*) that is still tied to perception (*Critique of Judgement*, 128; *Kritik der Urtheilskraft*, 275). However, what is most instructive about the distinction in the Analytic of the Sublime, is that even here, where an argument about the relation between cognition, reason, and madness is most wanting, nevertheless none is provided. Kant merely asserts the distinction premised on "the inscrutability of the idea of freedom [that] precludes all positive presentation" (ibid.), that is, by shifting the discussion to the distinction between negative and positive presentation.

17. Kant, *Anthropology*, 118. The text reads in German: "Bisweilen *kann es doch blos an den Ausdrücken liegen*, wodurch ein sonst helldenkender Kopf seine äußern Wahrnehmungen Anderen mittheilen will, daß sie nicht mit dem Princip des Gemeinsinnes zusammenstimmen wollen und er auf seinem Sinne beharrt. So hatte der geistvolle Verfasser der Oceana, Harrington, die Grille, daß seine Ausdünstungen (*effluvia*) in Form der Fliegen von seiner Haut absprangen. Es können dieses aber wohl elektrische Wirkungen auf einen mit diesem Stoff überladenen Körper gewesen sein, wovon man auch sonst Erfahrung gehabt haben will, und er damit *vielleicht nur eine Ähnlichkeit* seines Gefühls mit diesem Absprunge, nicht das Sehen dieser Fliegen andeuten wollen" (*Anthropologie*, 219–20, emphasis added).

18. Kant, *Anthropology*, 113; *Anthropologie*, 215: "das Gemüth durch Analogien hingehalten wird, die mit Begriffen einander ähnlicher Dinge verwechselt werden."

19. Kant, *Critique of Pure Reason*, trans. Werner S. Pluhar (Indianapolis: Hackett, 1996), A 25/B 39. For an intriguing account of the Transcendental Aesthet-

ic, see the final [sic] of Adorno's lectures on the first *Critique*, in *Kant's Critique of Pure Reason (1959)*, ed. Rolf Tiedemann, trans. Rodney Livingstone (Stanford: Stanford University Press, 2001).

20. It is at this point, where feeling and hence particularity necessarily reemerge as an issue, that a consideration of a (latent) Kantian politics beyond the hold of ideology may be possible. This would require a return to the *Critique of Judgement*, a move that is beyond the aims of the present discussion.

21. Jean Paul, *Clavis*, 1022.

22. Ibid., 1023.

23. Ibid., 1024.

24. "[M]uß jedes Bild und Zeichen zugleich auch noch etwas anderes sein als dieses, nämlich selber ein Urbild und Ding, das man wieder abbilden und bezeichnen kann u.s.f." (ibid.).

25. "Wenn nun der Philosoph seine Rechenhaut aufspannt und darauf die transzendente Kettenrechnung treiben will: so weiset ihm die bloße Sprache drei gewisse Wege an, sich zu—verrechnen" (ibid.). The normal translation of the conditional would have been: "Now, if the philosopher were to conduct the transcendent chain of calculation." The literal translation of the metaphor *Rechenhau aufspannt* has been preferred here, because Jean Paul often uses the image of the self's expanding epidermis to signify the solipsism of the idealist epistemology. See, for instance, the use of the same imagery in Jean Paul's *Vorschule*: "The absolute philosopher appropriates [*eignet sich*] the Carthage which he has encircled by his skin cut into an *infinitely* thin strip, as if he had thus covered the city [*das er mit seiner unendlich dünn-geschnittenen Haut unschnürt, so zu, als bedeck' ers damit*]. Since in the focus of philosophy all rays of the great concave mirror of all sciences intersect, he mistakes the focus of the mirror and the object, and believes the possessor of all scientific form to be the possessor of all scientific matter" (*Horn of Oberon: Jean Paul's School of Aesthetics*, trans. Margaret R. Hale [Detroit: Wayne State University Press, 1973], 287; *Vorschule der Ästhetik*, in *SämtlicheWerke*, 1.5:418). Carl Schmitt uses similar imagery to describe the individual of "political romanticism": "Die Gemeinschaft ist ein erweitertes Individuum, das Individuum eine konzentrierte Gemeinschaft; jeder geschichtliche Augenblick ein elastischer Punkt in der großen geschichtsphilosophischen Phantasie, mit der man über Völker und Äonen disponiert. Das ist der Weg, die romantische Herrschaft über die Realität zu sichern" (*Politische Romantik* [1925; Berlin: Duncker und Humblot, 1998], 84–85).

26. Jean Paul, *Clavis*, 1025.

27. Ibid.,1026.

28. Ibid., 1025.

29. *Die Nachtwachen des Bonaventura*, ed. and trans. Gerald Gillespie, vol. 6 of the Edinburgh Bilingual Library (Edinburgh: Edinburgh University Press, 1972), 247, translation slightly modified.

30. See the letter to Thieriot dated 14 January 1805, that is, only a few weeks after the *Nachtwachen* had been published. Jean Paul says: "Lesen Sie doch die

Nachtwachen von Bonaventura, d.h. von Schelling. Es ist eine treffliche Nachahmung meines Giannozzo" (*Jean Pauls Sämtliche Werke, historisch-kritische Ausgabe*, ed. Eduard Berend [Berlin: die Deutsche Akademie der Wissenschaften zu Berlin, 1961], 3.5:20).

31. Max Kommerell, *Jean Paul* (1933; Frankfurt am Main: Vittorio Klostermann, 1957), 347. For a contemporary look at Kommerell's remarkable book, see Walter Benjamin's review published in the *Frankfurter Zeitung* in 1934, "Der eingetunkte Zauberstab: Zu Max Kommerells Jean Paul," *Gesammelte Schriften*, ed. Rolf Tiedemann and Hermann Schweppenhäuser (Frankfurt am Main: Suhrkamp, 1991), abbreviated as *GS*, 3:409–17. For a recent evaluation, see Paul Fleming, "The Crisis of Art: Max Kommerell and Jean Paul's Gestures," *MLN* 115, no. 3 (2000): 519–43.

32. This is not to say, of course, that genres are to be rejected or the study of genres abandoned. The use of genres is still valid so long as it is not premised on laws superimposed onto the work. In other words, besides the classificatory system of genres, what has also be admitted is that the work itself can also exceed its genre. Jacques Derrida makes this point with reference to Blanchot's *La folie du jour* in "The Law of Genre," trans. Avita Ronnell, in *Acts of Literature*, ed. Derek Attridge (New York: Routledge, 1992), 223–52.

33. Jean Paul, *Titan*, 800.

34. Ibid., 766.

35. Ibid., 766–67.

36. Jean Paul, *Siebenkäs*, 66. The two different spellings of the word "Doppelgänger" were noted in the Introduction, n. 4.

37. Jean Paul, letter to Jacobi, 4 June 1799, as quoted in Wolfgang Harich, *Jean Pauls Kritik des philosophischen Egoismus: Belegt durch Texte und Briefstellen Jean Pauls in Anhang* (Leipzig: Reclam, 1968), 214. Harich's collection of all the relevant letters that deal with Jean Paul's response to "critical philosophy" will be used here for expedience, instead of the complete collection of letters in Berend's *Historisch-kritische Ausgabe*.

38. Letters to Jacobi, dated 4 October and 2 November 1799, respectively, in Harich, *Jean Pauls Kritik*, 215.

39. For the dedication to Jacobi, see *Clavis*, 1018.

40. Friedrich Heinrich Jacobi, "Jacobi an Fichte," in *Werke*, vol. 3, ed. Friedrich Roth and Friedrich Köppen (Darmstadt: Wissenschaftliche Buchgesellschaft, 1976), 9–10; "Jacobi to Fichte," in *The Main Philosophical Writings and the Novel Allwill*, ed. and trans. George di Giovanni (Montreal: McGill-Queen's University Press, 1994), 501.

41. Jacobi, "An Fichte," 49; "To Fichte," 524. Cf. chap. 3, "The Ideal of Pure Reason," of the Dialectic in the *Critique of Pure Reason*. Kant uses the disjunctive syllogism to argue, first, that there must be something that underlies all negations of reason and, second, that all the traditional proofs for the existence of God merely prove the existence of that something and not of God as a substantial being. Thus,

Jacobi, in his letter to Fichte, implicitly argues with Kant as well, although the complications introduced thereby are beyond the scope of this chapter.

42. Frederick C. Beiser, *The Fate of Reason: German Philosophy from Kant to Fichte* (Cambridge, Mass.: Harvard University Press, 1987), 80.

43. Jacobi, "An Fichte," 43; "To Fichte," 519.

44. Jacobi, "An Fichte," 44; "To Fichte," 519.

45. Fichte claims in the "Second Introduction to the Science of Knowledge" that, although Kant did not arrive at the system propounded by the *Wissenschaftslehre*, Kant had nevertheless a nascent conception of it that he never expounded except in fragments. See Johann Gottlieb Fichte, *Science of Knowledge: With the First and Second Introductions*, trans. Peter Heath and John Lachs (Cambridge: Cambridge University Press, 1982), 51; *Grundlage der gesammten Wissenschaftslehre als Handschrift für seine Zuhörer* [1794–95], in *Sämmtliche Werke*, ed. J. H. Fichte (Berlin: de Gruyter, 1965 [a faithful reprint of the 1845 edition]), 1:478–79.

46. The absolute I's intellectual intuition is not spelled out in the first *Wissenschaftslehre*. However, it is spelled out later in various texts, for instance, in Fichte, *Foundations of Transcendental Philosophy (Wissenschaftslehre) Nova Methodo 1796–99*, ed. and trans. Daniel Breazeale (Ithaca: Cornell University Press, 1998), 66.

47. Fichte denies that the self is a soul, following Kant's argument in the Paralogisms of the first *Critique*. Fichte is aware as early as the *Aenesidemus* review of the problems that arise from treating the subject as an object. See "Review of *Aenesidemus*," in *Fichte: Early Philosophical Writings*, trans. and ed. Daniel Breazeale (Ithaca: Cornell University Press, 1988), 59–77. For a cogent look at the way Fichte's absolute subject evolved out of the *Aenesidemus* review that deals directly with the problem of the subject as an object, see Frederick Neuhouser, *Fichte's Theory of Subjectivity* (Cambridge: Cambridge University Press, 1990), 68–86.

48. On space and reason in Fichte see John Sallis, "Hovering: Imagination and the Spacing of Truth," in *Spacings: Of Reason and Imagination in Texts of Kant, Fichte, Hegel* (Chicago: University of Chicago Press, 1987), 23–66.

49. As Fichte makes clear from the first paragraph of his "Concerning the Difference between the Spirit and the Letter within Philosophy," what offends him most of all is the mixing of "wordplay" and philosophy (*Early Philosophical Writings*, 193). The whole argument of the essay is premised on the assumption that linguistic usage presupposes a pure or correct meaning (see 196–97). Evidently, philosophy aspires to that pure meaning, although it is not clear how Fichte actually achieves this status when he ultimately has recourse to rhetorical flourishes like the following: "To try to think of oneself as nonexistent is pure nonsense" (207). The fact is that, as Paul de Man has forcefully argued, from the first moment of his system, from the self-positing of the absolute I, Fichte has recourse, without admitting it (and, in terms of Fichte's own System, illegitimately), to a linguistic act. See de Man, "The Concept of Irony," in *Aesthetic Ideology*, ed. Andrzej Warminski (Minneapolis: University of Minnesota Press, 1996), 163–84. Werner Hamacher

also contends that in Fichte's absolute self-positing, the I = I, the "I is only the fiction of its existence," in Hamacher, "Position Exposed: Friedrich Schlegel's Poetological Transposition of Fichte's Absolute Proposition," in *Premises: Essays on Philosophy and Literature from Kant to Celan*, trans. Peter Fenves (Cambridge, Mass.: Harvard University Press, 1996), 238. The performative aspect of the encounter between *das Ich* and *der Ich* as it relates to the philosophy of Fichte is absolutely crucial. It is therefore entirely inadequate to view the relation between the two egos in biographical terms and to equate the appearance of *der Ich* with Jean Paul's personal anxiety or his own mental state, as Otto Rank does in *Der Doppelgänger: Eine Psychoanalytische Studie* (Leipzig: Internationaler Psychoanalytischer Verlag, 1925), 50–51. Rank does not seem to be aware of the philosophical implications of this distinction or of Fichte's relevance here. The interplay between *der Ich* and *das Ich* is lost in the translation of Rank's book, *The Double: A Psychoanalytic Study*, trans. Harry Tucker Jr. (New York: Meridian, 1979).

50. The "green letter" was written at the height of the Atheism Controversy in spring 1799, and Jacobi makes explicit references in it to the Pantheism Controversy (see the reference to Spinoza, which informs the argument for the substantiality of the absolute ego) that took place a little over a decade earlier. For the Pantheism Controversy, see Beiser, *Fate of Reason*, and for the Atheism Controversy, see Anthony J. La Vopa, *Fichte: The Self and the Calling of Philosophy, 1762–1799* (Cambridge: Cambridge University Press, 2001).

51. For a discussion of substance in the metaphysical tradition that departs from the Aristotelean definition, see Adorno's fifth lecture in *Metaphysics: Concept and Problems (1965)*, ed. Rolf Tiedemann, trans. Edmund Jephcott (Stanford: Stanford University Press, 2000). Adorno shows that "this interpretation of substance, as that which needs nothing else in order to exist, has survived throughout the entire history of philosophy" (28). For instance, Spinoza—who was very much in Jacobi's mind in his polemic—provided the following definition of substance at the very beginning of his *Ethics*: "By substance I mean that which is in itself and is conceived through itself; that is, that the conception of which does not require the conception of another thing from which it has to be formed." Baruch Spinoza, *Ethics*, in *Complete Works*, trans. Samuel Shirley, ed. Michael L. Morgan (Indianapolis: Hackett, 2002), part 1, def. 3 (p. 217).

52. Aristotle *Categories* 2a.12–14. The definition of substance as it is given in Greek is: "οὐσία δέ ἐστιν κυριώτατά τε καὶ πρώτως καὶ μάλιστα λεγομένη, ἣ μήτε καθ' ὑποκειμένου τινὸς λέγεται, ἢ μήτ' ἐν ὑποκειμένῳ τινί ἐστιν, οἷον ὁ τὶς ἄνθρωπος ἢ ὁ τὶς ἵππος" (Aristotle, *The Categories; On Interpretation; Prior Analytics*, trans. Harold P. Cooke and Hugh Tredennick, Loeb Classical Library [Cambridge, Mass.: Harvard University Press, 1938], 18).

53. Jacobi, "To Fichte," 508; "An Fichte," 21–22: "in dem Begriffe eines reinen absoluten Ausgehens und Hingehens, ursprünglich—aus Nichts, zu Nichts, für Nichts, in Nichts." This is of course another way of saying that the absolute I has turned into "Messiah."

54. The "divinity" of the absolute I was not something noticed only by Jacobi. For instance, Schiller wrote to Goethe as early as October 1794 that by conceiving the world as "a ball that the I has thrown and that it receives again in reflection [Fichte] has really declared his divinity, as we really expected" (quoted in La Vopa, *Fichte*, 271).

55. Jean Paul, *Clavis*, 1021–22.

56. Ibid., 1016.

57. As Andrew Bowie has argued in chapter 2 of *From Romanticism to Critical Theory: The Philosophy of German Literary Theory* (London: Routledge, 1997), Jacobi's critique of Fichte can be seen as one of the crucial sources of German Romanticism's philosophy, which is in turn a foundation for critical theory and deconstruction. From this perspective, the suggestion is that the way he departs from, and augments, Jacobi places Jean Paul in an orbit of critical and philosophical developments after Romanticism. In addition, the doppelgänger is crucial in this undertaking after Romanticism.

58. Despite the intellectual as well as personal affinity between Jean Paul and Jacobi, it is important to avoid the easy solution of conflating their respective positions, as for instance Albrecht Decke-Cornill does. See his *Vernichtung und Selbstbehauptung: Eine Untersuchung zur Selbstbewußtseinsproblematik bei Jean Paul* (Würzburg: Königshausen + Neumann, 1987), 69–73.

59. This is an issue of technique, as will be argued in the final section of this chapter.

60. "Spuren seines ursprünglichen Vorsatzes, die Wissenschaftslehre lächerlich zu machen, schimmern noch überall im Clavis durch; und sooft er auch darin zu einem ihm schweren, ernsten, nüchternen Stil ausholt und ansetzt, so stellet er doch bald wieder (nach seinem kurzweiligen grotesken Naturell) alles in ein so komisches Licht, daß er einfältige Leser ordentlich dumm macht" (Jean Paul, *Clavis*, 1019–20).

61. This posturing is not merely a silly game, nor a mannerism. Rather, it opens up a site which allows for the unfolding of interpretation. This issue will be discussed later, as hypocrisy in Chapter 2 and as theatricality in Chapter 5.

62. For a review of the clinical debates around multiple personality as well as discussions of books and films, see Ian Hacking, *Rewriting the Soul: Multiple Personality and the Sciences of Memory* (Princeton: Princeton University Press, 1995). The problem with the criticism using multiple personality is that it easily lapses into the trap of the syncretism of the author's life and work, which was described in the Introduction. For an example of this, see Jeremy Hawthorn, *Multiple Personality and the Disintegration of Literary Character: From Oliver Smith to Sylvia Plath* (London: Edward Arnold, 1983). Conversely, multiple personality could resonate with the doppelgänger if Borch-Jacobsen's suggestion is followed, namely that it designates "the degree zero of consciousness" (Mikkel Borch-Jacobsen, "Who's Who? Introducing Multiple Personality," in *Supposing the Subject*, ed. Joan Copjec (London: Verso, 1994), 60). In

other words, multiple personality indicates that there is no ego as a "unifying pole of experience" (46),

63. The first time that Jean Paul uses the word "Doppeltgänger" he adds the following footnote: "Those are the people who see themselves [*So heißen Leute, die sich selber sehen*]" (*Siebenkäs*, 67). See also note 4 of the Introduction.

64. James George Frazer, *The Golden Bough: A Study in Magic and Religion*, 3d ed., part 2, *Taboo and the Perils of the Souls* (London: Macmillan, 1955), 77–100.

65. Michael Richardson, ed., *Double / Double* (Harmondsworth: Penguin, 1987), xiii.

66. Plato *Symposium* 189c–193e.

67. Tzvetan Todorov, *The Fantastic: A Structural Approach to a Literary Genre*, trans. Richard Howard (Ithaca: Cornell University Press, 1975), 160–61.

68. The expression "wrong Doppelgänger" is meant to indicate what was called in the Introduction a syncretism of life and work—namely, the attempt to show how the author's life gives rise to the doppelgänger. In this construal, the doppelgänger is displaced from the text and becomes instead a psychological or psychoanalytical category. As noted in the Introduction, this is one of the most common ways of missing the import of the doppelgänger. What will be argued here, in addition, is that this syncretism refers to the experience of the subject—indiscriminately defined as the author or the character—as being in a state of lack. For a general overview of the doppelgänger that follows this argument, see Clifford Hallam, "The Double as Incomplete Self: Toward a Definition of Doppelgänger," in *Fearful Symmetry: Doubles and Doubling in Literature and Film*, ed. Eugene J. Cook (Tallahassee: University Presses of Florida, 1981), 1–31.

69. Given this original openness, it is possible—even inevitable—to then inscribe specific content to it.

70. The discussion here concentrates only on the Freudian uncanny and that only insofar as it is connected to the doppelgänger. This is not meant to be a thorough study of the uncanny. Such a study should have to account for Heidegger's use of the term, at least in *Being and Time* and in *An Introduction to Metaphysics* where the choral ode to man in Sophocles' *Antigone* is addressed. It is regrettable that the first monograph on the uncanny published in English is content to make only occasional passing allusions to Heidegger and refrains from a sustained engagement with his work. See Nicholas Royle, *The Uncanny* (Manchester: Manchester University Press, 2003).

71. Sigmund Freud, "The 'Uncanny,'" trans. Alix Strachey and James Strachey, *Penguin Freud Library* (Harmondsworth: Penguin, 1991), 14:368; Sigmund Freud, "Das Unheimliche," in *Gesammelte Werke* (London: Imago, 1947), 12:259. All references to translations of Freud's writings are to the Penguin edition.

72. Sigmund Freud, *Fragment of an Analysis of a Case of Hysteria ("Dora")*, 8:92, 93.

73. Sigmund Freud, "Negation," 11:441. Freud's term is "die Verneinung," which is perhaps better translated literally as "denial." Although there are crucial

differences between the Fichtean "Vernichtung" and the Freudian "Verneinung," in particular because the former leads to an abstraction of subjectivity whereas the latter may be linked to its reduction to empirical content, the argument here is only that both conceptions lead to forms of absolutism. The difference—and ultimate coincidence—between those two types of absolutism of the subject will be taken up in the next chapter.

74. Andrew J. Webber, *The Doppelgänger: Double Visions in German Literature* (Oxford: Oxford University Press, 1996), 5–6, 10.

75. For instance, see ibid., 123–27, 145–47.

76. Ibid., 129.

77. See ibid., 123n, 129n. See also Hélène Cixous, "Fiction and Its Phantoms: A Reading of Freud's *Das Unheimliche* (The 'uncanny')," *New Literary History* 7, no. 3 (1976): 525–48.

78. Webber, *Doppelgänger*, 1.

79. Ibid., 5.

80. Freud, "The 'Uncanny,'" 361; "Das Unheimliche," 251. Neil Hertz, "Freud and the Sandman," in *End of the Line: Essays in Psychoanalysis and the Sublime* (New York: Columbia University Press, 1985), 101.

81. Freud, "The 'Uncanny,'" 339; "Das Unheimliche," 229–30.

82. Freud, "The 'Uncanny,'" 357; "Das Unheimliche," 147–48.

83. The first to point out the vertiginous consequences of this interplay between science and fantasy in Freud's paper was Cixous in "Fiction and Its Phantoms."

84. Freud is too reliant on the explanation of the uncanny in terms of narcissism, by his protégé, Otto Rank, which was first published in *Imago* in 1917, a couple of years before Freud's "Das Unheimliche." See Webber, *Doppelgänger*, 38–55, for a discussion of Rank and Freud.

85. Freud asserts this in contradistinction to Ernst Jentsch, for whom the uncanny is precisely intellectual uncertainty. See Jentsch, "On the Psychology of the Uncanny," trans. Roy Sellars, *Angelaki* 2, no. 1 (1995): 7–15.

86. My translation. The German reads: "In der Tat hat die Phantasiebearbeitung des Dichters die Elemente des Stoffes nicht so wild herumgewirbelt, daß man ihre ursprüngliche Anordnung nicht wiederherstellen könnte" ("Das Unheimliche," 244). The English translation is perhaps closer to Freud's intentions, but, as will soon become clear, this is precisely the reason it is inadequate. The Strachey translation reads: "In fact, Hoffmann's imaginative treatment of his material has not made such wild confusion of its elements that we cannot reconstruct their original arrangement." All references in this and the following paragraph are to the footnote in Freud, "The 'Uncanny,'" 353–54; "Das Unheimliche," 244–45.

87. Although there is a growing secondary literature on the chiasmus, the most succinct account of it remains Rodolphe Gasché's "Reading Chiasms," in *Of Minimal Things: Studies on the Notion of Relation* (Stanford: Stanford University Press, 1999). See esp. 277 ff., where Gasché demonstrates that the chiasmus is used to indicate the essential unfinishedness of texts.

88. The political implications of the ontology of the doppelgänger as the relationality between the mechanical and the ocular will be discussed in Chapter 4, where the relationality will be addressed in terms of autonomy and automaticity.

89. Freud, "Das Unheimliche," 244.

90. Freud, "The 'Uncanny,'" 341; "Das Unheimliche," 232.

91. Freud, "The 'Uncanny,'" 339; "Das Unheimliche," 229–30.

92. Freud, "The 'Uncanny,'" 356; "Das Unheimliche," 246.

93. Samuel Weber, "The Sideshow, or: Remarks on a Canny Moment," *MLN* 88, no. 6 (1973): 1111.

94. Ibid., 1112. Gilles Deleuze and Félix Guattari hold a similar position. For instance, they write about Kafka: "[I]t's not Oedipus that produces neurosis; it is neurosis—*that is, a desire that is already submissive and searching to communicate its own submission*—that produces Oedipus" (Deleuze and Guattari, *Kafka: Towards a Minor Literature*, trans. Dana Polan [Minneapolis: University of Minnesota Press, 1986], 10). This reversal, Deleuze and Guattari show, avoids representation.

95. Weber, "Sideshow," 1114.

96. This is a summary of ibid., 1130–33.

97. This problematic is taken up in greater detail in the final chapter, under the rubric of theatricality.

98. "Der Clavis ist ursprünglich das letzte Glied im *komischen Anhang* zum Titan; er löset aber von der alten Naide ab, um sich freier und durch Gesperre zu bewegen, wodurch ihm der korpulente Titan nie nachkann" (Jean Paul, *Clavis*, 1013).

99. Ibid., 1130.

100. Reference here is to the proposition discussed above that "whatever the human understanding cannot explain as mad is not pure philosophy for us" (ibid., 1022), although the same point is raised throughout the *Clavis*.

101. Ibid., 1016–17.

102. Ibid., 1017.

103. As Winfried Menninghaus has shown, nonsense in German literature as well as the philosophy of the time, has a similar function, namely it designates that which not only is incoherent but does not even stake a claim to coherence. See Menninghaus's remarkable *In Praise of Nonsense: Kant and Bluebeard*, trans. Henry Pickford (Stanford: Stanford University Press, 1999).

104. It should be stressed here that the discussion is restricted to Jean Paul's conception of the doppelgänger and that no claim is made about Romantic irony in general. In relation to Romantic irony, and more specifically the question of whether it is dialectical or nondialectical, de Man offers an interesting critique of Peter Szondi's "Friedrich Schlegel and Romantic Irony, with Some Remarks on Tieck's Comedies," in *On Textual Understanding and Other Essays*, trans. Harvey Mendelsohn (Minneapolis: University of Minnesota Press, 1986), 57–73. De Man argues that Szondi's conflation of irony with comedy essentially makes the former dialectical, or in de Man's words, Szondi stays with "the aesthetic of *Aufhebung* of irony by means of the notion of distance" ("The Concept of Irony," 182). Con-

versely, de Man insists on the nondialectical nature of irony, or that "irony is the *radical negation*, which, however, reveals as such, by the undoing of the work, the absolute toward which the work is under way" (183, emphasis added). Thus, as de Man points out, his own notion of irony is much more akin to Walter Benjamin's extrapolation of irony in the dissertation on criticism in Romanticism.

105. Jean Paul, *Clavis*, 1013.

106. Ibid.,1014.

107. "Durch *Steftenstücke* täuscht uns die Philosophie am besten" (ibid.).

108. "So heißet der Taschenspieler die Stücke, wozu er einen zweiten Mann braucht" (ibid.).

109. Ibid., 1014–15.

110. See Daniel Breazeale, "Philosophy and the Divided Self: On the 'Existential' and 'Scientific' Tasks of the Jena *Wissenschaftslehre*," *Fichte Studien* 6 (1994): 117–47.

111. Fichte, *Science of Knowledge*, 189–90; *Wissenschaftslehre*, 210–11.

112. "It [the self] is at once the agent and the product of action; the active and what the activity brings about; action and deed are one and the same, and hence the 'I am' expresses an Act, and the only possible one" (Fichte, *Science of Knowledge*, 97; *Wissenschaftslehre*, 96).

113. See Günter Zöller, *Fichte's Transcendental Philosophy: The Original Duplicity of Intelligence and Will* (Cambridge: Cambridge University Press, 1998).

114. Fichte, *Science of Knowledge*, 225; *Wissenschaftslehre*, 225: "*ausser* demselben ist nichts. . . . Mithin fass . . . das Ich in sich alle, d.i. eine unendliche, unbeschränkte Realität."

115. Fichte, *Science of Knowledge*, 227; *Wissenschaftslehre*, 256.

116. Fichte, *Science of Knowledge*, 233; *Wissenschaftslehre*, 264. As Fichte puts it: "ohne ein Streben überhaupt kein Object möglich ist." For a review of the secondary literature on Fichte's striving, as well as of the check, see Simon Lumsden's "Fichte's Striving Subject," *Inquiry* 47, no. 2 (2004): 123–42.

117. Fichte, *Science of Knowledge*, 233–34 (trans. slightly modified); *Wissenschaftslehre*, 264–65.

118. Fichte, *Science of Knowledge*, 226; *Wissenschaftslehre*, 255.

119. Fichte, *Science of Knowledge*, 30; *Wissenschaftslehre*, 454. The "Second Introduction" was written after the first version of the *Wissenschaftslehre* and published in 1797.

120. Fichte, *Science of Knowledge*, 238; *Wissenschaftslehre*, 270.

121. It is true that Fichte attempts to include art in his philosophical project, when he claims that a judgment of the type "A is beautiful" has the same thetic structure as the first principle of the *Wissenschaftslehre*, the positing of the I in the judgment "I am" (*Science of Knowledge*, 115; *Wissenschaftslehre*, 117). However, as Andrzej Warminski has shown in "Returns of the Sublime: Positing and Performative in Kant, Fichte, and Schiller," *MLN* 116, no. 5 (2001): 964–78, this reference to the judgment of taste in the *Wissenschaftslehre* leads to aporias that ultimately un-

dermine Fichte's proclaimed autonomy of philosophy. Further, for a discussion of the influence that Fichte had on Romantic poetry and on the conception of political praxis, see Jan Mieszkowski, "The Syntax of the Revolution," *European Romantic Review* 13, no. 2 (2002): 207–13.

CHAPTER 2: THE SUBJECT OF MODERNITY

1. G. W. F. Hegel, *Phenomenology of Spirit*, trans. A. V. Miller (Oxford: Oxford University Press, 1977), 56–57.

2. Jose Saramago, *The Double*, trans. Margaret Jull Costa (2002; London: Harvill, 2004). For a characteristic doppelgänger tale by E. T. A. Hoffmann, see his "The Doubles," in *Tales of E. T. A. Hoffmann*, ed. and trans. Leonard J. Kent and Elizabeth C. Knight (Chicago: University of Chicago Press, 1972), 234–79.

3. This problematic is, broadly speaking, the Romantic response to the literary and critical task. See on this Maurice Blanchot's influential article "Literature and the Right to Death," in *The Work of Fire*, trans. Charlotte Mandell (Stanford: Stanford University Press, 1995). Further, it should be highlighted that death, in this sense, is intricately linked to a political project, as, for instance, in the opening pages of Maurice Blanchot's *Le pas au-delà* (Paris: Gallimard, 1973).

4. The Serapionic principle—to narrate something fantastic based on personal experience, as if it has been seen by you—is formulated in the conversation between Cyprian and the monk Serapion at the beginning of the collection, and it is also reiterated throughout the volume. E. T. A. Hoffmann, *Die Serapionsbrüder*, in *Sämtliche Werke*, vol. 4, ed. Wulf Segebrecht (Frankfurt am Main: Deutscher Klassiker Verlag, 2001).

5. Cesare Beccaria, *On Crimes and Punishments and Other Writings*, trans. Richard Davies, ed. Richard Bellamy (Cambridge: Cambridge University Press, 1995), 92. See also Michel Foucault's discussion of Beccaria's treatise in *Discipline and Punish: The Birth of the Prison*, trans. Alan Sheridan (Harmondsworth: Penguin, 1979).

6. See Stathis Gourgouris, *Does Literature Think? Literature as Theory for an Antimythical Era* (Stanford: Stanford University Press, 2003), chap. 2, titled "Enlightenment and *Paranomia*." For modernity see passim and in particular page 54.

7. Michel Foucault, *The Order of Things: An Archaeology of the Human Sciences* (London: Routledge, 2002), 338. Foucault illustrates this zone of exclusion in the first chapter of *The Order of Things* with a memorable analysis of Velasquez's *Las Meninas*.

8. Foucault, *The Order of Things*, 347.

9. Ibid., 356.

10. Ibid., 361.

11. Ibid., 370.

12. Cf. Jean-Luc Nancy, *Hegel: The Restlessness of the Negative*, trans. Jason Smith and Steven Miller (Minneapolis: University of Minnesota Press, 2002).

13. Ἀλέξανδρος Παπαδιαμάντης, Ἡ φόνισσα, Ἅπαντα, ed. Ν. Δ. Τριανταφυλλόπουλος (1903; Athens: Domos, 1997), 3:520; Alexandros Papadiamantes, *The Murderess*, trans. Peter Levi (London: Writers and Readers, 1983), 127. References are provided to Levi's translation, although it is deficient, especially because of unjustified omissions in the last two chapters. Levi's translation has often been modified. One note on the transcription of the Greek: in citing Papadiamantes, the old spelling (polytonic) has been retained, while all other citations and titles are converted to monotonic.

14. For a distinction between modernism and modernity, see *Introduction to Modernity*. For modernity in terms of the distinction between style and appearance, see Andrew Benjamin, *Style and Time: Essays on the Politics of Appearance* (Evanston, Ill.: Northwestern University Press, 2006).

15. Papadiamantes' anonymous translation of Dostoevsky's *Crime and Punishment* was serialized in one hundred and six installments, published in Εφημερίς from 14 April to 1 August 1889. Not until 1992 was the translation published in book form for the first time. Θ. Δοστογέφκη, *Τὸ ἔκλημα καὶ ἡ τιμωρία* (Athens: Ideogramma, 1992). For information about the original publication details, see Eugenia Makrygianne's addendum to the book.

16. See Henry Buchanan, *Dostoevsky's Crime and Punishment: An Aesthetic Interpretation* (Nottingham: Astra Press, 1996), 64. Cf. Harriet Murav, *Holy Foolishness: Dostoevsky's Novels and the Poetics of Cultural Critique* (Stanford: Stanford University Press, 1992), 63–64. For the most influential study on the doppelgänger in Dostoevsky's work, see Dmitri Chizhevsky, "The Theme of the Double in Dostoevsky," in *Dostoevsky: A Collection of Critical Essays*, ed. René Wellek (Englewood Cliffs, N.J.: Prentice-Hall, 1962), 112–29. See also Robert B. Anderson, *Dostoevsky: Myths of Duality* (Gainesville: University of Florida Press, 1986). See also Karl Miller, *Doubles: Studies in Literary History* (Oxford: Oxford University Press, 1987). chap. 7.

17. Foucault, *The Order of Things*, 340.

18. See Papadiamantes, Ἡ φόνισσα, 515–16 and 519; *Murderess*, 123, 124.

19. Papadiamantes, Ἡ φόνισσα, 520; *Murderess*, 127. These are the final words of *The Murderess*.

20. James Hogg, *The Private Memoirs and Confessions of a Justified Sinner*, ed. John Carey (Oxford: Oxford University Press, 1990).

21. Linda Sue Singer Bayliss, "Mirrors: Literary Reflection as Psychic Process," Ph.D. diss., Michigan State University, 1984, reproduced by U.M.I., 1992, 33–34. This transference of attributes from Hermes to the devil may be connected with the apocryphal twinship between Jesus and Judas—where the former is the son and envoy of God, while the latter is the devil. Cf. F. C. Keppler, *The Literature of the Second Self* (Tucson: University of Arizona Press, 1972), 21–22. In any case, a thorough historical study of this connection cannot concentrate solely on the attributes, but it must also consider the way that those attributes and their transference were used in the dispensation of power structures. Such a study must avoid

reducing the evil to an affect. This is Robert Rogers's approach, when he asserts that Hogg's *Private Memoirs and Confessions of a Justified Sinner* "presents us with the paradox of a study which dwells on the subject of evil, largely in psychological terms, yet fails to involve our emotions deeply because of the way in which evil is accentuated and isolated in a diabolical other self" (33). Rogers presupposes an affective relation not only between the reader and the characters in the novel but also in the doppelgänger itself. However, it remains unclear how this dual affect can be sustained, other than by evoking the author's biography, and hence by repudiating the literary potential of the doppelgänger—a move already noted in the Introduction. Robert Rogers, *A Psychoanalytic Study of the Double in Literature* (Detroit: Wayne State University Press, 1970).

22. The gods' message "must always be taken to mean exactly what it says, even though it is couched in deceptive, double-edged oracular terms. . . . [E]ven the Father of Lies in Hogg's novel never once tells a real lie." Bayliss, "Mirrors," 24. In other words, the pronouncements of the doppelgänger cannot be fitted into a binary true-or-false logic. However, as it will be shown later, allegory also rejects that binary.

23. Ibid., 254.

24. Jacques Derrida has argued for the political nature of lying in "History of the Lie: Prolegomena," trans. Peggy Kamuf, *Graduate Faculty Philosophy Journal* 20, no. 1 (1997): 129–61. Lying destabilizes the hegemony of reason whose pursuit is truth. And, to the extent that reason is a marker of a masculine notion of discourse and politics, then lying brings about a different notion of the political. Such a notion implies a feminist critique of the political—a critique that will have to start with the body and the particular. Although this point is suggested through the present chapter, it has not been taken up in any detail. For a cogent investigation, see Ewa Płonowska Ziarek's remarkable *An Ethics of Dissensus: Postmodernity, Feminism, and the Politics of Radical Democracy* (Stanford: Stanford University Press, 2001). Lying will be further discussed in the section "Lying with Benjamin," in Chapter 5.

25. Lying will be further elaborated in terms of theatricality in Chapter 5.

26. Papadiamantes, Ἡ φόνισσα, 3:446; *The Murderess*, 36.

27. Papadiamantes, Ἡ φόνισσα, 418; *The Murderess*, 2. Levi translates the expression "εἶχε 'παραλογίσει'" as "she had lost track of reason." Although the same expression has been translated here as "she goes 'crazy,'" Levi's translation is also correct. Papadiamantes uses the same expression in chapter 5, in a passage that will be discussed in what follows. It will be argued there that madness and being aside or beside reason (παρά τον λόγο, or παραλογίζω) are related conceptions, which are related to Gourgouris's notion of *paranomia* (being aside or beside the law).

28. Papadiamantes, Ἡ φόνισσα, 459, 494; *The Murderess*, 52–53, 94.

29. Papadiamantes, Ἡ φόνισσα, 485, 489; *The Murderess*, 83, 88.

30. Only after the police track her down in the mountains does she decide to go

to the church, remembering that a "saint" protected even the killer of his brother from the authorities (Ἡ φόνισσα, 516; *The Murderess*, 123).

31. Papadiamantes, Ἡ φόνισσα, 516; *The Murderess*, 123. Notice that while Papadiamantes says that the hermit Akakios would have let her escape if he wanted, the English translation mistakenly says that Hadoula of her own accord could have escaped on a passing boat. Irrespective of what is confessed to Akakios, Hadoula is well aware that the act of confessing will place her within the purview of the divine law.

32. This presentation of confession in *The Murderess* is different from Papadiamantes' presentation of confession in his early work *The Merchants of the Nations*. For a detailed reading of confession in the latter work, see Dimitris Vardoulakis, "Confession and Time: The Subject in Papadiamantes's *The Merchants of the Nations*," *MLN* 124, no. 5 (2009): 1091–115.

33. Papadiamantes, Ἡ φόνισσα, 429–30; *The Murderess*, 16.

34. This is explained immediately after the passage quoted above.

35. Papadiamantes, Ἡ φόνισσα, 498; *The Murderess*, 100.

36. Papadiamantes, *Hapanta*, 2:77–81.

37. Even before interpretation begins, the conjunction of Papadiamantes and Dostoevsky points to a complicity between them that is both a secret and a nonsecret, thus opening up the structure of self-confession. The conjunction is not a secret to the extent that the novels present a plot in which a killer, for whatever reasons, feels justified in committing a murder. Yet the conjunction remains secretive because until relatively recently it was largely unknown that Papadiamantes was the translator of Dostoevsky's novel *Crime and Punishment*. Thus, Aggelos Terzakis, a prominent Greek intellectual and competent critic, observed in an article about Papadiamantes' influences that there is an affinity between *The Murderess* and *Crime and Punishment*, "a foreign work which Papadiamantes must have read when it was translated as feuilleton." Terzakis, "Οι 'επιδράσεις'," *Nea Hestia* 355 (1941): 55. This complicity between authors has important ramifications for criticism, as it will be argued in the next chapter in relation to Blanchot and Jean Paul.

38. Fyodor Dostoevsky, *Crime and Punishment*, trans. David McDuff (1866; Harmondsworth: Penguin, 1991), 613.

39. For a translation of Alexander Pushkin's story, see *The Queen of Spades and Other Stories*, trans. Rosemary Edmonds (Harmondsworth: Penguin, 1962). For the most influential interpretation of the numerology in the story, which also links the story to the Decembrist uprising, see Lauren G. Leighton, *The Esoteric Tradition in Russian Romantic Literature: Decembrism and Freemasonry* (University Park: Pennsylvania State University Press, 1994), passim, esp. chaps. 6 to 8. For another important study on Freemasonry and Russian literature, see S. L. Baehr, *The Paradise Myth in Eighteenth-century Russia: Utopian Patterns in Early Secular Russian Literature and Culture* (Stanford: Stanford University Press, 1991).

40. See Charles E. Passage, *Character Names in Dostoevsky's Fiction* (Ann Arbor, Mich.: Ardis 1982), 65–66.

41. For the dream in *Crime and Punishment*, see 626–28. This concluding redemption in *Crime and Punishment* is not necessarily a revelation. Importantly, Dostoevsky returns to the same dream in different contexts only to ridicule it. For one of the later versions in which Dostoevsky clearly adopts an ironic distance, see "A Strange Man's Dream: A Fantastic Story," trans. Malcolm Jones, in *The Penguin Book of Russian Short Stories*, ed. David Richards (Harmondsworth: Penguin, 1981).

42. Besides irreducible divergences in terms of historico-political context, language, genre and so on, an important difference in relation to the discussion here is that in *Crime and Punishment* the identity of the killer is revealed to the other characters through Raskolnikov's confession to Sonya, which is overheard, while in *The Murderess* the public prosecutor's suspicion is never corroborated by an admission. This difference can be further underscored with a juxtaposition to Camus's *The Outsider*. Camus inverted the plot of *Crime and Punishment* in the sense that, while in Dostoevsky the murderer is unknown, in *The Outsider* the murderer is known all along. Papadiamantes in *The Murderess* stands between the two, since there are neither direct witnesses to Hadoula's murders, nor does she admit to her crimes. Consequently, the evidence against Hadoula in a court of law would have remained circumstantial. Although the relation between Dostoevsky's *Crime and Punishment* and *The Murderess* has often been mentioned, there are no detailed comparative studies. An interesting comparison can be found in Κωστής Παπαγιώργης (Kostis Papagiorgis), *Αλέξανδρος Αδαμαντίου Εμμανουήλ* (Athens: Kastaniotis, 1998), 200–216. Dostoevsky's relation to Camus has often been pursued, especially through *The Man from the Underground*, the book that most influenced Camus. See Ray Davison, *Camus: The Challenge of Dostoevsky* (Exeter: University of Exeter Press, 1997).

43. *Selected Letters of Fyodor Dostoyevsky*, trans. R. MacAndrew, ed. Joseph Frank and David I. Goldstein (New Brunswick, N.J.: Rutgers University Press, 1987), 222. The letter, which survives only in draft form, was written at Wiesbaden in September 1865.

44. Papadiamantes, *Ή φόνισσα*, 424–25; *The Murderess*, 10. "She did this under the pretence of propriety. 'I won't have that little Witch "build me an early-one" [νὰ μοῦ σκαρώσῃ κανένα πρωιμάδι],' she had said. You can see that she took the metaphor from her husband's boat trade. But she really said it so as not to be compelled to give a bigger dowry."

45. Papadiamantes, *Ή φόνισσα*, 444–45; *The Murderess*, 34–35. "He had his caprices and his demands and his eccentricities. Today he wanted one thing, tomorrow another: one day so much, and the next day a lot more. Before the match, he had often listened to mean and envious people, paid heed to slander from this direction and that, involved himself in sleek intrigues, and just not wanted to get settled. And then just after the engagement he installed himself in his mother-in-law's house, and 'built' suddenly 'an early-one.' And all the time he had to be 'Yes sir, No sir.' And then in the end, after an age of ten thousand troubles and anguish unnarratable, someone manages to persuade a son-in-law like that to come to the altar."

46. Papadiamantes, Ἡ φόνισσα, 422, 439, 470. For her looming skills and for her powers of prognostication see page 448 and chapter 4 passim and especially page 444.

47. A law that is both human as is represented by the police, but also divine, because, as Amersa tells her mother, "sin is pursuing you." Papadiamantes, Ἡ φόνισσα, 474; *The Murderess*, 70.

48. Papadiamantes, Ἡ φόνισσα, 446; *The Murderess*, 36.

49. Papadiamantes, Ἡ φόνισσα, 468; *The Murderess*, 62.

50. Papadiamantes, Ἡ φόνισσα, 446–47; *The Murderess*, 36–37.

51. Papadiamantes, Ἡ φόνισσα, 447; *The Murderess*, 37.

52. Papadiamantes, Ἡ φόνισσα, 447; *The Murderess*, 37.

53. Papadiamantes, Ἡ φόνισσα, 447–48; *The Murderess*, 38.

54. Hadoula's insanity is always related to the act of strangulation. For instance, see the description of the attempted strangulation of Lyringo's daughter, where Hadoula is described as being "ἐν ἀλλοφροσύνῃ," that is, "mad." Papadiamantes, Ἡ φόνισσα, 498; *The Murderess*, 100.

55. Papadiamantes, Ἡ φόνισσα, 435; *The Murderess*, 23.

56. Papadiamantes, Ἡ φόνισσα, 444; *The Murderess*, 32.

57. Papadiamantes, Ἡ φόνισσα, 448; *The Murderess*, 38.

58. Papadiamantes, Ἡ φόνισσα, 460; *The Murderess*, 53: "If I was right, dear Saint John, send me a sign today [νὰ μοῦ δώσῃς σημεῖο σήμερα] . . . to do a good deed, for my soul and my poor heart to be at peace! . . . " Notice the urgency of Hadoula's request, to be given a sign *today*. Here, another difference between confession and self-confession could be discerned: while the former always waits for something that does not come, the latter does not wait; its mode is one of urgency.

59. Papadiamantes, Ἡ φόνισσα, 462; *The Murderess*, 56: "'There! . . . Saint John has sent me the sign, [Νά! . . . μοῦ ἔδωκε τὸ σημεῖο ὁ Ἅις-Γιάννης]' said Frankojannou to herself almost involuntarily, as she saw the two girls . . . "

60. Papadiamantes, Ἡ φόνισσα, 471; *The Murderess*, 66.

61. See, e.g., Papadiamantes, Ἡ φόνισσα, 467, 490, 497, 502.

62. See Jacques Derrida, "How to Avoid Speaking: Denials," trans. Ken Frieden, in *Languages of the Unsayable: The Play of Negativity in Literature and Literary Theory*, ed. Sanford Budick and Wolfgang Iser (New York: Columbia University Press, 1989), 3–70.

63. See Vardoulakis, "Confession and Time."

64. Papadiamantes has customarily been called ο φτωχός άγιος των ελληνικών γραμμάτων, the poor saint of Greek letters. Papadiamantes has been called "poor" because he was a κοσμοκαλόγερος, a secular monk, someone who renounced earthly wealth and comforts, but still stayed in the community in order to draw inspiration and assist in its betterment. And Papadiamantes was a "saint" because he shouldered the obligation to reveal the manner or means for that betterment. This secular saintliness is usually supported by Papadiamantes' own self-professed adherence to Greek Orthodox dogma, yet it need not lead

to an explicitly theological interpretation of his works, and *The Murderess* in particular.

65. Dimitris Tziovas expresses this attitude's foundational assertion: "the narrator acts as the guardian of truth" ("Selfhood, Natural Law, and Social Resistance in *The Murderess*," in *The Other Self: Selfhood and Society in Modern Greek Fiction* (Lanham, Md.: Lexington, 2003), 87). Tziovas ultimately sides with a sociopolitical interpretation, but does so by assuming that Papadiamantes delivers a true message, or at least a message that Papadiamantes regards as true (98), thereby surreptitiously shifting the province of truth from the narrator to the "real" author.

66. Guy (Michel) Saunier, *Εωσφόρος και άβυσσος: Ο προσωπικός μύθος του Παπαδιαμάντη* (Athens: Agra, 2001), 57. It should also be noted that Saunier translated *The Murderess* into French. See Alexandre Papadiamantes, *Les petites filles et la mort*, trans. Michel Saunier (Arles: Actes Sud, 2003).

67. Saunier, *Εωσφόρος και άβυσσος*, 260. And a page later: "Frankojannou IS [sic] . . . Papadiamantes." In other words, the secret of the novella must have a content, which is a representation of the author's repressions. This is the structure that underlies the most sustained interpretation of confession by a psychoanalyst, Theodor Reik's lectures in *The Compulsion to Confess: On the Psychoanalysis of Crime and Punishment* (1925; New York: Farrar, Straus and Cudahy, 1959). Reik insists throughout the lectures that the repressed can return and the secret can be revealed as confession. However, this presupposed that the confession is only an admission of guilt, a *Geständnis*, never a theological confession, a *Beichte*. This framework does not allow for a notion of self-confession, that is, for an articulation that puts different legislative frameworks in jeopardy. This is not surprising given that Reik is working on the old Freudian model of repression, which is understood through the content of the repressed. Conversely, as it was argued in "The Return of Negation" in Chapter 1, there is another Freudian repression that is formal and which gives rise to the chiastic ontology of the doppelgänger. For a nuanced discussion about the relation between religious confession and psychoanalysis, see Judith Butler, "Bodily Confessions," *Undoing Gender* (New York: Routledge, 2004), 161–73.

68. For another psychoanalytical approach which does not avoid similar traps, see E. Γ. Ασλανίδης (E. G. Aslanidis), *Το Μητρικό Στοιχείο στη Φόνισσα του Παπαδιαμάντη: Ψυχαναλυτικό Δοκίμιο* (Athens: Rappa, 1988).

69. Γ. Βαλέτας (G. Valetas), *Παπαδιαμάντης: Η ζωή, το έργο, η εποχή του* (Athens: Vivlos, 1957), 608. Valetas is not alone in reading *The Murderess* as a praise of Hadoula's aims. This is common in sociological interpretations. For instance, Mary N. Layoun contends that "the oppression and hardship of Greek peasant life . . . makes Frankojannou's actions, if not laudable, at least eminently comprehensible." Layoun, *Travels of a Genre: The Modern Novel and Ideology* (Princeton: Princeton University Press, 1990), 38. For other similar interpretations, see the collected volume n. ed., *Η κοινωνική διάσταση του έργου του Αλέξανδρου Παπαδιαμάντη* (Athens: Odysseas, 2000).

70. Valetas, Παπαδιαμάντης, 610–11.

71. Ibid., 610.

72. Kokolis see this very clearly when he interprets the relation between divine and human law as "the teleology of nature." Ξ. Α. Κοκόλης (X. A. Kokolis), *Για τη "Φόνισσα" του Παπαδιαμάντη: Δύο μελετήματα* (Thessalonica: University Studio Press, 1993), 58. Of course, it is Kant's third *Critique* that has convincingly shown that the dichotomy of creation and nature always implies a teleology.

73. The issue of the genre will be taken up in some detail in Chapter 3. Suffice it to say here that genre cannot be reduced to a dispensation of a subject—it is not a reflection of an author's subjectivity.

74. This affinity between a sociological reading and psychoanalysis stems from the fact that they both insist on starting with particularity. However, viewing a work of art as an autobiographical admission inevitably leads to psychologisms about the author's inspirations, motives, aims, and so on. Just to give one example, for Kargakos's *New Sociological and Political Interpretation of Papadiamantes* (as the subtitle of the book reads), the "key to the interpretation of *The Murderess*" lies in Papadiamantes' huge personal burden and impossible obligation to provide a dowry for his four sisters (23). This has the effect of splitting Papadiamantes' ego with schizophrenic tendencies. So while one ego remains religious, moral, and so on, the other seeks a revolution but only inside itself. Papadiamantes' "psychic resistances are transferred to his character. . . . In particular Frankojannou is Papadiamantes' alter ego, his secret self" (36–37). Frankojannou's schizophrenia, "her mind going on a high," has the consequence "that she has no murderous temperament" (51). Καργάκος Σαράντος (Kargakos Sarantos), *Ξαναδιαβάζοντας τη "Φόνισσα": Μια νέα κοινωνική και πολιτική θεώρηση του Παπαδιαμάντη* (Athens: Gutenberg, 1987).

75. Στέλιος Ράμφος (Stelios Ramfos), *Η παλινωδία του Παπαδιαμάντη* (Athens: Kedros, 1976), 90

76. Ibid., 93, 78.

77. Ibid., 81. The terms *achrony* is borrowed from Papagiorgis, Αλέξανδρος Αδαμαντίου Εμμανουή, 125, and 134 where Ramfos's argument is being summarized and taken up. A conception of a time dimension that is separated from "real" time and which is underwritten by the presence of God is a common denominator in the religious interpretations of Papadiamantes. For instance, Kolyvas writes that Papadiamantes' characters "partake of a religiously determined norm and ethical rules," and thus "revelation enlightens the truth and conceptualizes time and human life," and the truth leads to "a futural interpretation of past and present." Ιωακείμ-Κίμων Κολυβάς (Ioakim-Kimon Kolyvas), *Λογική της αφήγησης και ηθική του λόγου: Μελετήματα για τον Παπαδιαμάντη* (Athens: Nefeli,1991),16, 19, 20.

78. Ramfos, *Η παλινωδία του Παπαδιαμάντη*, 81, 83.

79. Ibid., 101.

80. Ibid., 102.

81. Ibid.,103.
82. Ibid.,106-7.
83. Ibid., 84-86. Ramfos very rigorously insists that Hadoula's madness has to be placed within the opposition of nature and law, which is completely excluded from the divine. The problem is that, as will be argued in a moment, such an exclusion cannot be sustained. An indication of this impossibility is Galateia Sarante's article on the phrase "her mind went on a high," which reaches the same conclusion about Hadoula's evil, but by conversely arguing that Hadoula eliminates all exclusions: "She has escaped human measure. . . . She corrects nature. . . . She becomes a judge, she becomes God." Γαλάτεια Σαράντη (Galateia Sarante), "'Είχε ψηλώσει ο νους της,'" in Φώτα ολόφωτα: Ένα αφιέρωμα στον Παπαδιαμάντη, ed. Ν. Δ. Τριανταφυλλόπουλος (N. D. Triantafyllopoulos) (Athens: Ε.Λ.Ι.Α., 1981), 348.
84. Ramfos, Η παλινωδία του Παπαδιαμάντη, 88-89.
85. Ibid., 97.
86. Ibid., 95.
87. The politics of revelation have often been discussed and will not be pursued in the present context. For one of the clearest and most sustained critiques of the ideology of revelation, see Paul Ricoeur, "Toward a Hermeneutic of the Idea of Revelation," *Harvard Theological Review* 70, no. 1–2 (1977): 1–37.
88. This is the meaning of the word παλινωδία in the title of Ramfos's book. Lakis Proguidis presents a sustained critique of that position. Λάκης Προγκίδης (Lakis Proguidis), Η κατάκτηση του μυθιστορήματος: Από τον Παπαδιαμάντη στον Βοκκάκιο, trans. Γιάννης Κιουρτσάκης (Athens: Hestia, 1998), 225–40. Proguidis's monograph is one of the most insightful on Papadiamantes. It has been the subject of a thematic issue of the journal *Nea Hestia* 145 (1999). Of interest also are Proguidis's articles and lectures collected in Ο Παπαδιαμάντης και η Δύση. Πέντε μελέτες (Athens: Hestia, 2002).
89. Papadiamantes, Οι έμποροι των εθνών [*The Merchants of the Nations*], *Hapanta*, 1:249. This is precisely what Odysseas Elytis terms "Papadiamantes's magic": "The magical mirror in all its glory. Earth's dynamism reflects onto the heavens, and the heavens' onto the earth." Οδυσσέας Ελύτης (Odysseas Elytis), Η μαγεία του Παπαδιαμάντη (Athens: Hypsilon, 1996), 33.
90. Papadiamantes, Οι έμποροι των εθνών, 249. Cf. Vardoulakis, "Confession and Time."
91. Longinus, *On the Sublime*, trans W. H. Fyfe, rev. trans. D. A. Russell (Cambridge Mass.: Harvard University Press, 1995), 188, translation significantly modified.
92. Longinus' notion of ὕψος has customarily been translated as "sublime," and as such its historicity is intricately connected to the sublime. However, it should not be confused with the same sublime in Edmund Burke or the *Erhabene* in Kant. As Ernesto Grassi has shown, Longinus' ὕψος is outside metaphysics and logocentrism. Ernesto Grassi, "The Experience of the Word," in *The Primordial Metaphor*,

trans. Laura Pietropaolo and Manuela Scarci (Binghamton, N.Y.: Medieval and Renaissance Texts and Studies, 1994), chap. 5.

93. Neil Hertz, in the first chapter of *End of the Line*, offers a remarkable reading of Longinus, starting from chapter 9 of *Peri Hupsous*. Hertz links ὕψος to a Freudian uncanny very similar to the one described in Chapter 1 of this book (Neil Hertz, *End of the Line: Essays in Psychoanalysis and the Sublime* [New York: Columbia University Press, 1985], 18). Thus Hertz also presents a link between the Longinian sublime and the doppelgänger.

94. Papadiamantes, Ἡ φόνισσα, 470; *The Murderess*, 66.

95. Papadiamantes, Ἡ φόνισσα, 471; *The Murderess*, 66.

96. The ambiguity of the law when it comes into contact with myth will be taken up in chapter 5.

CHAPTER 3: THE TASK OF THE DOPPELGÄNGER

1. F. C. Keppler, on the contrary, insists, in *The Literature of the Second Self* (Tucson: University of Arizona Press, 1972), on the separation of the author from the critical task that addresses the doppelgänger. According to Keppler, only "the work itself is direct and solid knowledge" (xii). Yet this distinction itself becomes precarious only a few lines later, when Keppler argues that the "more one sees the Double in literature the more it appears that he is the product not of tradition but of individual experience, and a new experience on the part of each writer who has made use of it" (xii–xiii). Later on Keppler specifies what he means by the use of the term "second self": duplicity can either be external or internal, and a literature of the "second self" cannot be only the former. Thus the motif of the shadow is dispensed with (6), alongside works that have been traditionally read as narratives of the double, such as *Jekyll and Hyde* (8), because the shadow as well as Stevenson's character with a split personality can be "objectively" separated from the psychological workings of the self. From what has been said in the preceding two chapters of this book, it will be clear that a distinction in the doppelgänger between the internal and the external cannot be maintained. The doppelgänger is precisely that subject which does not allow for a notion of individual subjectivity that can segregate the inside from the outside. Two conclusions follow: *pace* Keppler, the author must also be amenable to the doppelgänger; and, also, the doppelgänger will be the subject that is not founded on a movement of exclusion, a foundational exception, but rather the doppelgänger adheres to inclusivity and thus to a notion of friendship.

2. Maurice Blanchot, *The Step Not Beyond*, trans. Lycette Nelson (Albany: State University of New York Press,1982), 2; Maurice Blanchot, *Le pas au-delà* (Paris: Gallimard, 1973), 9.

3. Throughout his writings Blanchot addresses this nexus. One of the most famous places is the last part of *The Infinite Conversation*, titled "The Absence of the Book," where, for instance, Blanchot talks about the *il*, meaning both a

"he" and an "it," the third person pronoun that can be as much neuter as masculine. In this undecidability the subject and the work are intertwined under the rubric of writing. For instance, Blanchot says: "Thus we can see that the 'he' has split in two: on the one hand, there is something to tell, the *objective* real such as it is immediately present to an interested gaze; on the other hand, this real is reduced to a constellation of individual lives, of *subjectivities*—a multiple and personalized 'he,' an 'ego' manifest under the voice, sometimes fictive, sometimes without mask, can be heard more or less accurately" (Maurice Blanchot, *The Infinite Conversation*, trans. Susan Hanson (Minneapolis: University of Minnesota Press, 1997), 381; Maurice Blanchot, *L' entretien infini* (Paris: Gallimard, 1969), 559.

4. Maurice Blanchot, "The Task of Criticism Today," trans. Leslie Hill, *Oxford Literary Review* 22 (2000): 19; Maurice Blanchot, "Qu'en est-il de la critique?" in *Lautréamont et Sade* (Paris: Éditions de Minuit, 1963), 9. See Leslie Hill's incisive reading of Blanchot's "The Task of Criticism Today," which also examines Blanchot's critical project. Hill, "'Affirmation without Precedent': Maurice Blanchot and Criticism Today," in *After Blanchot: Literature, Criticism, Philosophy*, ed. Leslie Hill, Brian Nelson, and Dimitris Vardoulakis (Newark: University of Delaware Press, 2005), 58–79.

5. That is what Ernst Robert Curtius calls a "humility formula," which was used, for instance, before speaking about the divine. See his *European Literature and the Latin Middle Ages*, trans. Willard R. Trask (Princeton: Princeton University Press, 1990), 407–13.

6. Blanchot, "The Task of Criticism Today," 19; "Qu'en est-il de la critique?" 9.

7. Blanchot, "The Task of Criticism Today," 21; "Qu'en est-il de la critique?" 11.

8. Blanchot, "The Task of Criticism Today," 20; "Qu'en est-il de la critique?"10.

9. Blanchot, "The Task of Criticism Today," 21; "Qu'en est-il de la critique?" 11–12.

10. Blanchot, "The Task of Criticism Today," 22; "Qu'en est-il de la critique?" 12.

11. Maurice Blanchot, *Death Sentence*, trans. Lydia Davis, in *The Station Hill Blanchot Reader: Fiction and Literary Essays* (Barrytown, N.Y.: Station Hill Press, 1999), 129–87; Maurice Blanchot, *L'arrêt de mort* (Paris: Gallimard, 1948). References here will be to the original 1948 printing of the story.

12. J. Hillis Miller, "Death Mask: Blanchot's *L'arrêt de mort*," in *Versions of Pygmalion* (Cambridge, Mass.: Harvard University Press, 1990), 179–210. On the "double bind" in *L'arrêt de mort* see Jacques Derrida's compelling article "Living On: Border Lines," trans. James Hulbert, in *Deconstruction and Criticism* (New York: Seabury Press, 1979), 75–176.

13. Blanchot, *Death Sentence*, 132; *L'arrêt de mort*, 10.

14. Maurice Blanchot, *The Space of Literature*, trans. Smock (Lincoln: University of Nebraska Press, 1982), 172; Maurice Blanchot, *L'espace littéraire* (Paris: Gallimard, 1955), 180.

15. Since the 1971 edition of *L'arrêt de mort* the final two paragraphs were de-

leted. These two paragraphs constituted in the 1948 edition a separate section that has customarily been viewed as a metatext or as coda to the text.

16. Blanchot, *Death Sentence*, 132; *L'arrêt de mort*, 11.

17. Blanchot, *Death Sentence*, 167; *L'arrêt de mort*, 99.

18. Maurice Blanchot, *The Most High*, trans. Allan Stoekl (Lincoln: University of Nebraska Press, 1996), 222.

19. Blanchot, *Death Sentence*, 182; *L'arrêt de mort*, 137.

20. Of interest here is Michael Holland, "Nathalie ou 'le supplément du roman,'" in *L'œuvre du féminin dans l'écriture de Maurice Blanchot*, ed. Eric Hoppenot (Grignan: Éditions Complicités, 2004), 133–56. Holland briefly discusses the figure of Nathalie as it appears in Jean Paul, concentrating on Goethe's novel and specifically in comparison to the way it was appropriated by the Romantic project of Schlegel in his review of the novel in *Athenaeum*.

21. Maurice Blanchot, *After the Fact*, trans. Paul Auster, in *The Station Hill Blanchot Reader*, 490–91; Maurice Blanchot, *Après coup* précédé par *Le ressassement eternel* (Paris: Éditions du Minuit, 1983), 92.

22. Blanchot, *Death Sentence*, 157–59; *L'arrêt de mort*, 74–79. *Siebenkäs*, [1796], in *Sämtliche Werke*, ed. Norbert Miller (Darmstadt: Wissenschaftliche Buchgesellschaft, 2000), 1.2:364–66.

23. Blanchot, *Death Sentence*, 177; *L'arrêt de mort*, 124.

24. Jean Paul, *Auswahl aus des Teufels Papieren* [1789], in *Sämtliche Werke*, ed. Norbert Miller (Darmstadt: Wissenschaftliche Buchgesellschaft, 2000), div. 2, vol. 2.

25. Jean Paul, *Siebenkäs*, chap. 20.

26. Ibid., 531.

27. For a discussion of the political aspect of Jean Paul's novel *Titan*, see Heinz Schlaffer, "Epic and Novel: Action and Consciousness. Jean Paul's *Titan*," in *The Bourgeois as Hero*, trans. James Lynn (Cambridge: Polity, 1989), 8–38. In *Titan* Jean Paul continues the story of the central male characters in *Siebenkäs*.

28. See Leslie Hill, *Blanchot: Extreme Contemporary* (London: Routledge, 1997), 142–57.

29. Heinrich was also the name of Jean Paul's brother, whose suicide had a profound influence on Jean Paul.

30. Hill, *Blanchot*, 145–50.

31. See Christophe Bident, *Maurice Blanchot: Partenaire invisible, essai biographique* (Seyssel: Champ Vallon, 1998), 103–9, 291–5.

32. This reduction to the empirical, whereby "themes" are related to historical events as if the meaning of both were to be given solely through their reciprocity, is what makes suspect the efforts to read in *L'arrêt de mort* either a supposedly rejected fascist ideology (Jeffrey Mehlman, *Genealogies of the Text: Literature, Psychoanalysis, and Politics in Modern France* [Cambridge: Cambridge University Press, 1995], chap. 6), or even "the narrator's passivity as a historical agent" (Steven Ungar, *Scandal and Aftereffect: Blanchot and France since 1930* [Minneapolis: University of Minnesota Press, 1995], 72).

33. Walter Benjamin, "The Concept of Criticism in German Romanticism," in *Selected Writings*, 4 vols., ed. Michael W. Jennings et al. (Cambridge, Mass.: Harvard University Press, 1997–2003), abbreviated as *SW*, 1:178–85.

34. This is Fragment 1 in the collection of Jean Paul's previously unpublished material, *Ideen-Gewimmel: Texte und Aufzeichnungen aus dem unveröffentlichten Nachlaß*, ed. Thomas Wirtz and Kurt Wölfel (Frankfurt am Main: Eichborn, 1996), 25.

35. Blanchot, *Space of Literature*, 111; *L'espace littéraire*, 111.

Jean Paul's real name was Johann Christian Richter. Blanchot, following the conventional practice in France when referring to Jean Paul, combines the hyphenated pseudonym with his real surname: Jean-Paul Richter.

There are various other references to Jean Paul in Blanchot's work. However, the most important is maybe the short text "De Jean-Paul à Giraudoux," *Journal des débats* (3 February 1944): 2–3, reprinted in *Maurice Blanchot: Récits critiques*, ed. Christophe Bident and Pierre Vilar (Tours: Farrago, 2003), 29–32. Blanchot starts by pointing out that Jean Paul has a "sosie exalté" in Giraudoux. For Blanchot, Jean Paul represents a "principle" within Romanticism whose "main characteristic is the recognition of an experience proper to literature." Blanchot mentions the humble origins of Jean Paul's family, as well as the vision of his own death, and advances a dual typology of Jean Paul's works. There follows a discussion of metaphor in Jean Paul, which assigns his prose to a "véritable frénésie." Also, Blanchot mentions in the article contemporary translations of Jean Paul's works into French and pays tribute to Stefan George's assessment of Jean Paul. For a reading of this article by Blanchot, which concentrates, however, on the figure of Giraudoux, see Christophe Bident, " . . . au point de vacillement (d'un ecart Blanchot à Giraudoux)," in *Maurice Blanchot: Récits critiques*, ed. Bident and Vilar, 505–22.

36. Cf. Blanchot, "De Jean-Paul à Giraudoux," 29.

37. See the editor's note in *Siebenkäs*, 1153. "The Speech of the Dead Christ" has an extremely complex development in Jean Paul's works, as is often the case with ideas or themes that preoccupied him. The first draft of this piece bears the title "The dead Shakespeare's Lament to dead listeners about the non-existence of God," in Jean Paul, *Sämtliche Werke*, 2.2:589–92; according to the editor's note, it was first written in 1791 (*Sämtliche Werke*, 2.4:419–20). It will not be expedient to digress here into an examination of the development of this speech, not least because its rendering in *Siebenkäs* is the most famous one and the one referred to by Blanchot. J. W. Smeed traces the different versions in *Jean Paul's Dreams* (London: Oxford University Press, 1966), passim, but see in particular 18–31.

38. Jean Paul, *Siebenkäs*, 513–14.

39. Ibid., 279. Blanchot uses the phrase "les hommes hauts" (in quotation marks) also in "De Jean-Paul à Giraudoux," 30, where the phrase "lofty men" indicates those characters of Jean Paul's who are prodigious but who nevertheless have to suffer life's difficulties. This seems to be a fair description of Siebenkäs and Leibgeber in *Siebenkäs*, although it represents for Blanchot one of the two mains types

of characters to be found in Jean Paul's work. The two uses of "les hommes hauts" are not incompatible, but it is also not inconceivable that Blanchot has mixed up his references when he quotes from memory in the later article.

40. *Siebenkäs*, 279.

41. Ibid., 280.

42. This is not to say that the only name of an author, the name "Kafka," that appears in *L'arrêt de mort* does not make an impact that is beyond a mere reference to the author of the *Castle* and which touches on Blanchot's very understanding of literature, as Leslie Hill has shown in *Bataille, Klossowski, Blanchot: Writing at the Limit* (Oxford: Oxford University Press, 2001), 206–26.

43. Eleanor Kaufman, *The Delirium of Praise: Bataille, Blanchot, Deleuze, Foucault, Klossowski* (Baltimore: Johns Hopkins University Press, 2001), 54.

44. Maurice Blanchot, *The Unavowable Community*, trans. Pierre Joris (Barrytown, N.Y.: Station Hill Press, 1988), 23.

45. Michel Foucault, "Maurice Blanchot: The Thought from Outside," trans. Brian Massumi, in *Foucault/ Blanchot* (New York: Zone Books, 1987), 47.

46. Jean Paul, *Siebenkäs*, 385.

47. Maurice Blanchot, *The Book to Come*, trans. Charlotte Mandell (Stanford: Stanford University Press, 2003), 6; Maurice Blanchot, *Le livre à venir* (Paris: Gallimard, 1959), 13.

48. See Derrida's discussion of Blanchot's *La folie du jour* in "The Law of Genre," trans. Avital Ronell, in *Acts of Literature*, ed. Derek Attridge (New York: Routledge, 1992), 223–52.

49. Jean Paul, *Siebenkäs*, 450.

50. Christophe Bident, "The Movements of the Neuter," trans. Michael FitzGerald and Leslie Hill, in *After Blanchot: Literature, Criticism, Philosophy*, ed. Leslie Hill, Brian Nelson, and Dimitris Vardoulakis (Newark: University of Delaware Press, 2005), 24. See also Bident's *Maurice Blanchot: Partenaire invisible*.

51. Blanchot, *Space of Literature*, 173–74; *L'espace littéraire*, 182. If there is here an affirmation of failure, there is also in Blanchot a suspicion about success. For instance, see in *Le très-haut* the story of the general who is worried only when his orders seem to be carried out: "So our success just demonstrates the fact that we're still in our hole, still totally impotent" (Blanchot, *The Most High*, 218).

52. Blanchot, *Space of Literature*, 175; *L'espace littéraire*, 184.

53. Blanchot, *Space of Literature*, 173; *L'espace littéraire*, 181.

54. Jean Paul, *Horn of Oberon: Jean Paul's School of Aesthetics*, trans. Margaret R. Hale (Detroit: Wayne State University Press, 1973), 38–40; *Vorschule der Ästhetik*, in *Sämtliche Werke*, div. 1, vol. 5, pp. 60–62. All subsequent references to the *Vorschule* are to section 13.

55. Jean Paul, *Siebenkäs*, 66–67. This is not accidental since, as it has been extrapolated thus far, the doppelgänger is that which undoes the imagistic conception of subjectivity, the disruption of self-reflection. The doppelgänger is also re-

sponsible, as it will be argued in Chapter 5, for a notion of subject that adheres to the prohibition against the "graven image."

56. Jean Paul, *Siebenkäs*, 541.

57. Blanchot, *Death Sentence*, 181; *L'arrêt de mort*, 134.

58. Leibgeber gave Siebenkäs this key in *Siebenkäs*, 531. For the meeting between Siebenkäs and Natalie, see 572 ff.

59. This is not meant as a criticism of Jean Paul. Instead, as will be obvious to any reader of Jean Paul and Blanchot, their respective projects are evidently not the same.

60. Blanchot, *Death Sentence*, 172; *L'arrêt de mort*, 112.

61. Blanchot, *Death Sentence*, 172; *L'arrêt de mort*, 112.

62. Blanchot, *Death Sentence*, 172; *L'arrêt de mort*, 113.

63. Blanchot, *Death Sentence*, 173; *L'arrêt de mort*, 113.

64. Blanchot, *Death Sentence*, 174; *L'arrêt de mort*, 117.

65. On singularity in Blanchot, see Andrew Benjamin, "Figuring Self-Identity: Blanchot's Bataille," in *Other Than Identity: The Subject, Politics and Art*, ed. Juliet Steyn (Manchester: Manchester University Press, 1997), 9–31. Although Benjamin looks at the way Bataille figures in *L'entretien infini*, his analysis is still pertinent since is deals with the more general problematic of subjectivity and difference.

66. Blanchot, *Death Sentence*, 175; *L'arrêt de mort*, 180.

67. Blanchot, *Death Sentence*, 175–76; *L'arrêt de mort*, 120.

68. Blanchot, *Space of Literature*, 173; *L'espace littéraire*, 182.

69. Blanchot, *Death Sentence*, 167; *L'arrêt de mort*, 99.

70. Blanchot, *Death Sentence*, 178; *L'arrêt de mort*, 126.

71. Blanchot, *Death Sentence*, 179; *L'arrêt de mort*, 129.

72. Blanchot, *Death Sentence*, 181; *L'arrêt de mort*, 135.

73. Blanchot, *Death Sentence*, 182; *L'arrêt de mort*, 136.

74. Blanchot, *Space of Literature*, 175; *L'espace littéraire*, 184.

75. Blanchot, *Death Sentence*, 182; *L'arrêt de mort*, 137.

76. Blanchot, *Death Sentence*, 184; *L'arrêt de mort*, 141.

77. Blanchot, *Death Sentence*, 186; *L'arrêt de mort*, 146.

78. Blanchot, *Death Sentence*, 177; *L'arrêt de mort*, 123.

79. Blanchot, *Death Sentence*, 187; *L'arrêt de mort*, 149.

80. Blanchot, *Space of Literature*, 25; *L'espace littéraire*, 19.

81. Blanchot, "The Task of Criticism Today," 24.

82. Hill, "Affirmation without Precedent," 75.

83. Cited ibid., 75–76.

84. Maurice Blanchot, "The Beast of Lascaux" [1953], trans. Leslie Hill, *Oxford Literary Review* 22 (2000): 10; Maurice Blanchot, *La bête de Lascaux* (Montpelier: Fata Morgana, 1982), 15.

85. Blanchot, "The Beast of Lascaux," 11; *La bête de Lascaux*, 19. This is fragment 93 in the Diels numbering system. See Heraclitus, *The Art and Thought of*

Heraclitus, ed. Charles H. Kahn (Cambridge: Cambridge University Press, 2001), 42.

86. Blanchot, "The Beast of Lascaux," 12; *La bête de Lascaux*, 21. It should be noted that this does not entail a coincidence between the prophet and the writer. The prophet speaks with a certainty imbued with ideological violence, while, as Blanchot observes in discussing the poetry of René Char, it "is the poem's chance to be able to escape the intolerance of the prophet" ("The Beast of Lascaux," 15; *La bête de Lascaux*, 30).

87. The most radical such reworking is, perhaps, *Thomas l'Obscur*, published first as a novel in 1941, and then as a récit of significantly reduced size in 1950. Blanchot would make less extensive changes as a matter of course whenever he collected his articles in books.

88. See Jacques Derrida, *Politics of Friendship*, trans. George Collins (Verso: London, 1997), and *Of Hospitality: Anne Dufourmantelle Invites Jacques Derrida to Respond*, trans. Rachel Bowlby (Stanford: Stanford University Press, 2000).

CHAPTER 4: THE POLITICS OF THE DOPPELGÄNGER

1. In his remarkable book *The Jew, the Arab: A History of the Enemy* (Stanford: Stanford University Press, 2003), Gil Anidjar traces the historicity of the distinction between friend and enemy from the point of view of the private and public distinction—or the (non)distinction between theology and politics. The figure of "the Jew, the Arab" interrupts the theologico-political by showing that at the heart of this ideology is the thesis that "the enemy is to be used," as Anidjar puts it (24). It will always be through a privileging of its utilitarian function that an ideology will be defended. However, if the historicity of this privileging is taken into account, is it possible, then, not so much to erase utility, but rather not to subsume under it the ideal? Anidjar attempts to respond to this problematic by presenting a historicity of the enemy. A similar attempt is carried out here through (that is, in the medium of) the doppelgänger.

2. See the section titled "The Return of Negation" in Chapter 1.

3. Étienne Balibar, "Subjection and Subjectivation," in *Supposing the Subject*, ed. Joan Copjec (London: Verso, 1994), 8. In emphasizing that subjection is part of what it is to be a subject, Balibar is following a neo-Marxist tradition that includes Louis Althusser. Thus, Althusser makes a similar point in "Ideology and Ideological State Apparatuses," in "Lenin and Philosophy" and Other Essays, trans. Ben Brewster (London: NLB, 1977), 169.

4. Balibar, "Subjection and Subjectivation," 9.

5. Ibid., 6.

6. Ibid., 4.

7. Ibid., 14.

8. Walter Benjamin, *Arcades Project*, trans. Howard Eiland and Kevin McLaughlin (Cambridge, Mass.: Belknap, 1999), K1, 2.

9. Friedrich Schiller, "The Nature and Value of Universal History," *History and Theory* 11, no. 3 (1972): 321–34; Friedrich Schiller, "Was heisst und zu welchem Ende studiert man Universalgeschichte?" *Werke in Drei Bände*, vol. 2, ed. Gerhard Fricke and Herbert G. Göpfert (Munich: Carl Hansen Verlag, 1966), 9–22. A more literal translation of the German title would be "What Is Universal History and to What End Is It Studied?"

10. Schiller was speaking in March 1789, a few months before the French Revolution, which set in motion forces that challenged the "harmonious" European coexistence—if it ever existed. What is of interest, however, is not so much that Schiller did not foresee the approaching terror and warfare, even though the progressibility operating within Universal History does purport to be speaking about the future, but that the bloodbath was consistently justified with recourse to the same liberal and republican principles of perfectibility evoked by Schiller.

11. For a discussion of the automaton and the doppelgänger, see Renate Böschenstein, "Doppelgänger, Automat, serielle Figur: Formen des Zweifels an der Singularität der Person," in *Androïden: Zur Poetologie der Automaten*, ed. Jürgen Söring and Reto Sorg (Frankfurt am Main: Peter Lang, 1997), 165–95; and Aglaja Hildenbrock, in *Das andere Ich: Künstlicher Mensch und Doppelgänger in der deutsch- und englischsprachigen Literatur* (Tübingen: Stauffenburg, 1986), 34–70.

12. It will be recalled that this distinction was crucial for Fichte, as it has been argued in the section titled "'Double Acts' and Transformation" in Chapter 1. It will also become clear later in the present chapter that the same move is made by Kant, for instance, in his paper on cosmopolitanism. It is well known, of course, that Schiller had read Kant's essay before writing his inaugural address, and even the term "Universalgeschichte" could be argued to be Schiller's translation of Kant's term "allgemeine Geschichte."

13. Schiller, "Nature and Value of Universal History," 322–33; "Was heisst und zu welchem Ende studiert man Universalgeschichte?" 10–11.

14. Schiller, "Nature and Value of Universal History," 232–34; "Was heisst und zu welchem Ende studiert man Universalgeschichte?" 11–12.

15. This is, of course, the symptom of Enlightenment. As Catherine Liu puts it, while referring to Walter Benjamin's chess-playing automaton: "The figure of the automaton mediates the representation of a catachrestic imperative: how has Enlightenment represented that machine as its infernal Other, while at the same time adopting a principle of mechanical reason to justify the giddy optimism of its expansionist project? Only historical materialism can answer this question" (Catherine Liu, *Copying Machines: Taking Notes for the Automaton* [Minneapolis: University of Minnesota Press, 2000], xi). Also, this point comes to the fore in Kant's essay on cosmopolitanism, as will be shown later in this chapter.

16. "Cooperation" here should not be understood as a parallel activity by distinct individuals, but as an operation with distinct yet inseparable elements, namely the autonomous and the automatic—that is, the cooperation that puts the subjectivist parallel activity into question. The issue of messianism in Benjamin has

generated a large secondary literature. For one of the most compelling studies, which emphasizes the Jewish provenance of the messianic, see Irving Wohlfarth's "On the Messianic Structure of Walter Benjamin's Last Reflections," *Glyph* 3 (1978): 148–212. The issue of conciliation, as one aspect of the messianic, will be taken up in Chapter 5.

17. Alasdair Gray, *Poor Things: Episodes from the Early Life of Archibald McCandless M.D. Scottish Public Health Officer, Edited by Alasdair Gray* (London: Bloomsbury, 1992), 47, 142.

18. The way that Benjamin adduces such a reconciliation in Thesis I, only in order to subvert it, will be shown in "The Pure Machine's Gambit," the first section of Chapter 5. What binds Benjamin's and Gray's projects is, as it will be argued, an emphasis on such a subversion. Although the subject may be claiming to have secured a totality, the operative presence of the doppelgänger will turn such statements into aberrant claims whose *hypo*-critical structure—as it will be shown—is linked to the ontology of the doppelgänger.

19. Thesis I is cited in its entirety at the beginning of Chapter 5, where it is read with recourse to Benjamin's source, an article on the Turk by Edgar Allan Poe.

20. Benjamin, *The Arcades Project*, N3, 3.

21. The idea of a comprehensive collection or record in Benjamin has often been tackled through the image or theme of the collector. For two of the most influential articles on this, see Susan Buck-Morss, "The Flaneur, the Sandwichman, and the Whore: The Politics of Loitering," *New German Critique* 39 (1986): 99–140; and, Irving Wohlfarth, "Et Cetera? The Historian as Chiffonier," *New German Critique* 39 (1986): 142–68. The emphasis on parataxis in this chapter aims to highlight that the activity of collecting and its relation to the subject and to history also of necessity raises the issue of writing. There is neither a complete rupture nor a reconciliation between history and historiography. Rather, their relation—as it is argued in the present section—is mediated by the interruptive power of judgment.

22. See Longinus, *On the Sublime*, trans W. H. Fyfe, rev. trans. D. A. Russell (Cambridge Mass.: Harvard University Press, 1995), §43.

23. "Of Experience," in *The Complete Works of Montaigne: Essays, Travel Journals, Letters*, trans. Donald M. Frame (Stanford: Stanford University Press, 1948), is the concluding essay of Montaigne's *Essays*, and it consists of an inventory of the author's bodily and habitual attitudes. On this famous essay, see Jean Starobinski, "The Body's Moment," trans. John A. Gallucci, *Yale French Studies* 64 (1983): 273–305; on Rabelais's lists, see Mikhail Bakhtin, *Rabelais and His World*, trans. Hélène Iswolsky (Bloomington: Indiana University Press, 1984), passim, and Mikhail Bakhtin, "Forms of Time and of the Chronotope in the Novel: Notes Towards a Historical Poetics," in *The Dialogic Imagination*, trans. Caryl Emerson and Michael Holquist (Austin: University of Texas Press, 1988), 167–206; on the use of lists in La Popelinière's "perfect history" see Zachary Sayre Schiffman, *On the Threshold of Modernity: Relativism in the French Renaissance* (Baltimore: Johns Hopkins University Press, 1991), chaps. 1, 2.

24. See Michel Foucault, Preface to *The Order of Things: An Archaeology of the Human Sciences* (London: Routledge, 2002), xvi–xxvi. The French title is *Les Mots et les choses* (1966).

25. This short summary of the sources of universal history does not pretend to be comprehensive. A historical examination of it will have to be extensive, because universal history—understood as the possibility of completeness within any attempt at recording knowledge—can be shown to be effective since Herodotus. If an extensive history of universal history were to be attempted, close attention would have to be paid to the various topologies seeking to tabulate argumentative strategies and knowledge. For a fascinating account of the mnemotechnics that this gave rise to from ancient Greece to the Italian Renaissance, see Frances A. Yates, *The Art of Memory* (1966; London: Pimlico, 2000). It would also have to include related conceptions, such as the seventeenth-century idea of a "universal library," as well as the Enlightenment's various understandings of the dictionary and the encyclopedia. For a succinct account of the development of the concept of the universal history from Schiller onward, as well as for its critique, see Odo Marquard, "Universal History and Multiversal History," in *In Defense of the Accidental: Philosophical Studies*, trans. Robert M. Wallace (New York: Oxford University Press, 1991), 50–70.

26. Benjamin, *The Arcades Project*, N18, 3. In other words, what is made clear here is the political significance of the messianic. For an authoritative account of the nexus of the theological and the political in Benjamin, see Howard Caygill, "Non-messianic Political Theology in Benjamin's 'On the Concept of History,'" in *Walter Benjamin and History*, ed. Andrew Benjamin (London: Continuum, 2005), 215–26. See also the essays in *Kapitalismus als Religion*, ed. Dirk Baecker (Berlin: Kadmos, 2003).

27. Walter Benjamin, "Paralipomena to 'On the Concept of History,'" in *Selected Writings*, 4 vols., ed. Michael W. Jennings (Cambridge, Mass.: Harvard University Press, 1997–2003), abbreviated as *SW*, 4:404; *Gesammelte Schriften*, ed. Rolf Tiedemann and Hermann Schweppenhäuser (Frankfurt am Main: Suhrkamp, 1991), abbreviated as *GS*, 1.3:1235.

28. Ibid., *SW* 4:404; *GS* 1.3:1235.

29. For the relation between Benjamin and the Frankfurt School, see Susan Buck-Morss, *The Origin of Negative Dialectics* (New York: Free Press, 1977).

30. Benjamin, *The Arcades Project*, N8, 1.

31. For Benjamin's attitude to Warburg vis-à-vis the independence of disciplines, or, as Benjamin also called it, "cultural history," see Howard Caygill, "Walter Benjamin's Concept of Cultural History," in *The Cambridge Companion to Walter Benjamin*, ed. David S. Ferris, (Cambridge: Cambridge University Press, 2004), 83–89. Another article on the relation between Benjamin and the Warburg school that deserves mention is Beatrice Hanssen's "Portrait of Melancholy (Benjamin, Warburg, Panofsky)," in *Benjamin's Ghosts: Interventions in Contemporary Literary and Cultural Studies*, ed. Gerhard Richter (Stanford: Stanford University Press,

2002), 169–88. Although Hanssen does not address explicitly the issue of the independence of disciplines, her reading is still valuable for the investigation of the subject of history in showing that what distinguishes Benjamin's method from Warburg's method is that for the former there is a "disappearance of the human" (186).

32. Benjamin, *The Arcades Project*, N3, 4.

33. Cf. Benjamin, "Paralipomena to 'On the Concept of History,'" *SW* 4:406; *GS* 1.3:1240.

34. Cf. Benjamin, *The Arcades Project*, N1a, 8.

35. Benjamin, "On the Concept of History," *SW* 4:395; *GS* 1.2:701.

36. Andrew Benjamin, "Benjamin's Modernity," in *Cambridge Companion to Walter Benjamin*, ed. Ferris, 113. For Benjamin's modernity, see also Samuel Weber, "Genealogy of Modernity: History, Myth and Allegory in Benjamin's *Origin of German Mourning Play*," *MLN* 106, no. 3 (1991): 465–500.

37. Benjamin, "On the Concept of History," *SW* 4:397; *GS* 1.2:704.

38. "The historical method is a philological method," writes Benjamin in a note from the Paralipomena titled "Dialectical Image" (*SW* 4:405; *GS* 1.3:1238). And the philologist is, according to the essay on the *Elective Affinities*, the chemist who investigates the ashes of the pyre—that is, the material content of the work of art, or the historical pile of catastrophes. The constructive principle of historical materialism presupposes destruction (cf. N7, 6).

39. Benjamin, "On the Concept of History," *SW* 4:396; *GS* 1.2:702–3.

40. Ibid., *SW* 4:396; *GS* 1.2:703.

41. See, e.g., Benjamin, *The Arcades Project*, N18, 3.

42. The culmination of historicism equates universal history with the third sense of historicism indicated earlier, the positivism claiming to present the facts as they "really were."

43. A similar spacing will be discovered in what Benjamin call the "middle world" of Kafka—see the section titled "Kafka's 'Lost Gesture'" in Chapter 5.

44. Benjamin, "Paralipomena to 'On the Concept of History,'" *SW* 4:406; *GS* 1.3:1240.

45. Ibid., *SW* 4:406; *GS* 1.3:1240. "(Die Idee einer Universalgeschichte steht und fällt mit der Idee einer universellen Sprache. Solange die letztere ein Fundament besaß, sei es ein theologisches wie im Mittelalter, sei es ein logisches wie zuletzt bei Leibniz, war die Universalgeschichte nicht Denkmögliches. Dagegen kann die Universalgeschichte, wie sie seit dem vorigen Jahrhundert betrieben wurde, immer nur eine Sorte von Esperanto sein.)"

46. Peter Fenves has produced the most compelling work on the relation between Benjamin and Leibniz. For instance, in relation to the discussion here, Fenves has shown that the importance of the monad consists in allowing for "a language wholly removed from the sphere of subjective intentionality" (Peter Fenves, "On Philosophical Style—from Leibniz to Benjamin," *boundary 2* 30, no. 1 [2003]: 78). This means that the nothing is constitutive of the subject: "Only a 'no one' in the strict sense—a constitutively inconsistent plurality—can be one" (82). This

constitutive presence of the nothing in the subject will be termed "self-inscription" in Chapter 5.

47. Benjamin, "On the Concept of History," *SW* 4:397; *GS* 1.2:704.

48. The metaphor of the positivist historian as a collector of index cards comes from Carl Becker, *Detachment and the Writing of History: Essays and Letters*, ed. Phil Snyder (Ithaca: Cornell University Press, 1958), 24–25.

49. Benjamin, "Paralipomena to 'On the Concept of History,'" *GS* 1.3:1239.

50. Walter Benjamin, "On Language as Such and on the Language of Man," *SW* 1:68; Walter Benjamin, "Über Sprache überhaupt und über die Sprache des Menschen," *GS* 2.1:148. This early paper has generated a lot of secondary literature. For one of the most original readings, see Winfried Menninghaus, *Walter Benjamins Theorie der Sprachmagie* (Frankfurt am Main: Suhrkamp, 1980).

51. Benjamin, "Paralipomena to 'On the Concept of History,'" *SW* 4:406; *GS* 1.3:1240.

52. Ibid., *SW* 4:406; *GS* 1.3:1240–41.

53. "The Storyteller" is, of course, much more complex. The argument unfolds partly as a contrast between storytelling and the novel. See Timothy Bahti, "Death and Authority: Benjamin's 'The Storyteller,'" in *Allegories of History: Literary Historiography after Hegel* (Baltimore: Johns Hopkins University Press, 1992), 226–54, for an incisive reading of the difference between the two genres in terms of the temporality of the end and of ending.

54. Walter Benjamin, "The Storyteller: Observations on the Works of Nikolai Leskov," *SW* 3:150; *GS* 2.2:449.

55. Ibid., *SW* 3:151; *GS* 2.2:450.

56. Ibid., *SW* 3:152; *GS* 2.2:450–51.

57. Ibid., *SW* 3:152–53; *GS* 2.2:451–52.

58. Ibid., *SW* 3:153; *GS* 2.2:452.

59. Benjamin, "On the Concept of History," *SW* 4:390; *GS* 1.2:694.

60. Benjamin, "The Storyteller," *SW* 3:154; *GS* 2.2:453.

61. Benjamin, "On the Concept of History," *SW* 4:390; *GS* 1.2:694.

62. Benjamin, "The Storyteller," *SW* 3:148; *GS* 2.2:445.

63. Ibid., *SW* 3:148; *GS* 2.2:446.

64. *Herodotus with an English Translation*, trans. A. D. Godley (Cambridge, Mass.: Harvard University Press, 1957), 2:21.

65. Cf. Benjamin, "Paralipomena to 'On the Concept of History,'" *SW* 4:406; *GS* 1.3:1241.

66. Benjamin, *The Arcades Project*, K1, 2.

67. The inadequacy of this question is indicated by the indecision as to who really is in control. Thus Jürgen Habermas discerns Benjamin's failed notion of history in that materialism cannot be fitted into theology, if the dwarf representing theology is taken to be in control ("Walter Benjamin: Consciousness-Raising or Rescuing Critique," in *On Walter Benjamin: Critical Essays and Recollections*, ed. Gary Smith [Cambridge, Mass: MIT Press, 1988], 113–14). Conversely, Bahti em-

phasizes Benjamin's assertion that the puppet takes the chess player into its service, and correctly shows that this reversal of control presents a chiasmus between the two terms (Bahti, "History as Rhetorical Enactment: Walter Benjamin's Theses 'On the Concept of History,'" in *Allegories of History*, 200–201). However, in relation to subjectivity Bahti's reading requires a further step: the subject is not presented in the reversal of control between man and puppet, but rather in the process of reversibility that the relation between man and puppet makes possible. Ian Balfour perceives this process of reversibility but concludes from this that "the puppet and dwarf . . . have to combine forces, and it is the cooperation of the two that guarantees victory in the chess game of history" ("Reversal, Quotation [Benjamin's History]," *MLN* 106, no. 3 [1991]: 627). This image of an alliance between the man and the puppet may be construed as purporting that they are independent entities. Reversibility must emphasize instead the complicity between man and puppet, which undoes any notion of cooperation between individual parties.

68. Alasdair Gray, in personal conversation, has recounted that he wanted to write a story that turned *Frankenstein* upside down: Bella, if she is a fabrication, is nothing like Mary Shelley's monster. Instead, Bella is both sexually irresistible and sexually liberated—a most attractive character in the novel.

69. Alasdair Gray's monumental *The Book of Prefaces* (London: Bloomsbury, 2000), an anthology of prefaces from the seventh century to the twentieth, testifies to Gray's fascination with what can be called "framing devices."

70. In fact, this polyphony spills out of the novel itself. In a hilarious but also serious review that appeared the day after the publication of *Poor Things*, Archie Hind attacked the book as a fabrication and not an earnest historical record. Hind is a close friend of Gray's whose name actually appears twice in *Poor Things* and who in the review adopted a stylistic mannerism that echoed Gray's own. However, the review is not merely a superficial joke; it is also serious, because it has highlighted better than any other review of *Poor Things* the impossibility of gaining control of the narrative—an impossibility at the heart of *Poor Things* itself. See Archie Hind, "Outré Tale of Victorian Glasgow," *Glasgow Herald*, 3 September 1992, 13. (See also Gray's reply published in the same paper on 12 September 1992, 10). Here is a sample of Hind's review: "In the interest of truth, for which this reviewer will always stand, I would like to complicate things with a speculation of my own. What if Gray had planted the supposed memoir by McCandless on to an innocent and understanding Donnelly? It follows that he could and almost likely did write the McCandless episodes himself and foist them on the public by carefully grafting his fiction on to real historical events and people. There is ample internal textual evidence for this."

71. The character's name is unstable throughout the novel. Her first name is also Victoria, and her nickname is Bell. Her second name is also Hattersley, Blessington, and McCandless. Stephen Bernstein provides a reading of some of these appellations, concluding correctly that their complexity prohibits "a unitary reading" of *Poor Things* (Stephen Bernstein, *Alasdair Gray* [Lewisburg, Penn.: Bucknell University Press, 1999], 111).

72. Gray, *Poor Things*, 317.

73. It would be possible at this point to offer a feminist reading of *Poor Things*, by emphasizing that what needs to be kept inside—by exorcising its externalization, so to speak—is always the feminine. Thus, the division would be between a feminine interior and a masculine exterior. The latter would be, of course, reason, whereas the former would be reason's enemy; in Hegel's formulation: "Since the community only gets an existence through its interference with the happiness of the Family, and by dissolving [individual] self-consciousness into the universal, it creates for itself in what is suppresses and what is at the same time essential to it an internal enemy—womankind in general" (G. W. F. Hegel, *Phenomenology of Spirit*, trans. A. V. Miller [Oxford: Oxford University Press, 1977], 288). The figure that exemplifies this generalized womankind for Hegel is Antigone. In a feminist reading of Antigone Judith Butler emphasizes the impossibility of drawing steadfast distinctions between the state and kinship in order to secure the ethical, but also concludes with an affirmation of multiplicity as the condition of personal identity. See Judith Butler, *Antigone's Claim: Kinship Between Life and Death* (New York: Columbia University Press, 2000). A similar feminist undertaking would be pertinent also to *Poor Things*. However, emphasizing the political and ethical aspect of such an interiority-exteriority distinction need not be pursued solely through the question of gender. Indeed, generalizing the affirmation of multiplicity would entail an affirmation of multiple approaches to the political and the ethical in relation to Antigone—Antigone as both a name, a mythical narrative, and as *Antigone* the play written by Sophocles. For example, one other locus could be the uncanniness that characterizes the human according to the first stasimon—which is crucial for Heidegger's interpretation in his *Introduction to Metaphysics*. (Both Stathis Gourgouris in *Does Literature Think? Literature as Theory for an Antimythical Era* [Stanford: Stanford University Press, 2003], and Andrew Benjamin in "Placing Speaking: Notes on the First Stasimon of Sophocles' Antigone," *Angelaki* 9, no. 2 [2004]: 55–66 have offered insightful readings of this ode, readings that are also critical of the Heideggerian project.) The point is that the proliferation of ambiguity as a result of a destabilized origin gives rise to a political project whose historical multifacetedness indicates at the very least that ambiguity is part of that project—it needs to be retained.

74. Gray, *Poor Things*, 45. Signing as "Victoria McCandless MD" a letter in which she gives her side of the story as to her own origins, she criticizes her husband for all the expense of commissioning illustrations for his vanity publication, and she contends that "the portrait of me [on p. 45] is copied from an illustrated newspaper of 1896, and strikes me as a good likeness. If you ignore the Gainsborough hat and the pretentious nickname [i.e., the caption "Bella Caledonia"] it shows I am a plain, sensible woman, not the naïve Lucrezia Borgia and La Belle Dame Sans Merci described in the text. So I post the letter to posterity" (251). The recipient of the letter as well as the book are warned not too make too much of this illustration. But would not this admonition, placed in the opening of her long let-

ter, also create the suspicion that something repressed manifests itself here that cannot be denied?

75. Gray acknowledges Carlyle's influence in an interview with Sean Figgis and Andrew McAllister in *Bête Noire* 5 (1988): 19. For Carlyle's impact on Gray's earlier novel *1982 Janine* (1984), see Christopher Harvie, "Alasdair Gray and the Condition of Scotland Question," in *The Arts of Alasdair Gray*, ed. Robert Crawford and Thom Nairn (Edinburgh: Edinburgh University Press, 1991), 87. However, as Dietmar Böhnke has correctly observed, "it is certainly [*Poor Things*] which is most clearly modelled on [Carlyle's] *Sartor [Resartus]*. As usual, Gray gives it away in one of his notes, where he refers to a book printed by 'Stillschweigen Verlag' at 'Weissnichtwo' [*Poor Things*, 290]. This is incidentally also the 'punisher' and place of publication of the book of Carlyle's professor [Diogenes Teufelsdröckh]" (Dietmar Böhnke, *Shades of Gray: Science Fiction, History and the Problem of Postmodernism in the Work of Alasdair Gray* [Glienicke, Berlin: Galda + Wilch, 2004], 73).

76. Three related points should be raised here, even in passing. First, the determination of cultural influences remains always problematic. Wolfgang Iser has tried to argue that it is possible to conceptualize a translatability of cultures that will remain outside discursive dominance. "There is no longer any overarching third dimension from which to predicate what cross-cultural relationships are like. . . . Thus any kind of thirdness can be exposed for what it is: an interest-governed stance" (Iser, "On Translatability," *Surfaces* 4 [1994]: 13). See also Iser, "The Emergence of a Cross-Cultural Discourse: Thomas Carlyle's *Sartor Resartus*," in *The Translatability of Cultures: Figurations of the Space Between*, ed. Sanford Budick and Wolfgang Iser (Stanford: Stanford University Press, 1996), 245–64, which is of interest not only as an extended version of the previous paper, but also because it takes as it case study Carlyle's work. In a roundtable discussion on Iser's paper, Jacques Derrida correctly points out that even if a third party is presumably denied in the relation between two cultures, there will always be "the third party effect," which will sustain an infinite process of negotiation. In other words, there can never be a pure cultural interchange. For the roundtable discussion, see *Surfaces* 6 (1996): 5–37 (Derrida's comment is on 9). Second, because of the "third party effect" it is impossible to isolate one or two specific cultures (however they are defined, across national borders or within different "periods" of a single nation), in order to determine the intercultural influence. To the extent that finitude is inseparable from culture, culture is imbued with an ineliminable and uncontainable excess. Thus, Beat Witschi's account of Gray's writing solely within the rubric of "Scottish letters" is from the beginning constrained to tame this excess. See Beat Witschi, *Glasgow Urban Writing and Postmodernism: A Study of Alasdair Gray's Fiction* (Bern: Peter Lang, 1991). Third, even on a strictly textual level, there is a labyrinthine network of references in *Poor Things*. To offer a few indicative examples, there are numerous and explicit reference to *Hamlet*, a continuation of Dostoevsky's *The Gambler* in chapter 14, a reworking of Naipaul's *In a Free State* in chapter 17, a mention of Proust's Duc de Germantes in chapter 18, and the in-

fluences of authors such as James Hogg and Mary Shelley are evident throughout. Could a detective-critical work uncover all the implicit and explicit references? And, if that is untenable, does not this indicate the limitations of the detective-uncovering procedure?

77. Gray, *Poor Things*, 47, 147.

78. Ibid., 47.

79. Franco Moretti, *The Way of the World: The* Bildungsroman *in European Culture* (London: Verso, 2000), 99: "We are automatism as well as spirit, and so these novels [the *Bildungsroman* novels] give us a structure composed of opposing and complementary meanings."

80. Ibid., 244. This may bring to mind Tzvetan Todorov's similar conclusion about the end of the doppelgänger narrative because of its "appropriation" by psychoanalysis (see the section "The Return of Negation" in Chapter 1).

81. Also, significantly, the "letter to posterity" composed by Victoria McCandless is dated "1st August, 1914" (276). The "letter to posterity" will be discussed in later.

82. The same argument about the untenability of determining a specific type of narrative, whether a detective narrative or a bildungsroman, for *Poor Things*, could be applied mutatis mutandis for all the works of Alasdair Gray. Although this issue cannot be pursued here, it has to be noted that Carola M. Jansen's neat distinction between the *Lebensgeschichte* narrating the entire life of a main character, and the *Krisensgeschichte* concentrating on points of crisis in the life of the main character is also untenable. According to Jansen, *Poor Things* belongs to the first category, to a *Lebensgeschichte*; but, then, this would be merely another name for the bildungsroman. Moreover, a bildungsroman could also be a narrative of crisis. In any case, where the moment of crisis begins and where the entire lifespan ends is always a matter of interpretation, and never that which makes interpretation possible. See Carola M. Jansen, *Die Welten und Mikrokosmen des Alasdair Gray* (Bern: Peter Lang, 2000), passim, and for the distinction between *Lebensgeschichte* and *Krisensgeschichte*, 15.

83. Gray, *Poor Things*, 262, 263.

84. The word "creature" is not arbitrary. In a letter to Robert Crawford, the editor of a collection of essays on his work, Gray wrote: "I have recently finished . . . a new novel called *Poor Creatures*." The letter is dated 13 June 1991 (*Poor Things* was published in September 1992). The letter is photographically reproduced at the end of the volume of essays, without page number. See *The Arts of Alasdair Gray*, ed. Crawford and Nairn. There is no documentary evidence about when or why the title was changed to *Poor Things*.

85. Gray, *Poor Things*, xi.

86. Ibid., 211.

87. Ibid., 251.

88. Ibid., 263.

89. Ibid.

90. Ibid., 253.

91. Ibid., 265.

92. Immanuel Kant, "Idea of a Universal History with a Cosmopolitan Purpose," [1784], in *Political Writings*, ed. H. S. Reiss, trans. H. B. Nisbet (Cambridge: Cambridge University Press, 2000), 41–42; Immanuel Kant, "Idee zu einer allgemeinen Geschichte in weltbürgerliche Absicht," in Immanuel Kant, *Werke*, ed. Wilhelm Weischedel (Darmstadt: Wissenschaftliche Buchgesellschaft, 1998), 6:34.

93. Kant, "Idea of a Universal History," 47–48; "Idee zu einer allgemeinen Geschichte," 41–43.

94. This may appear similar to Heidegger's move whereby the animal's being "poor in the world" leads to a separation between man and animal, giving rise to a politics of the Dasein. See Martin Heidegger, *The Fundamental Concepts of Metaphysics: World, Finitude, Solitude*, trans. William McNeill and Nicholas Walker (Bloomington: Indiana University Press, 1995). The difference with Heidegger, however, is that what is called here "poor thingliness" not only will not lead to a separation between man and animal but will also question the basis on which such a separation is effected as well as the politics toward which it points.

95. Cosmopolitanism and animality were intertwined already before Plutarch. On the one hand, according to the tradition, the first person who used the expression "citizen of the world" was Diogenes, a cynic—and cynicism's etymology is from κύων, meaning dog. Diogenes Laertius narrates the following story about Diogenes the cynic: "Asked where he came from, he said, 'I am a citizen of the world' [κοσμοπολίτης]" (Diogenes Laertius, *Lives of Eminent Philosophers*, "Diogenes," trans. R. D. Hicks [Cambridge, Mass.: Harvard University Press, 1958], 6.63). This is generally regarded as the earliest surviving use of the term "cosmopolitan." For the cynic sources of cosmopolitanism, see John L. Moles's articles "The Cynics and Politics," in *Justice and Generosity: Studies in Hellenic Social and Political Philosophy*, ed. André Laks and Malcolm Schofield (Cambridge: Cambridge University Press, 1995), 129–58; and "Cynic Cosmopolitanism," in *The Cynics: The Cynic Movement in Antiquity and Its Legacy*, ed. R. Bracht Branham and Marie-Odile Goulet-Cazé (Berkeley: University of California Press, 1996), 105–20. Diogenes Laertius also reports that Zeno the Stoic, whose *Republic* is purported to be the first cosmopolitan treatise, was instructed in philosophy by the cynic Crates—thus giving rise to the joke that he wrote the *Republic* on a dog's tail. "For a certain space, he [Zeno] was instructed by Crates, and when at this time he had written his *Republic*, some said in jest that he had written it on Cynosura, i.e. on the dog's tail" (Diogenes Laertius, *Lives of Eminent Philosophers*, "Zeno," 7.4). It should be noted that Kant was attuned to this tradition. For the Stoic sources of Kant's cosmopolitanism, see Martha Nussbaum, "Kant and Cosmopolitanism," in *Perpetual Peace: Essays on Kant's Cosmopolitan Ideal*, ed. James Bohman and Matthias Lutz-Bachmann (Cambridge, Mass.: MIT Press, 1997), 25–57. Nussbaum's article is informative, despite an overly optimistic belief in the power of reason and liberal democracy, which betrays more the rhetoric of an apologist than of an exegete.

96. Plutarch, "On the Fortune or the Virtue of Alexander the Great," in *Moralia*, vol. 4, trans. Frank Cole Babbitt (Cambridge, Mass.: Harvard University Press, 1957), 4:329a–d.

97. A cursory look at Liddell-Scott's Greek lexicon would show the extensive interlacing between the notion of law and feeding at a place. For instance, the noun νομάς, without even the shift of the accent, indicates, among other, pasturage and the legal notion of *possessio*.

Gilles Deleuze has been attuned to the complex relation between the two nouns derived from the common verb νέμω. However, Deleuze is still intent on sharply distinguishing them, arguing that law (νόμος) signifies something static whereas pasture (νομός) is dynamic. Hence, for Deleuze, it is only from the latter that "nomad" is derived. See Gilles Deleuze, *Difference and Repetition*, trans. Paul Patton (London: Continuum, 2001), 36–37, as well as 309 n. 6. Paradoxically, although Deleuze draws such a sharp boundary in order to privilege the meaning that refers to boundary crossing and deterritorialization, the sharp distinction in itself is nothing but an instance of the law, a symptom of territorialization.

The most interesting discussion of the relation between law (νόμος) and pasture (νομός) can be found in Carl Schmitt's "Nomos—Nahme—Name," in *The Nomos of the Earth in the International Law of the* Jus Publicum Europaeum, trans. G. L. Ulmen (New York: Telos Press, 2003), 336–50. Schmitt insists on the strong relation between the two meanings, arguing even that "the source of every distributive justice" is the meaning of *nomos* as pasture (345).

98. The classical elaboration of this distinction, which is at the core of the theologico-political constitution of sovereignty, is Ernst Kantorowicz's *The King's Two Bodies: A Study in Mediaeval Political Theology* (1957; Princeton: Princeton University Press, 1970).

99. This discussion of the "two Godwins" is partly in agreement but also partly in disagreement with Philip Hobsbaum's "Unreliable Narrators: Poor Things and Its Paradigms," *Glasgow Review* 3 (1995): 37–46. Hobsbaum asserts that *Poor Things* can be read as a different story or narrative, depending on whether Godwin is taken to be (A) an ingenious scientist or (B) the educator of Bella: "In *Poor Things* B, Godwin Baxter is metaphorically a God-figure, who takes over a runaway wife and remakes her personality.... In *Poor Things* A, Godwin Baxter is literally a God, who performs the miraculous operation of resurrecting a drowned body by implanting a foetal brain.... The novel is either (A) about a woman remade by a doctor of genius or (B) about a woman rescued by a doctor of considerable talent.... [N]o preference for the one narrator over the other can be established. This circumstance opens the door to a sub-genre of novel whose 'centre' is not implied by any evidence suggested in the text. Notwithstanding its antecedents, we are looking at a book which may well anticipate an unexpected phase in the convoluted history of prose fiction" (45–46). When Hobsbaum claims that a de-centered narrative is primarily about the novel's generic development, he reaches a much weaker conclusion than the evidence he has adduced would allow. If the center is given with refer-

ence solely to the institution called "the novel," then already the political has been denied. And it has been denied by ascribing it as exterior to the novel. However, such a clear-cut distinction is impossible, since "Gray's work addresses the illusory distinction between public and private" (George Donaldson and Alison Lee, "Is Eating People Really Wrong? Dining with Alasdair Gray," *Review of Contemporary Fiction* 15, no. 2 [1995], copied from ProQuest, document ID: 4592193, n.p.). Moreover, Hobsbaum concedes as much when he asserts that "in *Poor Things* B, Baxter is so potent a figure as to create a mythology which develops into the optimistic socialism displayed in 'A Letter to Posterity.' It is equally clear that in *Poor Things* A, he is that mythology itself" (46). Precisely, although this is not merely a technique that places and displaces narrative points of view, but also the construal of the political implications of a person who both constitutes and embodies what he constitutes. To question this double constitution is to displace sovereignty no less than to displace narrative centers. Through the figure of Godwin, Gray propagates a political technique, the technique of displacing power structures. Conversely, the limited claim that Gray's book both creates a new "sub-genre" as well as "is" that genre "itself," would merely turn Gray into a Godwin: either an ingenious creator or a political missionary—but never the one who puts that distinction into trial.

100. The formulation "transience" or "passing away" is borrowed from Walter Benjamin's "Theological-Political Fragment": "The rhythm of this eternally transient worldly existence, transient in its totality, in its spatial but also in its temporal totality, the rhythm of messianic nature, is happiness. For nature is messianic by reason of its eternal and total passing away. To strive for such a passing away—even the passing of those stages of man that are nature—is the task of world politics, whose method must be called nihilism" (*SW* 3:306; *GS* 2.1:204). It should be remembered, of course, that Benjamin counterposed to the transience of messianic happiness the weak messianic power of unhappiness in Thesis II of "On the Concept of History." For a reading of Thesis II, see Werner Hamacher, "Now: Walter Benjamin and Historical Time," in *Walter Benjamin and History*, ed. Andrew Benjamin, 38–68. For a nuanced reading of "transience" in Benjamin see Beatrice Hanssen, *Walter Benjamin's Other History: Of Stones, Animals, Human Beings, and Angels* (Berkeley: University of California Press, 1998).

101. Gray, *Poor Things*, 222–23.

102. Ibid., 185, and cf. 168.

103. This is not to say that Bella is "bare life," in Giorgio Agamben's sense. "Bare life" implies that the "poor thing" is excluded from the political. On the contrary, the argument here is that the "poor thing" can never be conceived in a way that would exclude the political, even if the grounds of exclusion *seem to*, or are *purported to* not rest with the "poor thing." For Agamben's extrapolation of "bare life," see *Homo Sacer: Sovereign Power and Bare Life*, trans. Daniel Heller-Roazen (Stanford: Stanford University Press, 1998), passim. See Dimitris Vardoulakis, "The Ends of Stasis: Spinoza, Reader of Agamben," *Culture, Theory and Critique* 51.2 (2010).

104. Gray, *Poor Things*, 142.

105. The first intimation of this corporeal memory comes immediately after Bella announces to Dr. Hooker and Mr. Astley she is a woman of the world (ibid., 142). Bella says that she has visited a lot of places and never seen real human unhappiness. Upon which Dr. Hooker describes "the innate depravity of the unredeemed human animal" and the state of poverty and misery in the world (142). Bella reports: "I left the table at once. I needed quietness to think of all the new strange things I had heard. Maybe my cracked knob [she had an injury on the head which was said to be the cause of her amnesia] is to blame but I feel less happy since Dr. H. explained there is nothing wrong which the Anglo-Saxons are not curing with fire and sword. Before now I thought everyone I met was part of the same friendly family, even when a hurt one acted like our snappish bitch. Why did you not teach me politics, God?" (143).

106. Ibid., 173–74; emphasis added.

107. Ibid., 163.

108. Astley's "bitter wisdom" exemplifies a cynical disposition directed merely toward the laws and customs that constitute the polity and that are in accord with the forms of subjection perpetuated by those laws.

109. Gray, *Poor Things*, 18–19.

110. Ibid., 22–23.

111. Ibid., 243.

112. Ibid., 38.

113. Ibid., 275.

114. Ibid., 308.

115. Irony here should be understood not merely as a trope, but as the figuration that expresses the pretenses of systematicity, the force that undercuts a complete system—that is, the notion of irony that was described in the last section of Chapter 1 as Jean Paul's ironic appropriation of Fichte. The irony in Bella's activism is also noted by John C. Hawley in "Bell, Book, and Candle: *Poor Things* and the Exorcism of Victorian Sentiment," *Review of Contemporary Fiction* 15, no. 2 (1995), copied from ProQuest, document ID: 6839096, n.p. And, this irony pervades all of Gray's work, given that the epigraph is repeated throughout his oeuvre. Just a few clarifications on how and where the epigraph is used—as far as it has been possible to determine, given a fairly complex publication history: First, it appears for the first time in *Unlikely Stories, Mostly* (Edinburgh: Canongate, 1983). According to Phil Moores: "The boards are dark blue.... The 'Work as if you were living in the early days of a better nation' motto runs along the top; 'SCOTLAND 1983' runs along the bottom" (Phil Moores, "An Alasdair Gray Bibliography," in *Alasdair Gray: Critical Appraisals and a Bibliography*, ed. Phil Moores (Boston Spa and London: The British Library, 2002), 191. However, in the 1984 paperback Penguin edition, the epigraph is rendered as "WORK AS IF YOU WERE IN THE EARLY DAYS OF A BETTER NATION" in capitals and as part of an illustration depicting a mermaid with an extended arm and finger pointing to the right. The illustration is on the first page inside the book. Above the arm of the mermaid are the words "Scotland 1984" and below "Dennis Lee." Second, in

the acknowledgments page of the first British edition of *Poor Things* is stated: "The epigraph on the covers is from a poem by Denis Leigh." However, this sentence was deleted in subsequent editions of *Poor Things*, which also do not have the epigraph on the cover. Third, with the exception of *Unlikely Story, Mostly*, the epigraph appears only in the British hardback first editions, and always on the boards, i.e., behind the covering jacket. There are exceptions, however; e.g., the epigraph does not appear in *A History Maker* (Edinburgh: Canongate, 1994). Fourth, the epigraph appears also in Gray's nonfiction, such as the first British edition of *The Book of Prefaces* (2000), as well as in books that Gray has illustrated, such as the above-mentioned *Alasdair Gray* edited by Moores and published by the British Library. Fifth, as far as it has been possible to verify, only the German translations of Gray's books also carry this epigraph. This is no doubt due to the friendship between Gray and his German translator Berndt Rullkötter and Gray's assistance in the design of the German editions. See, e.g., the translation of *Poor Things* into German, *Arme Dinge* (Hamburg: Roger & Bernhard, 1996), which reproduces the epigraph on the front board behind the jacket in capitals as "Arbeite als lebtest du in den frühen Tagen einer besseren Nation." Finally, Johanna Tiitinen's "Work as if You Live in the Early Days of a Better Nation": History and Politics in the Works of Alasdair Gray (Helsinki: University of Helsinki Press, 2004) should be mentioned, although it has been impossible to obtain a copy in Australia.

116. Alasdair Gray, *Why Scots Should Rule Scotland* (Edinburgh: Canongate, 1992; rev. ed. 1997). The pamphlet was timed to coincide with the parliamentary elections in 1992 and the revised edition with the 1997 elections.

117. Gray's regular references are not to Kant, but to the Scottish Enlightenment. Kant was acquainted with Scottish philosophy, such as Adam Smith's *The Wealth of Nations*, through the translation of Christian Garve in 1794. Although this cannot be taken up in detail here, the so-called conjectural history of the Scottish Enlightenment prefigures Kant's notion of universal history in his paper on cosmopolitanism. (The term "conjectural history" was invented by Dugald Stewart with reference to the work on the theory of history undertaken by Hume, Smith, and other Scottish philosophers. See Stewart, "Theoretical or Conjectural History," in *The Scottish Enlightenment: An Anthology*, ed. Alexander Broadie [Edinburgh: Canongate, 1997], 670–74.) For recent work on human rights from a philosophical perspective, see *And Justice for All? The Claims of Human Rights*, edited by Ian Balfour and Eduardo Cadava, a special issue of *The South Atlantic Quarterly* 103, no. 2/3 (2004).

118. The argument that cosmopolitanism must respond to local particularity and difference has been developed by many in recent years. See, e.g., Kwame Anthony Appiah, *The Ethics of Identity* (Princeton: Princeton University Press, 2005), chap. 6.

119. Gray, *Poor Things*, 186.

120. The notion of displacement and automaticity are found throughout George Didi-Huberman's *Invention of Hysteria: Charcot and the Photographic Iconography*

Notes

of the Salpêtrière, trans. Alisa Hartz (Cambridge, Mass.: MIT Press, 2003). For instance, the notion of transference is invented to describe a displaced somatic symptom: "Charcot admitted that the application of metals did not cure the symptom, but displaced it. . . . He baptized this mystery 'transference'" (214). The theoretical understanding of hypnosis as a model for hysteria is based on the automatism of the body; e.g., "For the hysterical body in the asylum, it was the result of yielding to transference, consenting to the experiment. An automaton—now inert, now thrashing about" (181).

121. Gray, *Poor Things*, 189.

122. See John Llewelyn's *The HypoCritical Imagination: Between Kant and Levinas* (London: Routledge, 2000), which puts forward a similar extrapolation of the hypocritical, although Llewelyn derives it with different means—with the reading of different texts.

123. I would like to thank Catherine Malabou for suggesting to me the expression "automatic cosmopolitan."

CHAPTER 5: SELF-INSCRIPTIONS

1. Walter Benjamin mentions the "lost gestus" once in "Franz Kafka: On the Tenth Anniversary of His Death" (Walter Benjamin, *Selected Writings*, 4 vols., ed. Michael W. Jennings [Cambridge, Mass.: Harvard University Press, 1997–2003], abbreviated as *SW*, 2:814; Walter Benjamin, *Gesammelte Schriften*, ed. Rolf Tiedemann and Hermann Schweppenhäuser [Frankfurt am Main: Suhrkamp, 1991], abbreviated as *GS*, 2.2:436), without distinguishing it explicitly from other gestures. The argument here is not only that such a distinction is implicit, it is also that such a distinction is crucial for Benjamin.

2. Theatricality plays a central role in Benjamin's thought. Thus, his theory of allegory in the habilitation of the mid-1920s relies on the mourning play or *Trauerspiel*. And, in his later writings, the idea of the dialectics at a standstill arose in the first draft of Benjamin's essay on Brecht. (See Walter Benjamin, "Was ist das epische Theater? Eine Studie zu Brecht," *GS* 2.2:519–31. In this version of the essay from early 1931 the expression "die Dialektik im Stillstand" [530] was used for the first time.) More emphatically, to the extent that theatricality and the figure of the doppelgänger are interlaced, then theatricality will pertain not only to explicit discussions about theater, but to Benjamin's conception of a subject nonreducible to presence. That is, to the subject as it figures in Benjamin's critical and political project. Obviously, this raises the stakes very high and calls for demonstrating that the doppelgänger, despite its not being specifically mentioned, is still a central figure in Benjamin's work—a figure that spans his theory of language and criticism, no less than the messianic politics of "On the Concept of History." Benjamin's essay on Kafka will be the focus of this chapter. "Franz Kafka: On the Tenth Anniversary of His Death" is a sustained meditation on theatricality. It was written in the mid-1930s, when Benjamin sought to combine his earlier theories of language,

law, and criticism with his work on historiography and the political. The urgency of this project was no doubt due to the "aestheticization of politics" under way in Germany and elsewhere, but it also gave rise to an understanding of modernity and time. Thus, theatricality offers a privileged entry point to Benjamin's thought, although, for obvious restrictions of space, this chapter will not refer to the entirety of Benjamin's works but will selectively focus on those aspects that have a bearing on his Kafka essay.

3. Walter Benjamin, "On the Concept of History," *SW* 4:389; *GS* 1.2:693.

4. Rebecca Comay, "Benjamin's Endgame," in *Walter Benjamin's Philosophy: Destruction and Experience*, ed. Andrew Benjamin and Peter Osborne (Manchester: Clinamen, 2000), 248.

5. Ibid.

6. Walter Benjamin, *The Arcades Project*, trans. Howard Eiland and Kevin McLaughlin (Cambridge, Mass.: Belknap, 1999).

7. See Catherine Malabou, *The Future of Hegel: Plasticity, Temporality and Dialectic*, trans. Lisabeth During (London: Routledge, 2004), 160–64.

8. Although there is no direct evidence, there is enough circumstantial evidence that makes Poe's article almost certainly Benjamin's source. (1) As Tiedemann argues, Poe's article was translated by Baudelaire in *Nouvelles histories extraordinaires*, which Benjamin had been using (Rolf Tiedemann, "Historische Materialismus oder politischer Messianismus? Politische Gehalte in der Geschichtsphilosophie Walter Benjamins," in *Materialien zu Benjamins Thesen "Über den Begriff der Geschichte": Beiträge und Interpretationen*, ed. Peter Bulthaup [Frankfurt am Main: Suhrkamp, 1975], 118). (2) There is internal evidence, since all the details of Benjamin's description of the Turk are in Poe's article. Thus, Poe mentions the hypothesis about the dwarf, the mirrors, and the strings—although, it should be noted, that Benjamin's summary is not faithful to Poe's conclusions. (3) Benjamin does not seem to be aware of the two articles that definitively showed how the Turk worked. The first was published anonymously in the *Maganize Pittoresque* in 1834 and has been attributed to Jacques-François Mouret, who had been one of the chess players hidden inside the Turk. The second was published twenty-three years later by Silas Weir Mitchell, the son of the last owner of the Turk and who witnessed how it worked. Both are reprinted in Gerlas M. Levitt, *The Turk, Chess Automaton* (Jefferson, N.C.: McFarland, 2000), 221–22 and 236–40, respectively. From all this, it is possible to infer that Benjamin almost certainly read the story in Poe's version. Cf. Joshua Robert Gold, "The Dwarf in the Machine: A Theological Figure and Its Sources," *MLN* 121, no. 5 (2006): 1224.

9. Johann Nepomuk Maelzel toured the Turk widely around the world and made the automaton famous. However, the automaton was in fact invented by Wolfgang von Kempelen at the behest of Empress Maria Teresa. Its first performance was at the Viennese court in spring 1770. Maelzel managed to raise the Turk's reputation around the globe because he was a gifted performer who sought to highlight the mystery around the automaton. Maelzel's theatrical presentation of the Turk was

so crucial that, as Tom Standage observes, "[W]ithout Maelzel's showmanship [after Maelzel's death] . . . the Turk had become a pitiful shadow of its former self" (Tom Standage, *The Turk: The Life and Times of the Famous Eighteenth-Century Chess-Playing Machine* [New York: Berkley Books, 2003], 191).

10. Edgar Allan Poe, "Maelzel's Chess-Player," in *The Works of the Late Edgar Allan Poe*, ed. Rufus Wilmot Griswold (New York: Redfield, 1856), 4:349. Poe's early journalistic article was first published in the *Southern Literary Messenger* in 1836.

11. Poe, "Maelzel's Chess-Player," 351.

12. Ibid., 352.

13. Ibid., 353.

14. Ibid., 354.

15. Ibid., 356–60.

16. Poe's article has attracted a lot of attention in the secondary literature on the American author. One of the areas of interest is that the image of man and machine working together in Poe's article offers a challenge to subjective autonomy, precisely because the idea of a "pure machine" is rejected. Thus, as James Berkley puts it, Poe's "vision of subjectivity hence implied a quite different relationship between organism and environment than had the subject of liberal humanism" (James Berkley, "Post-human Mimesis and the Debunked Machine: Reading Environmental Appropriation in Poe's 'Maelzel's Chess-Player' and 'The Man That Was Used Up,'" *Comparative Literature Studies* 41, no. 3 [2004]: 357). Moreover, it was a relationship that offers "the possibility of transcending the conventional limits of the individualized human subject" (358). The relationship mentioned by Berkley is precisely the type of relationality made possible by the doppelgänger, as it has been argued throughout this book.

17. Poe, "Maelzel's Chess-Player," 365.

18. The implication is, of course, that such a performative will undo the mimetic or representational structure. From this perspective, The notion of theatricality elaborated in this chapter has a "family resemblance" to Judith Butler's treatment of the performative. See, e.g., Judith Butler, *Gender Trouble: Feminism and the Subversion of Identity* (1990; London: Routledge, 2006).

19. Poe, "Maelzel's Chess-Player," 361.

20. See the section titled "The Black and the White Nothing: *Clavis Fichtiana*" in Chapter 1.

21. Walter Benjamin, "Kafka," *SW* 2:808; *GS* 2.2:427–8.

22. Benjamin's emphasis on the *Gestus* is linked to his preoccupation with the work of Bertolt Brecht. This is not to suggest that Benjamin's discussion of Kafka's gesture is shaped solely by Brecht. Meanwhile, Rainer Nägele is certainly correct in saying that Benjamin's "reading of Kafka shaped his perception of Brecht's work" (Rainer Nägele, *Theatre, Theory, Speculation: Walter Benjamin and the Scenes of Modernity* [Baltimore: Johns Hopkins University Press, 1991], 152). For a detailed presentation of the development of Benjamin's concept of the *Gestus* through his

contact with Brecht, see Brigid Doherty, "Test and *Gestus* in Brecht and Benjamin," *MLN* 115, no. 3 (2000): 442–81. Of interest here is also Patricia Anne Simpson, "In Citing Violence: Gestus in Benjamin, Brecht and Kafka," in *Jewish Writers, German Literature: The Uneasy Examples of Nelly Sachs and Walter Benjamin.* ed. Timothy Bahti and Marilyn Sibley Fries (Ann Arbor: University of Michigan Press, 1995), 175–203.

23. The function of failure is certainly related to Benjamin's notion of modernity, as is argued by Peter Osborne in "Small-Scale Victories, Large-Scale Defeats," in *Walter Benjamin's Philosophy*, ed. Benjamin and Osborne, 59–109. As Osborne argues, it is "the strategic significance of the attempt to translate the experience of modernity into the language of tradition—and its failure—that makes Kafka's work so central to Benjamin's thought" (71). The present argument will proceed from a different, yet not unrelated, route. The figure of Kafka—this "figure of failure" as Benjamin puts it in the letter to Scholem from 12 June 1938—also introduces arguments about the subject of modernity. The discussion here will concentrate primarily on those arguments.

24. For the "graven image" in Benjamin's thought, and especially in the debates with Theodor Adorno, see Rebecca Comay's significant article "Materialist Mutations of the *Bilderverbot*," in *Walter Benjamin and Art,* ed. Andrew Benjamin (London: Continuum, 2005), 32–59.

25. The first part of this latter is more or less identical to the review that Benjamin wrote of Max Brod's biography, "Review of Brod's *Franz Kafka*," SW 3:317–19; GS 3:526–29.

26. The stress here is on Brod's *justification* for proceeding with the publication of Kafka's writings. Benjamin never questioned that Kafka's instructions had to be disregarded and that his writings had to be published, so much so, that Benjamin publicly defended Brod's decision to publish Kafka's manuscripts (see "Kavaliersmoral," GS 4.1:466–68).

27. *The Correspondence of Walter Benjamin and Gershom Scholem*, ed. Gershom Scholem, trans. Gary Smith and André Lefevere (Cambridge, Mass.: Harvard University Press, 1992), 221; *Gesammelte Briefe*, ed. Christoph Gödde and Henri Lonitz (Frankfurt am Main: Suhrkamp, 1995–2000), 6:107.

28. Max Brod, *Franz Kafka: A Biography*, trans. G. Humphreys Roberts and Richard Winston (New York: Schocken, 1960), 49.

29. Kafka as the Job of Prague was the theme of one of the earliest and most influential theological interpretations of Kafka, Margarete Susman's "Das Hiob-Probleme bei Kafka" (1929), reprinted as "Früheste Dichtung Franz Kafkas," in *Gestalten und Kreise* (Stuttgart: Diana, 1954), 348–66. Max Brod also takes up this analogy in chapter 6 of his biography of Kafka, where he argues, for instance, that "Kafka disputes with God as Job once did."

30. Brod, *Franz Kafka*, 134.

31. The term "the Indestructible" here refers to God as conceived in Brod's formulation above. It should not be confused with "The Indestructible" in Maurice

Blanchot's *The Infinite Conversation*, trans. Susan Hanson (Minneapolis: University of Minnesota Press, 1997), 123–35 (the fifth chapter of the second part of *The Infinite Conversation*), which raises a completely different problematic. Although this difference cannot be pursued here, see Christopher Fynsk's remarkable reading of this chapter of *The Infinite Conversation* in his "Blanchot's 'The Indestructible,'" in *After Blanchot: Literature, Criticism, Philosophy*, ed. Leslie Hill, Brian Nelson, and Dimitris Vardoulakis (Newark: University of Delaware Press, 2005), 100–122.

32. Maurice Blanchot, "Reading Kafka," in *The Work of Fire*, trans. Charlotte Mandell (Stanford: Stanford University Press, 1995), 7, 9, 10.

33. As Benjamin puts it in the letter to Scholem, it is not because Kafka did not know his greatness that he instructed the destruction of his manuscripts. Rather, Kafka did not want to burden of posterity (*Correspondence of Benjamin and Scholem*, 221; *Gesammelte Briefe*, 6:107). This denial of posterity, as a denial of the future and hence of the utopian, does not stand in contradiction to Benjamin's insistence that Kafka's will observes the Mosaic Law. Rather, it signifies the failure of self-reflection that requires an "all the time," as it was argued in the preceding section. This failure is effected by the doppelgänger.

34. "Eigentlich hätte er ja mit diesen überschüssigen Geldern die Schuld des Vaters gegenüber dem Chef weiter abgetragen haben können" (Franz Kafka, *Die Verwandlung*, in *Drucke zu Lebzeiten*, in *Schriften Tagebücher: Kritische Ausgabe*, ed. Jürgen Born, Gerhard Neumann, Malcolm Pasley, and Jost Schillemeit (Frankfurt am Main: Fischer, 2002), 154. The other references to the *Metamorphosis* are, respectively, to pages 117, 125, and 128–29. All references to Kafka are to the *Kritische Ausgabe*.

35. Benjamin, "Kafka," *SW* 2:804; *GS* 2.2:422–23.

36. Benjamin, "Kafka," *SW* 2:797; *GS* 2.2:412.

37. Benjamin, "Critique of Violence," *SW* 1:249; *GS* 2.1:198–99.

38. Benjamin, "Kafka," *SW* 2:805; *GS* 2.2:424.

39. Ibid.

40. Benjamin, "Critique of Violence," *SW* 1:250; *GS* 2.1:199. Cf. Judith Butler's discussion on "mere life" in "Critique, Coercion, and Sacred Life in Benjamin's 'Critique of Violence,'" in *Political Theologies: Public Religions in a Post-Secular World*, ed. Hent de Vries and Lawrence E. Sullivan (New York: Fordham University Press, 2006), 201–19. Butler's argument can be read as a critique of Agamben's notion of "bare life." See also Judith Butler and Gayatri Chakravorty Spivak, *Who Signs the Nation-State? Language, Politics, Belonging* (London: Seagull Books, 2007), 35–43.

41. Benjamin, "Kafka," *SW* 2:805–6; *GS* 2.2:424.

42. Ibid., *SW* 2:806; *GS* 2.2:424–25.

43. Benjamin, [Notes on Kafka], *GS* 2.3:1262.

44. Benjamin, "Kafka," *SW* 2:804, 814; *GS* 2.2:422.

45. Ibid., *SW* 2:801; *GS* 2.2:418.

46. Ibid., *SW* 2:808; *GS* 2.2:428.

47. Ibid., *SW* 2:814; *GS* 2.2:435.

48. Ibid., *SW* 2:800; *GS* 2.2:417. Benjamin's anachronistic designation assigns to the last chapter of *America* a singular temporality. The temporality of a totally anonymous person, or a *Verschollener*, someone "lost" or "missing." Benjamin could not have known in 1934 that Brod had changed the original title *Der Verschollene* of Kafka's first novel to *Amerika*. Yet Benjamin's description of the entirely characterless actors of the nature theater may make sense of the title.

49. As it was shown in the third section of Chapter 1, "The Black Nothing and the White Nothing: *Clavis Fichtiana*," the Aristotelian definition of *housia* from *Categories* 2a.12–14 asserts that substance is that from which nothing that pertains to it can be excluded from it. It was also noted there that this definition of substance has essentially remained constant and unchallenged throughout the history of Western metaphysics.

50. Benjamin, "Kafka," *SW* 2:801; *GS* 2.2:417–18.

51. In the context of the essay, it is clear that Benjamin is referring here to the gestures that characterize the nature theater. Using the word *Welttheater* may be a simple mistake on Benjamin's part. Or it may be an indication of an error: the error of not distinguishing in the essay clearly enough between world theater and nature theater—which, as the note from 1935 mentioned above indicates, Benjamin intended to remedy in his planned book on Kafka. Or, it may be neither a mistake nor an error, but an implicit assertion that there is no steadfast separation between the world and the nature theaters. Indeed, as it will be argued, what matters for Benjamin is not so much the fact that they can be distinguished as their alliance in metaphysics and its implications for the acting subject.

52. Benjamin, "Kafka," *SW* 2:802; *GS* 2.2:419.

53. Ibid., *SW* 2:801; *GS* 2.2:419.

54. Ibid., *SW* 2:801; *GS* 2.2:419.

55. Benjamin, "Fate and Character," *SW* 1:202; *GS* 2.1:173.

56. Ibid., *SW* 1:201; *GS* 2.1:171.

57. Ibid., *SW* 1:202; *GS* 2.1:173.

58. Ibid.

59. Ibid., *SW* 1:204; *GS* 2.1:175.

60. Ibid.

61. Benjamin, "Kafka," *SW* 2:797; *GS* 2.2:412.

62. Benjamin, "Fate and Character," *SW* 1:201; *GS* 2.1:171, and "Critique of Violence," *SW* 1:248–50; *GS* 2.1:197–200.

63. Benjamin, "Fate and Character," *SW* 1:205; *GS* 2.1:177–78.

64. Ibid., *SW* 1:204–5; *GS* 2.1:178.

65. Significantly, as late as 4 February 1939, Benjamin wrote to Scholem that "more and more, the essential feature in Kafka seems to me to be humor" (*Correspondence of Benjamin and Scholem*, 243; *Gesammelte Briefe*, 6:220). A comparison with Deleuze and Guattari's emphasis on "Kafka's laughter" would have been interesting to pursue at this point. See Gilles Deleuze and Félix Guattari, *Kafka: To-*

wards a Minor Literature, trans. Dana Polan (Minneapolis: University of Minnesota Press, 1986), 41–42. There is a decisive political aspect for Benjamin as well as for Deleuze and Guattari, in that with "laughter" there is an overcoming of fate. However, the rhizomatic description of Kafka's world by Deleuze and Guattari seems very close to the pure differentiation that will be shown to characterize Benjamin's discussion of the nature theater. In other words, it appears that the "middle world" of Kafka that Benjamin insists on, as it will be shown in the next section, is missing from Deleuze and Guattari. The comparison between the two positions cannot be taken up here in any detail without detracting from the main concerns of the chapter. See Stephanie Polsky's interesting article on Kafka, Benjamin, Deleuze and Guattari, although it does not tackle the problematic outlined above. Stephanie Polsky, "Down the K. Hole: Walter Benjamin's Destructive Land-Surveying of History," in *Walter Benjamin and History*, ed. Andrew Benjamin (London: Continuum, 2005), 69–87.

66. Benjamin, "Fate and Character," *SW* 1:202; *GS* 2.1:173.

67. Ibid., *SW* 1:203; *GS* 2.1:174–75.

68. For a revealing discussion of how the graven image and the expressionless are connected to sublimity, see Winfried Menninghaus, "Walter Benjamin's Variations of Imagelessness," in *Jewish Writers, German Literature*, ed. Bahti and Fries, 155–73.

69. In one of his notes from the visit to Brecht at Svendborg in the summer of 1934 (that is, at the time that Benjamin was writing his Kafka essay), Benjamin recorded that after a game of chess Brecht expressed the wish to invent a new game: "A game in which the positions do not always remain constant, in which the functions of the pieces change after they have stood in the same place for a certain length of time" (*SW* 2:785; *GS* 6:526). If this means that the new game will be the formation of the rules in the progress of the game itself, it will then disclose the sameness underlying both indifference and pure differentiation—in which case, Brecht's position as a materialist will spontaneously combust to that of a theologian.

70. Benjamin, "Kafka," *SW* 2:799; *GS* 2.2:416. Harry Zohn in *Selected Writings* translates *Mittelwelt* as "intermediate world." Maybe the best translation would have been "me(ri)dian world" in order to capture the placing of this world between, as well as higher then, myth and redemption. The term "middle world" is preferred here because it is, on the one hand, as close as possible to *Mittelwelt* and, on the other, because the word "me(ri)dian" is cumbersome.

71. Benjamin, "Kafka," *SW* 2:798; *GS* 2.2:414.

72. Ibid.

73. Ibid., *SW* 2:799; *GS* 2.2:415.

74. Ibid., *SW* 2:800; *GS* 2.2:416.

75. Ibid., *SW* 2:810; *GS* 2.2:430.

76. Ibid., *SW* 2:814; *GS* 2.2:435.

77. Ibid., *SW* 2:807; *GS* 2.2:426–27. See also *SW* 2:812; *GS* 2.2:433, where Benjamin stresses that Kafka's world pertain to "our space" and to "our time."

78. Ibid., *SW* 2:800; *GS* 2.2:420–21.

79. Rodolphe Gasché, "Tearing at the Texture," in *Of Minimal Things: Studies on the Notion of Relation* (Stanford: Stanford University Press, 1999), 64.

80. Benjamin, "Notizen zu einer Arbeit über die Lüge II," *GS* 6:62.

81. Kafka, cited in Benjamin, "Kafka," *SW* 2:799; *GS* 2.2:415.

82. Gasché, "Kafka's Law: In the Field of Forces Between Judaism and Hellenism," *MLN* 117, no. 5 (2002): 992.

83. Ibid., 991.

84. Kafka, cited in Benjamin, "Kafka," *SW* 2:799; *GS* 2.2:415, emphasis added. This gesture by Ulysses is one that seeks to undo the power of myth, as Adorno and Horkheimer were well aware in the first chapter of the *Dialectic of Enlightenment*. Stathis Gourgouris, in his incisive "The Gesture of the Sirens," in *Does Literature Think? Literature as Theory for an Antimythical Era* (Stanford: Stanford University Press, 2003),161–97, discusses the Kafka text alongside the Benjamin and the Adorno and Horkheimer interpretations.

85. Benjamin, "Kafka," *SW* 2:809; *GS* 2.2:428.

86. It will be recalled that Benjamin associated this staging with the sublimity of the tragic hero. There is, indeed, a formulation of the sublime that presents such a staging. This is Longinus' formulation, according to which one is both on the stage (*On the Sublime*, §14.2) and also outside the stage (§35.2). This double staging, no less than Longinus' extrapolation of allegory which was discussed earlier in Chapter 2, indicates an affinity with Benjamin. See also supra, n. 67.

87. Benjamin, "Kafka," *SW* 2:809; *GS* 2.2:430.

88. Kurt J. Fickert, *Kafka's Doubles* (Berne: Peter Lang, 1979), 81, 82.

89. Ibid.,11.

90. Ibid., 34.

91. Benjamin, "Kafka," *SW* 2:815; *GS* 2.2:437.

92. Ibid., *SW* 2:814; *GS* 2.2:436.

93. Benjamin, [Notes on Kafka], *GS* 2.3:1246.

94. Benjamin, "Kafka," *SW* 2:802–3; *GS* 2.2:420. See the excellent discussion on unfolding in Josh Cohen, "Unfolding: Reading after Romanticism," in *Walter Benjamin and Romanticism*, ed. Beatrice Hanssen and Andrew Benjamin (New York: Continuum, 2002), 98–108.

95. Benjamin, "Kafka," *SW* 2:814; *GS* 2.2:435.

96. Benjamin, [Notes on Kafka], *GS* 2.3:1203–4.

97. It would be interesting here to look at the debate between Brod and Kafka about apperception. In February 1906 Brod published two articles in which he argued that beauty should be equated with the emergence of the new, and that the new then affords a novel conception of subjectivity, a new apperception. However, replied Kafka, if the subject is related to subjectivity in the way that perceptions are apperceived, and if perceptions are always changing, then apperception is impossible (*eine Apperception ist hier überhaupt unmöglich*). Kafka illustrates this with the example of an individual (*ein Mensch*) who arrives at Prague without a sense of

the place, as if in a strange or foreign city. This debate was first related by Brod in his *Der Prager Kreis* (Frankfurt am Main: Suhrkamp, 1979), 109–12. Kafka's reply is reprinted in the volume of Kafka's *Kritische Ausgabe* titled *Nachgelassene Schriften und Fragmente I*, ed. Malcolm Pasley (Frankfurt am Main: Fischer, 2002), 9–11.

98. The term "original act" is borrowed from Werner Hamacher, "The Gesture in the Name: On Benjamin and Kafka," in *Premises: Essays on Philosophy and Literature from Kant to Celan*, trans. Peter Fenves (Cambridge, Mass.: Harvard University Press, 1996), 336.

99. Benjamin, "Kafka," *SW* 2:813; *GS* 2.2:435, emphasis added.

100. Kafka, *Nachgelassene Schriften und Fragmente*, in *Kritische Ausgabe*, 2:373.

101. Benjamin, "Kafka," *SW* 2:814; *GS* 2.2:436.

102. Otto Rank's study on the doppelgänger, which has already been mentioned in the discussion of the uncanny in Chapter 1, first appeared in *Imago* in 1914 and as a book in 1925; thus Benjamin could have been aware of it. Otto Rank discusses Chamisso's *Peter Schlemihl* in *The Double: A Psychoanalytic Study*, trans. Harry Tucker Jr. (New York: Meridian, 1979), 10.

103. Karl Marx, *The Eighteenth Brumaire of Louis Bonaparte* (New York: International Publishers, 1968), 44.

104. It is interesting to compare here Friedrich Kittler's article "Romanticism—Psychoanalysis—Film: A History of the Double," in *Essays: Literature, Media, Information Systems* (Amsterdam: G + B Arts, 1997), which defines the doppelgänger in terms that bring to mind Benjamin's description of the subject that does not recognize itself in modern technological media.

105. Benjamin, "Kafka," *SW* 2:815; *GS* 2.2:437.

106. Kafka, cited in Benjamin, "Kafka," *SW* 2:815–6; *GS* 2.2:438.

107. Benjamin, [Notes on Kafka], *GS* 2.3:1220. This note was written in May or June 1934. Benjamin partly repeats the same thought to Scholem five years later, in a letter dated 4 February 1939. See *Correspondence of Benjamin and Scholem*, 243; *Gesammelte Briefe*, 6:220: "And concerning his friendship with Brod, I think I am on the track of the truth when I say: Kafka as Laurel felt the onerous obligation to seek out his Hardy—and that was Brod. However that may be, I think the key [*Schlüssel*] to Kafka's work is likely to fall into the hands of the person who *is able to extract the comic aspects from Jewish theology*." This in effect argues that from the perspective of Kafka's writings Brod can be regarded precisely as his doppelgänger. Thus, despite Benjamin's rejection of Brod's theological interpretation, Kafka's lost gesture still requires Brod. Benjamin had concluded an earlier letter to Scholem, dated 12 June 1938, with the observation that Kafka's "friendship with Brod is to me above all else a question mark which he chose to ink in the margin of his life [*das er an den Rand seiner Tage hat mallen wollen*]" (*Correspondence of Benjamin and Scholem*, 226; *Gesammelte Briefe*, 6:114).

108. Sylviane Agacinski, *Time Passing: Modernity and Nostalgia*, trans. Jody Gladding (New York: Columbia University Press, 2003), 20. Benjamin has been one of the most influential figures in this thinking of time in conjunction with the im-

age—as is made evident, for instance, in Agacinski's book. His essays on photography and on the reproducibility of the work of art have been hugely influential in thinking of the image as that which presents the condition of the possibility of an experience of and in time. For one of the most fruitful accounts of the image and temporality—or, more specifically, the instant, what Benjamin calls "now-time"—see David Ferris, "The Shortness of History or, Photography in *Nuce*: Benjamin's Attenuation of the Negative," in *Walter Benjamin and History*, ed. Benjamin, 19–37.

109. Eduardo Cadava, *Words of Light: Theses on the Photography of History* (Princeton: Princeton University Press, 1997), 111.

110. Ibid., 113.

111. Ibid., 115.

112. Ibid., 116. An important article which reads Benjamin's Kafka essay through the Potemkin episode is Henry Sussman's "The Herald: A Reading of Walter Benjamin's Kafka Study," *Diacritics* 7, no. 1 (1977): 42–54.

113. Another story from the *Odyssey* springs to mind here, Ulysses' deception of the cyclops Polyphemus by introducing himself as "No one." The nothing is inscribed in the signature. (Cf. Chapter 4, n. 45.) Philippe Lacoue-Labarthe brilliantly summarizes the difficulty faced at the juncture: "Propriation (identification) is carried out through naming—that designation that is fearful because it can be sacralized. The question is, therefore: how, if one has to ask 'Who?,' to avoid the fall of *who* into the sacralization of the name" (Lacoue-Labarthe, "The Response of Ulysses," in *Who Comes After the Subject?* ed. Eduardo Cadava, Peter Connor, and Jean-Luc Nancy [New York: Routledge, 1991], 205). To put Lacoue-Labarthe's problematic in the vocabulary of this book: the question is, how to refer to the signature (to the "who"), without letting the nothing within it become either purely logical or purely ontological. Because, as shown in Chapter 1, the bifurcation of the logical and the ontological within the nothing, as argued by Jacobi, inevitably leads to religion, whereas Jean Paul's doppelgänger specifically sought to undo such a binary opposition.

114. Both "lying withs" are forms of failure, but failures that give rise to a specific understanding of the critical task. And this task will have to persist in its particularity—here, Benjamin's interpretation of Kafka's failure. But this is not to lapse into a biographical correlation between Benjamin and Kafka. Failure, as already intimated, is a category that pertains to the relation between life and work. Thus, failure is not an unsuccessful endeavor; nor does it denote the psychological feeling of "being a failure" that might result therewith. For failure to become a concept that structures modernity and Benjamin's criticism of Kafka, what has to be avoided is precisely the sort of assertion made by Hans Mayer: that Benjamin "sought to demonstrate through Kafka's failure the necessity of his own failure—and probably its justification" (Mayer, "Walter Benjamin and Franz Kafka: Report on a Constellation," in *On Walter Benjamin: Critical Essays and Recollections*, ed. Gary Smith [Cambridge, Mass: MIT Press, 1988], 195). What has to be resisted is a syncretism of *Kritik* and biography, such as was shown in the previous section to operate in Fickert's reading of the doppelgänger in Kafka.

115. Benjamin, "Notizen zu einer Arbeit über die Lüge II," *GS* 6:64.

116. Cf. Jacques Derrida, "History of the Lie: Prolegomena," trans. Peggy Kamuf, *Graduate Faculty Philosophy Journal* 20, no. 1 (1997): 129–61.

117. It should be noted that lying is a crucial concern of Benjamin's, or at least for Benjamin in the period from his dissertation on Romantic criticism to his habilitation. Moreover, to the extent that lying may also be implicated in categories such as irony or allegory, it could also be argued to be seen in notions of the later Benjamin, such as the citation in the Kraus essay or the dialectics at a standstill. However, such a genealogy of the lie in Benjamin is fraught with difficulties given that Benjamin never explicitly thematized it; moreover, such a genealogy deserves a study on its own. Benjamin did take notes toward "A Work on the Lie" (*Eine Arbeit über die Lüge*) or, as he also called it in his correspondence, "Objective Mendacity" (*Objektive Verlogenheit*). Most of these notes are available as fragments 40 to 44 in *GS* 6. Although the project on the lie remained incomplete, it did inform essays from the same period, such as "Critique of Violence," as it will be shown forthwith.

118. It will not be possible to do justice here to the complexity of a seminal essay such as the "Critique of Violence." For a reading of this essay as well as for its implications for in theory, see Beatrice Hanssen's compelling and far-reaching *Critique of Violence: Between Poststructuralism and Critical Theory* (London: Routledge, 2000). See also Werner Hamacher's important article "Affirmative Strike: Benjamin's 'Critique of Violence,'" trans. Dana Hollander, in *Walter Benjamin's Philosophy*, ed. Benjamin and Osborne, 108–36.

119. Benjamin, "Critique of Violence," *SW* 1:236; *GS* 2.1:179.

120. Michael Mack has argued that "the Kafka essay can be read as *Zur Kritik der Gewalt*'s missing link" (Michael Mack, "Between Kant and Kafka: Benjamin's Notion of the Law," *Neophilologus* 85, no. 2 [2001]: 268) to the extent that it is a critique of liberalism, meanwhile insisting on the influence of the Mosaic law in the "Critique of Violence," which leads him to conclude that at the end of the essay there is a justification for "any form of violence" challenging positive law (269). The argument here is that if there is a connection between the Kafka essay and the "Critique of Violence," that connection needs to be sought in that which challenges—not that which perpetuates—the predominance of violence. And that element is lying.

121. Benjamin, "Critique of Violence," *SW* 1:244–45; *GS* 2.1:191–92.

122. See Butler, "Critique, Coercion, and Sacred Life in Benjamin's 'Critique of Violence.'" The danger of overlooking this sphere will ineluctably lead to the conclusion that there is too sharp an opposition between mythic and divine violence, as for instance Jacques Derrida has argued in "Force of Law: The 'Mystical Foundation of Authority,'" trans. Mary Quaintance, in Jacques Derrida, *Acts of Religion*, ed. Gil Anidjar (London: Routledge, 2002), 231–98. (It should be added, however, that Derrida returns to Benjamin, in oblique yet suggestive ways, for instance in *Spectres of Marx* and in *Archive Fever*.)

123. Peter Fenves, "Testing Right: Lying in View of Justice," *Cardozo Law Review* 13, no. 4 (1991): 1080–81.

124. Ibid., 1113.

125. Benjamin, "The Paradox of the Cretan," *SW* 1:211; *GS* 6:58.

126. Ibid., *SW* 1:210; *GS* 6:57.

127. Ibid.

128. Ibid., *SW* 1:210; *GS* 6:57–58.

129. A *dissos logos* is the juxtaposition of contradictory propositions. For *dissoi logoi* and their relevance to criticism, see Paul Gordon, *The Critical Double: Figurative Meaning in Aesthetic Discourse* (Tuscaloosa: University of Alabama Press, 1995), esp. 56–61, where Kafka's "Von den Gleichnissen" is discussed. Although Gordon lucidly explicates many aspects of the relation between the doppelgänger and criticism, what is conspicuously absent from his monograph on the *dissos logos* is any reference to antinomy, especial as it was understood by Kant. Thus Gordon's project is not strategically positioned to tackle the issue of self-reflection, or the underwriting of the subject by subjectivity—that is, the point that informs this book.

130. Benjamin, "The Paradox of the Cretan," *SW* 1:211; *GS* 6:58.

131. Ibid..

132. Ibid.

133. Ibid., *SW* 1:211–12; *GS* 6:59.

BIBLIOGRAPHY

Adorno, Theodor W. *Kant's Critique of Pure Reason (1959)*. Edited by Rolf Tiedemann. Translated by Rodney Livingstone. Stanford: Stanford University Press, 2001.

———. *Metaphysics: Concept and Problems (1965)*. Edited by Rolf Tiedemann. Translated by Edmund Jephcott. Stanford: Stanford University Press, 2000.

———. *Negative Dialectics*. Translated by E. B. Ashton. London: Routledge, 1990.

———. *Prisms*. Edited by Samuel and Shierry Weber. London: Neville Spearman, 1967.

Agacinski, Sylviane. *Time Passing: Modernity and Nostalgia*. Translated by Jody Gladding. New York: Columbia University Press, 2003.

Agamben, Giorgio. *Homo Sacer: Sovereign Power and Bare Life*. Translated by Daniel Heller-Roazen. Stanford: Stanford University Press, 1998.

Althusser, Louis. "Lenin and Philosophy" and Other Essays. Translated by Ben Brewster. London: NLB, 1977.

Anderson, Robert B. *Dostoevsky: Myths of Duality*. Gainesville: University of Florida Press, 1986.

Anidjar, Gil. *The Jew, the Arab: A History of the Enemy*. Stanford: Stanford University Press, 2003.

Appiah, Kwame Anthony. *The Ethics of Identity*. Princeton: Princeton University Press, 2005.

Aristotle. *The Categories; On Interpretation; Prior Analytics*. Translated by Harold P. Cooke and Hugh Tredennick. Loeb Classical Library. Cambridge, Mass.: Harvard University Press, 1938.

Aslanides, E. G. *Το Μητρικό Στοιχείο στη Φόνισσα του Παπαδιαμάντη: Ψυχαναλυτικό Δοκίμιο*. Athens: Rappa, 1988.

Baecker, Dirk, ed. *Kapitalismus als Religion*. Berlin: Kadmos, 2003.

Baehr, S. L. *The Paradise Myth in Eighteenth-century Russia: Utopian Patterns in Early Secular Russian Literature and Culture.* Stanford: Stanford University Press, 1991.

Bahti, Timothy. *Allegories of History: Literary Historiography after Hegel.* Baltimore: Johns Hopkins University Press, 1992.

Bahti, Timothy, and Marilyn Sibley Fries, eds. *Jewish Writers, German Literature: The Uneasy Examples of Nelly Sachs and Walter Benjamin.* Ann Arbor: University of Michigan Press, 1995.

Bakhtin, Mikhail. *The Dialogic Imagination.* Translated by Caryl Emerson and Michael Holquist. Austin: University of Texas Press, 1988.

———. *Rabelais and His World.* Translated by Hélène Iswolsky. Bloomington: Indiana University Press, 1984.

Balfour, Ian. "Reversal, Quotation (Benjamin's History)." *MLN* 106, no. 3 (1991): 622–47.

Balfour, Ian, and Eduardo Cadava, eds. *And Justice for All? The Claims of Human Right.* Special edition, *South Atlantic Quarterly* 103, no. 2/3 (2004).

Balibar, Étienne. "Subjection and Subjectivation." In *Supposing the Subject*, ed. Joan Copjec, 1–15. London: Verso, 1994.

Barthes, Roland. "The Death of Author." In *Image, Music, Text*, 142–48. Translated by Stephen Heath. New York: Hill and Wang, 1977.

Bayliss, Linda Sue Singer. "Mirrors: Literary Reflection as Psychic Process." Ph.D. dissertation, Michigan State University, 1984; reproduced by U.M.I., 1992.

Beccaria, Cesare. *On Crimes and Punishments and Other Writings.* Translated by Richard Davies. Edited by Richard Bellamy. Cambridge: Cambridge University Press, 1995.

Becker, Carl. *Detachment and the Writing of History: Essays and Letters.* Edited by Phil Snyder. Ithaca: Cornell University Press, 1958.

Beiser, Frederick C. *The Fate of Reason: German Philosophy from Kant to Fichte.* Cambridge, Mass.: Harvard University Press, 1987.

Benjamin, Andrew. "Benjamin's Modernity." In *The Cambridge Companion to Walter Benjamin*, edited by David S. Ferris, 97–114. Cambridge: Cambridge University Press, 2004.

———. "Placing Speaking: Notes on the First Stasimon of Sophocles' Antigone." *Angelaki* 9, no. 2 (2004): 55–66.

———. *Style and Time: Essays on the Politics of Appearance.* Evanston, Ill.: Northwestern University Press, 2006.

———. *Translation and the Nature of Philosophy: A New Theory of Words.* London: Routledge, 1989.

———. "Figuring Self-Identity: Blanchot's Bataille." In *Other Than Identity: The Subject, Politics and Art*, edited by Juliet Steyn, 9–31. Manchester: Manchester University Press, 1997.

———, ed. *Walter Benjamin and History*. London: Continuum, 2005.

Benjamin, Andrew, and Peter Osborne, eds. *Walter Benjamin's Philosophy: Destruction and Experience*. Manchester: Clinamen, 2000.

Benjamin, Walter. *The Arcades Project*. Translated by Howard Eiland and Kevin McLaughlin. Cambridge, Mass.: Belknap, 1999.

———. *The Correspondence of Walter Benjamin and Gershom Scholem*. Edited by Gershom Scholem. Translated by Gary Smith and André Lefevere. Cambridge, Mass.: Harvard University Press, 1992.

———. *Gesammelte Briefe*. Edited by Christoph Gödde and Henri Lonitz. Frankfurt am Main: Suhrkamp, 1995–2000.

———. *Gesammelte Schriften*. Edited by Rolf Tiedemann and Hermann Schweppenhäuser. Frankfurt am Main: Suhrkamp, 1991.

———. *Selected Writings*. Edited by Michael W. Jennings et al. 4 vols. Cambridge, Mass.: Harvard University Press, 1997–2003.

Berkley, James. "Post-human Mimesis and the Debunked Machine: Reading Environmental Appropriation in Poe's 'Maelzel's Chess-Player' and 'The Man That Was Used Up.'" *Comparative Literature Studies* 41, no. 3 (2004): 356–76.

Bernstein, Stephen. *Alasdair Gray*. Lewisburg, Penn.: Bucknell University Press, 1999.

Bident, Christophe. "... au point de vacillement (d'un ecart Blanchot a Giraudoux)," in *Maurice Blanchot: Récits critiques*, edited by Christophe Bident and Pierre Vilar, 505–22. Tours: Farrago, 2003.

———. *Maurice Blanchot: Partenaire invisible, essai biographique*. Seyssel: Champ Vallon, 1998.

———. "The Movements of the Neuter." Translated by Michael FitzGerald and Leslie Hill. In *After Blanchot: Literature, Criticism, Philosophy*, edited by Leslie Hill, Brian Nelson, Dimitris Vardoulakis, 13–34. Newark: University of Delaware Press, 2005.

Bident, Christophe, and Pierre Vilar, eds. *Maurice Blanchot: Récits critiques*. Tours: Farrago, 2003.

Blanchot, Maurice. *Après coup: précédé par, Le ressassement eternel*. Paris: Minuit, 1983.

———. *L'arrêt de mort*. Paris: Gallimard, 1948.

———. "The Beast of Lascaux." 1953. Translated by Leslie Hill. *Oxford Literary Review* 22 (2000): 9–18.

———. *La bête de Lascaux*. Montpelier: Fata Morgana, 1982.

———. *The Book to Come*. Translated by Charlotte Mandell. Stanford: Stanford University Press, 2003.

———. "De Jean-Paul à Giraudoux." In *Maurice Blanchot: Récits critiques*, edited by Christophe Bident and Pierre Vilar, 29–32. Tours: Farrago, 2003.

———. *L'entretien infini*. Paris: Gallimard, 1969.

———. *L'espace littéraire*. Paris: Gallimard, 1955.

———. *The Infinite Conversation*. Translated by Susan Hanson. Minneapolis: University of Minnesota Press, 1997.

———. *Lautréamont et Sade*. Paris: Éditions de Minuit, 1963.

———. *Le livre à venir*. Paris: Gallimard, 1959.

———. *The Most High*. Translated by Allan Stoekl. Lincoln: University of Nebraska Press, 1996.

———. *Le pas au-delà*. Paris: Gallimard, 1973.

———. *The Space of Literature*. Translated by Ann Smock. Lincoln: University of Nebraska Press, 1982.

———. *The Station Hill Blanchot Reader: Fiction and Literary Essays*. Barrytown, N.Y.: Station Hill Press, 1999.

———. *The Step Not Beyond*. Translated by Lycette Nelson. Albany: State University of New York Press, 1982.

———. "The Task of Criticism Today." Translated by Leslie Hill. *Oxford Literary Review* 22 (2000): 19–24.

———. *The Unavowable Community*. Translated by Pierre Joris. Barrytown, N.Y.: Station Hill Press, 1988.

———. *The Work of Fire*. Translated by Charlotte Mandell. Stanford: Stanford University Press, 1995.

Böhnke, Dietmar. *Shades of Gray: Science Fiction, History and the Problem of Postmodernism in the Work of Alasdair Gray*. Glienicke, Berlin: Galda + Wilch, 2004.

Borch-Jacobsen, Mikkel. "Who's Who? Introducing Multiple Personality." In *Supposing the Subject*, edited by Joan Copjec, 45–63. London: Verso, 1994.

Böschenstein, Renate. "Doppelgänger, Automat, serielle Figur: Formen des Zweifels an der Singularität der Person." In *Androïden: Zur Poetologie der Automaten*, edited by Jürgen Söring and Reto Sorg, 165–95. Frankfurt am Main: Peter Lang, 1997.

Bowie, Andrew. *From Romanticism to Critical Theory: The Philosophy of German Literary Theory*. London: Routledge, 1997.

Breazeale, Daniel. "Philosophy and the Divided Self: On the 'Existential' and 'Scientific' Tasks of the Jena *Wissenschaftslehre*." *Fichte Studien* 6 (1994): 117–47.

Brod, Max. *Franz Kafka: A Biography*. Translated by G. Humphreys Roberts and Richard Winston. New York: Schocken, 1960.

———. *Der Prager Kreis*. Frankfurt am Main: Suhrkamp, 1979.

Buchanan, Henry. *Dostoevsky's Crime and Punishment: An Aesthetic Interpretation*. Nottingham: Astra Press, 1996.

Buck-Morss, Susan. "The Flaneur, the Sandwichman, and the Whore: The Politics of Loitering." *New German Critique* 39 (1986): 99–140.

———. *The Origin of Negative Dialectics*. New York: Free Press, 1977.

Butler, Judith. *Antigone's Claim: Kinship Between Life and Death*. New York: Columbia University Press, 2000.

———. "Critique, Coercion, and Sacred Life in Benjamin's 'Critique of Violence.'" In *Political Theologies: Public Religions in a Post-Secular World*, edited by Hent de Vries and Lawrence E. Sullivan, 201–19. New York: Fordham University Press, 2006.

———. *Gender Trouble: Feminism and the Subversion of Identity*. 1990. London: Routledge, 2006.

———. *Undoing Gender*. New York: Routledge, 2004.

Butler, Judith, and Gayatri Chakravorty Spivak. *Who Signs the Nation-State? Language, Politics, Belonging*. London: Seagull Books, 2007.

Cadava, Eduardo. *Words of Light: Theses on the Photography of History*. Princeton: Princeton University Press, 1997.

Caygill, Howard. "Walter Benjamin's Concept of Cultural History." In *The Cambridge Companion to Walter Benjamin*, ed. David S. Ferris, 73–96. Cambridge: Cambridge University Press, 2004.

———. "Non-Messianic Political Theology in Benjamin's 'On the Concept of History.'" In *Walter Benjamin and History*, edited by Andrew Benjamin, 215–26. London: Continuum, 2005.

Chizhevsky, Dmitri. "The Theme of the Double in Dostoevsky." In *Dostoevsky: A Collection of Critical Essays*, edited by René Wellek, 112–29. Englewood Cliffs, N.J.: Prentice-Hall, 1962.

Cixous, Hélène. "Fiction and Its Phantoms: A Reading of Freud's *Das Unheimliche* (The 'uncanny')." *New Literary History* 7, no. 3 (1976): 525–48.

Coates, Paul. *The Double and the Other: Identity as Ideology in Post-Romantic Fiction*. London: Macmillan, 1988.

Cohen, Josh. "Unfolding: Reading after Romanticism." In *Walter Benjamin and Romanticism*, edited by Hanssen and Benjamin, 98–108.

Comay, Rebecca. "Benjamin's Endgame." In *Walter Benjamin's Philosophy*, edited by Benjamin and Osborne, 246–85.

———. "Materialist Mutations of the *Bilderverbot*." In *Walter Benjamin and Art*, edited by Andrew Benjamin, 32–59. London: Continuum, 2005.

Copjec, Joan, ed. *Supposing the Subject*. London: Verso, 1994.

Crabtree, Adam. *From Mesmer to Freud: Magnetic Sleep and the Roots of Psychological Healing*. New Haven: Yale University Press, 1993.

Crawford, Robert, and Thom Nairn, eds. *The Arts of Alasdair Gray*. Edinburgh: Edinburgh University Press, 1991.

Curtius, Ernst Robert. *European Literature and the Latin Middle Ages*. Translated by Willard R. Trask. Princeton: Princeton University Press, 1990.

Davison, Ray. *Camus: The Challenge of Dostoevsky*. Exeter: University of Exeter Press, 1997.

Decke-Cornill, Albrecht. *Vernichtung und Selbstbehauptung: Eine Untersuchung zur Selbstbewußtseinsproblematik bei Jean Paul*. Würzburg: Königshausen + Neumann, 1987.

Deleuze, Gilles. *Difference and Repetition*. Translated by Paul Patton. London: Continuum, 2001.

———. *The Logic of Sense*. Translated by Mark Lester and Charles Stivale. New York: Columbia University Press, 1990.

Deleuze, Gilles, and Félix Guattari, *Kafka: Towards a Minor Literature*, Translated by Dana Polan. Minneapolis: University of Minnesota Press, 1986.

De Man, Paul. *Aesthetic Ideology*. Edited by Andrzej Warminski. Minneapolis: University of Minnesota Press, 1996.

De Nooy, Juliana. *Twins in Contemporary Literature and Culture: Look Twice*. Hampshire: Palgrave Macmillan, 2005.

Derrida, Jacques. *Acts of Literature*. Edited by Derek Attridge. New York: Routledge, 1992.

———. "Force of Law: The 'Mystical Foundation of Authority.'" Translated by Mary Quaintance. In Jacques Derrida, *Acts of Religion*, edited by Gil Anidjar, 231–98. London: Routledge, 2002.

———. "History of the Lie: Prolegomena." Translated by Peggy Kamuf. *Graduate Faculty Philosophy Journal* 20, no. 1 (1997): 129–61.

———. "How to Avoid Speaking: Denials." Translated by Ken Frieden. In *Languages of the Unsayable: The Play of Negativity in Literature and Literary Theory*, edited by Sanford Budick and Wolfgang Iser, 3–70. New York: Columbia University Press, 1989.

———. "Living On: Border Lines." Translated by James Hulbert. In *Deconstruction and Criticism*, 75–176. New York: Seabury Press, 1979.

———. *Of Hospitality: Anne Dufourmantelle Invites Jacques Derrida to Respond*. Translated by Rachel Bowlby. Stanford: Stanford University Press, 2000.

———. *Politics of Friendship*. Translated by George Collins. Verso: London, 1997.

Didi-Huberman, George. *Invention of Hysteria: Charcot and the Photographic Iconography of the Sâlpetrière*. Translated by Alisa Hartz. Cambridge, Mass.: MIT Press, 2003.

Die Nachtwachen des Bonaventura. Edited and translated by Gerald Gillespie. Vol. 6 of the Edinburgh Bilingual Library. Edinburgh: Edinburgh University Press, 1972.

Diogenes Laertius. *Lives of Eminent Philosophers*. Translated by R. D. Hicks. Cambridge, Mass.: Harvard University Press, 1958.

Doherty, Brigid. "Test and *Gestus* in Brecht and Benjamin." *MLN* 115, no. 3 (2000): 442–81.

Donaldson, George, and Alison Lee. "Is Eating People Really Wrong? Dining with Alasdair Gray." *Review of Contemporary Fiction* 15, no. 2 (1995); copied from ProQuest, document ID: 4592193, n.p.

Doniger, Wendy. *The Bedtrick: Tales of Sex and Masquerade*. Chicago: University of Chicago Press, 2000.

Dostoevsky, Fyodor. *Crime and Punishment*. 1866. Translated by David McDuff. Harmondsworth: Penguin, 1991.

———. *Το έκλημα και η τιμωρία*. 1889. Translated by Alexandros Papadiamantes. Athens: Ideogramma, 1992.

———. *Selected Letters of Fyodor Dostoyevsky*. Translated by R. MacAndrew. Edited Joseph Frank and David I. Goldstein. New Brunswick, N.J.: Rutgers University Press, 1987.

———. "A Strange Man's Dream: A Fantastic Story." Translated by Malcolm Jones. In *The Penguin Book of Russian Short Stories*, edited by David Richards. Harmondsworth: Penguin, 1981.

Elytis, Odysseas. *Η μαγεία του Παπαδιαμάντη*. Athens: Hypsilon, 1996.

Fenves, Peter. "On Philosophical Style—from Leibniz to Benjamin." *boundary 2* 30, no. 1 (2003): 67–87.

———. "Testing Right: Lying in View of Justice." *Cardozo Law Review* 13, no. 4 (1991): 1081–113.

Ferreira, Maria Aline Selgueiro Seabra. *I Am the Other: Literary Negotiations of Human Cloning*. Westport, Conn.: Praeger, 2005.

Ferris, David S., ed. *The Cambridge Companion to Walter Benjamin*. Cambridge: Cambridge University Press, 2004.

———. "The Shortness of History or, Photography in *Nuce*: Benjamin's Attenuation of the Negative." In *Walter Benjamin and History*, edited by Benjamin, 19–37.

Fichte, Johann Gottlieb. *Fichte: Early Philosophical Writings*, Translated and edited by Daniel Breazeale. Ithaca: Cornell University Press, 1988.

———. *Foundations of Transcendental Philosophy (Wissenschaftslehre) Nova Methodo 1796–99*. Edited and translated by Daniel Breazeale. Ithaca: Cornell University Press, 1998.

———. *Sämmtliche Werke*. Edited by J. H. Fichte. Berlin: Walter de Gruyter, 1965. A faithful reprint of the 1845 edition.

———. *Science of Knowledge: With the First and Second Introductions*. Translated by Peter Heath and John Lachs. Cambridge: Cambridge University Press, 1982.

Fickert, Kurt J. *Kafka's Doubles*. Berne: Peter Lang, 1979.

Figgis, Sean, and Andrew McAllister. "Alasdair Gray Interview." *Bête Noire* 5 (1988): 17–44.

Fleming, Paul. "The Crisis of Art: Max Kommerell and Jean Paul's Gestures." *MLN* 115, no. 3 (2000): 519–43.

Foucault, Michel. *Discipline and Punish: The Birth of the Prison*. Translated by Alan Sheridan. Harmondsworth: Penguin, 1979.

———. *Madness and Civilization: A History of Insanity in the Age of Reason*. Translated by Richard Howard. New York: Vintage, 1988.

———. "Maurice Blanchot: The Thought from Outside." Translated by Brian Massumi. In *Foucault/ Blanchot*. New York: Zone Books, 1987.

———. *The Order of Things: An Archaeology of the Human Sciences*. London: Routledge, 2002.

Frazer, James George. *The Golden Bough: A Study in Magic and Religion*. 3d ed. Part 2: *Taboo and the Perils of the Souls*. London: Macmillan, 1955.

Frenzel, Elisabeth. *Motive der Weltliteratur: Ein Lexikon Dichtungsgeschichtlicher Längsschnitte*. Stuttgart: Alfred Kröner, 1988.

Freud, Sigmund. *Gesammelte Werke*. Vol. 12. London: Imago, 1947.

———. *Penguin Freud Library*. Harmondsworth: Penguin, 1991.

Fynsk, Christopher. "Blanchot's 'The Indestructible.'" In *After Blanchot*, edited by Hill, Nelson, and Vardoulakis, 100–122.

Gasché, Rodolphe. "Kafka's Law: In the Field of Forces Between Judaism and Hellenism." *MLN* 117, no. 5 (2002): 971–1002.

———. *Of Minimal Things: Studies on the Notion of Relation*. Stanford: Stanford University Press, 1999.

———. *The Tain of the Mirror: Derrida and the Philosophy of Reflection*. Cambridge, Mass.: Harvard University Press, 1986.

Goethe, Johann Wolfgang von. *Wilhelm Meister's Apprenticeship*. Translated by Eric A. Blackall and Victor Lange. In *Goethe's Collected Works*, vol. 9. New York: Suhrkamp, 1983.

Gold, Joshua Robert. "The Dwarf in the Machine: A Theological Figure and Its Sources." *MLN* 121, no. 5 (2006): 1220–36.

Gordon, Paul. *The Critical Double: Figurative Meaning in Aesthetic Discourse*. Tuscaloosa: University of Alabama Press, 1995.

Gourgouris, Stathis. *Does Literature Think? Literature as Theory for an Antimythical Era*. Stanford: Stanford University Press, 2003.

Goux, Jean-Joseph. *Oedipus, Philosopher*. Translated by Catherine Porter. Stanford: Stanford University Press, 1993.

Grassi, Ernesto. "The Experience of the Word." In *The Primordial Metaphor*, translated by Laura Pietropaolo and Manuela Scarci. Binghamton, N.Y.: Medieval and Renaissance Texts and Studies, 1994.

Gray, Alasdair. *Arme Dinge*. Translated by Berndt Rullkötter. Hamburg: Roger & Bernhard, 1996.

———. *The Book of Prefaces*. London: Bloomsbury, 2000.

———. *A History Maker*. Edinburgh: Canongate, 1994.

———. *Poor Things: Episodes from the Early Life of Archibald McCandless M.D. Scottish Public Health Officer*, Edited by Alasdair Gray. London: Bloomsbury, 1992.

———. *Unlikely Stories, Mostly*. Edinburgh: Canongate, 1983.

———. *Why Scots Should Rule Scotland*. 1992. Rev. ed. Edinburgh: Canongate, 1997.

Η κοινωνική διάσταση του έργου του Αλέξανδρου Παπαδιαμάντη. Athens: Odysseas, 2000.

Habermas, Jürgen. "Walter Benjamin: Consciousness-Raising or Rescuing Critique." In *On Walter Benjamin*, ed. Smith, 90–128.

Hacking, Ian. *Rewriting the Soul: Multiple Personality and the Sciences of Memory*. Princeton: Princeton University Press, 1995.

Hallam, Clifford. "The Double as Incomplete Self: Toward a Definition of Doppelgänger." In *Fearful Symmetry: Doubles and Doubling in Literature and Film*, edited by Eugene J. Cook, 1–31. Tallahassee: University Presses of Florida, 1981.

Hamacher, Werner. "Afformative Strike: Benjamin's 'Critique of Violence.'" Translated by Dana Hollander. In *Walter Benjamin's Philosophy*, edited by Benjamin and Osborne, 108–36.

———. "Now: Walter Benjamin and Historical Time." In *Walter Benjamin and History*, edited by Andrew Benjamin, 38–68. London: Continuum, 2005.

———. *Premises: Essays on Philosophy and Literature from Kant to Celan*. Translated by Peter Fenves. Cambridge, Mass.: Harvard University Press, 1996.

Hanssen, Beatrice. *Critique of Violence: Between Poststructuralist and Critical Theory*. London: Routledge, 2000.

———. "Portrait of Melancholy (Benjamin, Warburg, Panofsky)." In *Benjamin's Ghosts: Interventions in Contemporary Literary and Cultural Studies*, edited by Gerhard Richter, 169–88. Stanford: Stanford University Press, 2002.

———. *Walter Benjamin's Other History: Of Stones, Animals, Human Beings, and Angels*. Berkeley: University of California Press, 1998.

Hanssen, Beatrice, and Andrew Benjamin, eds. *Walter Benjamin and Romanticism*. New York: Continuum, 2002.

Harich, Wolfgang, *Jean Pauls Kritik des philosophischen Egoismus: Belegt durch Texte und Briefstellen Jean Pauls in Anhang*. Leipzig: Reclam, 1968.

Harvie, Christopher. "Alasdair Gray and the Condition of Scotland Question."

In *The Arts of Alasdair Gray*, edited by Robert Crawford and Thom Nairn, 76–89. Edinburgh: Edinburgh University Press, 1991.

Hawley, John C. "Bell, Book, and Candle: *Poor Things* and the Exorcism of Victorian Sentiment." *Review of Cotemporary Fiction* 15, no. 2 (1995); copied from ProQuest, document ID: 6839096, n.p.

Hawthorn, Jeremy. *Multiple Personality and the Disintegration of Literary Character: From Oliver Smith to Sylvia Plath*. London: Edward Arnold, 1983.

Hegel, G. W. F. *Phenomenology of Spirit*. Translated by A. V. Miller. Oxford: Oxford University Press, 1977.

Heidegger, Martin. *The Fundamental Concepts of Metaphysics: World, Finitude, Solitude*. Translated by William McNeill and Nicholas Walker. Bloomington: Indiana University Press, 1995.

Hennis, Wilhelm. *Politik und praktische Philosophie: Eine Studie zur Rekonstruktion der politischen Wissenschaft*. Neuwied am Rhein: Hermann Luchterhand, 1963.

Heraclitus. *The Art and Thought of Heraclitus*. Edited by Charles H. Kahn. Cambridge: Cambridge University Press, 2001.

Herdman, John. *The Double in Nineteenth-Century Fiction: The Shadow of Life*. New York: Martin's Press, 1991.

Herodotus. *Herodotus with an English Translation*. Translated by A. D. Godley. Cambridge, Mass.: Harvard University Press, 1957.

Hertz, Neil. *End of the Line: Essays in Psychoanalysis and the Sublime*. New York: Columbia University Press, 1985.

Hildenbrock, Aglaja. *Das andere Ich: Künstlicher Mensch und Doppelgänger in der deutsch- und englischsprachigen Literatur*. Tübingen: Stauffenburg, 1986.

Hill, Leslie. "'Affirmation without Precedent': Maurice Blanchot and Criticism Today." In *After Blanchot*, edited by Hill, Nelson, and Vardoulakis, 58–79.

———. *Bataille, Klossowski, Blanchot: Writing at the Limit*. Oxford: Oxford University Press, 2001.

———. *Blanchot: Extreme Contemporary*. London: Routledge, 1997.

Hill, Leslie, Brian Nelson, and Dimitris Vardoulakis, eds. *After Blanchot: Literature, Criticism, Philosophy*. Newark: University of Delaware Press, 2005.

Hind, Archie. "Outré Tale of Victorian Glasgow." *Glasgow Herald*, 3 September 1992, 13.

Hobsbaum, Philip. "Unreliable Narrators: *Poor Things* and Its Paradigms." *Glasgow Review* 3 (1995): 37–46.

Hoffmann, E. T. A. *Die Serapionsbrüder*. In *Sämtliche Werke*, vol. 4, edited by Wulf Segebrecht. Frankfurt am Main: Deutscher Klassiker Verlag, 2001.

———. *Tales of E. T. A. Hoffmann*. Edited and translated by Leonard J. Kent and Elizabeth C. Knight. Chicago: University of Chicago Press, 1972.

Hogg, James. *The Private Memoirs and Confessions of a Justified Sinner*. Edited by John Carey. Oxford: Oxford University Press, 1990.

Holland, Michael. "Nathalie ou 'le supplément du roman.'" In *L'œuvre du féminin dans l'écriture de Maurice Blanchot*, edited by Eric Hoppenot, 133-56. Grignan: Complicités, 2004.

Iser, Wolfgang. "The Emergence of a Cross-Cultural Discourse: Thomas Carlyle's *Sartor Resartus*." In *The Translatability of Cultures: Figurations of the Space Between*, edited by Sanford Budick and Wolfgang Iser, 245-64. Stanford: Stanford University Press, 1996.

———. "On Translatability." *Surfaces* 4 (1994): 5-13.

Jacobi, Friedrich Heinrich. *The Main Philosophical Writings and the Novel Allwill*. Edited and translated by George di Giovanni. Montreal: McGill-Queen's University Press, 1994.

———. *Werke*. Edited by Friedrich Roth and Friedrich Köppen. Darmstadt: Wissenschaftliche Buchgesellschaft, 1976. Reproduction of the Leipzig 1812-25 edition.

Jansen, Carola M. *Die Welten und Mikrokosmen des Alasdair Gray*. Bern: Peter Lang, 2000.

Jensen, Uffa. *Gebildete Doppelgänger: Bürgerliche Juden und Protestanten im 19. Jahrhundert*. Göttingen: Vandenhoeck & Ruprecht, 2005.

Jentsch, Ernst. "On the Psychology of the Uncanny." Translated by Roy Sellars. *Angelaki* 2, no. 1 (1995): 7-15.

Kafka, Franz *Die Verwandlung*. In *Drucke zu Lebzeiten*, in *Schriften Tagebücher: Kritische Ausgabe*, edited by Jürgen Born, Gerhard Neumann, Malcolm Pasley, and Jost Schillemeit. Frankfurt am Main: Fischer, 2002.

———. *Nachgelassene Schriften und Fragmente I-II*. Edited by Malcolm Pasley. Frankfurt am Main: Fischer, 2002.

Kant, Immanuel. *Anthropology from a Pragmatic Point of View*. Translated by Victor Lyle Dowdell. Revised by Hans H. Rudnick. Carbondale: Southern Illinois University Press, 1978.

———. *The Critique of Judgement*. Translated by James Creed Meredith. Oxford: Oxford University Press, 1952.

———. *Critique of Pure Reason*. Translated by Werner S. Pluhar. Indianapolis: Hackett, 1996.

———. *Gesammelte Schriften*. Edited by Königlich Preußischen Akademie der Wissenschaften / Deutsche Akademie der Wissenschaften zu Berlin. Berlin: Reimer/ De Gruyter, 1910-.

———. "Idea of a Universal History with a Cosmopolitan Purpose." 1784. In *Political Writings*, edited by H. S. Reiss and translated by H. B. Nisbet. Cambridge: Cambridge University Press, 2000.

———. *Werke*. Edited by Wilhelm Weischedel. Darmstadt: Wissenschaftliche Buchgesellschaft, 1998,

Kantorowicz, Ernst. *The King's Two Bodies: A Study in Mediaeval Political Theology*. 1957. Princeton: Princeton University Press, 1970.

Kargakos, Sarantos. Ξαναδιαβάζοντας τη *"Φόνισσα": Μια νέα κοινωνική και πολιτική θεώρηση του Παπαδιαμάντη*. Athens: Gutenberg, 1987.

Kaufman, Eleanor. *The Delirium of Praise: Bataille, Blanchot, Deleuze, Foucault, Klossowski*. Baltimore: Johns Hopkins University Press, 2001.

Keenan, Thomas. *Fables of Responsibility: Aberrations and Predicaments in Ethics and Politics*. Stanford: Stanford University Press, 1997.

Keppler, F. C. *The Literature of the Second Self*. Tucson: University of Arizona Press, 1972.

King, Debra Walker. "Introduction: Body Fictions." In *Body Politics and the Fictional Double*, edited by Debra Walker King. Bloomington: Indiana University Press, 2000.

Kittler, Friedrich. *Essays: Literature, Media, Information Systems*. Amsterdam: G + B Arts, 1997.

Kokolis, X. A. *Για τη "Φόνισσα" του Παπαδιαμάντη: Δύο μελετήματα*. Thessalonica: University Studio Press, 1993.

Kolyvas, Ioakeim-Kimon. *Λογική της αφήγησης και ηθική του λόγου: Μελετήματα για τον Παπαδιαμάντη*. Athens: Nefeli, 1991.

Kommerell, Max. *Jean Paul*. 1933. Frankfurt am Main: Vittorio Klostermann, 1957.

Krauss, Wilhelmine. *Das Doppelgängermotiv in der Romantik: Studien zum romantischen Idealismus*. Berlin: Verlag von Emil Ebering, 1930.

Laclau, Ernesto. *Emancipation(s)*. London: Verso, 1996.

Lacoue-Labarthe, Philippe. "The Response of Ulysses." In *Who Comes After the Subject?* edited by Eduardo Cadava, Peter Connor, and Jean-Luc Nancy, 198–205. New York: Routledge, 1991.

La Vopa, Anthony J. *Fichte: The Self and the Calling of Philosophy, 1762–1799*. Cambridge: Cambridge University Press, 2001.

Layoun, Mary N. *Travels of a Genre: The Modern Novel and Ideology*. Princeton: Princeton University Press, 1990.

Lefebvre, Henri. *Introduction to Modernity: Twelve Preludes, September 1959–May 1961*. Translated by John Moore. London: Verso, 1995.

Leighton, Lauren G. *The Esoteric Tradition in Russian Romantic Literature: Decembrism and Freemasonry*. University Park: Pennsylvania State University Press, 1994.

Levitt, Gerlas M. *The Turk, Chess Automaton*. Jefferson, N.C.: McFarland, 2000.

Liu, Catherine. *Copying Machines: Taking Notes for the Automaton.* Minneapolis: University of Minnesota Press, 2000.

Llewelyn, John. *The HypoCritical Imagination: Between Kant and Levinas.* London: Routledge, 2000.

Longinus. *On the Sublime.* Translated by W. H. Fyfe. Revised translation by D. A. Russell. Cambridge, Mass.: Harvard University Press, 1995.

Lumsden, Simon. "Fichte's Striving Subject." *Inquiry* 47, no. 2 (2004): 123–42.

Lyotard, Jean-François. *Lessons on the Analytic of the Sublime.* Translated by Elizabeth Rottenberg. Stanford: Stanford University Press, 1994.

———. "Sensus Communis." Translated by Marian Hobson and Geoff Bennington. *Paragraph* 11, no. 1 (1988): 1–23.

Mack, Michael. "Between Kant and Kafka: Benjamin's Notion of the Law." *Neophilologus* 85, no. 2 (2001): 257–72.

Mahoney, Dennis F. "Double into Doppelgänger: The Genesis of the Doppelgänger-motif in the Novels of Jean Paul and E. T. A. Hoffmann." *Journal of Evolutionary Psychology* 4, no. 1 (1983): 54–63.

Malabou, Catherine. *The Future of Hegel: Plasticity, Temporality and Dialectic.* Translated by Lisabeth During. London: Routledge, 2004.

Malpas, Jeffrey. *Place and Experience: A Philosophical Topography.* Cambridge: Cambridge University Press, 1999.

Marquard, Odo. *In Defense of the Accidental: Philosophical Studies.* Translated by Robert M. Wallace. New York: Oxford University Press, 1991.

Marx, Karl. *The Eighteenth Brumaire of Louis Bonaparte.* New York: International Publishers, 1968.

Mayer, Hans. "Walter Benjamin and Franz Kafka: Report on a Constellation." In *On Walter Benjamin,* ed. Smith, 185–209.

Mehlman, Jeffrey. *Genealogies of the Text: Literature, Psychoanalysis, and Politics in Modern France.* Cambridge: Cambridge University Press, 1995.

Menninghaus, Winfried. *In Praise of Nonsense: Kant and Bluebeard.* Translated by Henry Pickford. Stanford: Stanford University Press, 1999.

———. *Walter Benjamins Theorie der Sprachmagie.* Frankfurt am Main: Suhrkamp, 1980.

———. "Walter Benjamin's Variations of Imagelessness." In *Jewish Writers, German Literature,* edited by Bahti and Fries, 155–73.

Mieszkowski, Jan. "The Syntax of the Revolution." *European Romantic Review* 13, no. 2 (2002): 207–13.

Miller, J. Hillis. *Versions of Pygmalion.* Cambridge, Mass.: Harvard University Press, 1990.

Miller, Karl. *Doubles: Studies in Literary History.* Oxford: Oxford University Press, 1987.

Moles, John L. "Cynic Cosmopolitanism." In *The Cynics: The Cynic Movement in Antiquity and Its Legacy*, edited by R. Bracht Branham and Marie-Odile Goulet-Cazé, 105–20.Berkeley: University of California Press, 1996.

———. "The Cynics and Politics." In *Justice and Generosity: Studies in Hellenic Social and Political Philosophy*, edited by André Laks and Malcolm Schofield, 129–58. Cambridge: Cambridge University Press, 1995.

Montaigne, Michel Eyquem de. *The Complete Works of Montaigne: Essays, Travel Journals, Letters*. Translated by Donald M. Frame. Stanford: Stanford University Press, 1948.

Moores, Phil. "An Alasdair Gray Bibliography." In *Alasdair Gray: Critical Appraisals and a Bibliography*, edited by Phil Moores, 189–236. Boston Spa and London: The British Library, 2002.

Moretti, Franco. *The Way of the World: The Bildungsroman in European Culture*. London: Verso, 2000.

Murav, Harriet. *Holy Foolishness: Dostoevsky's Novels and the Poetics of Cultural Critique*. Stanford: Stanford University Press, 1992.

Nägele, Rainer. *Theatre, Theory, Speculation: Walter Benjamin and the Scenes of Modernity*. Baltimore: Johns Hopkins University Press, 1991.

Nancy, Jean-Luc. *Hegel: The Restlessness of the Negative*. Translated by Jason Smith and Steven Miller. Minneapolis: University of Minnesota Press, 2002.

Neuhouser, Frederick. *Fichte's Theory of Subjectivity*. Cambridge: Cambridge University Press, 1990.

Nussbaum, Martha. "Kant and Cosmopolitanism." In *Perpetual Peace: Essays on Kant's Cosmopolitan Ideal*, edited by James Bohman and Matthias Lutz-Bachmann, 25–57. Cambridge, Mass.: MIT Press, 1997.

Osborne, Peter. "Small-Scale Victories, Large-Scale Defeats." In *Walter Benjamin's Philosophy*, edited by Benjamin and Osborne, 59–109.

Papadiamantes, Alexandros. Ἅπαντα [*Complete Works*]. Edited by Ν. Δ. Τριανταφυλλόπουλος. 2d ed. Athens: Domos, 1997.

———. *Les petites filles et la mort*. Translated by Michel Saunier. Arles: Actes Sud, 2003. First published in 1976 in Paris by Maspero.

———. *The Murderess*. Translated by Peter Levi. London: Writers and Readers, 1983.

———. "Φύλλα εσκορπισμένα": Τα παπαδιαμαντικά αυτόγραφα (γνωστά και άγνωστα κείμενα), edited by Δ. Α. Δημητρακόπουλος and Γ. Α. Χριστοδούλου. Athens: Kastaniotis, 1994.

Papagiorges, Kostes. Ἀλέξανδρος Ἀδαμαντίου Ἐμμανουήλ. Athens: Kastaniotis, 1998.

Passage, Charles E. *Character Names in Dostoevsky's Fiction*. Ann Arbor, Mich.: Ardis 1982.

Paul, Jean. *Horn of Oberon: Jean Paul's School of Aesthetics*. Translated by Margaret R. Hale. Detroit: Wayne State University Press, 1973.

———. *Ideen-Gewimmel: Texte und Aufzeichnungen aus dem unveröffentlichten Nachlaß*. Edited by Thomas Wirtz and Kurt Wölfel. Frankfurt am Main: Eichborn, 1996.

———. *Sämtliche Werke*. Edited by Norbert Miller. Darmstadt: Wissenschaftliche Buchgesellschaft, 2000.

———. *Sämtliche Werke, historisch-kritische Ausgabe*. Edited by Eduard Berend et al. Berlin: die Deutsche Akademie der Wissenschaften zu Berlin, 1927–.

Plutarch. *Moralia*. Translated by Frank Cole Babbitt. Cambridge, Mass.: Harvard University Press, 1957.

Poe, Edgar Allan. "Maelzel's Chess-Player." In *The Works of the Late Edgar Allan Poe*, edited by Rufus Wilmot Griswold, 4:346–70. New York: Redfield, 1856.

Polsky, Stephanie. "Down the K. Hole: Walter Benjamin's Destructive Land-Surveying of History." In *Walter Benjamin and History*, edited by Benjamin, 69–87.

Proguidis, Lakis. *Η κατάκτηση του μυθιστορήματος: Από τον Παπαδιαμάντη στον Βοκκάκιο*. Translated by Γιάννης Κιουρτσάκης. Athens: Hestia, 1998.

———. *Ο Παπαδιαμάντης και η Δύση. Πέντε μελέτες*. Athens: Hestia, 2002.

Pushkin, Alexander. *The Queen of Spades and Other Stories*. Translated by Rosemary Edmonds. Harmondsworth: Penguin, 1962.

Ramfos, Stelios. *Η παλινωδία του Παπαδιαμάντη*. Athens: Kedros, 1976.

Rank, Otto. *Der Doppelgänger: Eine Psychoanalytische Studie*. Leipzig: Internationaler Psychoanalytischer Verlag, 1925.

———. *The Double: A Psychoanalytic Study*. Translated by Harry Tucker Jr. New York: Meridian, 1979.

Reik, Theodor. *The Compulsion to Confess: On the Psychoanalysis of Crime and Punishment*. 1925. New York: Farrar, Straus and Cudahy, 1959.

Richardson, Michael, ed. *Double / Double*. Harmondsworth: Penguin, 1987.

Ricoeur, Paul. "Toward a Hermeneutic of the Idea of Revelation." *Harvard Theological Review* 70, no. 1–2 (1977): 1–37.

Rogers, Robert. *A Psychoanalytic Study of the Double in Literature*. Detroit: Wayne State University Press, 1970.

Rosenfield, Claire. "The Shadow Within: The Conscious and Unconscious Use of the Double." In *Stories of the Double*, edited by Albert J. Guérard, 311–31. Philadelphia: J. B. Lippincott, 1967.

Royle, Nicholas. *The Uncanny*. Manchester: Manchester University Press, 2003.

Sallis, John. *Spacings: Of Reason and Imagination in Texts of Kant, Fichte, Hegel*. Chicago: University of Chicago Press, 1987.

Saramago, Jose. *The Double*. 2002. Translated by Margaret Jull Costa. London: Harvill, 2004.

Sarante, Galateia. "'Είχε ψηλώσει ο νους της.'" In *Φώτα ολόφωτα: Ένα αφιέρωμα στον Παπαδιαμάντη*, edited by Ν. Δ. Τριανταφυλλόπουλος. 347–49. Αθήνα: Ε.Λ.Ι.Α., 1981.

Saunier, Guy (Michel). *Εωσφόρος και άβυσσος: Ο προσωπικός μύθος του Παπαδιαμάντη*. Athens: Agra, 2001.

Schiffman, Zachary Sayre. *On the Threshold of Modernity: Relativism in the French Renaissance*. Baltimore: Johns Hopkins University Press, 1991.

Schiller, Friedrich. "The Nature and Value of Universal History." *History and Theory* 11, no. 3 (1972): 321–34.

———. "Was heisst und zu welchem Ende studiert man Universalgeschichte?" In *Werke in Drei Bände*, vol. 2, edited by Gerhard Fricke and Herbert G. Göpfert, 9–22. Munich: Carl Hansen Verlag, 1966.

Schlaffer, Heinz. "Epic and Novel: Action and Consciousness. Jean Paul's *Titan*." In *The Bourgeois as Hero*, translated by James Lynn, 8–38. Cambridge: Polity, 1989.

Schmemann, Alexander. *Confession and Communion: Confession and Communion: Report to the Holy Synod of Bishops of the Orthodox Church in America*. http://www.schmemann.org/byhim/confessionandcommunion.html . Date of access January 2007.

Schmitt, Carl. "Nomos—Nahme—Name." In *The Nomos of the Earth in the International Law of the* Jus Publicum Europaeum, translated by G. L. Ulmen, 336–50. New York: Telos Press, 2003.

———. *Politische Romantik*. 1925. Berlin: Duncker und Humblot, 1998.

Schwartz, Hillel. *The Culture of the Copy: Striking Likenesses, Unreasonable Facsimiles*. New York: Zone, 1996.

Simpson, Patricia Anne. "In Citing Violence: Gestus in Benjamin, Brecht and Kafka." In *Jewish Writers, German Literature*, edited by Bahti and Fries, 175–203.

Slethaug, Gordon E. *The Play of the Double in Postmodern American Fiction*. Carbondale: Southern Illinois University Press, 1993.

Smeed, J. W. *Jean Paul's Dreams*. London: Oxford University Press, 1966.

Smith, Gary, ed. *On Walter Benjamin: Critical Essays and Recollections*. Cambridge, Mass: MIT Press, 1988.

Sophocles. *Ajax, Electra, Oedipus Tyrannus*. Translated by Hugh Lloyd-Jones. Cambridge, Mass.: Harvard University Press, 2001.

Spinoza, Baruch. *Complete Works*. Translated by Samuel Shirley. Edited by Michael L. Morgan. Indianapolis: Hackett, 2002.

Standage, Tom. *The Turk: The Life and Times of the Famous Eighteenth-Century Chess-Playing Machine*. New York: Berkley Books, 2003.

Starobinski, Jean. "The Body's Moment." Translated by John A. Gallucci. *Yale French Studies* 64 (1983): 273–305.

Stern, Lucien. "*Wilhelm Meisters Lehrjahre* und Jean Pauls *Titan*." 1922. In *Jean Paul*, edited by Uwe Schweikert, 33–73. Darmstadt: Wissenschaftliche Buchgesellschaft, 1974.

Stewart, Dugald. "Theoretical or Conjectural History." In *The Scottish Enlightenment: An Anthology*, edited by Alexander Broadie, 670–74. Edinburgh: Canongate, 1997.

Susman, Margarete. "Das Hiob-Probleme bei Kafka" (1929) = "Früheste Dichtung Franz Kafkas." In *Gestalten und Kreise*, 348–66. Stuttgart: Diana, 1954.

Sussman, Henry. "The Herald: A Reading of Walter Benjamin's Kafka Study." *Diacritics* 7, no. 1 (1977): 42–54.

Szondi, Peter. *On Textual Understanding and Other Essays*. Translated by Harvey Mendelsohn. Minneapolis: University of Minnesota Press, 1986.

Terzakis, Aggelos. "Οι 'επιδράσεις.'" *Nea Hestia* 355 (1941): 54–56.

Tiedemann, Rolf. "Historische Materialismus oder politischer Messianismus? Politische Gehalte in der Geschichtsphilosophie Walter Benjamins." In *Materialien zu Benjamins Thesen "Über den Begriff der Geschichte": Beiträge und Interpretationen*, edited by Peter Bulthaup, 77–121. Frankfurt am Main: Suhrkamp, 1975.

Tiitinen, Johanna. *"Work As If You Live in the Early Days of a Better Nation": History and Politics in the Works of Alasdair Gray*. Helsinki: University of Helsinki Press, 2004.

Todorov, Tzvetan. *The Fantastic: A Structural Approach to a Literary Genre*. Translated by Richard Howard. Ithaca: Cornell University Press, 1975.

Tournier, Michel. *Friday*. Translated by Norman Denny. Baltimore: Johns Hopkins University Press, 1997.

———. *Gemini*. Translated by Anne Carter. London: Collins, 1981.

Tymms, Ralph. *Doubles in Literary Psychology*. Cambridge: Bowes and Bowes, 1949.

Tziovas, Dimitris. "Selfhood, Natural Law, and Social Resistance in *The Murderess*." In *The Other Self: Selfhood and Society in Modern Greek Fiction*, 83–101. Lanham, Md.: Lexington, 2003.

Ungar, Steven. *Scandal and Aftereffect: Blanchot and France since 1930*. Minneapolis: University of Minnesota Press, 1995.

Valetas, G. *Παπαδιαμάντης: Η ζωή, το έργο, η εποχή του*. Athens: Vivlos, 1957.

Vardoulakis, Dimitris. "Confession and Time: The Subject in Papadiamantes's *The Merchants of the Nations*." *MLN* 124, no. 5 (2009): 1091–1115.

———. "The Ends of Stasis: Spinoza, Reader of Agamben." *Culture, Theory and Critique* 51, no. 2 (2010).

Warminski, Andrzej. "Returns of the Sublime: Positing and Performative in Kant, Fichte, and Schiller." *MLN* 116, no. 5 (2001): 964–78.

Webber, Andrew J. *The Doppelgänger: Double Visions in German Literature*. Oxford: Oxford University Press, 1996.

Weber, Samuel. "Genealogy of Modernity: History, Myth and Allegory in Benjamin's *Origin of German Mourning Play*." *MLN* 106, no. 3 (1991): 465–500.

———. "The Sideshow, or: Remarks on a Canny Moment. *MLN* 88, no. 6 (1973): 1102–33.

Witschi, Beat. *Glasgow Urban Writing and Postmodernism: A Study of Alasdair Gray's Fiction*. Bern: Peter Lang, 1991.

Wohlfarth, Irving. "Et Cetera? The Historian as Chiffonier." *New German Critique* 39 (1986): 142–68.

———. "On the Messianic Structure of Walter Benjamin's Last Reflections." *Glyph* 3 (1978): 148–212.

———. "Wolfgang Iser's 'On Translatability': Roundtable Discussion." *Surfaces* 6 (1996): 5–37.

Yates, Frances A. *The Art of Memory*. 1966. London: Pimlico, 2000.

Ziarek, Ewa Płonowska. *An Ethics of Dissensus: Postmodernity, Feminism, and the Politics of Radical Democracy*. Stanford: Stanford University Press, 2001.

Ziolkowski, Theodore. *German Romanticism and Its Institutions*. Princeton: Princeton University Press, 1990.

Žižek, Slavoj. *Enjoy Your Symptom! Jacques Lacan in Hollywood and Out*. New York: Routledge, 1992.

———. *The Sublime Object of Ideology*. London: Verso, 1989.

Zöller, Günter. *Fichte's Transcendental Philosophy: The Original Duplicity of Intelligence and Will*. Cambridge: Cambridge University Press, 1998.

Zouboulakis, Stauros, and N. D. Triantafyllopoulos, eds. *Ο μυθιστοριογράφος Παπαδιαμάντης: Συναγωγή κριτικών κειμένων*. Athens: Hestia, 2003.

INDEX

Adorno, Theodor Wiesengrund, 1, 4, 254n7, 255n19, 259n51, 298n24, 302n84
Agacinski, Sylviane, 234, 303n108
Agamben, Giorgio, 292n103, 299n40
Alexander (the Great), 178
Anidjar, Gil, 280n1, 305n122
Appiah, Kwame Anthony, 294n118
Aristophanes, 9, 39
Aristotle, 12, 31, 253n1, 259n52
Aslanidis, E. G., 271n68

Bahti, Timothy, 285n53, 285n67, 297n22, 301n68
Bakhtin, Mikhail, 282n23
Balfour, Ian, 285n67, 294n117
Balibar, Étienne, 139–40, 280n3–7
Barthes, Roland, 249n1
Bataille, Georges, 106, 118, 134, 279n65
Bayliss, Linda Sue Singer, 74, 266n21, 267n22
Beccaria, Cesare, 69, 105, 265n5
Becker, Carl, 285n48
Beiser, Frederick C., 258n42, 259n50
Benjamin, Andrew, 151, 266n14, 279n65, 283n26, 284n36, 287n73, 292n100, 296n4, 298n24, 300n65, 302n94
Benjamin, Walter, 6, 52, 115, 138, 141, 143–65, 188–96, 199–203, 206–44, 257n31, 263n104, 281n15–16, 282n18, 282n21, 283n26, 282n29, 283n31, 284n43, 284n46, 285n67, 292n100, 295nn1–2, 296n8, 297n22, 298nn23–26, 299n33, 300n48, 300n51, 300n65, 301n69, 302n86, 303n102, 303n104, 303nn107–8, 305n117, 305n122; "A Little History of Photography," 234; "A Work on the Lie" (Notizen zu einer Arbeit über die Lüge), 305n117; "A Work on the Lie II" (Notizen zu einer Arbeit über die Lüge II), 302n80, 305n115; *Berlin Childhood Around 1900*, 234; "Critique of Violence," 208, 209, 215, 239, 241, 299n37, 299n40, 300n62, 305nn117–22; "Fate and Character," 214, 220, 221, 300n55, 300nn62–63, 301n66; "Franz Kafka: On the Tenth Anniversary of His Death," 202, 235, 295n1, 295n2, 297n21, 299nn35–36, 299nn38–39, 299nn44–46, 300n50, 300nn52–54, 300n61, 301nn69–77, 302n81, 302nn84–85, 302n87, 302nn91–92, 302nn94–95, 303n99, 303n101, 303nn105–6, 304n112, 304n114, 305n120; *Goethe's Elective Affinities*, 147, 221, 284n38; Notes on Kafka, 299n43, 302n93, 302n96, 303n107; "On Language as Such and the Language of Man," 155; "On the concept of history," 143, 144, 193, 207, 242, 284n35, 284n37, 284n39, 285n47, 285n59, 285n61, 285n65, 292n100, 295n2, 296n3; "Paralipomena to 'On the Concept of History'," 283n27, 284n44, 285n49, 285n51, 284n33, 284n38, 284n43, 285n49, 285n51, 285n65; *The Arcades Project*, 145, 146, 194, 225, 282n20, 283n26, 283n30, 284n32, 284n34, 284n41, 285n66, 296n6; "The Concept of Criticism in German Romanticism," 277n33; "Theological-Political Fragment," 292n100; "The Paradox of the Cretan" (Über den 'Kreter'), 242, 306n125, 306n130; Theses I, 143, 144, 165, 192, 193, 195, 196, 199, 207, 242, 282nn18–19; Thesis

II, 143, 145, 292n100; Thesis III, 158; Thesis XVII, 147, 152–55, 159, 163; "The Storyteller," 157, 159, 160, 285nn53–54, 285n60, 285n62 ; *Ursprung des deutschen Trauerspiels*, 52, 295n2; "Was ist das epische Theater? Eine Studie zu Brecht," 295n2
Berkley, James, 297n16
Bernstein, Stephen, 286n71
Bident, Christophe, 121, 276n31, 277n35, 278n50
Blanchot, Maurice, 5, 17, 18, 25, 106–122, 125, 128–132, 134, 205, 206, 257n32, 265n3, 268n37, 274n3, 275n4, 277n35, 277n37, 277n39, 278n42, 278n48, 278n51, 279n65, 280nn86–87; "After the Fact," 276n21; *Death Sentence (L'arrêt de mort)*, 111, 275nn11–13, 275n15, 276nn16–17, 276n19, 276nn22–23, 276n32, 278n42, 279n52, 279nn60–64, 279nn66–67, 279nn69–73, 279nn75–79; *Lautréamont et Sade*, 109, 129, 275n4; "Literature and the Right to Death," 265n3; "Orpheus's Gaze," 121; "Reading Kafka," 299n32; *Space of Literature (L'espace littéraire)*, 128, 275n14, 277n35, 278n51, 278nn52–53, 279n68, 279n74, 279n80; "The Beast of Lascaux" (La bête de Lascaux), 279nn84–85, 280n86; *The Book to Come (Le livre à venir)*, 278n47; *The Infinite Conversation (L' entretien infini)*, 254n13, 274n3, 298n31; The Most High, 112, 114, 276n18, 278n51; *The Step Not Beyond (Le pas au-delà)*, 121, 265n3, 274n2; "The Task of Criticism Today," 109, 110, 129, 130, 132, 275n4, 275nn6–10, 279n81; *The Unavowable Community*, 118, 134, 278n44; *The Work of Fire (La Part du feu)*, 265n3, 299n32; *Thomas l'Obscur*, 280n87
Bohman, James, 290n95
Borch-Jacobsen, Mikkel, 260n62
Böschenstein, Renate, 281n11
Breazeale, Daniel, 258n 46, 264n110
Brecht, Bertolt, 226, 243, 295n2, 297n22, 301n69
Broadie, Alexander, 294n117
Brod, Max, 202, 204–6, 228, 232, 298nn25–26, 298nn28–31, 300n48, 302n97, 303n107
Buchanan, Henry, 266n16
Buck-Morss, Susan, 282n21, 283n29

Budick, Sanford, 270n62, 288n76
Butler, Judith, 271n67, 287n73, 297n18, 299n40, 305n122

Cadava, Eduardo, 234–36, 294n117, 304n109, 304n113
Camus, Albert, 269n42
Carlyle, Thomas, 167, 288nn75–76
Carter, Anne, 253n5
Caygill, Howard, 283n26, 283n31
Chamisso, Adelbert von, 230, 303n102
Char, René, 280n86
Charcot, Jean-Martin, 182, 183, 188–91, 294n120
Chizhevsky, Dmitri, 266n16
Cixous, Hélène, 42, 262n77, 262n83
Coates, Paul, 12–14, 253n2
Cohen, Josh, 302n94
Comay, Rebecca, 194, 197, 296n4, 298n24
Crabtree, Adam, 251n12
Crates, 290n95
Crawford, Robert, 288n75, 289n84
Curtius, Ernst Robert, 275n5

Decke-Cornill, 260n58
Deleuze, Gilles, 253n5, 263n94, 291n97, 300n65
Derrida, Jacques, xi, xii, 75, 143, 249n4, 250n 5, 257n32, 267n 24, 270n62, 275n12, 278n48, 280n88, 288n76, 305n116, 305n122
Didi-Huberman, George, 189, 294n120
Diogenes, 290n95
Doherty, Brigid, 297n22
Donaldson, George, 291n99
Doniger, Wendy, 252n16
Dostoevsky, Fyodor, 69, 73, 80, 81, 92, 93, 266nn15–16, 268nn37–38, 269nn41–42, 288n76

Fenves, Peter, 240, 241, 258–59n49, 284n 46, 303n98, 306n123
Ferreira, Maria Aline Selgueiro Seabra, 251n9
Ferris, David S., 283n31, 284n36, 303n108
Fichte, Johann Gottlieb, 4, 14, 15, 26–39, 41, 54–68, 120, 142, 177, 227, 254n7, 258nn45–49, 260n54, 260n57, 264n116, 264n121, 281n12, 293n115; *Science of Knowledge*, 36, 60, 62, 258n58, 264n111–12, 264n114–121
Fickert, Kurt J., 223, 224, 302n88, 304n144

Figgis, Sean, 288n75
Foucault, Michel, 16, 17, 70, 71, 73, 75, 77, 104, 119, 139, 146, 194, 254n9, 265n5, 265nn7–11, 266n17, 278n45, 284n24
Francis I, Emperor, 157
Frazer, James George, 38, 261n64
Frenzel, Elizabeth, 249–50n 4
Freud, Sigmund, 7, 14, 16, 37, 39–52, 182, 186, 189, 251n10, 261nn70–73, 262nn80–86, 236nn89–92
Fries, Marilyn Sibley, 297n22, 301n68

Garve, Christian, 294n117
Gasché, Rodolphe, 5, 220, 221, 250n5, 262n87, 302n79, 302n82
Gaulle, Charles de, 130
George, Stefan, 277n35
Goethe, Johann Wolfgang von, 16, 17, 113, 115, 151, 221, 254n11, 260n54, 276n20
Gold, Joshua Robert, 296n8
Gordon, Paul, 306n129
Gourgouris, Stathis, 70, 265n6, 267n27, 287n73, 302n84
Goux, Jean-Joseph, xi, 249n1, 250n7
Grassi, Ernesto, 273n92
Gray, Alasdair, 143, 165, 166, 172, 173, 186, 282n18, 286n68, 286nn69–70, 288nn75–76, 289n82, 289n84, 291n99, 293n115, 294n117; *A History Maker*, 293n115; *Poor Things*, 6, 143, 165–78, 181, 182, 185, 186, 188, 189, 282n17, 286nn70–71, 287nn72–73, 288nn75–76, 289nn77–78, 289nn82–91, 299n99, 292nn101–2, 293nn109–15, 294n119, 295n121; *The Book of Prefaces*, 286n69, 293n115; *Why Scots Should Rule Scotland*, 186, 294n116; *Unlikely Stories, Mostly*, 293n115
Guattari, Felix, 263n94, 300n65

Habermas, Jürgen, 285n67
Hacking, Ian, 260n62
Hallam, Clifford, 261n68
Hamacher, Werner, 258n49, 292n100, 303n98, 305n118
Hanssen, Beatrice, 283n31, 292n100, 302n94, 305n118
Harich, Wolfgang, 257nn37–38
Harrington, James, 16, 18–21, 255n17
Hawley, John C., 293n115
Hebel, Johann Peter, 157–58
Hegel, Georg Wilhelm Friedrich, 4, 66, 67, 69, 74, 149, 250n7, 265n1, 287n73
Heidegger, Martin, 261n70, 287n73, 290n94
Heine, Heinrich, 249n4
Hennis, Wilhelm, 253n1
Heraclitus, 131, 279n85
Herdman, John, 251n14
Herodotus, 146, 159, 160, 162, 283n25, 285n64
Hertz, Neil, 43, 262n80, 274n93
Hildenbrock, Aglaja, 252n17, 281n11
Hill, Leslie, 115, 130, 275n4, 276n28, 278n42, 278n50, 279n84, 298n31
Hind, Archie, 286n70
Hobsbaum, Philip, 291n99
Hoffmann, E. T. A., 42, 45, 46, 48, 69, 189, 251n12, 254n7, 262n86, 265n2, 265n4
Hogg, James, 74, 266, 267nn20–22, 288n76
Holland, Michael, 276n20
Homer, 99, 100, 146
Horkheimer, Max, 148–51, 302n84
Hume, David, 294n117

Iser, Wolfgang, 272n62, 288n76

Jacobi, Friedrich Heinrich, 15, 27, 28, 30–34, 39, 40, 56, 58, 60, 62, 257nn37–41, 258nn43–44, 259nn50–51, 259n53, 260n54, 260nn57–58, 304n113
Jansen, Carola M., 289n82
Jensen, Uffa, 251n9
Jentsch, Ernst, 262n85

Kafka, Franz, 6, 191–93, 196, 200–38, 242, 243, 263n94, 278n42, 284n43, 295n2, 297n22, 298n23, 298n26, 298n29, 299n33, 300n51, 300n65, 301n77, 302n97, 303n107, 304n114; *America (Amerika)*, 203, 211, 300n48; *Metamorphosis*, 203, 205–7, 210, 214–17, 223, 299n34; *The Castle*, 210, 212, 278n42; *The Trial*, 212 ; "Von den Gleichnissen," 306n129
Kant, Immanuel, 4, 14–19, 21, 23, 29, 30, 32–35, 37, 39, 96, 139, 149, 170, 176, 177, 179, 187, 254n14, 255nn15–19, 257n41, 258n45, 258n47, 264n121, 272n72, 273n92, 281n12, 281n15, 290nn92–93, 290n95, 294n117, 306n129
Kantorowicz, Ernst, 291n98
Kargakos, Sarantos, 272n74
Kaufman, Eleanor, 118, 278n43
Keenan, Thomas, 250n6

Kempelen, Wolfgang von, 296n9
Keppler, F.C., 266n21, 274n1
Kierkegaard, Søren, 254n7
King, Debra Walker, 2, 3, 249n3
Kittler, 303n104
Kokolis, X. A., 272n72
Kommerell, Max, 24, 257n31
Krauss, Wilhelmine, 254n7

Laclau, Ernesto, 250n6
Lacoue-Labarthe, Philippe, 304n113
Laertius, Diogenes, 290n95
Layoun, Maryn, 271n69
Lee, Alison, 291n99
Lefebvre, Henri, xi, xii, 249n3
Leibniz, Gottfried Wilhelm, 154, 284nn45–46
Leigh, Dennis, 293n115
Leskov, Nikolai, 157, 159, 196
Levitt, Gerlas M., 296n8
Liu, Catherine, 281n15
Llewelyn, John, 295n122
Longinus, 99, 100, 146, 273n91, 274n93, 282n22, 302n86
Lutz-Bachmann, Matthias, 290n95
Lyotard, Jean-François, 255n15

Mack, Michael, 305n120
Maelzel, Johann Nepomuk, 196–99, 296n9
Mahoney, Dennis F., 254n7
Malabou, Catherine, 295n123, 296n7
Malpas, Jeffrey, 254n8
Man, Paul de, 258n49, 263n104
Marquard, Odo, 283n25
Marx, Karl, 230, 303n103
Mayer, Hans, 304n114
McAllister, Andrew, 288n75
Mehlman, Jeffrey, 276n32
Menninghaus, Winfried, 263n103, 285n50, 301n68
Mieszkowski, Jan, 264n121
Miller, J. Hillis, 111, 275n12
Miller, Karl, 252n17, 266n16
Mitchell, Silas Weir, 296n8
Moles, John L., 290n95
Montaigne, Michel de, 146, 160, 161, 282n23
Moores, Phil, 293n115
Moretti, Franco, 168, 289n79
Mouret, Jacques-François, 296n8

Nägele, Rainer, 297n22

Naipaul, V.S., 288n76
Nairn, Thom, 288n75, 289n84
Nancy, Jean-Luc, 265n12, 304n113
Nelson, Brian, 275n 4, 278n50, 298n31
Nietzsche, Friedrich, 4, 11, 14, 250n7
Nooy, Juliana de, 251n9
Nussbaum, Martha, 290n95

Osborne, Peter, 298n23
Ovid, 39

Palsey, Malcolm, 302n97
Papadiamantes, Alexandros, 66, 72–75, 77, 80, 83, 91–95, 98, 102, 103, 105, 106, 192, 266n13, 266n16, 267n27, 268nn31–32, 268n37, 269n42, 270n64, 271n65, 271n67, 272n74, 272n77, 273nn88–89 ; *Les petites filles et la mort*, 271n66; *The Merchants of the Nations* (Οἱ ἔμποροι τῶν ἐθνῶν), 95, 268n32, 273n89; *The Murderess* (Ἡ φόνισσα), 4, 72–77, 79–81, 83, 88–93, 95–98, 102, 105, 106, 266n13, 266nn18–19, 267nn26–30, 268nn32–35, 268n37, 269n42, 269nn44–45, 270nn47–61, 270n64, 271nn65–66, 271n69, 272n74, 274nn94–95
Papagiorgis, Kostis, 269n42, 272n77
Passage, Charles E., 268n40
Paul, Jean, 4, 5, 9, 13, 14–17, 19, 21–40, 43–45, 51, 52, 54–56, 58–60, 62–64, 66–69, 73, 106, 113–23, 126, 128, 133, 142, 143, 167, 200, 245, 249n4, 253nn5–6, 256n25, 256n30, 257n37, 258n49, 260n57, 261n63, 263n104, 268n37, 276n20, 276n29, 277n34, 277n35, 277n37, 277n39, 279n59, 293n115, 304n113; *Auswahl aus des Teufels Papieren*, 276n24; *Clavis Fichtiana*, 15, 24–28, 32, 33, 35, 36, 40, 41, 55–59, 64, 66, 120, 143, 167, 253n6, 254n7, 256n21, 256nn26–28, 257n39, 260n55, 260n60, 263nn98–102, 264n105, 257n36, 261n63 ; *Preschool to Aesthetics* (*Vorschule der Ästhetik*), 122, 278n54; *Siebenkäs*, 17, 26–28, 113–14, 116, 119–20, 122–23, 167, 249n4, 253n5, 276n22, 276nn25–26, 276n27, 277nn37–39, 278nn40–41, 278n46, 279n49, 278n55, 279n56, 279n58; *Titan*, 17, 24, 26–28, 30, 34, 55, 58, 167, 254n12, 257nn33–35, 276n27
Plato, 9, 131, 261n66
Plutarch, 178–80, 186, 187, 290n95, 291n96

Index

Poe, Edgar Allan, 69, 196, 197, 199, 282n19, 296n8, 297nn10–11, 297nn16–17, 297n19
Polsky, Stephanie, 300n65
Proust, Marcel, 288n76
Psammenitus, 159, 161, 162, 196
Pushkin, Alexander, 81, 268n39

Rabelais, Francois, 146, 282n23
Ramfos, Stelios, 93–95, 272n75, 272nn77–86, 273n88
Rank, Otto, 38, 39, 69, 230, 258n49, 262n84, 303n102
Reik, Theodor, 271n67
Ricoeur, Paul, 273n87
Rogers, Robert, 266n21
Rosenfield, Claire, 251n14
Rosenzweig, Franz, 212
Rossmann, Karl, 211, 212
Rullkötter, Berndt, 293n115

Saramago, Jose, 69, 265n2
Sarante, Galateia, 273n83
Saunier, Guy (Michel), 91, 271nn66–67
Schelling, Friedrich Wilhelm Joseph von, 24, 45, 256n30
Schiller, Friedrich, 135, 141–43, 177, 260n54, 281nn9–10, 281nn12–14, 283n25
Schlaffer, Heinz, 276n27
Schlegel, Friedrich von, 276n20
Schmitt, Carl, 291n97
Scholem, Gerhard, 202, 298n23, 298n27, 299n33, 300n65, 303n107
Schwartz, Hillel, 8, 252n15
Schweppenhäuser, Hermann, 257n31, 283n27, 295n1
Shelley, Mary, 286n68, 288n76
Simpson, Patricia Anne, 298n22
Slethaug, Gordon E., 250n8
Smeed, J.W., 277n37
Smith, Adam, 294n117
Smith, Gary, 285n67, 304n114
Socrates, 131
Sophocles, 249n2, 261n70, 287n73

Spinoza, Baruch, 259nn50–51
Spivak, Gayatri Chakravorty, 299n40
Starobinski, Jean, 282n23
Stern, Lucien, 254n12
Stevenson, Robert Louis, 69, 274n1
Susman, Margarete, 298n29
Sussman, Henry, 304n112
Szondi, Peter, 263n104

Terzakis, Aggelos, 268n37
Thieriot, Ferdinand, 256n30
Tiedemann, Rolf, 255n19, 257n31, 259n51, 283n27, 295n1, 296n8
Tiitinen, Johanna, 293n115
Todorov, Tzvetan, 8, 39, 251n14, 261n67, 289n80
Tournier, Michel, 253n 5
Tymms, Ralph, 8, 251n11, 251n13
Tziovas, Dimitris, 271n65

Ungar, Steven, 276n32

Valéry, Paul, 113
Valetas, G., 92, 271n69, 272n70
Vardoulakis, Dimitris, 268n32, 270n63, 273n90, 275n4, 278n50, 292n103, 298n31

Warminski, Andrzej, 258n49, 264n121
Webber, Andrew J., 7, 42, 249n4, 262n74, 262n78, 262n84
Weber, Samuel, 51, 52, 263n93, 263n95, 284n36
Wilde, Oscar, 69
Witschi, Beat, 288n76
Wohlfarth, Irving, 281n16, 282n21

Yates, Frances A., 283n25

Zeno, 178, 290n95
Ziarek, Ewa Plonowska, 267n24
Ziolkowski, Theodore, 254n10
Žižek, Slavoj, 253n4
Zohn, Harry, 301n70

www.ingramcontent.com/pod-product-compliance
Lightning Source LLC
Chambersburg PA
CBHW031232290426
44109CB00012B/269